THE DICKENS CIRCLE

CHARLES DICKENS
(1836)
From a pencil sketch by George Cruikshank

Frontispiece

THE
DICKENS CIRCLE

A NARRATIVE OF THE
NOVELIST'S FRIENDSHIPS

BY

J. W. T. LEY

WITH PORTRAITS AND OTHER ILLUSTRATIONS

SECOND EDITION

LONDON
CHAPMAN & HALL, Ltd.
1919

Printed in Great Britain by
Richard Clay & Sons, Limited,
Brunswick St., Stamford St., S.E. 1,
and Bungay, Suffolk

TO
MY WIFE

PREFACE

From the time when, as a very raw youth, I first came to know anything about Charles Dickens, I have been attracted by the magnetic personality of the man himself even more than by the men and women he created. The outstanding impression that I gained from my first reading of Forster's *Life of Charles Dickens* was of this magnetism of his personality which attracted to him so many of the most brilliant men and women of the time, and won for him their whole-hearted friendship. That impression was deepened as I read more widely. Youth, of course, discovers wonders continually which it is amazed to find are already well known to its parents, but the amazement in my case arose out of the fact that this very striking phase of Dickens's character—this extraordinary capacity of his for friendship—had not apparently been discovered. At any rate, it had never been adequately dealt with. I was struck by the fact that this man Dickens, comparatively unlettered as he was, who had had no material advantages in life, but, on the contrary, many disadvantages, should not merely have come to know so many of his peers—that was inevitable—but should have so won their affection; should have been so loved by old men like Landor and Leigh Hunt, and Jeffrey, by men of his own age like Forster, and Maclise, and Talfourd, and by men of a younger generation like Percy Fitzgerald, James Payn and Charles Kent; should have been accepted by them all as the sun of their firmament.

If it be true that the proper study for mankind is Man, it is equally true that men most reveal themselves in their relations with men. In my desire to gain a true notion as to what manner of man Dickens really was, I found Forster's book disappointing. I have no quarrel with him on that ground; he could not be expected to give more than a comprehensive portrait of his subject, with the lights and shades that he himself saw. But his book did little more than whet my appetite, as it were. Paragraphic

vii

references were made to famous men of brilliant and fascinating parts, little more than hints were given of the novelist's relations with some of those men. And so I sought elsewhere. I began to read widely in Victorian biography and autobiography, and thus I gained a knowledge, not only of Dickens, but of many other noble and worthy men of the period, which I could not have gained otherwise, and which has been helpful and inspiring to me.

The result of my labours—unhappy word!—is here. It has many faults, I have no doubt. I only claim that it has been done conscientiously by one who loves his subject. My difficulty has been to decide what to omit. I have been almost overwhelmed with material, but I all along tried to avoid anything in the nature of a Gradgrindish compilation. I am vain enough to hope that my fellow Dickensians will find this book a useful auxiliary to Forster. I am modest enough to have aimed at nothing higher.

I suppose it would be impossible for any man to write a book on Dickens to-day without having to acknowledge indebtedness to Mr. B. W. Matz. That gentleman has been one of my most valued personal friends for a good many years now. I succeeded him as Hon. General Secretary of the Dickens Fellowship, and sat with him on the Council of that remarkable organisation for five years; I was a member, with him, of the little Committee which, with fear and trembling, launched *The Dickensian*, that bright little magazine which he has so ably edited for fourteen years; I have been associated with him in innumerable Dickensian ventures; and time and time again I have been indebted to him for his advice and help—both ever ready and ever valuable— as well as for many personal kindnesses of a more intimate character. And now I want to say that but for him I could never have written this book. I have had to turn to him again and again. His unique knowledge was always at my disposal, so were the contents of his excellent library, and when he did not himself possess a book that I needed he begged or borrowed it for me. But for his persistent encouragement I doubt if I should ever have seriously tackled the work at all; but for his consistent help I know I could never have completed it.

There are others who have rendered help which I gratefully acknowledge. Mr. William Miller, another old Dickensian friend,

has answered many inquiries out of his marvellous store of knowledge, and loaned me books; Mrs. Perugini, too, has most kindly
answered inquiries; the Marquis of Crewe generously loaned to
me the originals of all Dickens's letters to his father and mother;
Lord Tennyson gave me some valuable information about his
father's friendship with Dickens, and authorised me to quote
from his Memoir of his father; Mr. Marcus Stone, R.A., gave me
a personal interview.

Of the books I have consulted I could not possibly give a complete list. Their name is Legion. But where I have quoted I
have made acknowledgment in the text or in a footnote.

J. W. T. LEY

Newport, Mon.,
June 1918.

CONTENTS

CONTENTS

LIST OF ILLUSTRATIONS

THE DICKENS CIRCLE

CHAPTER I

INTRODUCTORY

"My art has brought acquaintances by scores,
But to my character I owe my friends."

THERE is no surer test of a man's character than to ask, " Who are his friends? " For the unworthy man does not hold the friendship of worthy men. Few men come out of the test better than Charles Dickens. Many other great men have had big circles; many Davids have had their Jonathans; but no man ever had a bigger or more notable circle, and none was ever more loved by those who were admitted to his friendship. He had, indeed, the capacity for friendship in a superlative degree. Of the attractiveness of his personality many have written in terms of enthusiasm. They all bear testimony to the truth of Forster's declaration :

"His place was not to be filled by any other. To the most trivial talk he gave the attraction of his own character. It might be a small matter; something he had read during the day, some quaint odd fancy from a book, a vivid little outdoor picture, the laughing exposure of some imposture, or a burst of sheer mirthful enjoyment; but of its kind it would be something unique, because genuinely part of himself. This, and his unwearying animal spirits, made him the most delightful of companions; no claim on good-fellow-ship ever found him wanting; and no one so constantly recalled to his friends the description Johnson gave of Garrick, as the cheerfullest man of his age."

In another place Forster says :

"It was an excellent saying of the first Lord Shaftesbury, that, seeing every man of any capacity holds within himself

B

two men, the wise and the foolish, each of them ought freely to be allowed his turn; and it was one of the secrets of Dickens's social charm that he could, in strict accordance with this saying, allow each part of him its turn : could afford thoroughly to give rest and relief to what was serious in him, and, when the time came to play his gambols, could surrender himself wholly to the enjoyment of the time, and become the very genius and embodiment of one of his own most whimsical fancies."

These are the declarations of a man who loved Dickens as his life, but they are confirmed by a hundred witnesses. But he was something very much more than a bright and delightful companion. He won friendship, and he won it because he gave it. " Charles Dickens," says Lady Pollock, " was and is to me the ideal of friendship." " He was indeed a man of magnanimous and *practical* sympathy," wrote Mrs. Cattermole. Read of him cheering Macready in his lonely retirement; read of him going to see Stanfield in his illness and so cheering him by his description of Fechter's latest play, " fighting a duel with the washstand, defying the bedstead, and saving the life of the sofa-cushion," that the sick man " turned the corner on the spot." Read of him always glad to slap a friend on the back and felicitate him on a success; always first to cheer him in failure; always by to grasp his hand and say and do the right thing in sorrow and suffering; read of him helping to start capable young writers on the road that leads to success; read of him as an editor to whom nothing was too much trouble if he could advise or help a young and promising contributor; read of him the life and soul of children's parties. What wonder that this man should have attracted good men to him and wound their affections round his heart?

" Angels," says Young, " from Friendship gather half their joys." Dickens was, indeed, a happy man. Scarce a great man of his time but loved him. And, be it noted, in all his wide circle there was none who sought reflected glory. They all shone by their own unaided light. Many of them were famous before he had been heard of; there were few of them who were not better educated than he was, who had not had better opportunities in life. Herein, surely, lies proof of the man's innate greatness. It is a wonderful thing that this newspaper reporter who had had no opportunities but what he had made for himself, whose earliest admirers had been the frequenters of the bar-parlour at Chatham, who had had practically no schooling at all, whose chief mentors in his boyhood had been the inmates of a Debtors' prison, whose boyhood companions had been the drudges of a blacking ware-house—that this man should, before he was thirty years old, have been the dominating spirit in a circle which comprised some of the finest minds of a period which was so rich in fine minds.

Before he was thirty years old ! Nay, before he was twenty-six years old. He celebrated his thirtieth birthday in America, where he had already formed close friendships with Washington Irving, Longfellow, Felton, and others, whilst he had left behind him men like Macready, Maclise, Forster, Jerrold, Talfourd, Jeffrey, Landor, who loved him truly, with whom he was on terms of intimate friendship.

When he was yet some two or three years short of thirty he was one of the leading members of the Shakespeare Society, in association with Procter, Talfourd, Macready, Thackeray, Blanchard, Charles Knight, Douglas Jerrold, Maclise, Stanfield, Cattermole, Charles and Thomas Landseer, and Frank Stone. Every one of these names is that of a man of first-class abilities who called Dickens friend. And to them, even at this time, must be added Jeffrey, Leigh Hunt, Landor, Samuel Rogers, Carlyle, etc. A short three years before Dickens had been an utterly obscure newspaper reporter with never a book to his credit. Practically every one of these men had at that time achieved independent fame. Several of them were much older than Dickens; three of them were old enough to be his grandfather, and had been famous before he was born. They were exceptionally gifted men of widely differing temperaments, irresistibly attracted by the magnetism of this young writer. And as the years rolled on none of them drifted away. In one or two cases the friendships were temporarily clouded, but in all such cases the sun rose again, and the friendships were renewed to last unto death. The Circle grew steadily year by year, and each new friendship was cemented as the old ones had been.

It was his sheer joy in life, his frank, hearty, wholly unspoiled outlook, his joyous laugh, yet withal his realisation of the seriousness, as well as the joy of life, his love for human nature and his never-failing determination to take it at its best—these were the qualities that won for him such a host of friends. It has been noted that he was the dominating personality in all this great company. That surely is the most remarkable fact of all. He was not simply admitted to the company of his peers : it was they who formed the Dickens Circle. They were the planets and stars that circled round the Dickens sun. Let it be a Christmas party, a game at leap-frog, a trip to Cornwall, amateur theatricals, a public dinner to Macready or Thackeray, or a private dinner to Black—whatsoever it be, if Dickens is in it at all, he is the moving spirit. All his associates, great men as well as lesser men, are dominated by the personality of this man who, in social up-spring, education, and all that usually counts for so much, was their inferior.

It is no conscious, aggressive domination either; it is just the working of the natural law which forces the strong man to the top. He had learned self-reliance in a hard school. All he had achieved was due absolutely to his inborn genius and to his own force of character. He had faced fearful odds in his most impressionable years—the years during which the boy begets the man. He had conquered, and out of the fight he had come strong, self-reliant, clean-minded and pure-hearted, joyous at his victory, with no trace of bitterness in him. Those early struggles had made him what he was. They had had some ill-effects, no doubt, but the good far outweighed the ill, and at the age of twenty-five Dickens sprang before the world, fully equipped to take and to hold his place among men.

Let us spend a short time in the Dickens Circle. Let us see the man in the company of his friends. Thus shall we come to know him better even than we know him now, and to love him more. We shall see him the jolliest of companions for the social hour; we shall see him the kind sympathetic friend in times of sorrow and of sadness; we shall see him almost womanly in his tenderness when his friends are stricken; we shall see him ever ready to prove his friendship at whatsoever sacrifice; we shall see him winning and holding surely the whole-hearted love of scores of men who did not lightly give their love; we shall find that he was indeed " the ideal of friendship "—" the good, the gentle, high-gifted, ever friendly, noble Dickens, every inch of him an honest man."

CHAPTER II

FRIENDS OF BOYHOOD AND YOUTH

AND to imitate David Copperfield, and begin at the beginning, there are one or two friends of the novelist's early years who certainly must have mention. First, a couple of friends of his boyhood. Let Bob Fagin have pride of place. Scarcely entitled to a place in the Dickens Circle, you say. Well, no; but a friend of Dickens's all the same, a friend in the darkest days : Bob Fagin, the fellow-drudge in the blacking warehouse, who, when a third drudge, Poll Green, objected to the future novelist being treated as " the young gentleman," " settled him speedily " ; who, when " the young gentleman " was one day taken ill, was so kind to him, filled empty blacking-bottles with hot water, and applied relays of them to his side half the day, and when it came towards evening, refused to allow him to go home alone. " I was too proud to let him know about the prison," Dickens tells us, " and after making several efforts to get rid of him, to all of which Bob Fagin in his goodness was deaf, shook hands with him on the steps of a house near Southwark Bridge on the Surrey side, making believe that I lived there. As a finishing piece of reality, in case of his looking back, I knocked at the door, and asked, when the woman opened it, if that was Mr. Robert Fagin's home." Kind-hearted Bob Fagin, it was hardly fair, was it? to use your name so roughly in after years.

Then there were his schoolfellows at Wellington House Academy, whither he went when the days of drudgery were over—Daniel Tobin, Henry Danson, Owen R. Thomas, and Richard Bray. They were his chief associates in those days when the sun had begun to shine again. That the young Dickens made some impression on these boyish friends is evident from the fact that Thomas preserved a letter which the future Boz wrote to him when he was between thirteen and fourteen years old.

Writing to Forster after Dickens's death, Thomas said : " After the lapse of years I recognised the celebrated writer as the individual I had known so well as a boy, from having preserved this note ; and upon Mr. Dickens visiting Reading in December 1854 to give one of his earliest readings, . . . I took the opportunity of showing it to him, when he was much diverted therewith. On the same occasion we conversed about mutual schoolfellows, and among others Daniel Tobin was referred to, whom I remember to have been Dickens's *most* intimate companion in the school-days (1824 to 1826). His reply was that Tobin either was then, or had previously been, assisting him in the capacity of amanuensis; but there is a subsequent mystery about Tobin, in connection with his friend and patron, which I have never been able to comprehend; for I understood shortly afterwards that there was an entire separation between them, and it must have been an offence of some gravity to have sundered an acquaintance formed in early youth, and which had endured, greatly to Tobin's advantage, so long."

There was no mystery about it. "The offence," says Forster, "went no deeper than the having at last worn out even Dickens's patience and kindness." Forster records that he could recollect Dickens helping this old schoolfellow on many occasions, and he adds: "His applications for relief were so incessantly repeated, that to cut him and them adrift altogether was the only way of escape from what had become an intolerable nuisance."

Danson, who became a physician, also recorded at Forster's request, his recollections of those days, and it is interesting to note that he remembered that the boys had a small club for the lending and circulating of small tales written by Dickens. He also records that the theatrical instinct was even then strong in Dickens. The boys mounted small theatres, and got up very gorgeous scenery to illustrate "The Miller and his Men" (for which play Dickens retained a curious liking—I had nearly written affection—all his life) and "Cherry and Fair Star."

It will be seen that Dickens made no lasting friendship at school, though Tobin hung on to him for years; but with a school-fellow of his brother's he did form a friendship that endured till the end. This was Thomas Mitton, who was with the other Dickens boys at Mr. Dawson's school in Hunter Street, Brunswick Square. Afterwards, it is believed, he and Charles were fellow-clerks at Mr. Molloy's in New Square, Lincoln's Inn, where Dickens was employed for a few weeks between leaving school and going to Mr. Blackmore's. Mitton stuck to the law, and in 1838 we find him drafting his friend's will. And so late as June 13, 1865, we find a letter to him giving a full account of the Staplehurst accident.

There is a friend who should be mentioned here, though he only just walks across the stage, as it were. His name was Potter, and he was a fellow-clerk in the office of Mr. Blackmore, attorney, Gray's Inn. It is recorded of him that he did much to stimulate

Dickens's theatrical tastes. The pair took every opportunity, we are told by their employer, of going together to a minor theatre, where they not unfrequently engaged in parts. That is all we know about Potter, but he was Dickens's friend—or shall we say pal?—during a very interesting and not at all unimportant phase of the novelist's life, and so he is entitled to a place in the Circle.

We pass on to the next period in the career of *Pickwick's* author. In the big Dickens Circle see that John Black is given his proper place. He was not an intimate friend; I suppose he and Dickens rarely met on really equal terms; but Black was the first friend who influenced Dickens's career and encouraged him when he could as yet scarcely have dreamed of future fame. " Dear old Black ! my first out-and-out appreciator," Dickens wrote only a few weeks before he died. He never forgot that it was " this good old mirth-loving man " who flung the slipper after him, as he put it, who first recognised his genius and encouraged him. For Black was Editor of the " Morning Chronicle " when young Dickens was a reporter on that paper, and Charles Mackay, who was also a member of the staff, tells us that he repeatedly heard Black predict the future greatness of Charles Dickens. Indeed, says Mackay, it was because he had heard his Editor say this so often that he begged from him the letter which Dickens wrote proposing to write for the paper the *Sketches by Boz*. Dickens was an unknown man with no worldly prospects when he became a member of Black's staff, and undoubtedly he owed much to the Editor, who was then past his fiftieth birthday. He always acknowledged it and paid hearty tribute. In that well-known speech at the dinner of the Newspaper Press Fund in 1865, for instance, in which he recalled some of his journalistic experiences, he said : " Returning home from exciting political meetings in the country to the waiting press in London, I do verily believe I have been upset in almost every description of vehicle known in this country. I have been, in my time, belated in miry by-roads, towards the small hours, forty or fifty miles from London, in a wheelless carriage, with exhausted horses and drunken postboys, and have got back in time for publication, to be received with never-forgotten compliments by the late Mr. Black, coming in the broadest of Scotch from the broadest of hearts I ever knew." And I have already quoted what he said not long before he died. After he gave up journalism he saw but little of this excellent man, but they met occasionally, Black proud of his old reporter, Dickens loving and respecting his old Editor and never forgetting his indebtedness to him. In 1843 Black ceased to be Editor of the " Morning Chronicle," " in circumstances," says Forster, " strongly reviving all Dickens's sympathies." The novelist wrote : " I

am deeply grieved about Black. Sorry from my heart's core.
If I could find him out, I would go and comfort him this moment."
He did find him out, and he gladdened his old Editor's heart by
arranging in his honour a dinner at Greenwich. This is the last
record of any meeting between the two men, but I do not doubt
but that they did meet again, for Black lived another twelve years
not far from London.

Two of Dickens's colleagues on the "Morning Chronicle"
were Charles Mackay and Thomas Beard. The former calls for
no more mention than he has already had, but with Beard a very
close friendship was formed, which lasted right through the years
until that sad day in June 1870. Beard was the first friend he
made when he entered the gallery; indeed, he was the only friend
among his gallery colleagues, for Dickens seems to have kept
himself very much to himself in those days—a curious fact in
view of his great capacity for friendship and his great sociability
in all other periods of his career. Beard's was one of the familiar
faces at Twickenham in the summer of 1838; he was present
at the *Haunted Man* christening dinner; and he was a guest at
the wedding of Kate Dickens to Charles Collins in 1860; whilst
in 1862, when the novelist thought of going to America for a
reading tour, he proposed to this old friend to accompany him as
secretary.

There is one famous man whose place is in this chapter. He is
Wentworth Dilke, grandfather of a still more famous grandson.
He knew Dickens in the blacking warehouse days. He was
acquainted with the future novelist's father, with whom he one
day visited the warehouse, and gave the young drudge a half-
crown, receiving in return a low bow. In after years Dilke related
this story to Forster, who mentioned it to Dickens. "He was
silent for several minutes," says the biographer. "I felt that
I had unintentionally touched a painful place in his memory;
and to Mr. Dilke I never spoke of the subject again." A few weeks
later Dickens referred to the matter, however, and as a result of
the conversation that followed, related the whole story of his
unhappy boyhood. So that it is to Dilke that we owe the knowledge of that experience in the novelist's boyhood which helps us
so much to understand the whole of his subsequent career.
Through the after years Dilke remained a friend, though not a
very intimate one. They were associated in connection with the
Literary Fund, and were in opposite camps in respect of its
management. For some years, says Forster, he fought un-
successfully against Dilke in this matter, but there was no personal
feeling in the struggle.

CHAPTER III

SUDDENLY, at the age of twenty-four, Dickens sprang into fame as the author of *Pickwick*. Previously, however, the *Sketches by Boz*, appearing in the " Morning Chronicle," had attained a considerable degree of popularity, and a few of the more discerning had read into them the promise which was so soon fulfilled. Among these was William Harrison Ainsworth, who ascertained the identity of Boz, advised him to publish the *Sketches* in book form, and introduced him to a publisher and to an illustrator. There is something odd in the fact that the man who rendered Dickens two of the greatest services of his life, has almost the least mention of any of the novelist's friends in Forster's book. For he very materially influenced Dickens's life. He was not only the first to encourage him to publish a book, introducing him to publisher and illustrator—Macrone and George Cruikshank— but also first made the young writer and John Forster acquainted, thus bringing about one of the most memorable friendships in literary history. In view of these facts one would expect to find him filling a very prominent place in a biography of Dickens from the pen of Forster. Yet he is not mentioned more than about half a dozen times.

The explanation is that though Ainsworth was still alive when Forster wrote his book, he had completely dropped out of the old circle, and was almost completely forgotten. Further, after the first few years he ceased to be one of Dickens's really intimate friends. In the beginning he was, undoubtedly, and up to the late 'forties he was still welcomed as a pleasant companion, but the original intimacy disappeared. The truth is, I think, that Ainsworth had not those solid qualities of friendship that Dickens required, and found in others. But in his early manhood he must have been a striking and attractive personality, and, in addition, he was the first prominent literary man with whom Dickens associated on level terms.

Imagine what the youthful " Boz " would feel. See what his boyhood had been. See how he had passed through the successive states of drudgery. Then he writes a few " specials " for his

9

paper.   Imagine his elation when he discovers that these sketches
have been observed by no less a person than Harrison Ainsworth,
the novelist who has recently taken the town by storm with
" Rookwood " and that glorious description of Dick Turpin's ride
to York.   Is it surprising that he is elated by the honour of such
a man's friendship?   And naturally there is also a sense of
indebtedness to Ainsworth for suggesting and facilitating the
publication of the sketches in book form.

And so for a time the two young novelists are close friends and
constant companions.   But after a few years, as Dickens steadily
establishes himself and forms a circle of famous friends around
him, these two drift apart, until the old ties are severed altogether,
and they live on through year after year without ever meeting
at all.   Ainsworth seems to have lost almost all his friends in
much the same way.   Indeed, the story of his life makes sad
reading, for it is a tragic picture that it.presents in the 'seventies
of the old man, who thirty years before was one of the most
brilliant stars in the London firmament, now neglected and well-
nigh forgotten.   " I recall a dinner at Teddington in the 'sixties,"
says Mr. Percy Fitzgerald, " given by Frederic Chapman, the
publisher, at which were Forster and Browning.   The latter said
humorously : ' A sad, forlorn-looking being stopped me to-day,
and reminded me of old times.   He presently resolved himself
into—whom do you think?—Harrison Ainsworth !' ' Good
heavens ! ' cried Forster, ' is he still alive ? ' "   That is one of the
saddest anecdotes that I have ever read.

In the early days, however, when " Rookwood " was out-
distanced in popularity only by *Pickwick* itself, and Forster was
just beginning that career which was to make him one of the
greatest literary forces of his time, we may be sure that none of
the three ever foresaw the day when one should learn with surprise
that another was still alive.   It was at the Christmas of 1836
that Dickens and Forster met at Ainsworth's house, and for the
next few years the three were inseparable.   Forster does not tell
us that Ainsworth took part in those daily ridings which are
recalled with the sadness with which the memory of the happy
days of long ago must ever be tinged, but he certainly did.   Mr.
S. M. Ellis, in his delightful book, " William Harrison Ainsworth
and His Friends," makes that quite clear :

> " In the first few years of their friendship the three were
> devoted to horse exercise, and Dickens and Forster would
> ride out from town to Kensal Lodge to pick up Ainsworth.
> . . . The three *literati* would gallop off for miles into the
> lovely country that stretched away to the north and west.

Away by Twyford Abbey and the clear, winding Brent to tiny Perivale and Greenford, most sylvan of hamlets, through the green vale of Middlesex to Ruislip, and home by Stanmore and Harrow. Or another day away across breezy Old Oak Common to Acton, stopping for a few minutes at Berrymead Priory to exchange greetings with Bulwer Lytton. On through Acton's narrow High Street, with its quaint raised pavement and ancient red-tiled houses, past ' Fordhook,' Fielding's last and well-loved home, past Ealing's parks and long village green, round through orchard-bordered lanes to Chiswick, with its countless memories, and so by Shepherd's Bush to Wood Lane and the Scrubbs, home again."

Week-end trips, we are told, were also frequently indulged in together, and in view of the undoubted fact that there was this intimacy, we may, with Mr. R. Renton,[1] echo Mr. Ellis's regret that Forster " devotes but a few words to the social or convivial phase of Dickens in these first glorious years of youth and fame. He barely mentions the frequent rides through the lovely country surrounding the suburbs of London which Dickens delighted to take in company with his two intimates, Forster and Ainsworth, and the even more frequent dinings and festivities the trio enjoyed go almost unrecorded."

'Tis true, and pity 'tis, 'tis true. The only direct reference he makes to Ainsworth's share in the enjoyments of those days is when, writing of the summer of 1838, which Dickens spent at Twickenham, he says : " A friend now especially welcome, also, was the novelist, Mr. Ainsworth, who shared with us incessantly for the three following years in the companionship which began at his house, . . . and to whose sympathy in tastes and pursuits, accomplishments in literature, open-hearted generous ways, and cordial hospitality, many of the pleasures of later years were due."

As a matter of fact, Dickens was at Ainsworth's house, Kensal Lodge, very frequently indeed, and we are told that, " as the host's most intimate friend," he used to preside at one end of the table. Open house was kept at Kensal Lodge, but still more was this the case when Ainsworth moved to Kensal Manor House in 1841.

Ainsworth was one of the company at the dinner to celebrate the completion of *Pickwick*, of which he received a presentation copy—one of the three specially-bound copies sent to the author by his publishers, as witness this letter to Forster :

" Chapman and Hall have just sent me . . . three extra-super bound copies of *Pickwick*, as per specimen enclosed.

---

[1] " John Forster and his Friendships."

The first I forward to you, the second I have presented to our good friend Ainsworth, and the third, Kate has retained for herself."

Of the *Pickwick* dinner Ainsworth wrote to his friend, James Crossley :

" On Saturday last we celebrated the completion of *The Pickwick Papers*. We had a capital dinner, with capital wine and capital speeches. Dickens, of course, was in the chair. Talfourd was the Vice, and an excellent Vice he made. . . . Just before he was about to propose *the* toast of the evening the head waiter—for it was at a tavern that the carouse took place—entered, and placed a glittering temple of confectionery on the table, beneath the canopy of which stood a little figure of the illustrious Mr. Pickwick. This was the work of the landlord. As you may suppose, it was received with great applause. Dickens made a feeling speech in reply to the Serjeant's eulogy. . . . Just before dinner Dickens received a cheque for £750 from his publishers."

This is the most extended account of the dinner that exists. Ainsworth continued to be a guest at these christening dinners until *Dombey*, whilst Dickens was certainly present at the " Tower of London " dinner.

Mr. Ellis points out that Ainsworth had quite a marked influence on Dickens's earlier work. Undoubtedly it was the popularity of " Rookwood " that caused Sam Weller to select as his contribution to the harmony on a certain occasion the song, " Bold Turpin vunce on Hounslow Heath," and it is interesting to note also that the name of Turpin's companion robber was Sikes. But, above all, it was to Ainsworth that Dickens was indebted for an introduction to the brothers Grant, better known to the wide, wide world as the Cheeryble Brothers. That Dickens did actually meet the Grants is now established beyond any doubt at all. To James Crossley, on October 31, 1838, Ainsworth wrote : " Dickens has just started for Stratford-upon-Avon and Chester, accompanied by Mr. Browne (the ' Phiz ' of *Pickwick* and *Nickleby*), the artist. He will reach Manchester on Saturday, I believe. On Sunday next Forster starts, per railroad, to join him, and I suppose on Monday they will call on you, as they are armed with letters of introduction to you. Dickens's object is to see the interior of a cotton mill—I fancy with reference to some of his publications. I have given him letters to G. Winter and Hugh Beaver."

W. Harrison Ainsworth.

On the authority of one of Ainsworth's daughters, Dickens paid this visit with the definite object of meeting the Grants, as well as of seeing the inside of a cotton mill. Ainsworth had known them when he was a boy, for Manchester was his native city, and he had described them to his friend. He now gave Mr. Winter a hint, and that gentleman arranged a dinner to which Dickens and the Grants were invited. And so Ainsworth rendered a further great service to Dickens and to the world at large.

During this visit to Manchester the three friends went out to Cheadle Hall, Cheshire, in order to see Ainsworth's three little girls, who were at boarding-school there, and they " took with them three books, duly inscribed and autographed, to present to the three little girls, who had never seen their visitors before."

In 1839 Ainsworth had the gratification of visiting his native city in company with his famous friend, and of being entertained by the citizens at dinner. The position must have been an embarrassing one for him, as the following extract from a letter to Crossley shows :

" Now, in respect of the public dinner. Is it to be given to me or Dickens—or to both? Acting upon your former letter, I invited my friend to accompany *me*, imagining the dinner was to be given in my honour; but I have no feeling whatever in the matter, and only desire to have a distinct understanding about it. If the dinner is given expressly to Dickens, I think a letter of invitation should be sent him. But you are the best judge of the propriety of this step; and it might be only giving needless trouble, as he is sure to come if the dinner *is* to be given to me."

The spirit reflected by this letter is excellent. The truth appears to be that Ainsworth had been originally invited, and that he had invited Dickens to accompany him, and the citizens of Manchester rather allowed the glory of " Boz " to eclipse the glory of Ainsworth. But the latter was devoid of jealousy, and he was quite willing that the greater honour should go to his friend, whose genius he readily and frankly recognised. Needless to say, Forster kept them company on this visit. The three friends stayed with Mr. Hugh Beaver, at the Temple, Cheetham Hill. They arrived in Manchester on Saturday, January 12. On the Monday the public dinner was held, followed, on the Tuesday, by a dinner at Crossley's house, and on the Wednesday by a dinner at Winter's house.

One doubts if throughout his long life there was any incident upon which Ainsworth looked back with so much gratification as this visit to Manchester. To return to his native city a famous man, and to be fêted by the citizens, was in itself a notable and pleasing event, but to be accompanied by and fêted in company with the most popular writer of his time—whom he could call " friend "—it must have been a proud day indeed for him.

At about this time Dickens and Ainsworth had an interesting scheme in hand which was destined not to fructify. " I think I have told you," the latter wrote to Crossley, " that Dickens and I are about to illustrate ancient and modern London in a *Pickwick* form. We expect much from this." It would have been an almost ideal collaboration. Who could have dealt with ancient London so well as he who was to write " The Tower of London " and " Old Saint Paul's," and who could have dealt with modern London so delightfully as the author of *Sketches by Boz* and *Pickwick*? But the scheme was abandoned, and this is the only reference to it that exists.

There is no need to deal here with Dickens's dispute with Macrone. Ainsworth had nought to do with it, except that he was naturally interested and sorry that the unpleasantness should have arisen between the publisher and the author whom he had been instrumental in bringing together. There was, however, real danger of a rupture between the two novelists, arising out of Dickens's dispute with Bentley in 1839, which led to Ainsworth succeeding Dickens as Editor of " Bentley's Miscellany." A rumour got abroad to the effect that Forster had persuaded Dickens to break his agreement with the publisher, and Dickens wrote a letter to Ainsworth from which the following is an extract :

" If the subject of this letter, or anything contained in it, should eventually become the occasion of any disagreement between you and me, it would cause me very deep and sincere regret. But with this contingency—even this before me— I feel that I must speak out without reserve, and that every manly, honest, and just consideration impels me to do so. By some means . . . the late negotiations between yourself, myself, and Mr. Bentley have placed a mutual friend of ours in a false position, and one in which he has no right to stand, and exposed him to an accusation . . . equally untrue and undeserved. . . . However painful it will be to put myself in communication once again with Mr. Bentley, and openly appeal to you to confirm what I shall tell him, there is no alternative, unless you will frankly and openly, and for the sake of your old friend, as well as very intimate and valued one, avow to Mr. Bentley yourself that he (Forster) is not to blame. . . . Believe me, Ainsworth, that for your sake, no

less than on Forster's account, this should be done. . . . I
do not mean to hurt or offend you by anything I have said,
and I should be truly grieved to find that I have done so.
But I must speak strongly, because I feel strongly."

Happily the affair ended amicably, and there was no breach
between the friends.   This letter (which is given in full in Mr. Ellis's
book) was written in March 1839.   A month earlier Dickens had
handed over the Editorship of the " Miscellany " to Ainsworth
in the following words : " In fact, then, my child, you have changed
hands.   Henceforth I resign you to the guardianship and protection of one of my most intimate and valued friends, Mr.
Ainsworth, with whom, and with you, my best wishes will ever
remain." [1]

In 1842 Ainsworth was one of the party that gathered at
Greenwich to welcome Dickens home from America.   After that,
references to meetings of the two novelists are very few indeed.
In 1847 Ainsworth, during a Continental tour, met Dickens at
Lausanne, and the latter wrote to Forster : " I breakfasted with
him at the Hotel Gibbon next morning. . . . We walked about
all day, talking of our old days at Kensal Lodge."   Those old days
were not forgotten, but times had changed, and the two men who
once saw one another almost daily now but rarely met.   There
was in each a sentiment for the " day that is dead," however,
and in 1849 Dickens did a very graceful thing when he invited
Ainsworth to act as godfather to his sixth son (now Mr. Henry
Fielding Dickens, K.C.).   Four years later Ainsworth gave up
Kensal Manor House, and those glorious reunions were once for
all ended.

The last record of any meeting between Dickens and Ainsworth
is in June 1854, when the latter, who had gone to live in Brighton,
came up to London expressly to meet some of his old friends.
Thackeray tried to effect a reunion in 1857.   He proposed a
dinner at which Dickens, Ainsworth, Maclise, and himself should
meet once more and live again the old, far-off happy days.   But
his efforts failed.   " Ainsworth and ' Boz ' won't come," he wrote
to Maclise, " and press for delay.   Well, then, although I know,
from the state of the banker's account at present, next week there
will probably be about five shillings wherewith to buy a dinner,
yet let them have their will.   Something tells me that it may be
long before the banquet in question takes place—but it is their
wish—so be it.   The greatest of all the names of Allah (Goethe
says) is ' Amen.' "   And he wrote to Ainsworth : " Here comes
a note from Dickens, who begs, too, for a remission of the dinner.

---

[1] " Familiar Epistle from a Parent to a Child."

As I can't have it without my two roaring animals, and the play wouldn't be worth coming to with the part of Hamlet omitted, the great Titmarsh Banquet is hereby postponed, to be held on some other occasion, however, with uncommon splendour."

Thackeray's forebodings were realised, and it is certain that the two friends who had been so intimate in the first days of popularity and success, did not meet for some years prior to Dickens's death. For on July 7, 1870, Ainsworth wrote to Charles Kent : " I was greatly shocked by the sudden death of poor Dickens. I have not seen him of late years, but I always hoped that we might meet again, as of old."

The tone of this letter certainly suggests that there had been an estrangement, and the impression is confirmed by Thackeray's note to Maclise just quoted : " Ainsworth and ' Boz ' *won't* come." There is no direct evidence of an estrangement, however, and for memory's sake—the memory of those joyous early years—one hopes that the impression is false.

CHAPTER IV

GEORGE CRUIKSHANK

It must have been a red-letter day for the obscure young newspaper reporter on which he learned that his first book was to be illustrated by the great George Cruikshank. For George was famous before Dickens had left school, and in 1837 he was the most famous illustrator of the day. For an unknown author to have his name on the title-page of his book was a guarantee against failure. Sam Weller came into being almost simultaneously with the publication of the *Sketches*, so that Dickens did not owe so much to the artist as he might have done, but the fact remains that the first real distinction that he ever had was that of having a book illustrated by the great George Cruikshank. And we may regard it as likely that he would, in a sense, be " carried away " by this personal acquaintance with one whose name had been a household word when he was a boy. But after a while he began to make other and better friends, and gradually he became less enthusiastic about Cruikshank and about Ainsworth too. I think we are justified in assuming this. It implies no reproach to the novelist. To put it in somewhat colloquial language, whilst Cruikshank was a distinguished man to be on intimate terms with, and whilst he was all very well as a companion on a convivial evening—at a Greenwich or Richmond dinner, shall we say?—a little of his company would go a very long way.

For the *Sketches* sixteen illustrations were done, and the artist did a new frontispiece for the first cheap edition. It should be noted that in no fewer than five of these pictures, portraits of Dickens appear. In the title-page of the second series, both author and artist may be seen waving flags from the balloon; whilst in the illustration to the paper on *Public Dinners* we have author, artist, and publishers (Messrs. Chapman & Hall). It was at about this time also that Cruikshank drew the portrait of Boz which is well known to Dickensians. It is said that this was drawn on the spur of the moment at a meeting of the Hook and Eye Club.

For *Oliver Twist* as it ran through " Bentley's Miscellany "

Cruikshank did twenty-four etchings, and when the book was published in ten monthly parts in 1846 he designed the wrapper.

Here is the place to refer to Cruikshank's extraordinary claim that he was the real author of *Oliver Twist*. It was Shelton Mackenzie who first gave publicity to the claim in his *Life of Dickens*, published in America, shortly after the novelist's death. He said that Cruikshank made the assertion to him in 1847. Forster, in the first volume of his *Life of Dickens*, gave it the lie direct, whereupon the artist wrote a letter to "The Times" in which he said:

> "When 'Bentley's Miscellany' was started, it was arranged that Mr. Dickens should write a serial in it, and which was to be illustrated by me; and in a conversation with him as to what the subject should be for the first serial, I suggested to Mr. Dickens that he should write the life of a London boy, and strongly advised him to do this, assuring him that I would furnish him with the subject and supply him with all the characters, which my large experience of London life would enable me to do."

And then, after retelling Shelton Mackenzie's circumstantial story, he said: "Without going any further, I think it will be allowed from what I have stated that I am the originator of *Oliver Twist*, and that all the principal characters are mine." Supposing it to have been true, there was no reason why Cruikshank should not have been given the full credit of having suggested the general outline of the plot, and provided the ideas for the leading characters. Shakespeare did not invent all his plots. But it was not true, and Forster was able to prove it. He published in facsimile the following letter of Dickens's, written to the artist in 1838:

> "My dear Cruikshank,
>
> "I returned suddenly to town yesterday afternoon to look at the latter pages of *Oliver Twist* before it was delivered to the booksellers, when *I saw the majority of the plates in the last volume for the first time.*[1]
>
> "With reference to the last one—Rose Maylie and Oliver—without entering into the question of great haste or any other cause which may have led to its being what it is—I am quite sure there can be little difference of opinion between us with respect to the result. May I ask you whether you will object to designing this plate afresh and doing so *at*

---

[1] These italics are my own.

once, in order that as few impressions as possible of the present one may go forth?

" I feel confident you know me too well to feel hurt by this inquiry, and with equal confidence in you, I have lost no time in preferring it."

And, as all the world knows, the plate was designed afresh. And yet in a pamphlet entitled " The Artist and the Author," which Cruikshank published in 1872, he had the effrontery to say :

"... I, the artist, suggested to the author of those works the original idea, or subject, for them to write out— furnishing, at the same time, the principal characters and the scenes. And then, as the tale had to be produced in monthly parts, the writer, or author, and the artist, had every month to arrange and settle what scenes, or subjects, and characters were to be introduced, and the author had to *weave in* such scenes as I wished to represent."

If further evidence had been wanted of the falsity of this claim, it was provided in an article which appeared in the " Strand Magazine " in August 1897, on " Some Unpublished Sketches by George Cruikshank." One of these sketches represented *Bill Sikes* in the condemned cell, the burglar being depicted in prac- tically the identical attitude in which Fagin appears in the famous illustration. And yet, according to Shelton Mackenzie, it was the drawing of *Fagin* in the condemned cell which first attracted Dickens. Mackenzie wrote that Cruikshank told him that Dickens dropped in at his studio one day and ferreted out a bundle of drawings. " When he came to that one, which represents Fagin in the condemned cell, he silently studied it for half an hour." This unfinished sketch effectually disposes of that statement.

And yet the artist persisted in it, and in a speech at a tem- perance meeting in Manchester in 1874 he reiterated the whole story. His worst enemies never accused him of being a rogue. There can be no doubt but that he really had brought himself to believe this monstrous story. Dickens had touched him on a sore spot several times, also. The novelist had been one of his most doughty opponents on the teetotal question, and it is con- ceivable that he had hurt the artist's dignity in another way. That is to say, I think it is highly probably that Dickens had rather " cold shouldered " him in the last twenty years of his life. But this is not enough, for Cruikshank also claimed to have been the practical author of several of Harrison Ainsworth's novels. Indeed he claimed almost as much for himself as the less reasoning Baconians claim for their hero. In very truth, there can be no doubt but that his mind was none too well balanced in his old age.

In the Manchester speech to which I have referred, Cruikshank remarked that Dickens was a great enemy of teetotal doctrines, and that he called its advocates " Old Hogs." As a matter of fact, he called them " Whole Hogs," and in *Household Words*, August 23, 1851, he had an article with that title, in which he put it to those who listened to these people

> " whether they have any experience or knowledge of a good cause that was ever promoted by such bad means? Whether they ever heard of an association of people, deliberately, by their chosen vessels, throwing overboard every effort but their own, made for the amelioration of the conditions of men, unscrupulously villifying all other labourers in the vineyard; calumniously setting down as aiders and abettors of an odious vice which they know to be held in general abhorrence, and consigned to general shame, the great compact mass of the community—of its intelligence, of its morality, of its earnest endeavour after better things? If, upon consideration, they know of no such other case, then the inquiry will perhaps occur to them, whether, in supporting a so-conducted cause they really be upholders of Temperance, dealing with words, which should be the signs for Truth, according to the truth that is in them? "

Two years later Dickens had another tilt, and this time at Cruikshank personally. This took the form of an article entitled *Frauds on the Fairies*, which also appeared in *Household Words*. Cruikshank had rewritten certain fairy tales as Temperance tracts, and Dickens resented such " frauds on the fairies."

He satirised it with the story of Cinderella " ' edited ' by one of these gentlemen doing a good stroke of business and having a rather extensive mission." It was excellent, and perfectly legitimate criticism, but Cruikshank did not like it, and he replied in his magazine with " A letter from Hop-o'-my-thumb to Charles Dickens, Esq." But the blow had gone home, and his " Fairy Library " did not last long.

It should be added that in 1848 Dickens wrote a criticism of the artist's series of plates, " The Drunkard's Children," the sequel to " The Bottle." The criticism, which appeared in " The Examiner," opened with " a few words by way of gentle protest " :

"Few men have a better right to erect themselves into teachers of the people than Mr. George Cruikshank. Few men have observed the people as he has done, or know them better; few are more earnestly and honestly disposed to teach them for their good; and there are very few artists, in England or abroad, who can approach him in his peculiar and remarkable power. But this teaching, to last, must be fairly conducted. It must not be all on one side. When Mr. Cruikshank shows us, and shows us so forcibly and vigorously, that side of the medal on which the people in their crimes and faults are stamped, he is bound to help us to a glance at that other side on which the government that forms the people, with all *its* faults and vices, is no less plainly impressed. Drunkenness, as a national horror, is the effect of many causes. . . . It would be as sound philosophy to issue a series of plates under the title of the Physic Bottle, or the Saline Mixture, and, tracing the history of typhus fever by such means, to refer it all to the gin-shop, as it is to refer Drunkenness there and to stop there. Drunkenness does not begin there. . . . The hero of the bottle, and father of these children, lived in undoubted comfort and good esteem until he was some five-and-thirty years of age, when, happening unluckily to have a goose for dinner one day . . . he jocularly sent out for a bottle of gin and persuaded his wife . . . to take a little drop, after the stuffing, from which moment the family never left off drinking gin, and rushed downhill to destruction very fast. Entertaining the highest respect for Mr. Cruikshank's great genius, and no less respect for his motives in these publications, we deem it right, on the appearance of a sequel to 'The Bottle,' to protest against this."

Cruikshank, extremist that he was, could hardly have felt very friendly toward Dickens, in view of these numerous lusty blows that the latter dealt him.

In addition to *Sketches by Boz* and *Oliver Twist*, Cruikshank illustrated *The Public Life of Mr. Tulrumble*, and the *Mudfog Papers*; whilst he also did an etching for *The Lamplighter's Story*, which was Dickens's contribution to "The Pic-nic Papers," published for the benefit of Macrone's widow. He also illustrated the *Life of Grimaldi*, which Dickens edited. Thus all his artistic relations with Dickens were confined to the latter's very earliest years of fame. But in those early years the pair met pretty often, and they often dined at each other's house. Cruikshank formed one of the company at the Greenwich dinner at which Dickens's friends welcomed him home from America in 1842—the dinner of which the novelist wrote to Prof. Felton as follows : " I wish you had been at Greenwich the other day, when a party of friends gave me a private dinner; public ones I have refused. C—— was perfectly wild at the reunion, and after singing all manner of marine songs, wound up the entertainment by coming home (six miles) in a little open phaeton of mine, *on his head,* to the mingled delight and indignation of the metropolitan police. We were very jovial, indeed; and I assure you that I drank your health with fearful vigour and energy." There was only one member of the company on that occasion whose name began with C. " We were very jovial." No doubt they were, but whilst Dickens could enjoy this sort of thing once in a while, he did not care about it too frequently. Cruikshank did in those days.

It only remains to be noted that the artist was associated with the early amateur dramatic performances. He took Stanfield's place in the performances at Miss Kelly's theatre in 1845, and he again had a part in the performances in aid of Leigh Hunt and John Poole in 1847. But he was a very ordinary actor. Chosen as a stop-gap, he could not be got rid of afterwards. For we find Dickens writing to Forster : " I make a desperate effort to get C. to give up his part. Yet in spite of all the trouble he gives me I am sorry for him, he is so evidently hurt by his own sense of not doing well. He clutched the part, however, tenaciously; and three weary times we dragged through it last night."

We find Cruikshank prominently mentioned in the burlesque account of the tour of 1847, supposed to have been written by Mrs. Gamp, which Forster prints.

Dickens intended that the artist members of the company should illustrate this account of the trip, but they backed out for some unexplained reason, and the thing was never carried through. But one drawing has been preserved. It is by Cruikshank, and was published in the " Strand Magazine " for August 1897. It illustrates the scene in which he himself is supposed to be addressing Mrs. Gamp, and depicts him raising his hat in the most polite manner.

CHAPTER V

WE have seen that Dickens met Forster at Christmas 1836. Six months later Forster gave his new friend one of the greatest joys of his life. Under date June 16, 1837, William Charles Macready records in his Diary : " Forster [1] came into my room with a gentleman whom he introduced as Dickens, *alias* Boz. I was glad to see him." And the Editor of the Diary truthfully comments : " Thus began a friendship of the happiest and most genial description that was only terminated by Dickens's death, thirty-three years afterward."

And the fact is certainly worthy of note. One needs only to read Macready's Diary to know that he was not the easiest man in the world to get on with. Browning described him as one of the most admirable and fascinating characters he had ever known, and Sala's description of him as " high-minded, generous, just," was perfectly accurate, but his quick and violent temper tried the patience of his friends very often. With nearly every one of them he quarrelled at some time or another, and most of them come in for emphatic reference in his Diary. But never Dickens. He never had a misword with this friend, who is never referred to but in terms of affection. The novelist's frankness, geniality, and generosity seem to have exercised their spell over him always. And Dickens, on the other hand, saw beneath the sometimes forbidding exterior of his friend that " high-minded, generous, just spirit " which was the real man. As Forster says : " No swifter or surer perception than Dickens's for what was solid and beautiful in character; he rated it higher than intellectual effort, and the same lofty place, first in his affection and respect, would have been Macready's " if he had not been the greatest of actors.

For each other as artist as well as man they had the highest admiration. " Wonderful Dickens ! " exclaims Macready very often. " He is a great genius ! " is another entry. " As a great indulgence and enjoyment, walked out to call on Dickens," he

---

[1] Forster and Macready had been acquainted since 1833, when they had been introduced to each other at Edmund Kean's funeral.

writes in another place; and when one of Dickens's books is un-kindly reviewed in "The Times" we find him commenting: "Read the paper, in which was a most *savage* attack on Dickens and his last book—*The Cricket*—that looks to me like the heavy and remorseless blow of an enemy determined to disable his antagonist by striking to maim him or kill if he can, and so render his hostility powerless.[1] I was sorry to see in a newspaper so powerful as 'The Times' an attack so ungenerous, so unworthy of itself. . . . Alas! for my poor dear friend Dickens!" In 1847 he records how, on going to see Dickens after reading Number 5 of *Dombey*, "I could not speak to him for sobs. It is indeed most beautiful; it is true *genius*," and in October 1850, he writes: "Purchased two last numbers of *Copperfield* and read parts of each. Was very much affected and very much pleased with them. His genius is very great."

That Dickens had an equally high opinion of Macready's abilities as an actor is shown by the notices he wrote for the "Examiner" of his friend's performances of Lear and Benedict—performances which he placed on the highest pinnacle, whilst in many of his letters are to be found eulogies of Macready's acting.

It would be possible to give many quotations showing the regard the two men had for each other entirely apart from their respective arts. From that first meeting in 1837 there sprang up a heart-whole affection. From boyhood Dickens had adored Macready, and when at last he achieved success and was able to meet the object of his idolatry on level terms, none of his ideals was destroyed. The friendship which was to last unbroken, without a cloud to obscure its sunshine, was formed at once. Within a month Dickens was revealing to Macready his plan for a comedy that he desired to write for him. The suggestion, which arose out of Dickens's desire to assist his friend's Covent Garden enterprise, was taken up seriously, and towards the end of 1838 he wrote to Macready: "I have not seen you for the past week, because I hoped when we next met to bring *The Lamp-lighter* in my hand. It would have been finished by this time, but I found myself compelled to set to work first at *Nickleby*. . . . I am afraid to name any particular day, but I pledge myself that you shall have it this month." It is obvious that this letter, which is not dated, is wrongly placed in the collection of Dickens's "Letters." It follows a letter dated December 12, but it must have been written earlier than that, for on December 5 Macready has this entry in his Diary: "Dickens brought me his farce, which he read to me. The dialogue is very good, full of point, but I am not sure about the meagreness of the plot. He

---

[1] The reference is to the forthcoming publication of the "Daily News."

WILLIAM CHARLES MACREADY

reads as well as an experienced actor would—he is a surprising man." Six days later there is this entry : " Dickens came with Forster and read his farce. There was manifest disappointment. It went flatly; a few ready laughs, but generally an even smile, broken in upon by the horse-laugh of Forster, the most indiscreet friend that ever allied himself to any person. . . . It was agreed that it should be put into rehearsal, and, when nearly ready, should be seen and judged of by Dickens." On the next day, however, Macready records that the farce is to be withdrawn, and a day or two later we have this entry : " Wrote to Bulwer, and to Dickens about his farce, explaining to him my motive for wishing to withdraw it and my great obligation to him. He returned me an answer which is an honour to him. How truly delightful it is to meet with high-minded and warm-hearted men. Dickens and Bulwer have been certainly to me noble specimens of human nature."

And so the proposal fell through. But Dickens was still anxious to serve his friend if possible. He had sent Macready a copy of *The Strange Gentleman*, which Harley had produced at Drury Lane a year or two before, thinking it " barely possible you might like to try it." " Believe me," he added, " if I had as much time as I have inclination, I would write on and on, farce after farce, and comedy after comedy, until I wrote you something that would run. You do me justice when you give me credit for good intentions, but the extent of my goodwill and strong and warm interest in you personally and your great undertaking, you cannot fathom nor express." There is no further reference to this play in this connection. Macready certainly never acted in it. A month earlier Dickens had suggested that his friend might appear in a version of *Oliver Twist*, but Macready's comment was : " Nothing can be kinder than this generous intention of Dickens, but I fear it is not acceptable." He was convinced that the book was utterly impracticable for any dramatic purpose.

Frequent were the meetings between the two friends in these early days, and on November 18, 1837, Macready was one of the company that gathered at the Prince of Wales Tavern to celebrate the completion of *Pickwick*. A fortnight later Macready records the gift to him by Dickens of a copy of the book.

In 1839—on March 30—Dickens presided at a dinner given in honour of Macready by the members of the Shakespeare Club, of which they were both members, together with Thackeray, Talfourd, Maclise, Jerrold, Stanfield, etc., and Macready tells us that the novelist's " speech in proposing my health was most earnest, eloquent, and touching. It took a review of my enterprise at Covent Garden, and summed up with an eulogy on myself that quite overpowered me. . . . I rose to propose Dickens's health, and spoke my sincere opinion of him as the highest eulogy, alluding to the verisimilitude of his characters. I said that I should not be surprised at receiving the offer of an engagement from Crummles for the next vacation." Later in the same year Dickens was one of the speakers at a public banquet given in honour of Macready on the occasion of the termination of his Covent Garden management.

When the announcement of the actor's impending retirement from Covent Garden was made, Dickens wrote him the following delightful letter :

" I ought not to be sorry to hear of your abdication, but I am . . . for my own sake and the sake of thousands who may now go and whistle for a theatre—at least, such a theatre as you gave them; and I do now in my heart believe that for a long and dreary time that exquisite delight has passed away. If I may jest with my misfortunes, and quote the Portsmouth critic of Mr. Crummles's company, I say that, ' As an exquisite embodiment of the poet's visions and a realisation of human intellectuality, gilding with refulgent light our dreary moments, and laying open a new magic world before the mental eye, the drama is gone—perfectly gone.'

" With the same perverse and unaccountable feeling which causes a broken-hearted man at a dear friend's funeral to see something irresistibly comical in a red-nosed or one-eyed undertaker, I receive your communication with ghostly facetiousness; though on a moment's reflection I find better cause for consolation in the hope that, relieved from your most trying and painful duties, you will now have leisure to return to pursuits more congenial to your mind, and to move more easily and pleasantly among your friends. In the long catalogue of the latter there is not one prouder of the name, or more grateful for the store of delightful recollections you have enabled him to heap up from boyhood, than . . ."

And he thus referred to the event in a letter to Laman Blanchard : " Macready has, as Talfourd remarked in one of his speeches, ' cast a new grace round joy and gladness, and rendered mirth more holy ! ' Therefore we are preparing crowns and wreaths here to shower upon the stage when that sad curtain falls and kivers up Shakespeare for years to come. I try to make a joke of it, but, upon my word, when the night comes, I verily believe I shall cry."

Many years afterwards Dickens paid (in *All the Year Round*, 1869) a tribute to Macready's Covent Garden management in the following words :

"It is a fact beyond all possibility of question that Mr. Macready, in assuming the management of Covent Garden Theatre in 1837, did instantly set himself, regardless of precedent and custom down to that hour obtaining, rigidly to suppress this shameful thing,[1] and did rigidly suppress and crush it during his whole management of that theatre, and during his whole subsequent management of Drury Lane. That he did so, as certainly without favour as without fear; that he did so, against his own immediate interests; that he did so, against vexations and oppositions which might have cooled the ardour of a less earnest man, or a less devoted artist, can be better known to no one than the writer of the present words, whose name stands at the head of these pages."

Between the dates of the two dinners referred to, Dickens had stood godfather to Macready's son, Henry. " One to be proud of," comments the father in his Diary. Dickens's acceptance of the invitation to undertake the trust was as follows : " I feel more true and cordial pleasure than I can express to you in the request you have made. Anything which can serve to commemorate our friendship, and to keep the recollection of it alive among our children is, believe me, and ever will be, most deeply prized by me. I accept the office with hearty and fervent satisfaction; and, to render this pleasant bond between us the more complete, I must solicit you to become godfather to the last and final branch of a genteel small family of three which I am told may be looked for in that auspicious month when Lord Mayors are born and guys prevail." The invitation was accepted, the expected branch—but not the " last and final "—arrived in October, and on August 25, 1840, Kate Macready Dickens—now Mrs. Perugini—was christened.

In 1839 Dickens gave Macready another proof of the regard in which he held him by dedicating *Nicholas Nickleby* to him in the following terms : " To W. C. Macready, Esq., the following pages are inscribed, as a slight token of admiration and regard, by his friend, the Author." The completion of the book was celebrated by a dinner held at the Albion, Aldersgate Street, at which Macready proposed the toast of the evening, saying that the declara-

---

[1] "The outrage upon decency which the lobbies and upper-boxes of even our best Theatres habitually paraded within the last twenty or thirty years."

tion of Dickens in his dedication was a tangible manifestation to him that he was not wholly valueless, and that the friendship of such a man increased his self-respect.

Three weeks later Macready received from Boz a copy of the book with this letter : " The book, the whole book, and nothing but the book . . . has arrived at last, and is forwarded herewith. The red represents my blushes at its gorgeous dress; the gilding, all those bright professions which I do not make to you; and the book itself, my whole heart for twenty months, which should be yours for so short a term, as you have it always." Macready's comment in his Diary is : " Returned home, found a parcel with a note from Dickens, and a presentation copy of *Nickleby*. What a dear fellow he is ! ' "

Boz had no more assiduous and no more admiring reader than this friend, who was one of the many to plead with him to allow Little Nell to live. " Asked Dickens to spare the life of Nell in his story, and observed that he was cruel. He blushed, and men who blush are said to be proud or cruel. He is not proud, and therefore——, or, as Dickens added, the axiom is false." The very next entry perhaps explains why Dickens blushed. Nell was already dead. " Found at home notes from Ransom, and one from Dickens with an onward number of *Master Humphrey's Clock*. I saw one print in it of the dear dead child that gave a dead chill through my blood. I dread to read it, but I must get it over. I have read the two numbers. I never have read printed words that gave me so much pain. I could not weep for some time. Sensation, sufferings have returned to me, that are terrible to awaken. It is real to me; I cannot criticise it." Who can doubt but that that blush was caused by the thought that the death of Nell would reawaken the actor's recent grief !

Macready showed his friendship for Dickens when, in 1841, the latter, contemplating a visit to America, was perplexed as to what arrangements to make for the care of his children during his absence. Macready relieved him of his anxiety by offering to undertake the responsibility. The offer was gratefully accepted, and the little ones spent their days at the actor's house whilst their father travelled in the Western world. How much Dickens appreciated Macready's kindness is shown, not only by his letters to him, but by his letters to Forster and others. During his journey from Pittsburg to Cincinnati, for instance, he wrote to the actor : " God bless you, my dearest friend, a hundred times, God bless you ! I will not thank you (how can I thank you !) for your care of our dear children, but I will ever be, heart and soul, your faithful friend." And he was.

He sailed on January 4, and on the 1st he said " Farewell " to

Macready. " Dear Dickens called to shake hands with me. My heart was quite full; it is much to me to lose the presence of a friend who really loves me. He said there was no one whom he felt such pain in saying good-bye to—God bless him." Some of the most interesting of his American letters were written to Macready, and when he returned to England Macready was among the first whom he hastened to greet. " I was lying on my sofa when a person entered abruptly whom I glanced at as Forster?— no; Jonathan Bucknill?—no. Why, who was it but dear Dickens, holding me in his arms in a transport of joy, God bless him ! "

In December 1842 Macready spoke Dickens's Prologue to J. Westland Marston's new play, " The Patrician's Daughter," and, according to his own account, spoke it " tolerably well." A little less than a year later he set out on his first American tour. Prior to his departure he was entertained to dinner at the Star and Garter, Richmond, and Dickens, who was the prime organiser of the function, took the chair. He was also made the recipient of a testimonial at Willis's Rooms.

On the advice of Captain Marryat, Dickens did not go to see his friend off for the States, the fear—which Dickens shared— being that the *Nickleby* dedication would damage Macready. America was angry with the author of *American Notes* and *Martin Chuzzlewit*, and " If I were to go on board with him," he wrote to Forster, " I have not the least doubt that the fact would be placarded all over New York before he had shaved himself in Boston. And that there are thousands of men in America who would pick a quarrel with him on the mere statement of his being my friend I have no more doubt than I have of my existence." During his absence Macready received from Dickens a copy of the *Carol*—" a little book I published on the 17th of December, and which has been a most prodigious success—the greatest, I think, I have ever achieved. It pleases me to think that it will bring you home for an hour or two, and I long to hear you have read it on some quiet morning."

When Macready returned to England Dickens was in Italy. None the less, he was greeted by the following letter which he found awaiting him : " My very dear Macready,—My whole heart is with you ' at home.' I have not felt so far off as I do now, when I think of you there and cannot hold you in my arms. This is only a shake of the hand. I couldn't say much to you if I were to greet you. Nor can I write much when I think of you safe and sound—happy after all your wanderings. My dear fellow, God bless you twenty thousand times; happiness and joy be with you. I hope to see you soon. If I should be so unfortunate as to miss you in London, I will fall on you with a swoop of love in Paris. . . . Again, and again, and again, my own true friend, God bless you ! ''

They met in Paris, and Macready writes in December 1844 : " Dickens dined with us, and left us at half-past five, taking with him the last pleasant day I expect to pass in Paris." Macready had gone to the French capital to fulfil an engagement, and Dickens met him there on his way back to Genoa from London, whence he had gone to give that memorable reading of *The Chimes* at Forster's chambers. Macready was not present at that reading, but on the night before Dickens read the book to him, and in a letter to his wife the novelist wrote : " If you had seen Macready last night, undisguisedly sobbing and crying on the sofa as I read, you would have felt, as I did, what a thing it is to have power."

In the following year Dickens and his friends gave the first of that memorable series of amateur theatricals, playing " Every Man in His Humour " at Miss Kelly's theatre in Dean Street in September, and repeating that play, together with " The Elder Brother," at the same theatre in December. It is not surprising that Macready's help and advice were much sought after by the amateur actors. Nor need we be surprised if the amateurs irritated him occasionally. " Called on Forster," he records, " with whom I found Dickens, and gave them the best directions I could to two unskilled men, how to manage their encounter in the play of ' The Elder Brother.' " And again : " Went out with Edward to call on Forster. Found Dickens and his tailor at his chambers, he encased in his doublet and hose. It is quite ludicrous the fuss which the actors make about this play !—but I was sorry to hear of intemperate language between them, which should neither have been given nor received as it was."

In 1851 Macready said farewell to the stage, and on the day after he had made his last appearance he received a letter from his friend which contained the following :

" I cannot forbear a word about last night. I think I have told you sometimes, my much-loved friend, how, when I was a mere boy, I was one of your faithful and devoted adherents in the pit—I believe as true a member of that true host of followers as it has ever boasted. As I improved myself, and was improved by favouring circumstances in mind and fortune, I only became the more earnest (if it were possible) in my study of you. No light portion of my life arose before me when the quiet vision to which I am beholden, in I don't know how great a degree, or for how much—who does?—faded from my bodily eyes last night. And if I were to try to tell you what I felt—of regret of its being past for ever, and of joy in the thought that you could have taken your leave of *me* but in God's own time—I should only blot this paper with something that would certainly not be of ink, and give very faint expressions to very strong emotions. What is all this in writing? It is only some sort of relief to my full heart, and shows very little of it to you; but that's something, so I let it go."

The actor went to live at Sherborne, and there he lived a life of quiet and dullness. As the Editor of his Diary says: " On the whole, the period of his residence at Sherborne must have been a depressing one, and he looms out of its greyness for the most part a brooding, sombre, figure much engrossed with family cares, and more than once bowed down by a fresh stroke of bitter affliction." And Dickens, in a letter to Forster, struck a similar note. Macready visited him in Paris in 1857, and after his return the novelist wrote to Forster : " It fills me with pity to think of him away in that lonely Sherborne place. I have always felt of myself that I must, please God, die in harness, but I have never felt it more strongly than in looking at and thinking of him." It was in these days that Dickens proved the sincerity of those professions of friendship which, as we have seen, he had made in his letters through the years that had passed. Lady Pollock bears testimony to this. " When the weight of time and sorrow pressed him down, Dickens was his most frequent visitor. He cheered him with narratives of bygone days; he poured some of his own abundant warmth into his heart; he led him into new channels of thought; he gave readings to rouse his interest; he waked up in him again by his vivid descriptions, his sense of humour; he conjured back his smile and his laugh— Charles Dickens was and is to me the ideal of friendship." Could any man wish to have a better epitaph than that?

In 1859, however, Macready removed from Sherborne to Chel- tenham, where he spent the remaining years of his life. There Dickens visited him in January, 1862, and his old friend came to hear him read. In a letter to Miss Hogarth, Dickens relates the effect of the *Copperfield* reading on Macready. " When I got home . . . I found him quite unable to speak, and able to do nothing but square his dear old jaw all on one side, and roll his eyes (half closed) like Jackson's picture of him. And when I said something light about it he returned : ' No—er—Dickens ! I swear to Heaven that as a piece of passion and playfulness— er—indescribably mixed up together, it does—er—no, really,

Dickens—amaze me as profoundly as it moves me. But as a piece of art—and you know—er—that I—no, Dickens! By ——! have seen the best art in a great time—it is incomprehensible to me. How is it got at?—er—how is it done?—er—how one man can—well! It lays me on my—er—back, and it is of no use talking about it!' With which he put his hand upon my breast and pulled out his pocket-handkerchief, and I felt as if I were doing somebody to his Werner."

Seven years later Dickens again visited Cheltenham, and gave a special reading of the murder scene from *Oliver Twist* for the benefit of his friend—now a feeble old man. Its effect on Macready has been told by many, but by none better than by Dolby. The latter took him to Dickens's room at the conclusion of the reading, and there, after being seated on the sofa, he said : " You remember my best days, my dear old boy?—No, that's not it. Well, to make a long story short, all I have to say is—two Macbeths ! "

And Dolby has also given us an interesting, if pathetic, picture of the old tragedian that same evening, when he entertained Dickens at his house. " Dickens was all life and vivacity, and when he found his old friend relapsing into feebleness and forgetfulness, was equal to the occasion, and refreshed his memory by some question about the olden days which caused Macready's face to change from its usual stolidity to an expression of quite vivacious humour." He had an idea that in his retirement he was forgotten by the world, and Dickens delighted him by telling him that his old harlequin had desired to be remembered to him. Says Dolby : " The fact of Smith remembering Macready put the latter in such a good humour that he insisted on having another bottle of the ' old straw Madeira ' . . . brought into the room. This being done he cheered up, and proceeded to tell us anecdotes of his managerial days. . . . In the recital of these he seemed to have changed his nature, and, as Dickens remarked afterwards, it was difficult to imagine that Macready had ever been anything but a low comedian. This little incident, told here, can scarcely produce much effect, but the *vis comica* employed by Macready, and the manner in which Dickens contrived to enliven his friend by his brief visit—and especially the way these stories were extracted from him—formed a pantomimic treat not easily to be forgotten."

This was the last meeting of the two friends. Macready outlived Dickens by practically three years. His daughter Kate, it may be noted, was a contributor to *Household Words*.

CHAPTER VI

ROBERT BROWNING

WE are told by the Editors of *The Letters of Charles Dickens* that Robert Browning was a dear and valued friend of the novelist. That is undoubtedly true, and therefore it is a pity that so little record of their friendship exists. Their friendship was inevitable, of course, for, with the sole exception of Dickens, Browning was Forster's greatest friend, and he was the friend of Macready too. And a friendship between two such men as Dickens and Browning was very natural. True, one was a cultured man and the other had no learning at all, but Browning was no ponderous pedant, and had none of the eccentricities or posings that are too commonly associated with poets. Both men were optimists. Both were sure that " God's in His heaven, All's right with the world," and preached that gospel untiringly. Both loved their fellow-men; both believed in and taught the gospel of love, and faith, and hope. I have seen no reference to the poet's opinions of Dickens's works, but we know that Dickens appreciated the worth of Browning's work from the beginning. He read " Blot on the 'Scutcheon " in manuscript in 1842, Forster having privately passed it on to him; and this is what he wrote :

" Browning's play has thrown me into a perfect passion of sorrow. To say there is anything in its subject save what is lovely, true, deeply affecting, full of the best emotion, the most earnest feeling, and the most true and tender source of interest, is to say that there is no light in the sun, and no heat in the blood. It is full of genius, natural and great thoughts, profound and yet simple and beautiful in its vigour. I know nothing that is so affecting, nothing in any books I have ever read, as Mildred's recurrence to that ' I was so young—I had no mother.' I know no love like it, no passion like it, no moulding of a splendid thing after its conception, like it. And I swear it is a tragedy that MUST be played; and must be played, moreover, by Macready. There are some things I would have changed if I could (they

D
33

are very slight, mostly broken lines), and I assuredly would have the old servant *begin his tale upon the scene ;* and be taken by the throat, or drawn upon, by his master, in its commencement. But the tragedy I never shall forget, or less vividly remember than I do now. And if you tell Browning that I have seen it, tell him that I believe from my soul there is no man living (and not many dead) who could produce such a work."

Peculiar interest attaches to this letter. It never saw the light of day—Browning never knew of its existence, until it was published in Forster's *Life of Dickens*. The play was produced by Macready in 1843, and there was unpleasantness between the actor and the author over its production. It was a failure. In 1884 Browning wrote an account of the whole business in a letter to Mr. Hill, then Editor of the " Daily News." " Macready," he wrote, " accepted the play ' at the instigation ' of nobody—and Charles Dickens was not in England when he did so : it was read to him after his return, by Forster—and the glowing letter which contains his opinion of it, although directed by him to be shown to myself, was never heard of nor seen by me till printed in Forster's book some thirty years after."

Now, Dickens returned from America in July 1842 : that letter to Forster was written in the last week of November. Browning says that the play was accepted by Macready while he was still at the Haymarket theatre, to be produced at Drury Lane later on. He adds : " When the Drury Lane season began, Macready informed me that he should act the play when he had brought out two others—' The Patrician's Daughter,' and ' Plighted Troth '; having done so, he wrote to me that the former had been unsuccessful in money drawing, and the latter had ' smashed his arrangements altogether '; but he would still produce my play." Browning, writing forty years later, suggests that this was a hint from Macready that he would like to be relieved from his undertaking, but that he did not appreciate it at the time. He then goes on to suggest. unmistakably that Macready set himself to fulfil his undertaking in the letter only, doing all he could to discourage the author with a view to disgusting him into withdrawing it. That is clearly the only interpretation of the poet's letter.

Why did Forster, the friend of Browning, Macready, and Dickens, withhold the novelist's letter; with its passionate appreciation of the play? The poet's biographer, Mrs. Sutherland Orr, says that he felt it a just cause of bitterness that the letter, which " was clearly written to Mr. Forster in order that it might be seen, was withheld for thirty years from his knowledge, and that of the public whose judgment it might so largely have influenced." Not unnaturally. The publication of the letter would have been balm to the poet in those days when he was struggling for recognition; at a time when he was being so much worried over the production of the play it would have meant much to him indeed. Then why did Forster, his closest friend, withhold it? Suppose he was torn by the claims of two friends? We know that he apprized Browning's genius at its true value, that he was the first critic of real standing to do so, and to foresee the poet's greatness. Suppose he felt that by withholding the letter he would be doing the one friend—Macready—an immediate substantial service, and doing the other no lasting harm, knowing that the actor had to " make good " in the present, and that the poet was certain of greatness notwithstanding a present disappointment? Suppose he laid this point of view before Dickens, and the latter said : " Very well; but publish the letter some day, to show to the world that I recognised a genius when I saw him " ? On any other grounds than these Forster's conduct is simply inexplicable. Dickens must have acquiesced, for he and Browning were friends till the end of his life, and but for some reason for silence, the matter must have cropped up in the course of an intimacy extending over thirty years.

CHAPTER VII

" PHIZ "

AT the time that Cruikshank was illustrating *Sketches by Boz* a much younger artist was illustrating another book by the same author. *Sunday Under Three Heads* was published in the same year, and a young artist of promise was engaged to do the illustrations. He had not met the author, but was destined soon to do so, and to win immortality through an almost lifelong association with him. How that came about does not need to be retold in detail. The first number of *Pickwick* appeared on March 31, 1836. Immediately afterwards the artist, Seymour, committed suicide. R. W. Buss took his place, but after two more numbers he was deemed unsatisfactory, and Hablôt Knight Browne commenced an association with Dickens that was to last for practically a quarter of a century. Browne was barely twenty-one years old, but three years previously he had received a silver medal from the Society of Arts for a large engraving, " John Gilpin's Ride." Buss afterwards stated that at this time Browne was " quite incapable of ' biting-in ' and finishing his own designs." This, I believe, is quite true; it is confirmed, indeed, by Phiz's biographer, Mr. David Croal Thomson; but the artist was able to rely upon the assistance of his lifelong friend, Robert Young, who was one of the most expert engravers in London, in whose hands Phiz's work never suffered.

I think that Buss was not given quite a fair trial, but we have to remember, in fairness to Dickens and the publishers, that *Pickwick* was in parlous plight—that at this time it was almost a " toss up " whether the work should be persevered with or not. Browne had already illustrated a book of Dickens's to the author's satisfaction. What more natural than that he should say, " Try Browne " ? From Dickens's standpoint, Phiz was ideal in this way—he was, as one of his biographers puts it, " a marvel of pliability "; he was " amenable to discipline," so to speak. It was sufficient for Dickens to say, " I want this done in such and such a way "; he could rely upon it being so done. I fancy the relations between Dickens and Browne, as author and illustrator, resembled those of superior and subordinate. If Browne had been

36

a man of very strong individuality I doubt if he would have illustrated Dickens for twenty-three years. In effect, he was content to receive instructions from the novelist and to do his best to give satisfaction.

It is said that Thackeray was the first to inform Browne of his good fortune. The story is that when Titmarsh submitted his sketches to Boz, the latter informed him that Browne had been selected, and that thereupon he hunted out the lucky man and congratulated him. It would certainly be like Thackeray to do so. Phiz's first published illustration to Dickens was the one which " standardised " Sam Weller, and it appeared in the fourth number of *Pickwick*, which was the number that marked the commencement of the book's wondrous success. It was indeed an auspicious beginning.

It is totally unnecessary to go into details concerning Phiz's illustrations to Dickens : all we are concerned with is the personal relations between the two men. And I fancy we shall be correct if we say that there was a friendliness rather than a friendship. Their temperaments were totally unlike. Dickens was a man of the world, always at his best in company, to whom, indeed, company was as the breath of his nostrils; Browne was a shy retiring man, who almost dreaded company. It was most difficult to persuade him to meet a few friends, we are told, and when he did accept an invitation, he always tried to seclude himself in a corner of the room, or behind a curtain. Mr. Arthur Allchin says, " Into the social life of Dickens Browne could seldom be drawn," and the artist's son [1] tells us that his father " was by nature shy and given to self-effacement, and when he became a busy man and had consequently little time or opportunity for social amusements, these tendencies increased till his dread of strangers amounted to a detrimental feature in his character."

" It became very difficult to make him go anywhere. At the beginning of his career he was certainly considered a cheerful companion, and took a part, if he found himself in congenial company, in any fun that was going. . . . But by living so much alone in his study, having an innate dislike of push, and a sort of natural distrust of strangers, he gradually worked himself up until it was difficult to get him to see anybody except intimate friends. He did not realise that there must be a stage before intimacy."

It is rather curious that Browne should not have been present at the *Pickwick* dinner. Neither Forster, nor Macready, nor

[1] The late Dr. Edgar Browne, of Liverpool.

Ainsworth includes his name among the names of the guests. He was present at the *Nickleby* and *Clock* dinners, however, and I believe he was present at all the subsequent book dinners until his business associations with Dickens were severed in 1859.

Before *Pickwick* was finished author and artist were on such excellent terms that Browne accompanied Dickens and his wife to Flanders for a summer holiday in July 1837. In January of the following year the two young men made their trip to Yorkshire, which may almost be described as historic, their object being to obtain " local colour " and first-hand information for the Dotheboy scenes in *Nicholas Nickleby*. In November of the same year, they made another excursion together, with the object of securing material for the same book, going to Manchester, ostensibly to see the inside of a cotton mill, but in reality, as we know now, to see the Brothers Grant, who were unconsciously to pose for their portraits to the brilliant young novelist, and were to be immortalised by him as the Brothers Cheeryble.[1]

The last book that Phiz illustrated for Dickens was *A Tale of Two Cities*. That was in 1859. I can find no evidence of any quarrel. Mr. Arthur Allchin says : " His (Phiz's) reserved nature was becoming intensified as he grew older, while upon Dickens began to flow that stream of flattery and adulation which eventually urged him to break with publishers, with assistants, and with tried friends." Quite respectfully, I beg to state my opinion that this is absurd, and grossly unjust to Dickens. The man had his faults unquestionably, but that the flattery and adulation of the world ever caused him to turn from any friend of earlier years, no evidence exists to prove. It is true that Mr. Allchin quotes Phiz as saying : " I was about the last of those who knew him in early days with whom Dickens fell out, and considering the grand people he had around him and the compliments he perpetually received, it is a wonder we remained friends so long." Phiz may have written this, but it would be in a moment of perhaps not unnatural pique. I am very sure that this was not his true judgment of Dickens. The novelist had been receiving flattery and adulation, and had moved among the highest in the land, for twenty years. If such things were likely to turn his head, they would have done so long before 1859. Whatever else may be said of Dickens, it cannot be said with any show of justification that he was a snob.

Then Mr. Allchin goes on to make another suggestion. This is to the effect that Phiz was dropped because he refused to side with Dickens in his domestic troubles : " Browne," he says, " persistently refused to express an opinion or to interfere, and

---

[1] See chapter iii.

(PHIZ.)

though Dickens said nothing further at the time, the book then in progress, *A Tale of Two Cities*, was the last Browne was commissioned to illustrate." One would like to know exactly on what ground the suggestion is based. Browne himself seems to have had no definite explanation, as witness his letter to his friend Young :

> " By your enclosed, Marcus is no doubt to do Dickens. I have been a ' good boy,' I believe—the plates are all in hand in good time, so that I don't know what's up any more than you do. Dickens probably thinks a new hand would give his old puppets a fresh look, or perhaps he does not like my illustrating Trollope neck and neck with him, though, by Jingo ! he need fear no rivalry there ! Confound all authors and publishers, say I ; there is no pleasing or satisfying one or t'other. I wish I never had anything to do with the lot."

This letter was so obviously written in a moment of irritation— at the very time when Phiz knew that he was to be dropped—that it cannot be taken seriously. But it does prove that, at the time, at any rate, Browne had no idea what was the reason for his having been dropped. Years afterwards he wrote the following letter to one of his sons, referring to *A Tale of Two Cities* :

> " A rather curious thing happened with this book : Watts Phillips, the dramatist, hit upon the very same identical plot ; they had evidently both of them been to the same source in Paris for their story. Watts's play came out with great success with stunning climax at about the time of Dickens's sixth number. The public saw that they were identically the same story, so Dickens shut up at the ninth number instead of going on to the eighteenth as usual. All this put Dickens out of temper, and he squabbled with me amongst others, and I never drew another line for him."

It will be noted that in the letter to Young written at the time, Phiz makes no mention of any squabble. I have been unable to find any confirmation of the statement that Dickens reduced the length of *A Tale of Two Cities* by one half ; there certainly is no internal evidence to support it. Nor have I found any confirmation of the assertion that Dickens was out of temper because of the success of " A Dead Heart "—though the coincidence must have been exceedingly annoying.

But, after all, there is a likely explanation for Dickens's change of illustrator. His old friend, Frank Stone, died in 1859, and he promptly exerted himself on behalf of young Marcus Stone, of whose abilities as an artist he had a very high opinion. As witness this letter that he wrote to Thomas Longman, the publisher :

" I am very anxious to present to you, with the earnest hope that you will hold him in your remembrance, young Mr. Marcus Stone, son of poor Frank Stone. . . . You know, I daresay, what a start this young man made in the last Exhibition, and what a favourable notice his picture attracted. He wishes to make an additional opening for himself in the illustration of books. He is an admirable draughtsman, has a most dexterous hand, a charming sense of grace and beauty, and a capital power of observation. These qualities in him I know well to my own knowledge. He is, in all things, modest, punctual, and right, and I would answer for him, if it were needful, with my head. If you will put anything in his way, you will do it a second time, I am certain."

Given a young artist of whom he had such a glowing opinion, given the desire to help him as the son of a very dear friend, given the opportunity presented by the publication of a new book— what more natural than that he should commission Marcus Stone to illustrate *Our Mutual Friend*? It may be, too, that Dickens felt that a change was desirable even though such a capable young artist, with such strong claims upon him had not been ready to hand. Phiz had been illustrating his works for twenty-three years; times had changed, tastes had changed; the style of illustration that was popular in 1836 was not so adapted to the tastes of 1860. We may well understand Phiz feeling hurt : nothing could be more natural; but assuredly Dickens had a very strong case indeed—a case possibly greatly strengthened by Phiz's action in joining the staff of " Once a Week."

But we have it on the authority of the late F. G. Kitton that relations were not strained for long, and that just after Dickens's death Phiz was " considerably affected by the mere mention of the name of the illustrious novelist, which seemed to stir up feelings of regret at losing such a friend."

CHAPTER VIII

THOMAS NOON TALFOURD

Pickwick appeared in volume form in the autumn of 1837, with a dedication to Thomas Noon Talfourd, with whom a close friendship had been formed while the book was appearing in parts. Dickens had first been drawn to Talfourd by the latter's activity in the cause of copyright. Sitting in the Press Gallery of the old House of Commons, he looked down, as we know, with something very like contempt upon the nation's legislators. But for a couple of Sessions before he left, he had the opportunity of watching the young barrister who had entered the House in 1835, and had been enthusiastic in the copyright cause. As a young author—not, of course, dreaming of the greatness that lay before him, but still conscious of abilities and hopeful for success—he welcomed Talfourd's efforts, and we may at least accept it as probable that his appreciation of those efforts led him to seek the acquaintance of the Member for Reading, who had just gained some fame as the author of " Ion," which Macready had staged.

Acquaintance ripened into friendship very quickly, and it is not surprising. In Talfourd Dickens found a man, not of genius, perhaps, but of great gifts and undoubted versatility. More than that, he had been one of Charles Lamb's intimate friends, and had known every member of that great company of stars that had had the gentle Elia for its sun; he had scored a success with " Ion," and he was a friend of the great actor who had staged the piece, for whom Dickens had from boyhood entertained feelings of the greatest admiration. To become personally acquainted with such a man must have been a great joy to Boz.

And so, by the time *Pickwick* was finished, they had formed a friendship that was never to be clouded. It is true that *Pickwick* was dedicated to Talfourd largely out of gratitude for his efforts in respect of copyright, but that was not all. The dedication was a tribute to the personal friendship which existed between the men. Talfourd was selected to occupy the vice-chair at the dinner which was held to celebrate the completion of this book. " And an excellent Vice he made," wrote Ainsworth; " he speaks with great fervour and tact, and being really greatly interested

41

on the occasion, exerted himself to the utmost." Whilst Macready records in his Diary : " Talfourd proposed Dickens's health in a very good speech."

Talfourd could scarcely have been a man of strongly-marked personality, otherwise the friend of Lamb, and Coleridge, and Dickens would be better known to posterity than he is. But he must have been a lovable man. " Facile and fluent of kindliest speech," Forster says he was. " Those who knew him," says Ballantine, " will never forget his kindly and genial face, the happiness radiating from it when imparting pleasure to others, and his generous hospitality," and Edmund Yates tells us that he was a " kindly host, with . . . beaming face." And when, in 1854, he died suddenly while addressing the Grand Jury at Stafford, Dickens paid a noble tribute in *Household Words* to his fine qualities :

> " So amiable a man, so gentle, so sweet-tempered, and of such noble simplicity, so perfectly unspoiled by his labours, and their rewards, is very rare upon this earth. . . . The chief delight of his life was to give delight to others. His nature was so exquisitely kind, that to be kind was its highest happiness.
> " An example in his social intercourse to those born to station, an example equally to those who win it for themselves ; teaching the one class to abate its stupid pride, the other to stand upon its eminence, not forgetting the road by which it got there and fawning upon no one. The conscientious judge, the charming writer and accomplished speaker, the gentle-hearted, guileless, affectionate man, has entered on a brighter world. Very, very many have lost a friend ; nothing in creation has lost an enemy.
> " The hand that lays this poor flower on his grave was a mere boy's when he first clasped it—newly come from the work in which he himself began life, little used to the plough it has followed since—obscure enough, with much to correct and learn. Each of its successive tasks through many intervening years has been cheered by his warmest interest, and the friendship then begun has ripened to maturity in the passage of time ; but there was no more self-assertion or condemnation in his winning goodness at first than at last. The success of other men made as little change in him as his own."

The man of whom that could be written, even by his most partial friend, must have been a good man, a man worthy of

Yours' faithfully

T N Talfourd

friendship, a man with whom the world ought to be better acquainted than it is.

Talfourd was one of the select circle in the days of Dickens's earliest happiness. In 1839 he was at the *Nickleby* dinner; two years later he presided at the dinner to celebrate the second volume of *Master Humphrey's Clock*. In 1842 he was one of those who entertained Dickens to dinner at Greenwich on his return from America, and he was at many other of these delightful gatherings.

In 1844 Talfourd was disappointed in what had seemed to be a grand opportunity of rendering his friend some signal service. The story of how Dickens's novels were plagiarised and pirated is well known, and it is equally common knowledge how strongly the novelist felt about it. At last, in a case of peculiar flagrancy in respect of the *Carol*, he took action in response to Talfourd's and Forster's urging. But the case was so flagrant that the Vice-Chancellor would not even hear Talfourd, who, of course, had been briefed by Dickens, and Forster comments : " What it cost our dear friend to suppress his speech by very much exceeded the labour and pains with which he had prepared it." After leaving the court, Dickens wrote to Forster : " Oh ! the agony of Talfourd at Knight Bruce's not hearing him ! He had sat up till three in the morning, he says, preparing his speech, and would have done all kinds of things with the affidavits."

The author of " Ion " was of course a great admirer of Dickens's works, and we are told that for the Artful Dodger he evinced a particular regard. As Jeffrey pleaded that Little Nell might live, so Talfourd pleaded for the Dodger " as earnestly in mitigation of judgment as ever at the bar for any client he most respected." And when the book in which the Dodger appears was completed he wrote the following sonnet :

" Not only with the author's happiest praise
    Thy work shall be rewarded ; 'tis akin
    To deeds of men who, scorning ease to win
A blessing for the wretched, pierce the maze
Which heedless ages nurture round the ways,
    Where fruitful sorrow tracks its parent sin,
    Content to listen to the wildest din
Of passion, and in fearful shapes to gaze,
    So they may earn the power that intercedes,
    Wills the bright world and melts it ; for within
Wan childhood's squalid haunts, where barest needs
    Make tyranny more bitter, at thy call
An angel face with plaintive sweetness pleads,
    For infant suffering, to the heart of all." [1]

It is sometimes said that Talfourd was the original of Tommy

---

[1] Another version of this Sonnet appeared in *The Dickensian* in 1905.

Traddles. I can find no proof of this, but there is just enough internal evidence to justify suspicion, so to speak. As Mr. Percy Fitzgerald says, " he may have offered suggestions for the character." Traddles's lovable ways and qualities of friendship may well have been taken from Talfourd. It is certainly conceivable that the latter's elevation to the bench just when the last numbers of *Copperfield* were being written suggested Traddles's destiny to Dickens. For though he has not yet donned the ermine when the book closes, we know he did so ultimately.

In 1846 Talfourd and his wife visited Dickens at Lausanne. In 1841 commenced the " splendid strolling " on behalf of Leigh Hunt and John Poole, and at one of the earliest performances— at Manchester—Dickens delivered a prologue written by Talfourd. In 1849 this valued friend was raised to the bench, which, says Forster, " he adorned with qualities which are justly the pride of that profession, and with accomplishments which have become more rare in its highest places than they were in former times." And he adds : " Talfourd assumed nothing with the ermine but the privilege of more frequent intercourse with the tastes and friends he loved, and he continued to be the most joyous and least affected of companions. Such small oddities or foibles as he had made him secretly only dearer to Dickens, who had no friend he was more attached to, and the many happy nights made happier by the voice so affluent in generous words, and the face so bright with ardent sensibility, come back to me sorrowfully now."

Upon his elevation Talfourd visited Dickens at Bonchurch, and the novelist wrote to Forster : " Talfourd delightful, and amuses me mightily. I am really quite enraptured at his success, and think of his happiness with uncommon pleasure." To that visit he also referred in the *Household Words* article from which I have already quoted :

" In the first joy of his appointment to the judicial bench, he made a summer's visit to the seashore, to ' share his exultation in the gratification of his long-cherished ambition with the friend '—now among the many friends who mourn his death and lovingly recall his virtues. Lingering in the bright moonlight at the close of a happy day, he spoke of his new functions, of his sense of the great responsibility he undertook, and of his placid belief that the habits of his professional life rendered him equal to their efficient discharge; but, above all, he spoke, with an earnestness nevermore to be separated in his friend's mind from the murmur of the sea upon a moonlight night, of his reliance on the strength of his desire to do right before God and man. He spoke with his own singleness of heart, and his solitary hearer knew how deep and true his purpose was."

Among the earliest public readings given by the novelist was one at Reading for Talfourd's sake. That was in 1854, not long before his friend's death. Talfourd was a native of Reading, and he represented the town in Parliament from 1835 to 1841, and from 1847 until he became a judge in 1849, and it was a pleasing thing for Dickens to respond to his friend's appeal to give a reading there.

Apropos of the fact that Talfourd sat for Reading from 1835 to 1841, it is interesting to note that it was in the latter year that Dickens was approached with a view to his standing for that constituency. I have never seen this fact noted before, but it is decidedly interesting, and it is scarcely fanciful to imagine that Talfourd must have recommended his friend as the man who might succeed him.

We may close with the story of a little joke that Dickens and Talfourd once played on Macready. Let it be related in the actor's own words. On December 6, 1839, he writes, "Dickens gave me a play to read called 'Glencoe,'" and on the following day, "Finished the play of 'Glencoe,' which has so much to praise in it." Then, on December 12, the entry is as follows:

"Went to dine with Talfourd. . . . Talfourd, Forster, and self. After dinner the conversation turned on plays. I mentioned one I had of a striking character upon a popular subject. Talfourd asked me the title. I told him 'Glencoe.' He questioned me about its possible melodramatic tendency. I told him that the treatment avoided the melodrama of the stage, that the style was an imitation of his writing, but without the point that terminated his speeches; that the story was well managed and dramatic, and that I intended to act it. At last, to my utter astonishment, he pulled out two books from his pocket, and said : ' Well, I will no longer conceal it—it is my play '—and he gave us each a copy ! I never in my life experienced a greater surprise. . . . I laughed loud and long."

CHAPTER IX

ANOTHER very notable friendship that was formed during the time that *Pickwick* was appearing in parts was that with Walter Savage Landor, to whom Dickens was introduced by Forster, who had met the poet in the summer of 1836. "That there should have been this communion of sympathy between two men of such widely different temperaments is a fact that can only be regarded as extraordinary." Thus commented a well-known newspaper upon the friendship of Dickens and Landor when, in February 1903, memorial tablets to both men were unveiled at Bath. And this particular newspaper was not alone; almost every leader-writer who dealt with the event wrote to similar effect. As a matter of fact, this point of view arises from the common mistaken notion of the sort of man that Landor was. He certainly was a very hot-headed man, but he was as certainly a warm-hearted man; though it is true that he was often wrong-headed, it is also true that he was always right-hearted. Though he quarrelled violently very many times in the course of his long life, he made many friends who truly honoured him. There is nothing surprising to me in the fact that such a man should have appealed to Dickens, with his appreciation of " thorough-going, ardent, and sincere earnestness," and his ever-present divine sense of humour. Landor's impetuosity, " the very fury of his superlatives, which seemed to go off like blank cannons, and hurt nothing," would but serve to strengthen the appeal that he would have for Dickens, who knew that he was " such a true gentleman in his manner, so chivalrously polite, his face lighted by a smile of so much tenderness," and that he " had nothing to hide, but showed himself exactly as he was." What, after all, is there so extraordinary in the fact that the novelist should have conceived an affection for a man whom he could thus describe?

And that Landor should have reciprocated the regard is no more remarkable. It seems to me to be the most natural thing in the world that a man of his enthusiasm for liberty, hatred of chicanery and humbug, and fundamental tenderness, should have welcomed the entry into the lists of so sturdy a champion as Charles Dickens, and formed an admiration for this young writer who moved to laughter and to tears, and almost in a day had gained the ear of the public in the cause of the suffering and oppressed.

Landor was sixty-one years old before the first number of *Pickwick* appeared. He was almost the doyen of literary men when " Boz " at an unusually early age started his great career. He had lived through great and stirring and epoch-making events, which had already receded into history; to Dickens he must have seemed like the survivor of a past heroic age. On the novelist's side there were reverence and enthusiasm for a " grand old man "; on Landor's there was a whole-hearted welcome for a young writer who promised to carry on the great fight against oppression and corruption, that he himself had waged all his life, and whose earnestness and frank joy of life must have had an irresistible appeal for him. There was, in short, a mutual admiration that developed into genuine affection, almost as of parent and child.

The poet's first message to Dickens is recorded by Forster as having been entrusted to him in April 1839 : " Tell him he has drawn from me more tears and more smiles than are remaining to me for all the rest of the world, real or ideal." The friendship quickly ripened, and on Landor's next birthday—January 30, 1840—Dickens and Forster, with Mrs. Dickens, and also Maclise, visited the old man at Bath, where he was then living. This visit is, of course, historic, because it was marked by the birth of the idea which subsequently took the form of Little Nell. It was a happy circumstance, for, as Forster tells us, " No character in prose fiction was a greater favourite with Landor. He thought that upon her, Juliet might for a moment have turned her eyes from Romeo and that Desdemona might have taken her hair-breadth escapes to heart, so interesting and pathetic did she seem to him." In lines which he addressed to Dickens in " The Examiner " in 1844, Landor wrote :

> "Write me few letters; I'm content
> With what for all the world is meant;
> Write then, for all; but since my breast
> Is far more faithful than the rest,
> Never shall any other share
> With little Nelly nestling there."

Forster adds that when the circumstance referred to was mentioned to Landor some years later " he broke into one of those whimsical bursts of extravagance out of which arose the fancy of Boythorn. With tremendous emphasis he confirmed the fact, and added that he had never in his life regretted anything so much as his having failed to carry out an intention he had formed respecting it; for he meant to have purchased that house, 35 St. James's Square, and then and there to have burnt it to the ground, to the end that no meaner association should ever desecrate the birthplace of Nell. Then," adds the biographer, " he would pause a little, become conscious of his absurdity, and break into a thundering peal of laughter."

For many years Dickens and Forster travelled to Bath on January 30, to help to make their friend happy on his birthday, and Mrs. Lynn Linton has told us something about the visit of 1849—Landor's 75th birthday. " Dickens," she says, " was bright, gay, and winsome, and while treating Mr. Landor with the respect of a younger man for an older, allowed his wit to play about him, bright and harmless as summer lightning."

According to Forster, it was on this occasion that Landor spoke of the many tears that *David Copperfield* had caused him to shed, " to which the author of that delightful book himself replied by a question, which, from so powerful and so gentle a master of both laughter and tears, startled us. . . . ' But is it not yet more wonderful that one of the most popular books on earth has absolutely nothing in it to cause any one either to laugh or cry?'" The reference was to " Robinson Crusoe." Here Forster's memory obviously played him false. This conversation is reported as having taken place in 1849, but as a matter of fact Forster is recalling a conversation which took place seven years later, and at which Landor was not present. This is proved by the fact that Dickens wrote the following letter to the poet on July 5, 1856 :

" . . . I have just been propounding to Forster, if it is not a wonderful testimony to the homely force of truth, that one of the most popular books on earth has nothing in it to make any one laugh or cry? Yet I think, with some confidence, that you never did either over any passage in ' Robinson Crusoe.' In particular I took Friday's death as one of the least tender, and (in the true sense) least sentimental things ever written. It is a book I read very much; and the wonder of its prodigious effect on me and every one, and the admiration thereof, grows on me the more I observe this curious fact."

After Landor left Bath [1] those birthday parties ceased to be, and when Dickens visited the city in 1869, poor in health, there was sadness in remembrance. " Landor's ghost," he wrote to

---

[1] He returned to the City some years later, but not to St. James's Square.

WALTER SAVAGE LANDOR
From a painting by Boxall, R.A.

Photo

LANDOR'S HOUSE AT BATH

T. W. Tyrrell

Forster, " goes along the silent streets here before me. . . . The place looks to me like a cemetery which the Dead have succeeded in rising and taking. Having built streets of their old grave-stones, they wander about scantly trying to ' look alive.' A dead failure."

Shortly after that first visit to Landor at Bath, in 1840, Forster was amused to receive from the poet, with the query, " What on earth does it all mean ? " a letter which Dickens had written to him :

> " Society is unhinged here (wrote the novelist) by her Majesty's marriage, and I am sorry to add that I have fallen hopelessly in love with the Queen, and wander up and down with vague and dismal thoughts of running away to some uninhabited island with a maid of honour, to be entrapped by conspiracy for that purpose. Can you suggest any par-ticular young person, serving in such a capacity, who would suit me ? It is too much, perhaps, to ask you to join the band of noble youths (Forster is in it and Maclise) who are to assist me in this great enterprise, but a man of your energy would be invaluable. I have my eye upon Lady ——, principally because she is very beautiful and has no strong brothers. Upon this, and other points of the scheme, however, we will confer more at large when we meet; and meanwhile burn this document, that no suspicion may arise or rumour get abroad." [1]

It is not difficult to understand that Landor should have been puzzled by the receipt of such an effusion ! It was all a wildly irresponsible joke, of course, " encouraged," Forster records, " to such whimsical lengths not alone by him, but (under his influence) by the two friends named, that it took the wildest forms of humorous extravagance." But it must have been sadly bewilder-ing to poor Landor !

In 1841 Dickens gave the poet marked proof of the esteem in which he held him, by inviting him to act as godfather to his second son. And he conveyed the invitation in a letter that must have sent a glow through the old man's heart. It would give the child something to boast of, to be called Walter Landor, he wrote, and to call him so would do his own heart good. For, as to himself, whatever realities had gone out of the ceremony of christening, the meaning still remained in it of enabling him to form a relationship with friends he most loved; and as to the

---

[1] About eighteen years ago, I saw this letter quoted quite seriously in a London newspaper as evidence of Dickens's occasional lack of mental balance !

E

boy, he held that to give him a name to be proud of was to give him also another reason for doing nothing unworthy or untrue when he came to be a man.

In December of that year the christening took place, and Landor came up from Bath for the event. " We had some days of much enjoyment," says Forster. The poet always took a keen interest in his godson's progress, one of his most winning qualities being his love of children. In 1851, when Dickens was engaged in that " splendid strolling," with the famous company of distinguished amateur actors, he wrote to his wife from Clifton as follows : " I saw old Landor at Bath, who has bronchitis. When he was last in town, Kenyon drove him about, by God, half the morning, under a most damnable pretence of taking him to where Walter was at school, and they never found the confounded house ! He had in his pocket on that occasion a souvenir for Walter in the form of a Union shirt pin, which is now in my possession, and shall be duly brought home."

In 1852, Dickens paid his friend another compliment by painting a full-length portrait of him in *Bleak House*—a portrait of him as he was when they were first acquainted, and undoubtedly as accurate a portrait as was ever produced of any man.

" We all conceived a prepossession in his favour," says Esther Summerson, " for there was a sterling quality in his laugh, and in his vigorous healthy voice, and in the roundness and fullness with which he uttered every word he spoke, and in the very fury of his superlatives, which seemed to go off like blank cannons and hurt nothing. But we were hardly prepared to have it so confirmed by his appearance, when Mr. Jarndyce presented him. He was not only a very handsome old gentleman—upright and stalwart as he had been described to us—with a massive grey head, a fine composure of face when silent, a figure that might have become corpulent but for his being so continually in earnest that he gave it no rest, and a chin that might have subsided into a double chin but for the vehement emphasis in which it was constantly required to assist; but he was such a true gentleman in his manner, so chivalrously polite, his face was lighted by a smile of so much sweetness and tenderness, and it seemed so plain that he had nothing to hide, but showed himself exactly as he was —incapable . . . of anything on a limited scale, and firing away with those blank great guns, because he carried no small arms whatever—that really I could not help looking at him with equal pleasure as he sat at dinner, whether he smilingly conversed with Ada and me, or was led by Mr.

Jarndyce into some great volley of superlatives, or threw up his head like a bloodhound, and gave out that tremendous ha, ha, ha ! ' "

And not only in regard to the broad outline of the character did Dickens draw upon his knowledge of his friend. One very important event in Landor's life is given with a disguise that must have been far from impenetrable to the poet's friends. We all remember the dispute that Boythorn had with his neighbour, Sir Leicester Dedlock, at Chesney Wold.

" ' But how do you and your neighbour get on about the disputed right of way ? ' said Mr. Jarndyce.

" ' By my soul ! ' exclaimed Mr. Boythorn, suddenly firing another volley, ' that fellow is, and his father was, and his grandfather was, the most stiff-necked, arrogant, imbecile, pig-headed, numskull, ever, by some inexplicable mistake of nature, born in any station of life but a walking-stick's ! The whole of that family are the most solemnly conceited and consummate blockheads ! But it's no matter; he should not shut up my path if he were fifty baronets melted into one, and living in a hundred Chesney Wolds, one within another, like the ivory balls in a Chinese carving. The fellow, by his agent, or secretary, or somebody writes to me, " Sir Leicester Dedlock, Baronet, presents his compliments to Mr. Lawrence Boythorn, and has to call his attention to the fact that the green pathway by the old parsonage house, now the property of Mr. Lawrence Boythorn, is Sir Leicester's right of way, being in fact a portion of the park of Chesney Wold; and that Sir Leicester finds it convenient to close up the same." I write to the fellow, " Mr. Lawrence Boythorn presents his compliments to Sir Leicester Dedlock, Baronet, and has to call *his* attention to the fact that he totally denies the whole of Sir Leicester Dedlock's positions on every possible subject, and has to add, in reference to closing up the pathway, that he will be glad to see the man who may undertake to do it." The fellow sends a most abandoned villain with one eye, to construct a gateway. I play upon that execrable scoundrel with a fire-engine, until the breath is nearly driven out of his body. The fellow erects a gate in the night, I chop it down and burn it in the morning. He sends his myrmidons to come over the fence, and pass and repass. I catch them in humane man-traps, fire split peas at their legs, play upon them with the engine—resolve to free mankind from the insupportable burden of the existence of those lurking ruffians. He brings actions for trespass : I bring actions for trespass. He brings actions for assault and battery; I defend them, and continue to assault and batter. Ha, ha, ha!'"

Forster relates several stories of Landor's quarrels with his neighbours at Llanthony, in Monmouthshire, and in those stories there are many touches which might have been taken from the pages of *Bleak House*. Here, for instance, is an extract from a letter of Landor's relating to the troubles he had with one of his tenants. The man referred to deserved the vituperation heaped upon him, it may be said, but the point is that the whole passage is entirely in the Boythorn spirit.

" I have mentioned only a few instances of this fellow's roguery and ingratitude; but enough for you to judge of him. All his brothers—three certainly—have abandoned every visible means of procuring an honest livelihood, and are with him; although his poor labourers are starving, and he has actually borrowed money from them. In fact, he thinks it more reputable to be convicted of roguery than suspected of poverty. He has embezzled the money I allowed for the repairs of the house, because I insisted on no written agreement and relied on his honour. He has discharged me and my gamekeeper from shooting on his farm."

Some time before that Landor, in view of the obvious need that existed for a Justice of the Peace in his district, appealed to the Lord Lieutenant, the Duke of Beaufort, to recommend him for the Commission. The Duke declined, and Landor wrote to Lord Chancellor Eldon. Here is an extract from the letter :

" When the Duke of Beaufort thought proper to decline my offer, I wrote again to him with perfect temper, and requested him to appoint one better qualified. He had no reply to make. . . . What honour it will confer on the Lord Lieutenant to have rejected the public and gratuitous service of such a man, is worth his consideration rather than mine. It certainly will bestow on him a more lasting celebrity than any other Duke of Beaufort has acquired. I did not believe him to have been so ambitious. But if it should appear that any Lord Lieutenant has erred in pursuing game by a track so unfrequented and so cheerless, your lordship at least has the power of preventing the ill consequences which would arise from his stupid precipitancy or his unruly passion. . . . It is possible that a Lord Lieutenant may have been instructed in little else than in the worming of hounds, the entrapping of polecats, the baiting or worrying of badgers and foxes; that he may be a perverse, and ignorant, and imbecile man; that he may be the passive and transferable tool of every successive administration; and that he may consider all whose occupations are more becoming, the gentleman and the scholar who is wiser or more independent than himself, as a standing and living reproach."

Does not Boythorn himself speak here?

Dickens pictures many of Landor's most winning traits. Every reader will remember Boythorn's pet canary which would be perched on its master's forehead, or on his finger eating out of his hand, what time he would be pouring out the most tremendous denunciations in the most thunderous of voices. Well, it is all a transcript from life. As one of Landor's friends wrote : " He was an enthusiastic friend, and as far as sound violence, and unmeasured vituperation went, a bitter hater; but beyond unsparing vituperation, he would not have injured an enemy. He would certainly not have lent a hand to crush him." And another friend wrote : " He had the reputation of being a violent man. . . . But I never saw anything but the greatest gentleness and courtesy in him, especially to women." In almost similar words Esther Summerson writes of Boythorn over and over again. And if Boythorn had his canary, Landor had his dormice and his pet dog. The latter—a Pomeranian named Pomero—was his especial favourite for many years. " By Heaven," says Boythorn, " he is the most astonishing bird in Europe ! He *is* the most wonderful creature ! I wouldn't take ten thousand guineas for that bird. I have left an annuity for his sole support, in case he should outlive me. He is, in sense and attachment, a phenomenon."

Writes Landor to Forster : " Pomero was on my knee when your letter came. He is now looking out of the window; a sad male gossip as I often tell him. I dare not take him with me to London. He would most certainly be stolen, and I would rather lose Ipsley or Llanthony." And when a lady asked him if he would care to part with the dog, he replied, " No, madam, not for a million of money ! " " *Not for a million !* " she exclaimed. " Not for a million," he added. " A million would not make me at all happier, and the loss of Pomero would make me miserable for life."

In 1853 we find Dickens acknowledging a dedication in these terms :

"My Dear Landor,

"I am in town for a day or two, and Forster tells me I may now write to thank you for the happiness you have given me by honouring my name with such generous mention, on such a noble place, in your great book. . . . You know how heartily and inexpressibly I prize what you have written to me, or you never would have selected me for such a distinction. I could never thank you enough, my dear Landor, and I will not thank you in words, any more. Believe me, I receive the dedication like a great dignity, the worth of which I hope I thoroughly know. The Queen could give me none in exchange that I wouldn't laughingly snap my fingers at."

Landor spent the last few years of his life in Italy, and in one of the last letters he wrote from Florence he sent his love to " noble Dickens." The friends had met for the last time just before his departure in 1858, which was in consequence of a libel action in which the old man had got himself embroiled at Bath. Passing through London, he stayed a night at Forster's house. Dickens was of the party there to meet him, but Landor did not join the company. Dickens left the room to greet his friend. " I thought," wrote one of the company, " that Landor would talk over with him the unpleasant crisis; and I shall never forget my amazement when Dickens came back into the room laughing, and said that he found him very jovial, and that his whole conversation was upon the character of Catullus, Tibullus, and other Latin poets."

Landor died in 1864, and in *All the Year Round* Dickens paid a tribute to his memory in a review of Forster's biography of their " mutual friend."

" In a military burial-ground in India, the name of Walter Landor is associated with the present writer's over the grave of a young officer. No name could stand there, more inseparably associated in the writer's mind with the dignity of generosity; with a noble scorn of all littleness, all cruelty, oppression, fraud, and false pretence."

Twenty years before, Dickens, about to journey to Italy, had asked Landor what he would most wish to have in remembrance of that land, and he had been told " An ivy leaf from Fiesole." Dickens had plucked a leaf and sent it to the poet " with his love." When Landor died, that ivy leaf was found among his treasures.

CHAPTER X

" DEAR OLD MAC "

Young Dickens—still not twenty-six years old—was now fairly launched on the sea of success. Instantaneously almost, he had sprung right into the front rank. At a bound he had become the most popular author that England had ever known. How popular he was has been told by many, and it is not my purpose to recount it yet again; but it is true to say that his name was a household word. He had awakened to find himself famous, his name on everybody's lips, he himself sought after by the most famous men of the time, who a bare two years ago had not heard of his existence, with whom, two years previously, he could scarcely have dared to dream that he might ever be on speaking terms. Yet here he was already on intimate terms with Ainsworth and Macready and Landor, and forming new friends as brilliant and as famous almost daily. Among these Daniel Maclise was the favourite. For years he played a very big part in Dickens's life, and a rare friendship existed. They were to drift apart to some extent in after years, but there was to be no quarrel or ill-feeling. Maclise was to meet with disappointment and injustice in the pursuit of his art, and it was to lead him into a waywardness (as Dickens called it) which was to cause him to drift out of the circle of friends who held him in such true esteem; but there was to be no real rupture of the friendship with Boz. The affection which was formed in the beginning was to last until the end.

In the early days, when each was in the first flush of his success, when hearts were young, and every month was May, they, with Forster, spent many happy hours. Other friends were with them sometimes—Ainsworth most often—but these three were " choice spirits," and every one who knew them at this time, tells how inseparable they were, and how they gave themselves up, heart and soul, to the enjoyment of life's morning. Scarcely a day passed but they met; scarcely a day but they were off riding or tramping together. Sometimes one would tempt the others; sometimes two would conspire to tempt the third. As thus :

" Mr. John Forster (of Lincoln's Inn Fields), and Mr. Charles Dickens (of universal popularity), request the favour of Mr. Maclise's company at supper, at the Parthenon Club to-night at half-past ten o'clock precisely.

" Thinking it possible that Mr. Maclise may have gone to Court at an early hour this morning, they address this letter both to his private house, and to the Athenæum; and but for the veneration due to their youthful sovereign, they would forward a duplicate to the Palace at Pimlico."

All records tell us that Maclise—this " dear and familiar friend " —must have been a glorious companion at this time—a companion after Boz's own heart. Handsome, brilliant, loyal, full of buoyant animal spirits, and yet with a full appreciation of the seriousness of life, he was a soul very much akin to Dickens Forster, in describing the summer spent by the novelist at Twickenham in 1838, tells us : ". . . the social charm of Maclise was seldom wanting, nor was there anything that exercised a greater fascination over Dickens than the grand enjoyment of idleness, the ready self-abandonment to the luxury of laziness, which we both so laughed at in Maclise, under whose easy swing of indifference, always the most amusing at the most aggravating events and times, we knew that there was artist-work as eager, energy as unwearying, and observation almost as penetrating as Dickens's own."

And he adds, " A greater enjoyment than the fellowship of Maclise at this period it would be difficult to imagine. Dickens hardly saw more than he did, while yet he seemed to be seeing nothing, and the small esteem in which this rare faculty was held by himself, a quaint oddity that in him gave to shrewdness itself an air of Irish simplicity, his unquestionable turn for literature, and a varied knowledge of books not always connected with such love and such unwearied practice of one special and absorbing art, combined to render him attractive far beyond the common. His fine genius and his handsome person, of neither of which he seemed himself to be in the slightest degree conscious, completed the charm."

It is scarce an exaggeration to say that not even Forster himself was better loved in the early days than Maclise, and there is something peculiarly sad in the record of the artist's cares and disappointments, causing him gradually to change his habits, until he " shut himself up within himself," and drifted away from the friends who loved him so well.

But " sufficient unto the day——" Let us not leave those early days yet. Dickens spent the summer of 1839 at Petersham,

DANIEL MACLISE, R.A.

and here, we read, he and Maclise were the most prominent in all sorts of sports. "Bar-leaping, bowling, and quoits," says Forster, "were among the games carried on with the greatest ardour. . . . Even the lighter recreations of battledore and bagatelle were pursued with relentless energy."

Of course, Maclise was present at the dinner given to Macready in 1839, over which Dickens presided. In this same year, too, he was one of the company that gathered at The Albion to celebrate the completion of *Nicholas Nickleby*. It was a happy thought of those concerned to hang his recently executed portrait of Dickens in the room. This, of course, was the painting known as the "Nickleby portrait," which now hangs in its rightful place, the National Portrait Gallery. It was bequeathed to the nation by Sir E. R. Jodrell, who bought it at the Gad's Hill sale in 1870 for £693. There are many portraits of the novelist in existence, but it is the unanimous testimony of all who knew him at this time, that this is by far the best. As a likeness, said Thackeray, "it is perfectly amazing; a looking-glass could not render a better facsimile. Here we have the real identical man, Dickens; the artist must have understood the inward Boz as well as the outward, before he made this admirable representation of him." It was painted for Messrs. Chapman & Hall for reproduction as a frontispiece to the first volume edition of *Nickleby*, and after it had been duly engraved for that purpose, it was presented by the publishers to Dickens—a graceful act. It was exhibited at the Royal Academy in 1840.

In 1840, Maclise accompanied Dickens and his wife and Forster to Bath, on that visit to Landor, during which Dickens first conceived the idea of *Little Nell*. This was but one of many trips in which Maclise accompanied the novelist. In April of this same year, for instance, the launching of *Master Humphrey's Clock* was celebrated by a trip to Stratford-on-Avon. The party was the same that had visited Bath. The *Clock* met with a huge sale, and so the holiday was extended somewhat, Lichfield being visited as well as Shakespeare's native town. In the same year, Maclise and Forster met Dickens on his way back from Broadstairs, where he had spent the summer, and they "passed two agreeable days in re-visiting well-remembered scenes" at Chatham, Rochester, and Cobham.

Naturally Maclise was to the fore in welcoming Dickens home from America in 1842. "By the sound of his cheery voice," says Forster, "I first knew that he was come, and from my house we went together to Maclise, also without a moment's warning." "Dear Old Mac" was present at the Greenwich dinner, of course, but, says Forster, "the most special celebration was reserved for the autumn, when, by way of challenge to what he had seen while abroad, a home journey was arranged with Stanfield, Maclise, and myself for his companions, into such of the most striking scenes of a picturesque English county as the majority of us might not before have visited; Cornwall being ultimately chosen."

The trip duly came off, and surely never did four schoolboys let loose for the holidays have a more rollicking time. Three weeks the tour lasted, and in that time " land and sea yielded each its marvels to us."

" Blessed star of morning," wrote Dickens to Prof. Felton, " such a trip as we had into Cornwall . . . ! . . . We went down into Devonshire by railroad, and there we hired an open carriage, from an innkeeper, patriotic in all Pickwick matters, and went on with post horses. Sometimes we travelled all night, sometimes all day, sometimes both. I kept the joint-stock purse, ordered all the dinners, paid all the turnpikes, conducted facetious conversations with the postboys, and regulated the pace at which we travelled, . . . and Maclise, having nothing particular to do, sang songs. Heavens ! If you could have seen the necks of bottles . . . peering out of the carriage pockets ! . . . If you could have followed us into the earthy old churches we visited, and into the strange caverns on the gloomy seashore, and down into the depths of mines, and up to the tops of giddy heights where the unspeakably green water was roaring, I don't know how many hundred feet below ! If you could have seen but one gleam of the bright fires by which we sat in the big rooms of ancient inns at night, until long after the small hours had come and gone, or smelt but one steam of the hot punch . . . which came in every evening in a huge broad china bowl ! I never laughed in my life as I did on this journey. It would have done you good to hear me. I was choking and gasping and bursting the buckle off the back of my stock, all the way. . . . Seriously, I do believe there was never such a trip. And they made such sketches, those two men, in the most romantic of our halting-places, that you would have sworn we had the Spirit of Beauty with us, as well as the Spirit of Fun."

Maclise's principal contribution to the artistic products of the tour was " The Nymph of the Waterfall." For the figure of the nymph, Miss Georgina Hogarth posed; the waterfall was that of St. Knighton. This picture was exhibited at the Academy in 1843, and Forster tells us that " so eager was Dickens to possess

CHARLES DICKENS

(1839)

From an engraving by Finden of a painting by Daniel Maclise, R.A

this landscape . . . yet so anxious that our friend should be spared the sacrifice which he knew would follow an avowal of his wish, that he bought it under a feigned name before the Academy opened, and steadily refused to take back the money which on discovery of the artifice Maclise pressed upon him." The artist, indeed, returned Dickens's cheque, with the following letter :

> " MY DEAR DICKENS,
>   " How could *you* think of sending me a cheque for what was to me a matter of gratification? I am almost inclined to be offended with you. May I not be permitted to give some proof of the value I attach to your friendship? I return the cheque with regret that you should have thought it necessary to send it to yours faithfully,
>   " DANIEL MACLISE."

To which Dickens replied :

> " Do not be offended. I quite appreciate the feeling which induced you to return what I sent you; notwithstanding, I *must* ask you to take it back again. If I could have contemplated for an instant the selfish engrossment of so much of your time, and extraordinary power, I should have had no need (knowing you, I knew that well) to resort to the little artifice I played off. I will take anything else from you at any time that you will give me, and any scrap from your hand; but I entreat you not to disturb this matter. I am willing to be your debtor for anything else in the whole wide range of your art, as you shall very readily find whenever you put me to the proof."

Maclise put his friend to the proof five years later. He then painted a portrait of Mrs. Dickens as a companion to the *Nickleby* portrait of the novelist, and this was accepted as a token of his friendship. The " Nymph of the Waterfall " was purchased after Dickens's death by Forster for 610 guineas, and is now in the Forster Collection at South Kensington.

In addition to the more extended trips, and to the daily ridings and trampings, to which reference has been made, there were frequent junketings. Macready, for instance, records on July 30, 1841, " Prepared for our long-promised expedition; Stanfield came to accompany us; we set out together, calling for Mrs. Dickens; went to Belvedere; arrived there, found the other carriage with Dickens, Forster, Maclise, and Cattermole. . . .

Leaving Belvedere, we lunched at the small inn, and returned to Greenwich, where we saw the hospital, and meeting Drs. Elliotson and Quin, and Mr. Roberts, we dined at the Trafalgar." On another date the actor writes, " Catherine called for me, and we went to Greenwich to dine with Stanfield. Our party consisted of the Dickenses, Quin, Liston, Maclise, E. Landseer, Grant, Allan and niece, Forster, who was *stentorian*, Ainsworth, etc.; cheerful day." Again, " Went to Richmond—Star and Garter; met Forster, Mr. and Mrs. Dickens, Miss Hogarth, Maclise, and Stanfield; we had a very merry—I suppose I must say *jolly* day—rather more tumultuous than I like."

And yet again : " Stanfield, Maclise, Mr. and Mrs. Horace Twiss arrived; then Mr. and Mrs. Dickens, Miss Hogarth, and Catherine, and Troughton, and we sat down to one of those peculiar English banquets, a whitebait dinner. We were all very cheerful—very gay; all unbent, and without ever forgetting the respect due to each other; all was mirth unrestrained and delighted gaiety. Songs were sung in rapid succession, and jests flung about from each part of the table. Choruses broke out, and the reins were flung over the necks of the merry set. After, ' Auld Lang Syne,' sung by all, Catherine giving the solos, we returned home in our hired carriage and an omnibus hired for the house, Kenyon and I on the box of the carriage. A very happy day."

Maclise's pencil was often at the service of his friend. For instance, Dickens took with him to America a delightful drawing of his children; and in the following year the well-known sketch of Dickens, his wife, and his sister-in-law was executed, of which, Forster says, " never did a touch so light carry with it more truth of observation. The likenesses of all are excellent. . . . Nothing ever done of Dickens himself has conveyed more vividly his look and bearing at this yet youthful time. He is in his most pleasing aspect; flattered, if you will; but nothing that is known to me gives a general impression so life-like and true of the then frank, eager, handsome face." Maclise took no part in the amateur theatricals, but there is in existence a fine painting by him of Forster as Kiteley in " Everyman in his Humour," whilst in the Dyce and Forster Collection at South Kensington, is a playbill of this play (September 20, 1845) bearing a pencil sketch by Maclise of Forster as Kiteley and Dickens as Bobadil. He immortalised, too, the famous reading of *The Chimes* at Forster's house on December 2, 1844. Further, he executed a drawing of Dickens's house at Devonshire Terrace, whilst his " Apotheosis of the Raven " is also well known.

Last, but very far from least, Maclise contributed illustrations to three of the Christmas Books—two each to *The Chimes* and

THE FOUR ELDER CHILDREN OF CHARLES DICKENS

Charley, Mamie, Katey, and Wally, with Grip the raven

From a drawing by Daniel Maclise, R.A., 1842

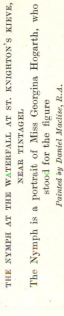

THE NYMPH AT THE WATERFALL AT ST. KNIGHTON'S KIEVE, NEAR TINTAGEL

The Nymph is a portrait of Miss Georgina Hogarth, who stood for the figure

Painted by Daniel Maclise, R.A.

The Cricket on the Hearth, and four to *The Battle of Life*, and also one picture, Nell and the Sexton, to *The Old Curiosity Shop*. " It is a delight," wrote Dickens to Forster with reference to *The Battle of Life*, " to look at these little landscapes of the dear old boy. How gentle and elegant, and yet how manly and vigorous they are ! I have a perfect joy in them."

Of Maclise's opinion of Dickens's work there is only one piece of evidence. In a letter to Forster when *Dombey and Son* was appearing in numbers, he wrote : " I think it very good—the old nautical instrument seller novel and most promising. I'm never up to his young girls—he is so very fond of the age of ' Nell,' when they are most insipid. I hope he is not going to make another ' Slowboy '—but I am only trying to say something and to find fault when there is none to find. *He is absolutely alone*."

It need hardly be said that Dickens had a very high opinion of Maclise's gifts, but that waywardness, to which reference has been made, and which is remarked on by several who knew him, was very early observed by the novelist. " He is such a discursive fellow," Dickens wrote to Felton, " and so eccentric in his might, that on a mental review of his pictures I can hardly tell you of them as leading to any one strong purpose. . . . He is a tremendous creature, and might be anything. But, like all tremendous creatures, takes his own way, and flies off at unexpected breaches in the conventional wall." To the same friend he also wrote, " You asked me long ago, about Maclise. . . . He is such a wayward fellow in his subjects, that it would be next to impossible to write such an article as you were thinking about. . . . He is in great favour with the Queen, and paints secret pictures for her to put upon her husband's table on the morning of his birthday, and the like. But if he has a care, he will leave his mark on more enduring things than palace walls." [1]

And with his inherent generosity towards his friends he wrote in " Douglas Jerrold's Shilling Magazine," August 1845, a fine appreciation of Maclise's cartoon, " The Spirit of Chivalry," which he described as " a composition of such marvellous beauty, of such infinite variety, of such masterly design, of such vigorous and skilful drawing, of such thought and fancy, of such surprising and delicate accuracy of detail, subserving one grand harmony, and one plain purpose, that it may be questioned whether the Fine Arts in any period of their history, have known a more remarkable performance." This cartoon was painted for Westminster Hall to the order of the Commissioners. How meanly and despicably Maclise was treated by that body of circum-

[1] It is curious that to-day Maclise is known to most people only by his frescoes on the walls of the Houses of Parliament—the Palace of Westminster.

locutionists is known, and Dickens, bursting with indignation at this treatment of his friend, whose genius he knew and understood, gave full vent to his indignation in this article, which breathes throughout the spirit of chivalry itself.[1]

As already stated, it was the bitterness arising from his treatment by the Commissioners that caused Maclise to lose his interest in life. His health had never been good, and it steadily broke now. He died but a few weeks before his great friend—on April 27, 1870. " Like you at Ely, so I at Higham, had the shock of first reading at a railway station of the death of our dear old friend and companion," wrote Dickens to Forster. " What the shock would be, you know too well. It has been only after great difficulty, and after hardening and steeling myself to the subject, by at once thinking of it and avoiding it in a strange way, that I have been able to get command over it and over myself. If I feel at the time that I can be sure of the necessary composure, I shall make a reference to it at the Academy to-morrow."

The reference was made at the Academy banquet on May 1. Having replied to the toast of " Literature," Dickens said :

> " I cannot forbear, before I resume my seat, adverting to a sad theme to which H.R.H. the Prince of Wales also made allusion, and to which the President referred with the eloquence of genuine feeling. . . .
>
> " For many years I was one of the two most intimate friends and most constant companions of the late Mr. Maclise. Of his genius in his chosen art I will venture to say nothing here, but of his prodigious fertility of mind and wonderful wealth of intellect I may confidently assert that they would have made him, if he had been so minded, at least as great a writer as he was a painter. The gentlest and most modest of men, the greatest as to his generous appreciation of young aspirants, and the greatest and largest hearted as to his peers, incapable of a sordid or ignoble thought, gallantly sustaining the true dignity of his vocation, without one grain of self-ambition, wholesomely natural at the last as at the first; in wit a man, simplicity a child; no artist, of whatsoever denomination, I make bold to say, ever went to his rest leaving a golden memory more pure from dross, or having devoted himself with a truer chivalry to the art goddess whom he worshipped."

" The words came from his lips, I have been told," says Dickens's daughter, Mrs. Perugini, " as though he were inspired, and after

---

[1] See *Miscellaneous Papers.*

the sound of his voice died away, there was for a few instants a great silence in the room, then all the artists and other guests present crowded round him, thanking and congratulating him." One of these guests has recorded that other toasts and speeches were to have followed, but after this magnificent tribute to the memory of a dear friend, the company, moved by a common instinct, rose and departed. All felt that nothing should follow such a speech as had just been made. To quote Forster once more : " These were the last public words of Dickens, and he could not have spoken any worthier of himself, or better deserved than by him of whom they were spoken."

CHAPTER XI

GEORGE CATTERMOLE

GEORGE CATTERMOLE, who was one of the most welcome visitors to Twickenham in that summer of 1838, had married a distant relative of Dickens's, and it was through his engagement that the novelist came to know him. Dickens was at his wedding, and, we are told, hilariously pelted the couple with rice. The following day he wrote from Petersham :

> " You know all I would say from my heart and soul on the auspicious event of yesterday; but you don't know what I would say about the delightful recollections I have of your ' good lady's ' charming looks and bearing, upon which I discoursed most eloquently here last evening, and at considerable length. As I am crippled in this respect, however, by a suspicion that possibly she may be looking over your shoulder while you read this note (I would lay a moderate wager that you have looked round twice or thrice), I shall content myself with saying that I am ever heartily, my dear Cattermole, Hers and yours."

Writing of Cattermole in those early days Forster says that he " had then enough and to spare of fun as well as fancy to supply ordinary artists and humorists by the dozen, and wanted only a little more ballast and steadiness to possess all that could give attraction to good-fellowship." This must not be taken too literally. It is merely a not very happy way of saying that Cattermole was not a practical man. Given the two alternatives that the late Mr. Peter Keary offered to every man, Cattermole would have " got out." He was a brilliant artist with a rare gift of fancy, who, if he had had anything of Forster's practical nature, would have made a fortune, and left a bigger name behind him than he did. But the artistic temperament was too strong in him, self-consciousness was a failing with him, it was not in him to " push " himself, and so he has suffered an effacement which ought not to have been his. He lacked those qualities of " push and go " which are worshipped with rather an excess

Photo

T. W. Tyrrell

4 AILSA PARK VILLAS, TWICKENHAM, WHERE DICKENS RESIDED IN 1838

of adoration in these days. He lacked anything like worldly ambition, and in 1839 refused a knighthood.

Dickens liked him immensely, and was frequently at his house, and the artist's son recalls the dinners at Clapham Rise, which, he says, " had a charm of their own." And Mrs. Cattermole speaks of the many kind and successful excursions that Dickens made to comfort and console him in the time of intense grief. " It was here," she says, " that Charles Dickens was the *friend ;* he could ' weep with those that wept and rejoice with those that did rejoice.' He was indeed a man of magnanimous and *practical* sympathy."

But, of course, Cattermole is known to Dickensians chiefly as one of the illustrators of *Master Humphrey's Clock.* It was in January 13, 1840, that Dickens wrote to him :

" I am going to propound a mightily grave matter to you. My new periodical work appears . . . on Saturday the 28th of March. Instead of being published in monthly parts at a shilling each only, it will be published in weekly parts at threepence and monthly parts at a shilling; my object being to baffle the imitators and make it as novel as possible. The plan is a new one—I mean the plan of the fiction—and it will comprehend a great variety of tales. . . .

" Now, among other improvements, I have turned my attention to the illustrations, meaning to have woodcuts dropped into the text and no separate plates. I want to know whether you would object to make me a little sketch for a woodcut—in indian ink would be quite sufficient— about the size of the enclosed scrap; the subject, an old quaint room with antique Elizabethan furniture, and in the chimney-corner an extraordinary old clock—the clock belonging to Master Humphrey, in fact, and no figures. This I should drop into the text at the head of my opening page."

And so Cattermole became an illustrator of *The Old Curiosity Shop* and *Barnaby Rudge.* He did 39 of the 194 illustrations for the *Clock,* and these comprised 14 for *The Old Curiosity Shop,* 15 for *Barnaby Rudge,* and 10 for the *Clock* chapters. For the most part he confined himself to the architectural subjects. How much Dickens appreciated his work is shown by what he wrote at the conclusion of *The Old Curiosity Shop* :

" I cannot close this hasty note, my dear fellow, without saying that I deeply felt your hearty and most invaluable co-operation in the beautiful illustrations you have made for

F

the last story, that I look at them with a pleasure I cannot describe to you in words, and that it is impossible for me to say how sensible I am of your earnest and friendly aid. Believe me that this is the very first time any designs for what I have written have touched and moved me, and caused me to feel that they expressed the idea I had in mind. I am most sincerely and affectionately grateful to you, and am full of pleasure and delight."

Indeed, he asked for finished water-colour paintings of two of the illustrations, and here is his acknowledgment of their receipt :

" It is impossible for me to tell you how greatly I am charmed with those beautiful pictures, in which the whole feeling and thought and expression of the little story is rendered to the gratification of my inmost heart; and on which you have lavished those amazing resources of yours with a power at which I fairly wondered when I sat down yesterday before them.

" I took them to Mac,[1] straightway, in a cab, and it would have done you good if you could have seen and heard him. You can't think how moved he was by the old man in the church, or how pleased I was to have chosen it before he saw the drawings.

" You are such a queer fellow and hold yourself so much aloof, that I am afraid to say half I would say touching my grateful admiration; so you shall imagine the rest."

Reference was made to those paintings and to Cattermole's aloofness in a letter written many years later (in 1868) to the artist's wife when he was sick unto death. The old intimacy had passed away—owing to Cattermole's aloofness—but the old friendship remained :

" My old affection for him has never cooled. The last time he dined with me, I asked him to come again that day ten years, for I was perfectly certain (this was my small joke) that I should not set eyes upon him sooner. The time being fully up, I hope you will remind him, with my love, that he is due. His hand is upon these walls here, as I should like him to see for himself, and *you* to see for *yourself*, and in this hope I shall pursue his complete recovery."

But it was not to be. The old friend had entered the Spirit World ere the year was out.

[1] Maclise.

Why Cattermole was never invited to illustrate any more of Dickens's books is a mystery that I cannot pretend to solve. But if the friends were never again to be thus associated, they were associated in another sphere of art, for Cattermole took part in some of the amateur theatricals.

He played Wellbred in " Every Man in his Humour " at Miss Kelly's theatre in 1845, and retained the part in the subsequent performance at the St. James's Theatre in November, and again in the London and provincial performances in 1847 on behalf of Leigh Hunt and John Poole. It is curious that Forster does not record the participation in these performances of so old and so close a friend.

After this there is practically no record of the friendship. Cattermole's appearances in the social circle became very rare. But the friendship, as we have seen, remained unaffected, and in 1852 we find Dickens writing this delightful letter :

" I was going to let off a tremendous joke about the new number coming out by and bye resplendently ' in parts ' (you perceive the subtle point ?) when my spirits were dashed and my intention balked by your not having told me the sex—which was absolutely necessary to the elaboration of the idea. But for this notification I should have had nothing but pleasure in the receipt of your note, on account of the baby, on account of the mother, on account of the father, on account of the welcome I give your handwriting and any sort of communication with you, however shadowy—on all accounts and for all sorts of loving reasons. . . . Now, don't you think . . . DON'T you think you COULD manage to dine here at the family board either next Sunday or next Sunday after that at five exactly ? . . . If you come I'll ask Sloppy to meet you, and we'll have a leg of mutton from Tuckersesesesesescscsesesesesesis in the Strand, where I understand they are perpetually a hulloxinin of Devonshire sassageses round the corner."

Forster does not quote this letter, but he explains the joke. " Sloppy " was a character—a " waterman " at the Charing Cross cabstand, first discovered by Cattermole, " whose imitations of him were a delight to Dickens, and adapted themselves in the exuberance of his admiration to every conceivable variety of subject." Forster adds : " ' Sloppy ' had a friend ' Jack ' in whom he was supposed to typify his own early and hard experiences before he became a convert to temperance; and Dickens used to point to ' Jack ' as the justification for himself and Mrs.

Gamp for their portentous invention of Mrs. Harris. It is amazing nonsense to repeat, but to hear Cattermole, in the gruff hoarse accents of what seemed to be the remains of a deep bass voice enveloped in wet straw, repeat the wild proceedings of ' Jack,' was not to be forgotten."

CHAPTER XII

WILLIAM MAKEPEACE THACKERAY

IT is not at all easy to arrive at any positive impression as to what were Dickens's relations with Thackeray, with whom he was already well acquainted at this time, but it seems clear that there was never an intimate friendship. For years they were on terms of cordiality; Thackeray was certainly a frequent visitor at Dickens's house from very early days, and they got along together very well until Edmund Yates brought about an estrangement; but they were men of totally dissimilar temperaments and up-bringing, and it is difficult to conceive of a real intimacy ever having existed. Thackeray had been well educated and moved in the atmosphere of the drawing-room and the club. Dickens " may be said to have educated himself "; he belonged to a totally different strata of Society, and could have had but little in common with his great contemporary. The one viewed life, so to speak, from the stalls, the other from the gallery. Thackeray's (superficially) cynical outlook on life must have irritated Dickens, whose boisterous, unashamed enjoyment of all good things could never have been understandable to the other.

One writer has said : " Dickens was a man of great vanity, wholly, or almost wholly free from pride. Thackeray was a man of great pride, wholly, or almost wholly without vanity. Dickens was vain of his literary distinction; Thackeray was too proud to be vain of his rank as an author. Indeed . . . he seems to be always more than half ashamed of his calling. Thackeray was without literary envy; Dickens had more than a little of that great defect of the literary character. Dickens was vain of his friendship with great folks; Thackeray was too proud of his natural title to be one of themselves to be vain of associating with the aristocracy." There is probably much truth in this. Thackeray's lack of pride in his art was the most serious defect Dickens saw in him. In the " In Memoriam " article in the " Cornhill Magazine " Dickens wrote :

" We had our differences of opinion. I thought that he too much feigned a want of earnestness, and that he made a pretence of undervaluing his art, which was not good for the art that he held in trust.   But when we fell upon these topics it was never very gravely, and I have a lively image of him in my mind, twisting both his hands in his hair, and stamping about laughing, to make an end of the discussion."

A lack of earnestness, real or feigned, was something with which Dickens had no patience at all, and whether we call it vanity or pride, he certainly held his art in the highest esteem, and was very jealous of it.

Much has been made by many writers of a jealousy which they allege Thackeray entertained of Dickens, but I believe that no such feeling existed.   Mr. Percy Fitzgerald tells us that in the 'fifties there were two " parties " in the literary world—a Thackeray party and a Dickens party; and that feeling ran high between them.   That is true, but, we may be certain that the feeling did not extend to the men themselves.   We have on record one or two outbursts of Thackeray's that most assuredly do not reflect the real spirit of the man.   They are cherished by people who cannot re-create for us the circumstances or the tone of voice in which they were uttered, and if we were to judge Thackeray by them we should be doing him an injustice.   James Cordy Jeaffreson says :

" It is certain that Thackeray, from the dawn of his celebrity to the last year of his life, was greatly desirous of surpassing Dickens in the world's favour, and at times was keenly annoyed by his inability to do so.   I question whether Thackeray had a familiar friend who did not at some time or other hear the author of ' Vanity Fair ' speak of himself as Dickens's rival, and declare his chagrin at failing to out-rival him."

Lord William Lennox relates that one night he dined at a house where both Thackeray and Dickens were among the guests.   After dinner, a young man, who sat next to Dickens and immediately opposite Thackeray, began to praise Dickens to his face in a fulsome manner.   " All of a sudden," says the narrator of the incident, " Thackeray stopped in the midst of a sentence, turned his chair round as if to escape from the sound of the flatterer's tongue, and whispered, ' Do you hear that ?   I go nowhere but I am subject to it.   I should not mind Bulwer-Lytton praised to the skies, for I own my inferiority, but—— ! ' "   Frankly, if I swallow this story at all, I do so with a spoonful of salt.   Thackeray acknowledging inferiority to Lytton is beyond belief.

WILLIAM MAKEPEACE THACKERAY 71

We are told—and it is a much more credible story—that on one occasion Thackeray exclaimed : " Dickens is making ten thousand a year. He is very angry with me for saying so; but I *will* say it, for it is true. He doesn't like me. He knows that my books are a protest against his—that if the one set are true, the other must be false." But of this I am very sure; there was nothing at all petty in his envy of Dickens. He was conscious of his greatness in his art, conscious, no doubt, of his superiority to Dickens in some respects, but no man more readily or more generously recognised and paid tribute to his great contemporary's genius. If there are on record many expressions of his envy, there are also on record many more expressions of his appreciation of Dickens's genius. Jeaffreson says that this envy was not a passion mean in itself : " An essentially and uniformly generous passion, it was attended with a cordial recognition of the genius of Charles Dickens, and with enthusiastic admiration of his finer artistic achievements. Though he often spoke to me of Dickens and his literary doings, I never heard him utter a word of disparagement of the writer whom he laboured to outshine." He further records that Thackeray once said to him : " What is the use of my trying to run before that man ? I cannot touch him—I can't get near him." Whilst on another occasion he said : " I am played out. All I can do now is to bring out my old puppets and put new bits of ribband on them. But if he lives to be ninety, Dickens will still be creating new characters. In his art that man is marvellous."

James Payn tells us that " what Thackeray . . . wrote of Dickens he also certainly felt. I had once a long conversation with him upon the subject ; it was before the shadow (caused by a trivial matter, after all) had come between them, but I am sure that would not have altered his opinion. Of course, there were some points on which he was less enthusiastic than on others; the height of the literary pedestal on which Dickens sat was, he thought, for some reasons, to be deplored for his own sake. ' There is nobody to tell him when anything goes wrong,' he said; ' Dickens is the Sultan, and Wills is his Grand Vizier '; but on the whole his praise was as great as it was generous."

And read this from Thackeray's own pen :

" As for the charities of Mr. Dickens, the multiplied kindnesses which he has conferred upon us all, upon our children, upon people educated and uneducated, upon the myriads who speak our common tongue, have not you, have not I, all of us, reason to be thankful to this kind friend who so often cheered so many hours, brought pleasure and sweet laughter to so many homes, made such multitudes of children happy, endowed us with such a sweet store of gracious thoughts, fair fancies, soft sympathies, hearty enjoyment? I may quarrel with Mr. Dickens's art a thousand and a thousand times; I delight and wonder at his genius. I recognise it—I speak with awe and reverence—a commission from that divine Beneficence Whose blessed task we know it will one day be to wipe every tear from every eye. Thankfully, I take my share of the feast of love and kindness which this noble and generous and charitable soul has contributed to the happiness of the world. I take and enjoy my share, and say a benediction for the meal."

Verily, here is no evidence of a petty or ignoble envy. In his lecture on Sterne he said : " The foul satyr's eyes leer out of the leaves constantly. . . . I think of these past writers, and of one who lives amongst us now, and am grateful for the innocent laughter and the sweet unsullied pages which the author of *David Copperfield* gives to my children." Then there is the famous eulogy of the *Carol* :

" And now there is but one book left in the box, the smallest one; but, oh! how much the best of all. It is the work of the master of all the English humorists now alive; the young man who came and took his place calmly at the head of the whole tribe, and who has kept it. Think of all we owe Mr. Dickens since those half-dozen years, the store of happy hours that he has made us pass, the kindly and pleasant companions whom he has introduced to us; the harmless laughter, the generous wit, the frank, manly, human love which he has taught us to feel! Every month of those years has brought us some kind token from this delightful genius. His books may have lost in art, but could we afford to wait? . . . Who can listen to objections regarding such a book as this? It seems to me a national benefit, and to every man or woman who reads it a personal kindness. The last two people I heard speak of it were women; neither knew the other or the author, and both said, by way of criticism, ' God bless him! ' . . . As for Tiny Tim, . . . there is not a reader in England but that little fellow will be a bond of union between the author and him; and he will say of Charles Dickens, as the women just now, ' God bless him! ' What a feeling is this for a writer to be able to inspire, and what a reward to reap! "

Of *David Copperfield* he wrote in " Punch " : " How beautiful it is, how charmingly fresh and simple! In those admirable touches of tender humour—and I shall call humour, Bob, a mixture of love and wit—who can equal this great writer?" There is, too, the well-known story of how, going into the " Punch " office, he threw a copy of the fifth number of *Dombey and Son* on to the table before Mark Lemon, and exclaimed : " There's no writing against such power as this—one has no chance! Read the chapter describing young Paul's death : it is unsurpassed—it is stupendous."

And, finally, we have the story that he told in the course of one of his lectures in 1855. He was speaking of Dickens :

> " All children love him. I know two that do, and read his books ten times for once they peruse the dismal preach-ments of their father. I know one who, when she is happy, reads *Nicholas Nickleby*; when she is unhappy, reads *Nicholas Nickleby*; when she is tired, reads *Nicholas Nickleby*; when she is in bed, reads *Nicholas Nickleby*; when she has nothing to do, reads *Nicholas Nickleby*; and when she has finished the book, reads *Nicholas Nickleby* again. This critic, at ten years of age, said : ' I like Mr. Dickens's books better than yours, papa,' and frequently expressed her desire that the latter author should write a book like one of Mr. Dickens's books. Who can?"

Has ever more charming tribute been paid by one author to another? It drew from Dickens the following acknowledgment :

> " I have read in ' The Times ' to-day an account of your last night's lecture, and cannot refrain from assuring you in all truth and earnestness that I am profoundly touched by your generous reference to me. I do not know how to tell you what a glow it spread over my heart. Out of its fulness I do entreat you to believe that I shall never forget your words of commendation. If you could wholly know at once how you have moved me, and how you have animated me, you would be the happier, I am sure."

No; it may be—probably is—true that Thackeray felt annoy-ance at the fact that such popularity as Dickens had won was not his, but he was too great a man, he possessed too big a heart, to be capable of such petty jealousy as some writers suggest. Was there any such feeling on Dickens's side? How could there be? From the day that Sam Weller saw the light, Dickens, until the day of his death, was the idol of his countrymen, and his books sold better than the books of any other author in the world.   Jeaffreson never met Dickens, and he was a friend of Thackeray's, so that on this point we may listen to him with confidence.   He says that Dickens never regarded himself as a competitor with Thackeray, and that " from the dawn of Thackeray's success to the hour of his death, the rivalry of the two novelists was a one-sided rivalry."   He adds : " Jealousy does not appear to have been one of Dickens's failings.   He had quite as much reason to be jealous of Sir Edward Bulwer-Lytton and of Wilkie Collins, when they were in the fulness of their powers and popularity, as he had to be jealous of Thackeray; but he lived in friendliness with them, and invited them to write for him."

Thackeray seems to have felt that Dickens did not like him personally.   What reason he may have had I do not know, but it is difficult to believe that if it were true he would have been a welcome guest at Dickens's home for twenty years.   At any rate, we do know that when Thackeray was going to America Dickens came to London from Folkestone especially to preside at the farewell dinner.   Forster tells us that there was a muster of more than sixty admiring entertainers, and that " Dickens's speech gave happy expression to the spirit that animated all, telling Thackeray not alone how much his friendship was prized by those present, and how proud they were of his genius, but offering him in the name of tens of thousands absent who had never touched his hand or seen his face, lifelong thanks for the treasures of mirth, wit, and wisdom within the yellow-covered numbers of ' Pendennis ' and ' Vanity Fair.' "   And in 1858, when Thackeray presided at the annual dinner of the General Theatrical Fund, Dickens, in proposing his health, said :

" From the earliest days of this institution I have ventured to impress on its managers, that they would consult its credit and success by choosing its chairmen as often as possible within the circle of literature and the arts; and I will venture to say that no similar institution has been so presided over by so many remarkable and distinguished men.   I am sure, however, that it never has had, and that it never will have, simply because it cannot have, a greater lustre cast upon it than by the presence of the noble English writer who fills the chair to-night.   It is not for me at this time, and in this place, to take on myself to flutter before you the well-thumbed pages of Mr. Thackeray's books, and to tell you to observe how full they are of wit and wisdom, how out-speaking, and how devoid of fear or favour; but

I will take leave to remark, in paying my due homage and respect to them, that it is fitting that such a writer and such an institution should be brought together. Every writer of fiction, although he may not adopt the dramatic form, writes, in effect, for the stage. He may never write plays; but the truth and passion which are in him must be more or less reflected in the great mirror which he holds up to nature. Actors, managers, and authors are all represented in this company, and it may be supposed that they have all studied the deep wants of the human heart in many theatres; but none of them could have studied its mysterious workings in any theatre to greater advantage than in the bright and airy pages of ' Vanity Fair.' To this skilful showman who has so often delighted us, and who has charmed us again to-night, we have now to wish God-speed, and that he may continue for many years to exercise his potent art. To him fill a bumper toast, and fervently utter, God bless him ! ' "

Temperamentally, I suppose, no two men could be more unlike than Dickens and Thackeray, but we may be sure of this—that Dickens never subscribed to the very common but very superficial judgment of Thackeray as a cynic. Ruskin says : " Those who are naturally proud and envious will learn from Thackeray to despise humanity; those who are naturally gentle to pity it; those who are naturally shallow to laugh at it." This is truer than many of Ruskin's literary judgments, but there is no profundity in it. If it is true that all great works of art reveal the personalities of their authors, then " The Newcomes," and " Pendennis," and " Vanity Fair " tell us that Thackeray was a man of wonderful tenderness, with a genuine love for humanity. His early sorrow had not embittered him, and if he laughed at humanity, it was always a sweet and tender laugh of toleration. He did not wear his heart on his sleeve, as Dickens, perhaps, was apt to do, but beneath the apparently cynical smile there was an almost womanly sensitiveness. As " Punch " said, when he died :

> " . . . if he smiled
> His smile had more of sadness than of mirth—
> But more of love than either."

Trollope was a very enthusiastic Thackeray worshipper, but there is no exaggeration in the following :

" He who knew Thackeray will have a vacancy in his heart's innermost casket which must remain vacant till he dies. One loved him almost as one loves a woman, tenderly, and with thoughtfulness—thinking of him when away from him as a source of joy that cannot be analysed, but is full of comfort."

We may be sure that Dickens never entertained any feeling of dislike for such a man. The truth is much more likely to be that Thackeray never really understood the author of *Pickwick*.

The first meeting of these two novelists is historic. Thackeray himself told the story at a Royal Academy banquet at which Dickens was present. Responding to the toast of " Literature," he said :

> " Had it not been for the direct action of my friend who has just sat down, I should most likely never have been included in the toast which you have been pleased to drink, and I should have tried to be not a writer, but a painter or designer of pictures. That was the object of my early ambition. I can remember when Mr. Dickens was a very young man, and had commenced delighting the world with some charming humorous works . . . that this young man wanted an artist to illustrate his writings; and I recollect walking up to his chambers in Furnival's Inn, with two or three drawings in my hand, which, strange to say, he did not find suitable. But for the unfortunate blight which came over my artistical existence, it would have been my pride and my pleasure one day to find a place on these walls for one of my performances."

One hesitates to hazard a guess at how much those drawings would fetch if they could be put on the market to-day. It is not the least of the debts that the world owes to Dickens that it was he who drove Thackeray to write, and thus to enrich our literature and to give us such friends as Col. Newcome and Major Dobbin. It is said, indeed, that at the time Thackeray remarked, " Well, if you won't let me draw, I will write."

The next time they met was at Harrison Ainsworth's house, and then we read of Thackeray as one of the welcome visitors at Twickenham in 1838. Thackeray endeared himself to Dickens's children : for this " cynic " was ever in his element when in the company of the little ones, and we have Mrs. Perugini's word for it that he was loved by her and by her brothers and sisters. He was a guest at the Children's Theatricals at Tavistock House, and Forster records how, on hearing one of the youngsters sing the ballad of Miss Villikins, the author of " Vanity Fair " rolled off his chair " in a burst of laughter that became absurdly contagious."

W. M. THACKERAY

DICKENS AND HIS FRIENDS IN CORNWALL
The carriage contains Daniel Maclise, Clarkson Stanfield, Charles Dickens,
and John Forster

From a sketch by W. M. Thackeray

In 1849 Thackeray was present at the dinner to celebrate the publication of the first number of *David Copperfield*. We read, too, of pleasant meetings in France. And here it should just be recalled that although Thackeray was not one of the party that made the Cornish trip in 1842, he produced a souvenir of that memorable jaunt in the shape of a rough drawing depicting Dickens, Forster, Stanfield and Maclise in the carriage in which they did their travelling. That they were certainly very good friends at this time is shown by the fact that in 1843 Dickens presented Thackeray with a copy of the *Carol* with the following autograph inscription : " W. M. Thackeray, from Charles Dickens (whom he made very happy once a long way from home)." I have been unable to trace the allusion here. That copy of the *Carol* has an interesting history, for, when, after Thackeray's death, his belongings were sold by auction, Queen Victoria sent an unlimited commission to buy it, becoming its possessor for £25 10*s*.

It is an ever-to-be-regretted fact that the friendship between these two great men should have been severed through the unmannerly conduct of a young journalist who, at the time, at any rate, was of no importance. Yates had started a paper called " Town Talk," and to this, in the autumn of 1858, he contributed an article on Thackeray. That article contained the following :

" No one meeting him can fail to recognise in him a gentleman; his bearing is cold and uninviting, his style of conversation either openly cynical or affectedly good-natured and benevolent; his *bonhommie* is forced, his wit biting, his pride easily touched; but his appearance is invariably that of the cool, *suave*, well-bred gentleman, who, whatever may be rankling within, suffers no surface display of his emotions. . . . His success with ' Vanity Fair ' culminated with his ' Lectures on the English Humorists of the Eighteenth Century,' which were attended by all the court and fashion of London. The prices were extravagant, the lecturer's adulation of birth and position was extravagant, the success was extravagant. No one succeeds better than Mr. Thackeray in cutting his coat according to his cloth. Here he flattered the aristocracy; but when he crossed the Atlantic, George Washington became the idol of his worship, the ' Four Georges ' the objects of his bitterest attacks. . . . Our own opinion is, that his success is on the wane. . . . There is a want of heart in all he writes, which is not to be balanced by the most brilliant sarcasm and the most perfect knowledge of the workings of the human heart."

There can be no two opinions : this article was grossly offensive. It may be said that Thackeray might have ignored the rudeness of an unimportant young journalist, but Yates and he were members of the same club, and I cannot but think that he acted in the only possible way. He wrote to Yates :

" As I understand your phrases, you impute insincerity to me when I speak good-naturedly in private, assign dishonourable motives to me for sentiments which I have delivered in public, and charge me with advancing statements which I have never delivered at all. Had your remarks been written by a person unknown to me, I should have noticed them no more than other calumnies; but as we have shaken hands more than once and met hitherto on friendly terms (you may ask one of your employers, Mr. ——, whether I did not speak of you very lately in the most friendly manner), I am obliged to take notice of articles which I consider to be not offensive and unfriendly merely, but slanderous and untrue. We meet at a club where, before you were born, I believe, I and other gentlemen have been in the habit of talking without any idea that our conversation would supply paragraphs for professional vendors of ' Literary Talk '; and I don't remember that out of that club I have ever exchanged six words with you. Allow me to inform you that the talk which you have heard there is not intended for newspaper remark, and to beg—as I have a right to do—that you will refrain from printing comments upon my private conversations; that you will forego discussions, however blundering, upon my private affairs; and that you will henceforth please to consider any question of my personal truth and sincerity as quite out of the province of your criticism."

Yates, writing long afterwards, says : " I think it must be admitted by the most impartial reader that this letter is severe to the point of cruelty; that whatever the silliness and impertinence of the article, it was scarcely calculated to have provoked so curiously bitter an outburst of personal feeling against its writer; that in comparison with the offence committed by me, the censure administered by Mr. Thackeray is almost ludicrously exaggerated." I cannot follow the argument. Yates's article had been not merely silly and impertinent; it had been libellous; it had impugned the personal honour of one of the best-known men of the time. If Yates had promptly apologised the matter would have gone no further. But, with all the " cleverness " and

" smartness " of youth, he " put himself on his dignity " and adopted an utterly impossible attitude. He drafted a reply to Thackeray's letter, reminding that writer how he himself had lampooned many of his fellow-authors. The letter was never sent—unhappily, as Yates says. He submitted it to Dickens, and Dickens was of opinion that it was " too flippant and too violent." Together they compiled the following letter, which was duly forwarded :

> " I have to acknowledge receipt of your letter. . . . You will excuse my pointing out to you that it is absurd to suppose me bound to accept your angry ' understanding ' of my ' phrases.' I do not accept it in the least : I altogether reject it. I cannot characterise your letter in any other terms than those in which you characterise the article which has given you so much offence. If your letter to me were not both ' slanderous and untrue,' I should readily have discussed its subject with you and avowed my earnest and frank desire to set right anything I may have left wrong. Your letter being what it is, I have nothing to add to my present reply."

The article had been libellous; this letter was both " silly " and " impertinent." It is astounding that Dickens could have assisted in the drafting of it. If Thackeray's letter had been four times as severe as it was, that would not have altered the fact that Yates had been guilty of inexcusable conduct, and could not have released him from the obligations of a gentleman. On the receipt of this letter, Thackeray decided to take more drastic action. He reported the matter to the Committee of the Garrick Club—the club referred to in his letter. The Committee decided that " the practice of publishing such articles, being reflections by one member of the club against any other, will be fatal to the comfort of the club, and is intolerable in a society of gentlemen." There surely can be no disputing such a proposition. Yates was called upon either to make an ample apology or to retire from the club. He declined to do either, and appealed to a General Meeting. At that meeting, Dickens, Wilkie Collins, and Samuel Lover were among those who spoke in his defence, but the decision went against him. He then started an action at law. It was at this stage that Dickens made his serious mistake. He had all through acted as Yates's leading counsel, yet now he actually proposed to act as a mediator. He wrote to Thackeray :

" . . . .

Can any conference be held between me, as representing

Mr. Yates, and an appointed friend of yours, as representing you, with the hope and purpose of some quiet accommodation of this deplorable matter, which will satisfy the feelings of all concerned?

" It is right that, in putting this to you, I should tell you that Mr. Yates, when you first wrote to him, brought your letter to me. He had recently done me a manly service I can never forget, in some private distress of mine (generally within your knowledge), and he naturally thought of me as his friend in an emergency. I told him that his article was not to be defended; but I confirmed him in his opinion that it was not reasonably possible for him to set right what was amiss, on the receipt of a letter couched in the very strong terms you employed.

" When you appealed to the Garrick Committee, and they called their General Meeting, I said at that meeting that you and I had been on good terms for many years, and that I was very sorry to find myself opposed to you; but that I was clear that the Committee had nothing on earth to do with it, and that on the strength of my conviction I should go against them.

" If this mediation that I have suggested can take place, I shall be heartily glad to do my best in it—and God knows in no hostile spirit towards any one, least of all to you. If it cannot take place, the thing is at least no worse than it was; and you will burn this letter, and I will burn your answer."

Of course it could not take place. It was a most futile pro-position, seeing that Dickens held such strong views. Thackeray replied :

" I grieve to gather from your letter that you were Mr. Yates's adviser in the dispute between me and him. His letter was the cause of my appeal to the Garrick Club for protection from insults against which I had no other remedy.

" I placed my grievance before the Committee of the Garrick Club as the only place where I have been accustomed to meet Mr. Yates. They gave their opinion of his conduct and of the reparation which lay in his power. Not satisfied with their sentence, Mr. Yates called for a General Meeting; and, the meeting which he had called having declared against him, he declines the jurisdiction which he had asked for, and says he will have recourse to lawyers.

" Ever since I submitted my case to the club, I have had, and can have, no part in the dispute. It is for them to judge if any reconcilement is possible with your friend."

He added that he had forwarded Dickens's letter to the Committee of the club, and enclosed a copy of his covering letter. In the latter he had written that he was still, as ever, prepared to abide by their decision. What other reply could he have given to Dickens? The Committee did not accept the latter's offer. The legal proceedings fell through on a technicality, but Yates resigned his membership of the club, and Dickens walked out with him.

The whole story is a sorry one, and I scarcely think it can be wondered at if the knowledge of the part played by Dickens embittered Thackeray. An estrangement ensued that lasted for years. Yates says : " There is no doubt it was pretty generally said at the time, as it has been said since, and is said even now, that this whole affair was a struggle for supremacy or an outburst of jealousy between Thackeray and Dickens, and that my part was merely that of a scapegoat or shuttlecock." This is nonsense, for when Thackeray first reported the matter to the Committee of the Garrick Club, he had no suspicion that Dickens was behind Yates.

What were Dickens's feelings we do not know, but we do know—on the evidence of Dickens's daughter—that after a time Thackeray entertained feelings of genuine regret at the estrangement, and on more than one occasion expressed to her a wish that there could be a reconciliation. It came eventually, and it was the " cynic " who made the first advance. Sir Theodore Martin was a witness of the incident. He was standing, he tells us, talking to Thackeray in the hall of the Athenæum Club, when Dickens came out of the room where he had been reading the morning papers, and, passing close to them without making any sign of recognition, crossed the hall to the staircase that led to the library. Suddenly, Thackeray broke away, and reached Dickens just as the latter had his foot on the staircase.

" Dickens turned to him, and I saw Thackeray speak and presently hold out his hand to Dickens. They shook hands, a few words were exchanged, and immediately Thackeray returned to me, saying, ' I'm glad I have done this : I said, " It is time this foolish estrangement should cease, and that we should be to each other what we used to be. Come; shake hands." ' Dickens, he said, seemed at first rather taken aback, but held out his hand, and some friendly words

G

were exchanged. Thackeray also said, ' I love the man, and I could not resist the impulse.' "

Thirteen days later Dickens was standing at the graveside of his friend in Kensal Green cemetery. In September 1870, three months after Dickens himself had been laid to rest, an anonymous writer in " Harper's Magazine " recorded : " I remember Dickens at the grave of Thackeray. . . . On the day when that great and true man was laid in his grave in Kensal Green . . . Dickens had a look of bereavement in his face which was indescribable. When all others had turned aside from the grave he still stood there, as if rooted to the spot, watching with almost haggard eyes every spadeful of dust that was thrown upon it. Walking away with some friends, he began to talk, but presently in some sentence his voice quivered a little, and shaking hands all round rapidly he went off alone."

That chance meeting at the Athenæum Club must have been held by Dickens in precious remembrance when he wrote shortly afterwards in the " Cornhill Magazine " :

" The last words he ever corrected in print were, ' And my heart throbbed with an exquisite bliss.' God grant that on that Christmas Eve, when he laid his head back on his pillow and threw up his hands, as he was wont to do when very weary, some consciousness of duty done, and Christian hope throughout life humbly cherished, may have caused his own heart to throb when he passed away to his Redeemer's rest ! "

CHAPTER XIII

DOUGLAS JERROLD

With Douglas Jerrold, Dickens undoubtedly had much more in common than with Thackeray, and there were very few of his friends whom he held in greater esteem. To the average man of the present generation Jerrold is hardly a figure of flesh and blood. It is a pity, because in reality, beneath his cold exterior, behind the biting wit, there beat a tender heart; behind the satirist, there was a man of a lovable and winsome nature, who could be the most delightful of companions and truest of friends to those who had once won his confidence. And who more likely to win his confidence than the Boz of the late 'thirties and early 'forties? Both had studied in hard schools, and both had come out of the ordeal with a passionate desire to do something to make the world brighter for those who should come after them. Those early experiences had made Jerrold angry with the world; they had not taught him the broad, good-humoured tolerance that they had taught Dickens, but they had made him, as they had made the other, tender and sympathetic towards those who suffered from the world's cruelty and neglect. To a man of Jerrold's nature, the friendship of Dickens must have meant much. And he valued it : saving only Blanchard's, there was no friendship that he valued more. And that Dickens had a great regard for him, there is plenty of evidence to show.

Yet even Dickens could not win Jerrold's confidence at once. They met first in 1835, and in 1844 we find Dickens writing : " I wish we had not lost so much time in improving our personal knowledge of each other." They had been friends all those nine years, but there had been none of that mutual confidence which is the highest manifestation of friendship. Henceforth, however, it existed, and with a brief unhappy interruption, it lasted to the end.

Macready mentions many dinner-parties at which the friends were present, and Blanchard Jerrold, in his biography of his father, recalls a happy evening at his home when the host and Dickens and Forster and Maclise and Macready " indulged in a most active game of leap-frog, the backs being requested to turn in any obtrusive ' twopenny,' with the real zest of fourteen ! "

83

And he adds : " Never were boys more completely possessed of the spirit of the game in a seminary playground." It is not easy to conjure up the picture in its completeness. Dickens and Maclise and Forster?—yes; Jerrold?—h'm, well, yes; but Macready !—the staid and sedate W. C. M. playing at leap-frog ! It almost baffles imagination !

In 1843 Dickens and Jerrold had an amusing correspondence. Benjamin Webster set the ball rolling by offering a prize of £500 for the best five-act comedy. Jerrold allowed his wit to play round this, and rallied all his friends as possible competitors. To Dickens he wrote :

> " Of course, you have flung *Chuzzlewit* to the winds, and are hard at work upon a comedy. Somebody—I forget his name—told me that you were seen at the Haymarket door, with a wet newspaper in your hand, knocking frantically for Webster. . . . Mind, you must send in your play by Michaelmas—it is thought Michaelmas day itself will be selected by many of the competitors; for, as there will be about five hundred (at least) comedies, and as the Committee cannot read above two at a sitting, how—unless, indeed, they raffle for choice—can they select the true thing—the phœnix from the geese—by January 1st, 1844 ? You must make haste, so don't go out o' nights."

To which Dickens entering into the spirit of the fooling, as he so well knew how to do, replied as follows :

> " Yes, you have anticipated my occupation. *Chuzzlewit* be d—d. High comedy and five hundred pounds are the only matters I can think of. I call it *The One Thing Needful*, or *A Part is Better than the Whole*.

> " But I have my comedy to fly to. My only comfort ! I walk up and down the street at the back of the theatre every night and peep in at the green-room window, thinking of the time when ' Dickens ' will be called for by excited hundreds, and won't come till Mr. Webster . . . shall enter from his dressing-room, and quelling the tempest with a smile, beseech that wizard, if he be in the house (here he looks up at my box), to accept the congratulations of the audience, and indulge them with a sight of the man who has got five hundred pounds in money, and it's impossible to say how much in laurel. Then I shall come forward, and bow once — twice —thrice—roars of approbation—Brayvo—brarvo—hooray—

hoorar—hooroar—one cheer more; and asking Webster home to supper, shall declare eternal friendship for that public-spirited individual . . .

> "I am always, my dear Jerrold,
> "Faithfully your Friend,
> "THE CONGREVE OF THE NINETEENTH CENTURY

(which I mean to be called in the Sunday papers).

> "P.S.—I shall dedicate it to Webster, beginning: 'My dear Sir,—When you first proposed to stimulate the slumbering dramatic talent of England, I assure you I had not the least idea,'—etc., etc., etc."

Dickens and Jerrold had a true admiration for each other's work. Several times Dickens writes appreciatively of his friend's books, and Forster tells us that he derived special enjoyment from "The Story of a Feather." Jerrold's admiration of his friend's work was no less enthusiastic. In 1843 he wrote a most appreciative notice of the *Carol* in "Punch," and in other journals with which he was associated he paid tribute to Dickens's genius.

The "Punch" notice of the *Carol* drew from Dickens (then at Cremona) a long letter in which he wrote : "It was very hearty and good of you, Jerrold, to make that affectionate mention of the *Carol* in 'Punch,' and I assure you it was not lost on the distant object of your manly regard, but touched him as you wished and meant it should." The letter also included this hearty invitation :

> "You rather entertained a notion once of coming to see me at Genoa. I shall return straight, on the ninth of December, limiting my stay in town to one week. Now couldn't you come back with me? One journey, that way, is very cheap, costing little more than twelve pounds; and I am sure the gratification to you would be high. I am lodged in quite a wonderful place, and could put you in a painted room, as big as a church and much more comfortable. There are pens and ink upon the premises, orange trees, gardens, battledores and shuttlecocks, rousing wood-fires for evenings, and a welcome worth having.
> "Come! . . . Letter from a gentleman in a country gone to sleep to a gentleman in a country that would go to sleep too, and never wake again, if some people had their way. You can work in Genoa. The house is used to it. It is exactly a week's post. Have that portmanteau looked to, and when we meet, say : 'I am coming!'"

The temptation to the hard-worked and none too affluent Douglas Jerrold must have been sore indeed. The forthcoming meeting referred to in this letter was that historic gathering at Forster's home on December 2, 1844, when Dickens read *The Chimes* to a few of his most intimate friends. Jerrold was there at the novelist's express wish—" Jerrold I should particularly wish," he had written to Forster. And in the letter from which we have just quoted he had conveyed the invitation in these words : " Forster has told you, or will tell you, that I very much wish you to hear my little Christmas book; and I hope you will meet me at his bidding in Lincoln's Inn Fields. I have tried to strike a blow upon that part of the brass countenance of wicked Cant; when such a compliment is sorely needed at this time, and I trust that the result of my training is at least the exhibition of a strong desire to make it a staggerer. If *you* should think at the end of the four rounds (there are no more) that the said Cant in the language of ' Bell's Life,' ' comes up piping,' I shall be very much the better for it."

Upon his return to Italy, Dickens renewed the invitation, and at last Jerrold was able to respond. He and Forster and Maclise met Dickens at Brussels on his way home, and the party passed a delightful week in Flanders. Writing of that week long after, Dickens said: " He was the delight of the children all the time, and they were his delight. He was in his most brilliant spirits and I doubt if he were ever more humorous in his life. But the most enduring impression that he left upon us who are grown up —and we have all often spoken of it since—was that Jerrold, in his amiable capacity of being easily pleased, in his freshness, in his good nature, in his cordiality and in the unrestrained openness of his heart, had quite captivated us."

In subsequent years, when Dickens was in France and Italy writing *Dombey*, he extended further invitations to his friend. To a letter containing one of these invitations, Jerrold replied :

> " Let me break this long silence with heartiest congratula-
> tion. Your book has spoken like a trumpet to the nation,
> and it is to me a pleasure to believe that you have faith in
> the sincerity of my gladness at your triumph. You have
> rallied your old thousands again; and, what is most delight-
> ful, you have rebuked and forever ' put down ' the small
> things, half knave, half fool, that love to *make* the failure
> they ' feed on.' They are under your boot—tread 'em to
> paste."

Then, after explaining that he had not written before because he had hoped against hope to be able to accept the invitation, he continued :

> " And so time went on, and *Dombey* comes out, and now, to be sure, I write. Had *Dombey* fallen apoplectic from the steam-press of Messrs. Bradbury and Evans, of *course* your letter would still have remained unanswered. But, with all England shouting ' Viva Dickens,' it is a part of my gallant nature to squeak through my quill, ' brayvo,' too."

Dickens's reply was as hearty :

> "This day week, I finished my little Christmas book[1] (writing towards the close the exact words of a passage in your affectionate letter received this morning : to wit, ' after all, life has something serious in it ') and ran over here for a week's rest. I cannot tell you how much true gratification I have had in your most hearty letter. Forster told me that the same spirit breathed through a notice of *Dombey* in your paper; and I have been saying since to Kate and Georgy that there is no such good way of testing the worth of literary friendship as by comparing its influence on one's view with any that literary animosity can produce. Mr. W. will throw me into a violent fit of anger for the moment, it is true; but his acts and deeds pass into the death of all bad things next day, and right out of my memory; whereas a generous sympathy like yours is ever present to me, ever fresh and new to me—always stimulating, cheerful and delightful. The pain of unjust malice is lost in an hour. The pleasure of a generous friendship is the steadiest joy in the world. What a glorious and comfortable thing that is to think of ! "

In 1856 Jerrold was once more able to snatch a brief holiday, and he spent some weeks with Dickens and Wilkie Collins at Boulogne. But it was not always Dickens who was the tempter, as witness the following :

> " My dear Dickens,
>
>   " When, *when* we can count upon a dry afternoon, won't you and the Hidalgo and Mac.—and the ladies, come down here " (Putney Lower Common) " to a cut of country lamb and a game of bowls ? Our turf is coming up so velvety. I intend to have a waistcoat sliced from it, trimmed with daisies. . . . I wish you could see (and eat) the dish of strawberries just brought in for breakfast by my girl Polly—' all,' as she says, ' big and square as pincushions.' "

---

[1] *The Cricket on the Hearth.*

In 1845 Jerrold was associated with Dickens in two of the most notable undertakings of the novelist's life. He was one of the founders of the "Daily News," and he was one of the instigators of the amateur theatricals. He was, in fact, almost the first to agree to serve under Dickens on the "Daily News," and he was appointed a leader-writer. He was very active in the preparations, and enthusiastic for the success of the undertaking. On the first night (in January 1846), he was a frequent and anxious visitor to the composing-room. When the paper had been printed, and started on its great career, around the "stone" in that room,

> "there gathered . . . an assembly of which Charles Dickens was the chief and informal president, and of which his various writers and the leading persons concerned in the newly established paper were the principal members. It was an interesting group, and the bulk of the little throng consisted of the compositors by whom the 'Daily News' had been set up. The object was to drink success to the enterprise, and a few pithy speeches were made. Charles Dickens probably expatiated in terms of general brotherhood, and invited the sympathy of the men of toil with the men of mind, whose efforts were to be devoted in this new channel for the common good. But a more express record has remained of a word spoken by Douglas Jerrold. His was a fit figure for such a scene. As he stood by the 'stone,' frail of build, with eager eyes, aquiline face and with hair flying back from his forehead down to his shoulders, he brought his fist down with a bang as he told the men, with emotion which was long remembered among them, how he had 'worked his way up through stony-hearted London.'" [1]

But it is by his association with the amateur theatricals that Jerrold is best known to Dickensians. I think it a sage assumption that it was he and Clarkson Stanfield who really instigated those performances. Long years before, these two had been comrades on board H.M.S. "Namur"; Jerrold had been middy, Stanfield foremast man. In those days they had frequently got up theatricals. Jerrold left the service in 1815, and the two met no more until they were brought face to face in 1832 at a rehearsal of Jerrold's "The Rent Day." Stanfield was the scene painter! The old friendship was renewed. Blanchard Jerrold writes :

[1] "The 'Daily News' Jubilee."

"Some years hence, they shall be sauntering in Richmond Park. . . . There shall be other friends with them. Matters theatrical shall bubble up in the careless ebb and flow of the conversation; and suddenly the 'Namur' middy . . . shall cry—'Let's have a play, Stanfield, like we had on board the "Namur."' Hence those many merry evenings passed among cordial friends; those hearty laughs over gross stage blunders, those genial suppers after rehearsals, those curious evenings spent upon the stage of Miss Kelly's little theatre, when the little figure of the 'Namur' midshipman might be dimly seen in the centre of the dark pit, all alive; but the presence of which was most authoritatively proved very often, when a clear voice chirped to the laughing actors some pungent witticism or queer turn of thought, provoking 'What, are you *there*, Jerrold?' as a good-natured reply from the victim."

The suggestion having once been made, Dickens, whose enthusiasm had been kindled by the amateur theatricals in Canada, entered into the scheme with all the zest of which he was capable, when he returned from Italy in the following year. Miss Kelly's theatre was taken, and "Every Man in His Humour" was the play selected, Jerrold taking the part of Master Stephen. Macready tells us that he did it very badly, but Macready's criticism and condemnations must not be taken too literally, and in this case he is not supported by any member who has left any record of that evening in September 1846. Then followed the performances on behalf of Leigh Hunt and John Poole. The net proceeds of these were five hundred guineas. This was not so much as had been hoped, so Dickens conceived the idea of increasing it by writing, in the character of Mrs. Gamp, an account of the journey to the north and of the performances. "It was to be," says Forster, "a new 'Pilgrims' Progress.' . . . Mrs. Gamp was to have always an invincible animosity towards Jerrold, for *Caudle* reasons." The first pages were written, but the artists who were to have illustrated the thing seem to have lacked enthusiasm, and so it was never completed. But in the fragment that Forster preserved, Mrs. Gamp expressed her feelings towards Jerrold in the following terms:

"Mrs. Harris, wen I see that little willain bodily before me, it give me such a turn that I was all in a tremble. If I hadn't lost my umbereller in the cab, I must have done him a injury with it! Oh the bragian little traitor! right among the ladies, Mrs. Harris; looking his wickedest and deceitfullest of eyes while he was a talking to 'em; laughing at his own jokes as loud as you please; holding his hat in one hand to cool his-self, and tossing back his iron-grey mop of a head of hair with the other, as if it was so much shavings—there, Mrs. Harris, I see him, getting encouragement from the pretty delooded creeturs, which never know'd that sweet saint, Mrs. C., as I did, and being treated with as much confidence as if he'd never wiolated none of the domestic ties, and never showed up nothing! Oh the aggrawation of that Dougledge! Mrs. Harris, if I hadn't apologiged to Mr. Wilson, and put a little bottle to my lips which was in my pocket for the journey, and which it is very rare indeed I have about me, I could not have abared the sight of him—there, Mrs. Harris! I could not!—I must have tore him, or have give way and fainted."

In the performances of 1848, in aid of the fund for the endowment of a perpetual curatorship of Shakespeare's home, Jerrold took no part, but he was to the fore again in 1851, in the Guild of Literature and Art performances, playing Mr. Shadowly Softhead in Lytton's "Not so Bad as we Seem," at Devonshire House, and taking equally prominent parts during the provincial tour.

After this "Splendid Strolling," there arrived that unhappy estrangement to which reference has been made. What was its cause, we shall never know, but we have Dickens's assurance that it was not on any personal subject, and did not involve an angry word. But months passed and they did not even see each other. And then the clouds were swept away. The old friends met in a London club. Each was with his own party, and they sat back to back without any recognition. Suddenly, however, Jerrold swung his chair round and with outstretched hands exclaimed, "For God's sake, let us be friends again. A life's not long enough for this." Those outstretched hands were grasped as lovingly as they had been offered, and the sun of friendship was never more obscured. A couple of years later, Jerrold was dead, and Dickens was writing to his son:

"Few of his friends, I think, can have had more favourable opportunities of knowing him in his gentlest and most affectionate aspect, than I had. He was one of the gentlest and most affectionate of men. I remember very well that when I first saw him about the year 1835, when I went into his sick room in Brittle Grove, Brompton, I found him propped up in a great chair, bright-eyed and quick and eager in spirit, but very lame in body, he gave me an impression of tenderness. It never became dissociated from him. There was nothing cynical or sour in his heart as I knew it. In the company of children and young people he was particularly happy, and showed to extraordinary advantage. He never was so gay, so sweet tempered, so pleasing and so pleased as then. Among my own children I have observed this many and many a time."

Jerrold left his family none too well off, and on the day of his funeral, Dickens, with that large-heartedness which dictated many similar enterprises, drew up a scheme for helping them. " I propose," he wrote to Forster, " that there shall be a night at a theatre, when the actors shall play ' The Rent Day ' and ' Black-Eyed Susan '; another night elsewhere, with a lecture from Thackeray; a day reading by me; a night reading by me; a lecture by Russell and a subscription performance of ' The Frozen Deep,' as at Tavistock House. . . . I have got hold of Arthur Smith as the best man of business I know, and go to work with him to-morrow morning. . . . My confident hope is that we shall get close upon two thousand pounds."

And Forster records that " the friendly enterprise was carried to a close with a vigour, promptitude and success that corresponded with this opening. In addition to the performances named, there were others in the country, also organised by Dickens, in which he took active personal part; and the result did not fall short of his expectations."

CHAPTER XIV

WRITING of that summer at Twickenham, Forster says: " Edwin Landseer, all the world's favourite, and the excellent Stanfield, came a few months later, in the Devonshire Terrace days." Landseer was one of the novelist's best-liked friends of his earlier years. For him, we are told, Dickens had the highest admiration and personal regard. He drifted somewhat from the circle as he grew in popularity; came to care more for the glamour of drawing-rooms and the admiration of Society than for the old happy intercourse with such congenial spirits as Maclise, Stanfield, Dickens, and Forster. " Indeed," says one of his biographers, Mr. James A. Manson, " his stiff behaviour and distant air were so painful that many of his older comrades preferred to stand aloof rather than behold the deterioration of his nature and character. This vexed him in turn, for in his innermost heart he felt that his friends were justified, and that he was to blame." The actual friendship with Dickens was never broken, and even so late as 1870 he was a guest at the dinner which the novelist gave at Hyde Park Place to celebrate Mr. Percy Fitzgerald's wedding. But the old intimacy vanished.

They became acquainted while *Nickleby* was running its course, and Landseer was quickly established as one of that brilliant circle of which Dickens was the bright particular star. It should be said that he was already an admirer of Dickens's works, and in this connection a capital story was told by the late W. P. Frith. While Frith was a student at the Royal Academy Schools, Landseer took his turn with the other R.A.s as a " Visitor at the Schools." He read the whole time, we are told, and one evening his father—very old and very deaf—came in with his speaking-trumpet, and said :

" You are not drawing then; why don't you draw? "

" Don't feel inclined," shouted the son down the trumpet.

" Then you ought to feel inclined. That's a fine figure; get out your paper and draw."

" Haven't got any paper," said the son.

"What's that book?" said the father.

"*Oliver Twist,*" said Edwin Landseer, in a voice loud enough to reach Trafalgar Square.

"Is it about art?"

"No, it's about Oliver Twist."

"Let me look at it. Ha! It's some of Dickens's nonsense, I see. You'd much better draw than waste your time upon such stuff as that."

In the Devonshire Terrace days, social foregatherings were frequent, and Landseer was a shining light at most of them. He was ever a popular guest at the children's theatricals too.

Landseer was among those whom Dickens specially desired to be invited to the private reading of *The Chimes* at Lincoln's Inn Fields in 1844, but he was not present. Two years later he did his only illustration for Dickens, namely a drawing of Boxer for *The Cricket on the Hearth.* He spent some time with Dickens in Paris in 1855, and they had some jolly times together, reminiscent of old days. After that they seem to have met very rarely, though, as I have said, the friendship stood until the end.

Landseer's two brothers, Tom and Charles, were also friends of Dickens's. Charles often joined the circle at Devonshire Terrace and elsewhere, but Tom was debarred from such delights owing to his deafness. They were both members of the Shakespeare Society, but Edwin does not seem to have belonged to that body. There is scarcely any reference to their association with Dickens, but the following letter of the novelist's to Macready serves to indicate the reality of the friendship he felt for Tom:

"Tom Landseer—that is the deaf one whom everybody quite loves for his sweet nature under a most deplorable infirmity—Tom Landseer asked me if I would present to you for him the accompanying engraving which he has executed from a picture by his brother Edwin; submitting it to you as a little tribute from an unknown but ardent admirer of your genius, which speaks to his heart, although it does not find its way there through his ears. I readily undertook the task, and send it herewith.

"I urged him to call upon you with me and proffer it boldly; but he is a very modest and delicately-minded creature, and was shy of intruding. If you thank him through me, perhaps you will say something about my bringing him to call, and so gladden the gentle artist and make him happy."

CHAPTER XV

" NOBLE OLD STANNY "

THE other friend specially mentioned by Forster in connection with the Devonshire Terrace days was Clarkson Stanfield—" Noble old Stanny," the best-loved friend that Dickens ever had. It seems a bold thing to say that there was one who came before Forster in Dickens's regard, but there is plenty of evidence to support it. Forster was the " guide, philosopher and friend," the entirely trustworthy adviser and confidant, the friend upon whom Dickens could lean, the solid common-sense guide; Stanfield was the lovable man, " the very spirit of kindly feeling," as Macready called him, the man for whom the novelist " always had a most tender love," the man who was ever ready at almost any sacrifice to serve his fellows, contriving to do it so that they were almost unconscious of the service.

Stanfield was introduced into the Dickens Circle by Jerrold, and quickly was an established favourite there. In 1839 we find him at the *Nickleby* dinner; in 1842 he was at the Greenwich dinner, and he was, as we have seen, one of the party that made that memorable trip into Cornwall. He was the oldest member of the party (Dickens was nineteen years his junior), but he was as young as any of them in spirit and in capacity for enjoyment. " . . . Stanfield got into such apoplectic entanglements," Dickens wrote to Prof. Felton, " that we were often obliged to beat him on the back with portmanteaus before we could recover him. Seriously, I do believe there never was such a trip." And in another part of the same letter he wrote : " Stanfield (an old sailor) consulted an enormous map on all disputed points of way-faring; and referred, moreover, to a pocket-compass and other scientific instruments." Among the souvenirs of the trip was a sketch by Stanfield of the Logan Stone, which, says Forster, " laughingly sketched both the charm of what was seen and the mirth of what was done, for it perched me on the top of the stone. It is historical, however, the ascent having been made."

In a letter to Stanfield written from Albaro a year or two later, Dickens made a humorous allusion to this trip :

94

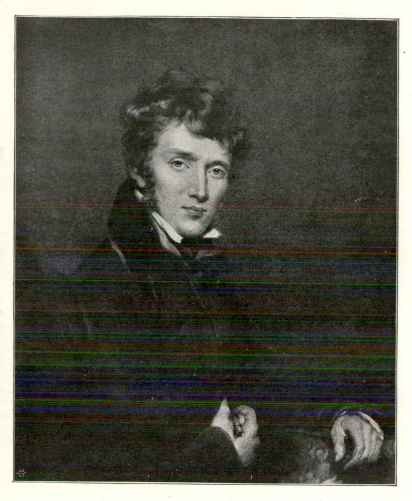

CLARKSON STANFIELD, R.A.

" I love you so truly, and have such pride and joy of heart in your friendship, that I don't know how to begin writing to you. When I think how you are walking up and down London in that portly surtout, and can't receive proposals from Dick [1] to go to the theatre, I fall into a state between laughing and crying, and want some friendly back to smite. ' Je-im ! ' ' Aye, aye, your honour,' is in my ears every time I walk upon the sea-shore here; and the number of expeditions I make into Cornwall in my sleep, the springs of Flys I break, and the bowls of punch I drink, would soften a heart of stone."

From this time no enjoyment seems to have been complete to Dickens unless it was shared by this friend. They were always exchanging visits, and Stanfield was one of the moving spirits at all parties at the novelist's house.

In the early days he often shared with Maclise and Forster in those jaunts to Hampstead which have made Jack Straw's Castle famous. Here is a letter to Forster : " Stanfield and Mac have come in, and we are going to Hampstead to dinner. I leave Betsy Prig, as you know, so don't you make a scruple about leaving Mrs. Harris. We shall stroll leisurely up, to give you time to join us, and dinner will be on the table at Jack Straw's at four." Humorous invitations of this kind were always passing between the friends.

In 1844 the artist was at the *Chuzzlewit* dinner. To this dinner he brought the eccentric Turner, who, Forster records, " had enveloped his throat, that sultry summer day, in a huge red belcher-handkerchief which nothing would induce him to remove." During that Italian stay Dickens wrote to Stanfield a long letter inviting him to pay him a visit : " I wish you would come this way and see me at that Palazzo Peschiere ! Was ever man so welcome as I would make you ! What a truly gentlemanly action it would be to bring Mrs. Stanfield and the baby. And how Kate and her sister would wave pocket-handkerchiefs from the wharf in joyful welcome ! Ah, what a glorious proceeding ! "

Stanfield contributed illustrations to four of the Christmas books—two to *The Chimes*, one to *The Cricket on the Hearth*, three to *The Battle of Life*, and three to *The Haunted Man*. For his *Chimes* illustrations he refused to accept any payment, and so Dickens gave him a silver claret jug which was inscribed, " In memory of *The Chimes*." With it he sent the following letter :

[1] Apparently a nickname of Stanfield's for Dickens. Some of the latter's letters to the painter are thus signed, and the name occurs in no other connection.

" MY DEAR STANNY,

" I send you a claret jug. . . . I need not say how much I should value another little sketch from your extraordinary hand in this year's small volume to which Mac. again does the frontispiece. But I cannot hear of it and will not have it (though the gratification of such aid to me is really beyond expression) unless you will so far consent to make it a matter of business as to receive without asking any questions a cheque in return from the publishers. Don't misunderstand me—though I am not afraid there is much danger of your doing so, for between us misunderstanding is, I hope, not easy. I know perfectly well that no terms would induce you to go out of your way in such regard for perhaps anybody else. I cannot, nor do I desire to, vanquish the friendly obligation which help from you imposes on me. But I am not the sole proprietor of these little books; and it would be monstrous in you if you were to dream of putting a scratch into a second one without some shadowy reference to the other partners; ten thousand times more monstrous in me if any consideration on earth could induce me to permit it, which nothing will or shall. So see what it comes to. If you will do me the favour on my terms, it will be more acceptable to me, my dear Stanfield, than I could possibly tell you. If you will not be so generous, you deprive me of the satisfaction of receiving it at your hands, and shut me out from that possibility altogether. What a stony-hearted ruffian you must be in such a case ! "

Despite this, Stanfield seems to have got his way. He did the illustrations, but refused to accept payment, and this time Dickens gave him a silver salver, inscribed, " Clarkson Stanfield from Charles Dickens." And in the following year he did " three morsels of English landscape which had a singular charm for Dickens at the time, and seem to me still of their kind quite faultless." [1] The novelist wrote to Forster : " It is a delight to look at these little landscapes of the dear old boy. How gentle and elegant, and yet how manly and vigorous they are ! I have a perfect joy in them." It ought also to be noted that Stanfield did a water-colour drawing of " The Britannia," in which Dickens crossed the Atlantic in 1842, with a view to its being used as a frontispiece to the first cheap edition of *American Notes*. This was purchased in 1870 by the Earl of Darnley for £110 5s.

In 1857 Dickens paid the " dear old boy " a tribute which was very truly appreciated by dedicating *Little Dorrit* to him.

[1] Forster's *Life of Dickens*.

Stanfield was one of the promoters of the Guild of Literature and Art, and worked as untiringly as Dickens for its success. As all the world knows, he rendered tremendous help in connection with the famous amateur theatricals, painting scenery for some of the plays, that ranks among his best work. He did not act, though when it was decided in 1845 to play " Every Man in his Humour," he was cast for the part of Downright, and even rehearsed twice. Then, however, he did what Maclise had done previously, " took fright and ran away," and Dudley Costello took his place.

In 1851 came the Guild performances. For " Not so Bad as we Seem," Stanfield painted one of the scenes—an open space near the river. Four years later came the performances of Wilkie Collins's " The Lighthouse " in " the smallest theatre in the world " at Tavistock House. It was for this play that Stanfield painted his famous drop-scene of the Lighthouse, which, at the Gadshill sale after Dickens's death, fetched one thousand guineas. Forster gives the following version of how this scene came to be painted. With Mark Lemon, Dickens walked across Hampstead to visit the artist. " He has been very ill," Forster quotes the novelist as writing, " and he told us that large pictures are too much for him, and he must confine himself to small ones. But I would not have this, I declared he must paint bigger ones than ever, and what would he think of beginning upon an act-drop for a proposed vast theatre at Tavistock House? He laughed and caught at this, we cheered him up very much, and he said he was quite a man again."

This scarcely tallies with Dickens's own published letters. This walk across Hampstead is recorded as having taken place in April, but on May 20 we find Dickens writing to Stanfield as follows :

" I have a little lark in contemplation, if you will help it to fly.

" Collins has done a melodrama (a regular old-style melodrama), in which there is a very good notion. I am going to act it, as an experiment, in the children's theatre here—I, Mark, Collins, Egg, and my daughter Mary, the whole *dram. pers.*; our families and yours the whole audience; for I want to make the stage large and shouldn't have room for above five-and-twenty spectators. Now, there is only one scene in the piece, and that, my tarry lad, is the inside of a lighthouse. Will you come and paint it for us, one night, and we'll all turn to and help? It is a mere wall, of course, but Mark and I have sworn that you must do it. . . . Write

H

me a line in reply. We mean to burst on an astonished world with the melodrama, without any note of preparation."

And two days later he wrote as follows (the italics are my own) :

" Your note came while I was out walking. Even if I had been at home I could not have managed to dine together to-day, being under a beastly engagement to dine out. Un less I hear from you to the contrary, I shall expect you here some time to-morrow, and will remain at home. I only wait your instructions to get the little canvases made. *O, what a pity it is not the outside of the light'us, with the sea a-rowling agin it !* Never mind, we'll get an effect out of the inside, and there's a storm and shipwreck ' off '; and the great ambition of my life will be achieved at last, in the wearing of a pair of very coarse petticoat trousers. So hoorar for the salt sea, mate, and bouse up ! Ever affectionately,
" DICKY."

This expression of regret that the scene is not to be " the outside of the light'us, with the sea a-rowling agin it," is irreconcilable with Forster's statement that Stanfield had actually been asked to paint such a scene a month before. However, the fact is that that scene was painted, as well as one of the interior. It took the artist just two mornings to execute, and it is one of his best achievements !

In 1856 " The Frozen Deep " was performed at Tavistock House, and again the ever-willing Stanfield was pressed into the service. " The priceless help of Stanfield had again been secured," says Forster, " and I remember finding him one day at Tavistock House in the act of upsetting some elaborate arrangements by Dickens, with a proscenium before him made up of chairs, and the scenery planned out with walking-sticks." The play-bill records, " The scenery and scenic effects of the second and third acts, by Mr. Stanfield, R.A., assisted by Mr. Danson. The act-drop, also by Mr. Stanfield, R.A." Afterwards, Dickens had the Lighthouse drop-scene framed, and " The Frozen Deep " drop-scene divided into two subjects—a British man-of-war, and an Arctic sea—and, says Forster, " the school-room that had been the theatre was now hung with sea-pieces by a great painter of the sea. To believe them to have been but the amusement of a few mornings was difficult indeed. Seen from the due distance there was nothing wanting to the most masterly and elaborate art."

Towards the end of his life, Stanfield had much anxiety and

PERFORMANCE OF "NOT SO BAD AS WE SEEM," BEFORE QUEEN VICTORIA
AND PRINCE ALBERT, AT DEVONSHIRE HOUSE, ON MAY 16, 1851

From a contemporary print

"THE LIGHTHOUSE"

Painted by Clarkson Stanfield, R.A., for the private theatricals

98

illness, and Dickens and Forster gave him ample evidence of the
sincerity of their friendship. He lived at Hampstead, and it was
the delight of his two friends to tramp across the Heath and pay
him surprise visits to cheer him up. Writing to Macready in
1863, Dickens says : " Stanfield was very ill for some months,
then suddenly picked up, and is really rosy and jovial again.
Going to see him when he was very despondent, I told him the
story of Fechter's piece " (then in rehearsal) " with appropriate
action ; fighting a duel with the washing-stand, defying the
bedstead, and saving the life of the sofa-cushions. This so kindled
his old theatrical ardour, that I think he turned the corner on
the spot."

The painter died in May 1867. Just a month before he had
received his last letter from Dickens—a letter breathing affection
in every line. On his death-bed this good man had performed an
act which was in keeping with his whole life. Dickens and Mark
Lemon had quarrelled some years previously, and had not spoken
since. With life nearing its close, the true-hearted Stanfield
pleaded with Dickens to resume his friendship with " Uncle Mark."
Dickens was the last man with whom such an appeal could be in
vain, and the two men once more clasped hands over " noble
old Stanny's " open grave.

When at last the end came, Dickens, in *All the Year Round*,
paid his final tribute :

" . . . The writer of these words had been his friend for
thirty years ; and when, a short week or two before his death,
he laid that once so skilful hand upon the writer's breast,
and told him they would meet again, ' but not here,' the
thoughts of the latter turned, for the time, so little to his
noble genius, and so much to his noble nature !

" He was the soul of frankness, generosity, and simplicity.
The most genial, the most affectionate, the most loving, and
the most lovable of men. . . .

" No Artist can ever have stood by his art with a quieter
dignity than he always did. Nothing would have induced
him to lay it at the feet of any human creature. To fawn,
or to toady, or to do undeserved homage to any one, was an
absolute impossibility with him. And yet his character was
so nicely balanced that he was the last man in the world to
be suspected of self-assertion, and his modesty was one of
his most special qualities.

" He was a charitable, religious, gentle, truly good man.
A genuine man, incapable of pretence or of concealment. . . .
There is no smile that the writer can recall, like his ; no

manner so naturally confiding and so cheerfully engaging. When the writer saw him for the last time on earth, the smile and the manner shone out once through the weakness, still : the bright unchanging Soul within the altered face and form.

.   .   .   .

" Gone ! And many and many a dear old day gone with him ! But their memories remain and his memory will not soon fade out, for he set his mark upon the restless waters, and his fame will long be sounded in the roar of the sea."

CHAPTER XVI

FRANCIS JEFFREY

THE friendship with Lord Jeffrey was formed in the early Devonshire Terrace days. It was one of the most striking friendships of the novelist's life. They could not meet often, of course, and when they did meet, Jeffrey could take no part in the almost daily ridings or in the frequent social entertainments, for he was an old man. But between the two men there sprang up a truly extraordinary affection. " I believe I have lost as affectionate a friend as I ever had, or shall have, in this world," wrote Dickens when Jeffrey died in 1850. It was true. They met in 1841 and cemented a friendship which had already commenced " autographically," and which must have meant very much to Dickens. Jeffrey was born in 1773, so that he was sixty-eight years old when he first met Dickens, who had not yet completed his thirtieth year, and his attitude towards the young novelist was almost that of a fond parent towards a brilliant son. His kindly criticism and his whole-hearted encouragement must have been invaluable to the young writer. Indeed, they must have meant more to him than he ever knew, or the world can ever estimate.

It is true that in respect of one of Jeffrey's criticisms (of some parts of *Dombey and Son*) we find Dickens writing to Forster : " I do not at heart, however, lay much real stress on his opinion, though one is naturally proud of awakening such sincere interest in the breast of an old man who has so long worn the blue and yellow "; none the less he could not ignore the opinions of such a man, and even though unconsciously, they cannot have failed to influence his work. Indeed, as we shall see later, Jeffrey did influence the plot of this very book in a very important particular.

But, in those early days, when Boz had just burst from obscurity into world-wide fame : just realising his strength as he was, the friendship and advice of this famous editor and critic could not but help to mould him, and to direct his genius in ways where it could wield its most potent influence.

Jeffrey loved Dickens with a love that is rare among men. The old man's heart warmed to the creator of Little Nell and Smike as it had warmed to few men in his long life, and throughout his letters to Dickens there is a note of affectionate interest that is most touching. Their first meeting was in April 1841, and in the following month, Jeffrey wrote to Lord Cockburn from London :

> " I have seen a good deal of —— and above all, of Charles Dickens, with whom I have struck up what I mean to be an eternal and intimate friendship. He lives very near to us, and I often run over and sit an hour *tête-à-tête*, or take a long walk in the park with him—the only way really to know or be known by either man or woman. Taken in this way I think him very amiable and agreeable. In mixed company, where he is now much sought after, he is rather reserved. He has dined here, and we with him, at rather too sumptuous a dinner for a man with a family, and only beginning to be rich, though selling 44,000 copies of his weekly issues." [1]

What strikes one as somewhat astonishing, is the fact that though the *Clock* dinner took place on April 10th, while Jeffrey was in London, he was not of the company, for though this was his first meeting with Dickens, they had corresponded previously. A month before, Dickens had written to Forster about Jeffrey in quite familiar terms, referring to a letter that had obviously come from that great man himself : " I had a letter from Edinburgh this morning, announcing that Jeffrey's visit will be the week after next ; telling me that he drives about Edinburgh, declaring there has been ' nothing so good as Nell since Cordelia,' which he writes also to all manner of people ; and informing me of a desire in that romantic town to give me greeting and welcome." We have also the well-known fact that Jeffrey pleaded earnestly with Dickens to allow Little Nell to live. That must have been before this visit to London in April 1841, for Nell was dead then.

We are told that in this visit Jeffrey was welcomed with many feasts and entertainments of which he partook very sparingly. Before he returned to Edinburgh, he had extracted a promise from Dickens to pay a visit to Scotland in the ensuing summer. That visit duly took place. The novelist and his wife arrived at the Royal Hotel, Edinburgh, on June 22nd, and he had, as Forster puts it, his " first practical experience of the honours his fame had won for him." During his stay in Scotland, he naturally saw much of his friend, and visited him several times at Craig-crook.

Records of meetings between the two men after this are lament-

[1] *Master Humphrey's Clock.*

ably scarce, but we do know, that henceforth Jeffrey visited Dickens in London about every spring, and that as the years passed the friendship deepened. Dickens paid another visit to Scotland in December 1847, for the purpose of opening the Glasgow Athenæum, and, of course, took in Edinburgh going and returning in order to spend some time with Jeffrey. During this visit an incident occurred which may be mentioned in this place. On the first day of the new year—1848—the novelist wrote to Forster : " Jeffrey, who is obliged to hold a kind of morning court in his own study during the holidays, came up here yesterday in great consternation, to tell me that a person had been to make and sign a declaration of bankruptcy, and that on looking at the signature he saw it was Sheridan James Knowles." With that promptness that characterised him in everything he ever did, he decided to do something to assist this famous play-wright. The help of friends was enlisted, and as a result, in the following May, performances of " The Merry Wives of Windsor " and " Love, Law and Physick " were given in London, Birming-ham, Manchester, Liverpool, Glasgow and Edinburgh with a view of endowing a curatorship of Shakespeare's house at Strat-ford-on-Avon, to be held by Knowles. The endowment was abandoned upon the town of Stratford taking charge of the house, but the proceeds of the performances, which amounted to £2551, went to the object really desired.

Dickens paid Jeffrey the two greatest compliments that were in his power to pay. He dedicated one of his books to him, and he invited him to act as godfather to one of his children. The book was *The Cricket on the Hearth*, the dedication reading : " To Lord Jeffrey, with the affection and attachment of his friend, Charles Dickens." The child to whom Jeffrey became godfather was the third son, named, of course, Francis Jeffrey, who was born on January 15, 1844, and became known in the family circle as " Chickenstalker." This was the old man's reply to his friend's invitation to him to act as the boy's godfather :

". . . about that most flattering wish, or, more probably, passing fancy, of that dear Kate of yours, to associate my name with yours over the baptismal font of your new-come boy. My first impression was that it was a mere piece of kind badinage of hers (or perhaps your own) and not meant to be seriously taken, and consequently that it would be foolish to take any notice of it. But it has since occurred to me, that if you had really meditated so great an honour for me, you would naturally think it strange if I did not in some way acknowledge it, and express the deep sense I should certainly have of such an act of kindness. And so I write now to say, in all fulness and simplicity of heart, that, if such a thing is indeed in your contemplation, it would be more flattering and agreeable to me than most things that have befallen me in this mortal pilgrimage; while if it was but the sportful expression of a happy and confiding play-fulness I shall still feel grateful for the communication, and return you a smile as cordial as your own, and with full permission to both of you to smile at the simplicity which could not distinguish jest from earnest."

What Jeffrey thought of Dickens's genius and of the products of that genius, is well known. Not the wildest enthusiast that ever lived was more extravagant in his appreciation of the novels than was this great critic. But for the fact that most of his letters to Dickens are preserved, it would be almost incredible that the man who was so feared as a critic should have held Boz in such high estimation, and should have enthused so extrava-gantly over his writings. The truth is that he saw in those writings a new humanising force. It was not Dickens the great humorist over whom he was so enthusiastic; but Dickens the tender-hearted, Dickens the lover of little children, Dickens the champion of the downtrodden and suffering. It was Smike who first touched his heart, and it was Nell who completed the conquest. How he wept over Nell, and how he pleaded that she might live, all the world knows, but I shall be forgiven for introducing one authenticated anecdote.

Mrs. Henry Siddons, a neighbour and intimate of Jeffrey's, opened his library door one day, and saw the old man sitting in his chair, with his head on the table, and apparently in deep grief. She was in the act of retiring silently, when he looked up, and beckoned her to remain. She saw that his eyes were suffused with tears. " Don't go, my dear friend," he said, " I shall be all right again in another minute." " I had no idea that you had had any bad news or cause for grief," said the lady, " or I would not have come. Is any one dead ? " " Yes, indeed," was the reply. " I'm a great goose to have given way so; but I could not help it. You'll be sorry to hear that little Nelly, Boz's little Nelly, is dead."

His love for this character never faded, and his references to her in his letters are frequent. To Mrs. Rutherford, for instance, in 1842, he wrote : " . . . I am verging with unreasonable celerity to decay, and am already in a condition which will require all the indulgence I now beseech of you. So you must be a good girl and play the *Nelly* to me now and then, keeping me out of scrapes, and cheering my failing spirit with the spectacle of your brightness and sustaining it by the strength of your affection."

It would be possible to fill many pages with extracts from Jeffrey's letters to Dickens proving how truly he appreciated his friend's writings, but I will confine myself to just one or two. In regard to *American Notes* he wrote :

> " Your account of the silent or solitary imprisonment system is as pathetic and powerful a piece of writing as I have ever seen; and your sweet airy little snatch, of the happy little woman taking her new babe home to her young husband, and your manly and feeling appeal on behalf of the poor Irish (or rather of the affectionate poor of all races and tongues), who are patient and tender to their children under circumstances which would make half the exemplary parents among the rich, monsters of selfishment and discontent, remind us that we have still among us the creator of Nelly, and Smike, and the schoolmaster, and his dying pupil, etc., and must continue to win for you still more of that homage of the heart, that love and esteem of the just and good, which, though it *should* never be disjoined from them, I think you must already feel to be better than fortune or fame."

Then there is the famous letter about the *Carol*. No one will wish to quarrel with me for quoting that :

> " Blessings on your kind heart, my dear Dickens ! and may it always be as light and full as it is kind and a fountain of kindness to all within reach of its beatings ! We are all charmed with your Carol, chiefly, I think, for the genuine *goodness* which breathes all through it, and is the true inspiring angel by which its genius has been awakened. The whole scene of the Cratchits is like the dream of a beneficent angel, in spite of its broad reality, and little *Tiny Tim*, in life and death, almost as sweet and as touching as Nelly. And then the school-day scene, with that large-hearted delicate sister, and her true inheritor, with his gall-lacking liver, and milk of human kindness for blood, and yet all so natural, and so humbly and serenely happy ! Well, you should be happy yourself, for you may be sure you have done more good, and not only fostered more kindly feelings, but prompted more positive acts of beneficence by this little publication than can be traced to all the pulpits and confessionals in Christendom, since Christmas 1842."

This is what he wrote on the receipt of a copy of *The Chimes* :

" Blessings on your kind heart, my dearest Dickens, for *that*, after all, is your great talisman, and the gift for which you will be not only most loved, but longest remembered, your kind and courageous advocacy of the rights of the poor—your generous assertion and touching displays of their virtues, and the delicacy as well as the warmth of their affections, have done more to soothe desponding worth—to waken sleeping (almost dead) humanities—and to shame even selfish brutality, than all the other writings of the age, and make it, and all that are to come after, your debtors.

" Well, you will understand from this (though it was all true before) that the music of your *Chimes* has reached me, and resounded through my heart, and that I thank you with all that is left of it. . . .

" The aldermen and justices, friends and fathers, etc., and, in short, all the tribe of selfishness and cowardice and cant, will hate you in their hearts, and cavil when they can; will accuse you of wicked exaggeration and excitement to discontent, and what they pleasantly call disaffection ! But never mind—the good and the brave are with you, and the truth also, and in that sign you will continue."

And then, with reference to the fifth number of *Dombey*—the number containing the death of little Paul :

" Oh, my dear, dear Dickens ! What a No. 5 you have now given us ! I have so cried and sobbed over it last night, and again this morning; and felt my heart purified by those tears, and blessed and loved you for making me shed them; and I never can bless and love you enough. Since that divine Nelly was found dead on her humble couch, beneath the snow and ivy, there has been nothing like the actual dying of that sweet Paul, in the summer sunshine of that lofty room. And the long vista that leads us so gently and sadly, and yet so gracefully and winningly, to that plain consummation ! Every trait so true and so touching, and yet lightened by that fearless innocence which goes *playfully* to the brink of the grave, and that pure affection which bears the unstained spirit, on its soft and lambent flash, at once to its source in eternity. In reading of these delightful children, how deeply do we feel that ' of such is the kingdom of heaven '; and how ashamed of the contaminations which *our* manhood has received from the contact of earth, and wonder how *you* should have been admitted into that pure communion, and so ' presumed, an earthly guest, and drawn empyreal air,' though for our benefit and instruction."

As I have said, he did not value Dickens's humour and tragic power so much. As witness his comment on some of the more powerful passages in *Dombey* : " I am proud that you should thus show us new views of your genius—but I shall always love its gentler magic the most; and never leave Nelly and Paul and Florence for Edith. . . . I am prepared, too, in some degree, for being softened towards Dombey ; for you *have* made me feel sincere pity for Miss Tox; though, to be sure, only by making her the victim of a still more hateful and heartless creature than herself." The last letter which Dickens ever received from him referred to some of the earlier chapters of *David Copperfield*. He had not taken very kindly to the Micawbers : " Uriah is too disgusting; and I confess I should have been contented to have heard no more of the Micawbers."

It is interesting to note that Jeffrey influenced the plot of *Dombey and Son* in one very important point. He raised the question whether the end might not come by other means than Edith's death, and bringing with it a more bitter humiliation for her destroyer. When Edith arranged to flee with Carker, Dickens meant her to be what she seemed to be. Jeffrey, however, positively refused to believe that she was Carker's mistress, and the result was that Dickens decided upon an alteration, and gave us that scene of her undeceiving the villain and " giving him to know that she never meant that."

I have said that Jeffrey always treated Dickens more as a much-loved son than as a friend. He himself described his relationship to the novelist as that of an elder brother. Not only did he encourage Boz with whole-hearted praise, but he sought his confidence in regard to more intimate and personal affairs. For instance, in February 1844, we read in one of his letters : " I shall not be satisfied if the profits of the *Carol* do not ultimately come up to my estimate. I want amazingly to see you rich, and independent of all irksome exertions. . . . And so, God be with you." Then in 1847 we find him writing :

" I certainly did not mean to ask you for the full and clear, if not every way satisfactory statement you have trusted me with. But I do feel the full value of that confidence, and wish I had any better return to make to it than mere thanks, and idle, because general, advice. I am rather disappointed, I must own, at finding your *embankment* still so small. But it is a great thing to have made a beginning, and laid a foundation; and you are young enough to reckon on living many years under the proud roof of the completed structure, which even I expect to see ascending in its splendour. But when

I consider that the public has, upon a moderate computa-tion, paid at least £100,000 for your works (and had a good bargain too at the money), it is rather provoking to think that the author should not have — in bank, and have never received, I suspect, above ——. There must have been some mismanagement, I think, as well as ill-luck, to have occasioned this result—not extravagance on your part, my dear Dickens—nor even excessive beneficence—but improvi-dent arrangements with publishers—and too careless a control of their proceedings. . . . I am as far as possible from grudg-ing you the elegances and indulgences which are suitable to your tasteful and liberal nature, and which you have so fully earned; and should indeed be grieved not to see you sur-rounded, and your children growing up, in the midst of the refinements which not only gratify the relishes, but improve the capacities, of a cultivated mind. All I venture to press on you is the infinite importance and unspeakable comfort of an achieved and secure *independence;* taking away all anxiety about decay of health or mental alacrity, or even that impatience of task work which is apt to steal upon free spirits who would work harder and better if redeemed from the yoke of necessity. But this is twaddle enough, and must be charitably set down to the score of my paternal anxiety and senile caution. . . . And so God bless you and your dear Kate, and my charming boy, and all his brothers and sisters, and all whom you love, and love you—with you, or at a distance. . . . Give my love to Kate, and do not let her forget me. Name me, too, sometimes to the boy."

And here, in the same year, is an intimate note which Dickens was not the sort of man to tolerate from *any*body :

" Well, but how have you been ? And how is the poor child who was so cruelly hustled against the portals of life at his entry ? And his dear mother ? And my bright boy ? And all the rest of the happy circle ? . . . And how does the People's Edition prosper ? And how does *the embankment* proceed ? And do you begin to feel the germs of a prudent avarice and anticipated pride of purse working themselves into your breast ? And whom do you mostly live with, or wish to live with ? And among whom, and in what condition, do you most aspire to die ? Though I am not exactly your father confessor, just know I always put you through your Catechism, and I do expect and require an answer to all these interrogatives. . . . So God bless you ! my dear Dickens ;

SIR DAVID WILKIE, R.A.

FRANCIS JEFFREY

PROFESSOR JOHN WILSON

and with truest love to my true-hearted Kate, and all true Dickenses, believe me, always, ever and ever yours."

Dickens, in 1848, evidently became remiss, for here is an extract from a letter written by Jeffrey in November :

> "MY DEAR DICKENS,
>
> "We must not grow quite out of acquaintance, if you please ! You have put my name alongside of your own, on a memorable little page, and have solemnly united them again on the head of a child, who will live, I hope, neither to discredit the one, nor to be ashamed of the other. And so, for the sake even of decent consistency, you must really take a little notice of me now and then, and let me have some account, as of old, of your health and happiness—of your worldly affairs, and your spiritual hopes and experiences —of your literary projects and domestic felicities—your nocturnal walks and dramatic recreations—of the sale of cheap copies, and the conception of bright originals—of your wife and children; in short, your autumn migrations and winter home—of our last parting, which was more hurried than usual, and our next meeting, which, alas, I feel to be more and more uncertain."

Assuredly it was something to have inspired such feelings of friendship in such a man !

Jeffrey died in January 1850. Less than a year before he had written to his much-loved friend :

> "MY EVER DEAR DICKENS,
>
> "I have been very near dead; and am by no means sure that I shall *ever* recover from the malady which has confined me mostly to bed for the last five weeks, and which has only, within the last three days, allowed me to leave my room for a few hours in the morning. But I must tell you that, living or dying, I retain for you, unabated and unimpaired, the same cordial feelings of love, gratitude and admiration, which have been part of my nature, and no small part of my pride and happiness, for the last twenty years.[1] . . . I am better, however, within these last days; and hope still to see your bright eye, and clasp your open hand, once more at least before the hour of final separation. In the meantime, you will be glad, though I hope not surprised, to hear that I have no acute suffering, no disturbing apprehen-

---

[1] A great exaggeration, of course.

sions or low spirits; but possess myself in a fitting, and indeed cheerful tranquillity, without impatience, or any unseemly anxiety as to the issue I am appointed to abide."

Of this letter, Dickens wrote to Forster : " I had a letter from Jeffrey yesterday morning, just as I was going to write to him. He has evidently been very ill, and I begin to have fears for his recovery. It is a very pathetic letter, as to his state of mind; but only in a tranquil contemplation of death, which I think very noble." Less than three weeks before he died, the old man wrote his last letter to Dickens, and in that he struck an equally noble and beautiful note :

" We are all tolerably well here, I thank you; Mrs. Jeffrey, I am happy to say, has been really *quite well* for many months, and, in fact, by much the most robust of the two. My fairy grandchild, too, is bright and radiant through all the glooms of winter and age, and fills the house with sunshine and music. I am old and vulnerable, but still able for my work, and not a bit morose or querulous; ' And by the mass the heart is in the trim.' I love all that is lovable, and can respond to love as intensely as in youth, and hope to die before that capacity forsakes me."

The death of this earnest admirer and true friend was, Forster tells us, a great sorrow to Dickens. He wrote to Forster : " Poor dear Jeffrey ! I bought a ' Times ' at the station yesterday morning, and was so stunned by the announcement, that I felt it in that wounded part of me, almost directly; and the bad symptoms (modified) returned within a few hours. . . . I sent him proof-sheets of the number only last Wednesday. I say nothing of his wonderful abilities and great career, but he was a most affectionate friend to me; and though no man could wish to live and die more happily, so old in years and yet so young in faculties and sympathies, I am very, very deeply grieved for his loss."

CHAPTER XVII

SIR DAVID WILKIE

SIR DAVID WILKIE, to whose memory Dickens proposed a toast at the Edinburgh banquet in 1841, was a very intimate friend in 1839 and 1840, and was one of those with whom in those years there were " frequent social entertainments." But towards the end of the latter year he went abroad in a vain quest of health, and died off Gibraltar in June 1841. In that month Dickens paid his first visit to Edinburgh and was entertained at a great public dinner, " and," says Forster, " it was while we were all regretting Wilkie's absence abroad, and Dickens with warrantable pride was saying how surely the great painter would have gone to this dinner, that the shock of his sudden death came, and there was left but the sorrowful satisfaction of honouring his memory." Dickens, we are told, refused to believe the sad news at first, and wrote to Forster : " My heart assures me Wilkie liveth. He is the sort of man who will be very old when he dies." But the news was true, and at the dinner on June 15, Dickens had to propose the memory of his friend :

" One of the gifted of the earth has passed away, as it were, yesterday; one who was devoted to his art, and his art was nature—I mean David Wilkie. He was one who made the cottage hearth a graceful thing—of whom it might truly be said that he found ' books in the running brooks,' and who has left in all he did some breathing of the air which stirs the heather. But however desirous to enlarge on his genius as an artist, I would rather speak of him now as a friend who has gone from amongst us. There is his deserted studio—the empty easel lying idly by—the unfinished picture with its face turned to the wall, and there is that bereaved sister, who loved him with an affection death cannot quench. He has left a name in fame clear as the bright sky; he has filled our minds with memories pure as the blue waves which roll over him. Let us hope that she

111

who more than all others mourns his loss, may learn to reflect that he died in the fulness of his fame, before age or sickness had dimmed his powers—that she may yet associate with feelings as calm and pleasant as we do now the memory of Wilkie."

CHAPTER XVIII

SOME SCOTCH FRIENDS

DURING that memorable visit to Scotland in 1841 Dickens met most of the famous men in Edinburgh, and formed with one or two of them pleasant acquaintanceships which lasted for some years. First of all there was John Wilson, "Christopher North," who presided at the great dinner in Jeffrey's absence through ill health. They were introduced by Jeffrey, and thus Dickens describes him in a letter to Forster. "A bright, clear-complexioned, mountain-looking fellow, he looks as though he had just come down from the Highlands and had never in his life taken pen in hand. . . . He is a great fellow to look at and talk to; and if you could divert your mind of the actual Scott, is just the figure you would put in his place." Wilson was in poor health at this time, and the speech at the dinner was a great effort to him, but it was an admirable speech, and it was hearty in its appreciation of Dickens's work.[1]

I cannot find that Dickens and Wilson ever met after 1841, but during the visit they saw much of each other, and the novelist clearly took a very strong liking to the professor. This meeting of the two men aroused great interest in Scotland, and a Scotch artist, A. Lesage, celebrated it in caricature, in which he showed Dickens being introduced to Wilson by Jeffrey. Wilson is leaning upon the shoulder of Peter Robertson, with whom Dickens also spent several pleasant hours during his visit. He was " a large, portly, full-faced man, with a merry eye, and a queer way of looking under his spectacles which is characteristic and pleasant." Dickens added : " He seems a very warm-hearted earnest man, too, and I felt quite at home with him forthwith." Three years later Peter Robertson, now become Lord Robertson, visited the novelist at Albaro, and was heartily welcome. Still later we find him a frequent guest at Devonshire House, where he was in great request for his Scotch mimicries.

Others whom he came to know during this Scotch visit were Sir William Allan, who " squired him about " all one morning, Adam Black, the publisher, Sir Archibald Alison (with whom he

---

[1] It was reprinted in full in *The Dickensian*, October 1916.

became very friendly during his second visit to Edinburgh in 1847), Lord Murray, Lord Gillies, Joseph Gordon, Macvey Napier and J. C. Colquhoun.   After the banquetings Dickens journeyed through the Highlands, accompanied by Angus Fletcher as guide. He was an eccentric who never settled down to any occupation and preferred a wandering life to that of home.   " His unfitness for an ordinary career," says Forster, " was perhaps the secret of such liking for him as Dickens had.   Fletcher's eccentricities and absurdities, divided often by the thinnest partition from a foolish extravagance, but occasionally clever, and always the genuine though whimsical outgrowth of the life he led, had a curious charm for Dickens.   He enjoyed the oddity and humour; tolerated all the rest; and to none more freely than to Kindheart during the next few years, both in Italy and in England, opened his house and hospitality."   Fletcher's eccentricities during this Highlands tour were a great source of merriment to Dickens.

At Albaro in 1844 Fletcher—Mr. Kindheart, as Dickens called him—made a long stay with the novelist, and numerous are the references to his eccentricities; numerous, too, are the references to his simple kindliness.   He loved Dickens greatly, and in his zeal once instigated the people of Carrara to organise a demonstrative welcome for his friend.   He himself was staying there, and knowing that Dickens was coming, took steps to see that the novelist was given a special welcome.   " There is a beautiful little theatre there, built of marble; and they had it illuminated that night, in my honour.   There was really a very fair opera. . . . It was crammed to excess, and I had a great reception; a deputation waiting upon us in the box, and the orchestra turning out in a body afterwards and serenading us at N. Walton's."

Fletcher died in 1862, and Dickens wrote: " Poor Kindheart !   I think of all that made him so pleasant to us, and am full of grief."

CHAPTER XIX

A DISTINGUISHED GROUP

THERE are many other friends yet to be noted before we pass on to the Gore House days, and some of these may be grouped into one chapter.

Dr. John Elliotson is, I suppose, best remembered as the person to whom Thackeray dedicated " Pendennis," but that is by no means his only claim to fame. For instance, he was one of the founders of University College Hospital. He lost his professorship at London University in 1838 because of his conversion to mesmerism, and it was probably his reputation in this direction that first attracted Dickens to him. "He had," says Forster, "always sympathised almost as strongly as Archbishop Whately did with Doctor Elliotson's mesmeric investigations." And for the man personally Dickens had a great regard. " What a good fellow Elliotson is," he wrote to Macready in 1841, and Forster writes of this friend as " the kind physician, Dr. Elliotson, whose name was for nearly thirty years a synonym with us all for unwearied, self-sacrificing, beneficent service to every one in need." So early as 1840 Elliotson was of the inner circle, and in 1846 we find him spending a few days with Dickens at Lausanne— " an enjoyment without a drawback "; and right through the years, though we know very little of their associations, the friendship remained as close and earnest as at the beginning.

Lord Normanby, " whose many acts of sympathy and kindness had inspired strong regard in Dickens," was an early friend and a very valued one indeed. Through very many years a steady and very close friendship lasted, and Dickens paid his tribute to it by dedicating *Dombey and Son* to his friend's wife. It is particularly to be regretted that no record of this friendship exists, for Lord Normanby was one of Boz's earliest admirers; but a couple of references in Forster's book is all I have been able to find. His Lordship was in the chair at the Greenwich dinner in 1844, he and Dickens saw a great deal of each other in Paris at different times, and they were often guests at each other's homes. And that is all we know.

Albany Fonblanque was a friend of these very early days. He

was much more Forster's friend than Dickens's, with whom he was never really intimate, but none the less, he was well liked by the novelist, and he is entitled to special mention for the reason that he was one of the first to discern the genius of Boz. Indeed, it was from him that Forster himself first heard of the existence of this young writer whose works bore such promise. The *Sketches by Boz*, says Dickens's biographer, were much more talked about than the first two or three numbers of *Pickwick*, " and I remember well with what hearty praise the book was named to me by my dear friend, Albany Fonblanque, as keen and clear a judge as ever lived, either of books or men." Later it was Forster's pleasure to make Fonblanque and Boz acquainted. The famous journalist's admiration for the genius of Dickens was great. He writes on one occasion :

> " I have been laid up with one of my attacks, which I mention only in honour of Dickens, who carries me through such sore afflictions. Last year I took to my bed in company with *Barnaby Rudge* at Paris. This season *Martin Chuzzlewit* has carried me through my intestine troubles. The Togers (*sic*) made me laugh between such fits as Gil Blas should have had to warrant his roars in the cavern. An author like Dickens cannot know the good he does in his manifold services to humanity and alleviating ministrations under distress."

He became a welcome guest at Dickens's house, but I think there can be no doubt but that he came into the Dickens Circle chiefly by virtue of his great friendship with Forster. He was a good-hearted man of brilliant parts, but he was not a strong personality, and I can find no evidence that he had any great appeal for Dickens. The novelist valued him as a critic, of course, and particularly wished him to be invited to the reading of *The Chimes* at Lincoln's Inn Fields in 1844. He was not there, but when the reading was repeated a day or two later he attended. Says Forster, " Such was the report made by it that once more, on the pressing intercession of our friend, Thomas Ingoldsby (Mr. Barham), there was a second reading to which the presence and encouragement of Fonblanque gave new zest."

R. H. Barham, of " Ingoldsby " fame, was undoubtedly held in considerable regard by Dickens, but he died in 1845, and there is very little record of the friendship between the brother humorists. It would appear probable that they were acquainted in 1838. In December of that year Dickens wrote a delightful letter to one Master Hastings Hughes, who had written to him stating his wishes as to the various rewards and punishments to be meted out to the characters in *Nickleby*. The boy's letter, we are told, was forwarded to him through Barham, which makes it pretty certain that Ingoldsby and Boz were acquainted. In 1842, as we have seen, Barham was at the Greenwich dinner. Certainly from that time he was a frequent guest at Dickens's house. Further evidence that they were on particularly friendly terms is provided by the fact which has just been noted that in December 1844 the novelist gave a second private reading of *The Chimes* for Barham's express benefit.

It surely is surprising that Dickens and Charles Lever were not closer friends than they were. There is such a buoyant joyousness in the books of both men, reflecting truly their natures, that one would have thought they would have come together as steel and magnet. One would have thought they had almost everything in common. Both were great humorists, both had large hearts, and loved their kind, both loved good-fellowship and joviality. Yet there was scarcely any friendship between them. As a matter of fact, for years there was a most regrettable coolness. Lever's biographer, Mr. W. J. Fitzpatrick, offers an explanation. When " Lorrequer " was published, he says, a reviewer declared that he would rather be its author than the author of all the *Pickwicks* or *Nicklebys* in the world. This passage was used, with others of a similar description, in advertisements, " giving much annoyance to Dickens, who at last responded ungraciously to a civil letter of Lever's, and it was not for years that friendly relations were resumed." Mr. Fitzpatrick adds that with the comparison or advertisements Lever had nothing to do. One is glad to have the assurance, for such methods surely were in bad taste.

But the ill-feeling passed away after some years, and in the 'sixties Dickens asked Lever to write a story for *All the Year Round*. Lever responded with " A Day's Ride, a Life Romance." Says his biographer : " It proved, however, a fatiguing failure, and Lever was long sore from the effect of it. Dickens complained that it had the effect of depressing the circulation of *All the Year Round*; and at last resorted to the unusual step of advertising the day on which the prolonged ' ride ' was to end. He admitted that a few good glimpses of men and scenes were obtained— among others of Algernon Potts, the predestinarian, whose adventures elicited the remark that ' Lever, letting off a good deal of Bohemia, is at his best in the wild vagaries of this reckless daydream.' " Mr. Percy Fitzgerald tells the same story. " A Day's Ride, a Life Romance," he says, brought the Journal into very parlous state, and Dickens had to start *Great Expectations*.

There is nothing much else to be recorded. Lever's story,

" St. Patrick's Eve," was founded on his experiences of the great sufferings of the Irish peasantry during the cholera epidemic, and, says his biographer, " though not avowed, was suggested by Dickens's *Chimes*, which had just scored a success." Another interesting fact is that in " Davenport Dunn, the Man of one Day," Lever made use of some leading incidents in the life of the notorious John Sadler, whom Dickens took for the original of Mr. Merdle in *Little Dorrit.*

One would naturally expect to find a friendship between Sydney Smith and Dickens, and one did exist, though it was not of an intimate character. They met early in the novelist's career. In the published collection of Dickens's Letters, we find one to William Longman, in which the novelist writes : " I wish you would tell Sydney Smith that of all the men I ever heard of and never saw, I have the greatest curiosity to see and the greatest interest to know him." That letter, which is undated, is placed among the letters of the year 1839, but that is clearly a mistake, for in the previous year we find Smith writing to Dickens in a vein which proves they were already pretty well acquainted. The letter refers to some ladies of Smith's acquaintance who wished to meet Dickens at dinner, and it proceeds : " My friends have not the smallest objection to being put into a number, but on the contrary would be proud of the distinction; Lady Charlotte in particular you may marry to Newman Noggs."

Curiously enough, the great wit did not enjoy *Pickwick.* In 1837 Tom Moore records that he met Smith at a dinner in the Row, and that the wit cried Dickens down, " and evidently without having given him a fair trial." *Nickleby* conquered him, however, and it was the number in which Mrs. Nickleby imparts her confidences to Miss Knagg that clinched the victory. He wrote to Sir George Phillips : " *Nickleby* is *very good.* I stood out against Mr. Dickens as long as I could, but he has conquered me."

From that time Dickens had no greater admirer.

The following letter, written in 1842, soon after the novelist's return from America, is proof of Smith's personal regard for Dickens : " I accept your obliging invitation conditionally. If I am invited by any man of greater genius than yours, or by one in whose works I have been more completely interested, I will repudiate you, and dine with the more splendid phenomenon of the two."

By 1840 they were on very friendly terms, and Forster records that in that year they met at many social entertainments. And so it was till the end. They often met socially and they had a true regard for each other's character and genius. The last time they met was in 1844 at a dinner at Osnaburgh Terrace on May 28.

Smith died in the following year, and two years later Dickens paid a very striking tribute to his memory, by naming his fifth son after him—Sydney Smith Haldimand Dickens.

Charles Buller was at the dinner to Black, so that Dickens must have known him fairly well, but he was never really one of the novelist's circle. If Lytton's description of him was correct, he could not have been very acceptable to Boz. He was clever, wrote the author of " Pelham," but superficial—always wanting in earnestness, and ironically pert. Southwood Jones, another of the company at that dinner to Black, was a much better liked friend, who was often at Dickens's house.

In 1841 Dickens became greatly interested in the improvements that had taken place in the London prisons during recent years, and, says Forster, " he took frequent means of stating what in this respect had been done, since even the date when his *Sketches* were written, by two most efficient public officers at Clerkenwell and Tothill Fields, Mr. Chesterton and Lieutenant Tracey, whom the course of these inquiries turned into private friends." These two gentlemen were officials of the kind that are not so common as they ought to be—keen for beneficial reform, refusing to be hidebound by Red Tape; and Dickens had a high admiration of the valuable work they did. They became private friends, but not intimate friends, and never had an important place in the Dickens Circle.

CHAPTER XX

WILLIAM JERDAN

In this place shall William Jerdan have mention, because, like Fonblanque, he early discerned the genius of Boz. Nay, it is to his credit that he went out of his way to offer encouragement to the young writer.

"With Dickens" (he says), "I can claim long friendly relations, and with Thackeray hardly less amicable inter· course. In the first morning beam of public delight upon the former I felt the full glow, and looked with prophetic gladness to the bright day which I was sure must follow so auspicious a dawning. When Sam Weller appeared on the canvas, I was so charmed with the creation that I could not resist the impulse to write to the author and counsel him to develop the novel character largely—to the utmost. My urgency was taken in good part, and we improved our alliance so genially that when *Pickwick* was triumphantly finished and a ' semi-business Pickwickian sort of dinner ' ensued, I was invited to be of the party with the compliments of the author : ' I depend upon *you* above everybody. . . .' I cannot describe my gratification. The party was delightful, with Mr. Sergeant Talfourd as V.P., and there the pleasant and uncommon fact was stated . . . that there never had been a line of written agreement, but that the author, printer, artist, and publisher, had all proceeded on simple verbal assurances, and that there never had arisen a word to interrupt or prevent the complete satisfaction of every one."

We may readily believe that the receipt of such a letter from so powerful a person as the Editor of the " Literary Gazette " was a very gratifying event to the young novelist. H. F. Chorley says that Jerdan was " the puppet of certain booksellers, and dispensed praise and blame at their bidding, and, it may be feared, ' for a consideration.' " The value of Chorley's opinion is discounted by the fact that he was a shining light of the " Athenæum," and, moreover, Jerdan meets this very charge in his " Auto-

biography " and pretty conclusively disposes of it. Nevertheless, Jerdan wielded tremendous power, and praise or blame from
him very often meant the making or the marring of a young writer.
Therefore, his letter of praise and encouragement must have
meant a great deal to the twenty-four-years-old Boz.

Jerdan was also at the *Nickleby* dinner : " On a later occasion
of the same kind," he says, " I was flattered by the nomination
to occupy the post of honour at the bottom of the table, and am
happy to remember that I acquitted myself so creditably of its
onerous duties as to receive the approbation of the giver of the
feast, his better half, and the *oi polloi* unanimously." In a footnote to this, he says : " I slyly introduced in something I had to
say about a portrait of her " (Mrs. Dickens's) " husband which I
knew she longed to possess ; and the hint was taken in the right
quarter and the painting presented to her." The reference
obviously is to Maclise's famous picture. Here again Jerdan is
laying flattering unction to his soul. He may have given the
" sly hint," and he may have assumed, when he knew that the
painting was in Dickens's possession, that his hint had been acted
upon, but, of course, the gift was to Dickens himself, and it
was a spontaneous act of Chapman and Hall's without any
reference to " sly hints " from Jerdan or anybody else.

Reference to this painting of Maclise's reminds us of a very
curious link between Dickens and Jerdan to which reference has
been made by Mr. Percy Fitzgerald. He points to the fact that
Mr. Pickwick had his portrait painted, and that it was a portrait
" which he did not wish to be destroyed when he grew a few years
older." Mr. Fitzgerald sees in this an allusion to an incident
that created a sensation in the spring of 1836—just at the time
that *Pickwick* was in the first dawn of its popularity. Maclise
had painted a portrait of Sir John Soane, the famous architect,
and the donor to the nation of the Soane Museum. Sir John had
been a generous donor to the Literary Fund, and he offered the
portrait for hanging in the Committee room. It was a good
portrait, and he was very pleased with it, until somebody put
it into his head that it made him look older than he really was.
Then he demanded that it should be replaced by a portrait by Sir
Thomas Lawrence, which he offered to present.

Maclise demanded his painting back ; Sir John insisted that it
should be handed to him. The Committee were saved from their
dilemma by some one cutting the portrait to shreds. That some
one was Jerdan. Macready, in his Diary confirms Mr. Fitzgerald's statement, for on May 10, 1836, he writes : " Went to
rehearsal, calling on Forster by the way, who related to me and
showed me a statement in the ' Chronicle ' of the occurrence that

Jerdan had cut to pieces (as he had said at Elstree he would do) Maclise's portrait of Sir John Soane, who has been absurdly and tetchily desirous of destroying that too faithful record of his personal appearance." Mr. Fitzgerald's suggestion that Dickens had this incident in mind when he wrote the sentence quoted is at least reasonable.

Jerdan was associated with Dickens in the adjustment of the difficulties with Bentley. He says that when Dickens decided to repurchase a share of the copyright of *Oliver Twist*, " upon my table the sum of £2250 was handed over to Mr. Bentley, and both parties perfectly satisfied." This must not be taken too literally, for the agreement, according to Forster, was that the £2250 was deducted from the purchase money—£3000—of *Barnaby Rudge*. But it is true that Jerdan had a hand in the negotiations. Forster says that it was a note from Jerdan on behalf of Bentley that opened those negotiations.

Dickens and Jerdan continued to be friendly acquaintances, visiting one another occasionally, meeting sometimes in social life, but there never existed, I am very sure, any fellowship. Dickens was one of the guests at the dinner which was held to celebrate the twenty-fifth birthday of the " Literary Gazette," accepting the invitation in the following terms :

" I was going into Yorkshire on Monday morning, but having fortunately been able to take a place for Tuesday, can accept your kind invitation.

" Be sure that among all the congratulations which will be offered to you in the delightful occasion of our meeting there will be none more cordial and warm-hearted than mine. By the time we dine together again to celebrate the fiftieth birthday of your healthy offspring, I shall study to find appropriate things to clothe them in ; till then, however, I fear they must remain locked up in my heart—where they will at any rate keep warmer than on the lips of, my dear Jerdan, yours most faithfully,

" CHARLES DICKENS."

That was in 1852. Subsequently they do not seem to have met so frequently as of yore, and the only further occasion on which I can find their names linked is in the following year, when Dickens was one of the Committee that organised a testimonial to Jerdan on his retirement from the " Literary Gazette." It should, however, be recorded that Jerdan occasionally contributed to *Household Words* and *All the Year Round*.

CHAPTER XXI

JOHN GIBSON LOCKHART

WITH Scott's son-in-law Dickens was acquainted from his very earliest days of authorship. Ainsworth has recorded that Lockhart thought that *Pickwick* was "all very well—but damned low!" Which is interesting in view of the facts that at the time *Pickwick* was written Lockhart was Editor of the "Quarterly Review"—which Dickens parodied as the "Quarrelly Review" for the purpose of some dummy book-backs in his library—and that the "Quarterly's" was the only authoritative voice raised even in mild criticism. For it was in October 1837 that the famous article appeared which warned Dickens—quite properly, in view of the facts—that he was writing too much and too often, and that, having gone up like the rocket, if he was not careful, he might come down like the stick.

Lockhart seems to have had many qualities that made it difficult to love him, and especially from 1837, in which year the first of a series of painful domestic sorrows came upon him, he seems to have tried the patience of his friends pretty sorely. That caustic wit of his was not exactly an asset to him in social relations, and when his trials came upon him he developed an irritability and a moroseness that did not tend to win for him affection. In her "Life" of her father, Professor Wilson ("Christopher North"), Mrs. Gordon says of him that he was "cold, haughty, supercilious in manner," and that he "seldom won love and not infrequently caused his friends to distrust it in him, for they sometimes found the warmth of their own feelings thrown back upon them in the presence of this cold indifference."

All this is true, but if he had his faults they were on the surface. He was generous and just, and bore no malice. Beneath an exterior that was often unpleasing there was a tender and affectionate heart, and by those who took the trouble to get beneath the surface and to understand him he was held in high esteem. Carlyle, for instance, who was not easy to please, spoke of him, we are told, as he seldom spoke of any man, and between them there was a trusting confidence quite remarkable. Dickens, too, saw and loved the real man, and a letter written eight years after

Lockhart's death is evidence of the regard he had for him. Mrs. Lynn Linton wrote a review of Mrs. Gordon's book for *All the Year Round,* and in it she made some reference to Scott's son-in-law and biographer, which Dickens struck out.

> " Will you tell Mrs. Linton " (he wrote to Wills) " that in looking over her admirable account (*most* admirable) of Mrs. Gordon's book I have taken out the references to Lockhart? Not because I in the least doubt their justice, but because I knew him, and because one bright day at Rome I walked about with him for some hours when he was dying and all the old faults had faded out of him, and the mere ghost of the handsome man I had first known when Scott's daughter was at the head of his house had little more to do with this world than she in her grave, or Scott in his, or little Hugh Littlejohn in his. Lockhart had been anxious to see me all the previous day (when I was at Campagne), and as we walked about I knew very well that *he* knew very well why. He talked of getting better, but I never saw him again. This makes me stay Mrs. Lynn Linton's hand, gentle as it is."

Verily Dickens was a friend worthy the name.

I do not know when Dickens and Lockhart met. Forster says that in 1839, after his return from a trip into Wales, Dickens " had pleasing communications with Lockhart, dining with him at Cruikshank's a little later; and this was the prelude to a ' Quarterly Review ' article on *Oliver* by Mr. Ford, written at the instance of Lockhart, but without the raciness he would have put into it, in which amends were made for previous less favourable notices in that Review. Dickens had not, however, waited for this to express publicly his hearty sympathy with Lockhart's handling of some passages in his admirable ' Life of Scott ' that had drawn down upon him the wrath of the Ballantynes. This he did in the ' Examiner.' " [1]

It would not be unnatural to infer that this was their first acquaintanceship, but the reference by Dickens in his letter quoted above to his recollection of Lockhart when " Scott's daughter was at the head of his house " proves that the inference would be wrong, for Mrs. Lockhart died in 1837. So that Boz and the Editor of the " Quarrelly Review " must have known each other when *Pickwick* was still the one topic of conversation. They remained very good friends, dining at each other's homes occasionally, and more often meeting at what Forster calls " social foregatherings."

[1] Two articles, entitled " Scott and his Publishers," in the " Examiner," March 31 and September 29, 1839. Reprinted in *Miscellaneous Papers.*

CHAPTER XXII

SAMUEL ROGERS

SAMUEL ROGERS was another friend of these days, who must have special prominence here because Dickens dedicated *The Old Curiosity Shop* to him. Of all the novelist's friendships there surely is none at first thought more puzzling than this one. We find Dickens always speaking or writing of him in terms of regard, or of friendly feeling, yet scarcely a writer who knew the man and has left anything like a portrait of him, has painted a pleasant picture. I am not so sure that I would accept William Jerdan's estimate of any man too literally, but his estimate of Samuel Rogers is unpleasantly in accord with the portraits preserved for us by most other writers of the time. " . . . It did not appear," he says, " that the nonagenarian (whatever he might have enjoyed half a century before) had any friends. I never saw about him any but acquaintances or toadies. Had he out-lived them? No; he was not of a nature to have any friends. . . . The posthumous laudation lavished upon him by his political cronies was purely of the *de mortuis nil nisi bonum* kind. He never received that coin when alive; for, if the truth be told, his liberality and generosity were small specks which could not bear blazon, and he was radically ill-tempered."

How are we to reconcile this with the terms of Dickens's dedication of *The Old Curiosity Shop*?

To
SAMUEL ROGERS,
ONE OF THE FEW MEN
WHOM RICHES AND HONOUR
HAVE NOT SPOILED,
AND WHO HAVE PRESERVED
IN HIGH PLACES
ACTIVE SYMPATHY WITH
THE POOREST
AND HUMBLEST
OF THEIR KIND.

Puzzling, is it not? Yet, Barry Cornwall gives corroborative testimony. "It has been rumoured," says Procter, "that he was a sayer of bitter things. I know he was a *giver* of good things—kind and amiable where a potion was wanted, never ostentatious or oppressive, and always a friend in need." I suppose the truth is that Rogers had a soft spot somewhere in his heart, and that only men of genuine human sympathy, such as Dickens and Procter were, were able to see beneath a decidedly forbidding surface. All the same, I think the old man was not much more than an acquaintance of Dickens's. There was a friendliness rather than a friendship. We have to observe that to a young writer like Dickens there was a glamour surrounding a man who belonged to a generation that had passed away. Rogers was, indeed, a relic of the past, more so than Leigh Hunt, more so, even, than Landor; for Hunt was but little past the prime of life when Dickens sprang into fame, and though Landor was much older, his joy in life had not abated—he lived still in the present. Rogers was yet older than Landor. To Dickens, I fancy, he was more of a curiosity than anything else—though it is certain that the novelist liked him, and does seem to have been a favourite. I cannot but think that Dickens was admitted to greater intimacy than Jerdan and some others; I cannot but think that the bright, joyous young Boz, overflowing, in the first flush of his success, with the joy of life, must have capti- vated—so far as it was possible for such a man to be captivated— the cynical old banker-poet.

This friendship—or friendliness—between Boz and the wizened old poet was assuredly a quaint association. But, after all, Rogers had moved in literary and artistic circles—had been the centre of a brilliant circle for a couple of generations or more— and to the young Boz, fresh from poverty and drudgery, it must have meant much to be admitted to such a circle. That Rogers liked him there is plenty of evidence to show. It was not Dickens's books that attracted him, for we are told that " he did not recog- nise how great a genius was that of Charles Dickens," whilst Mr. H. Ellis Roberts says [1] that " when Dickens published the *Christmas Carol* in 1843, he sent a copy to Rogers, hoping he would like the slight fancy it embodied, but the old man was now beyond appreciating the new genius : he fell asleep over the first half-hour's reading because he found it so dull; the next hour was so painful that he had to finish it in order to remove the impression."

No, it was not Dickens's books that attracted Rogers. May it not have been that the presence of the buoyant young writer was to the old man as the first sight of the blue sky and green fields is to the invalid who has just risen from a sick-bed with

---

[1] " Samuel Rogers and his Circle."

SAMUEL ROGERS

From a drawing by Sir Thomas Lawrence, P.R.A

hope that had been almost extinguished once more restored?
May it not have been that this young man's hearty enjoyment
of life carried its infection even into the heart of this rich old
bachelor, and brought back to him the days when he might have
written " The Pleasures of Hope " ?

Samuel Carter Hall—not a very charitable critic—tells us of
Rogers that " you could not fancy when you looked upon him
that you saw a good man. It was a repulsive countenance; to
say it was ugly would be to pay it a compliment, and I verily
believe it was indicative of the naturally shrivelled heart and
contracted soul." Henry Fothergill Chorley is less sweeping. He
tells us how perverse and inhuman Rogers could be where he did
not like, and how uncivil he could be, but he also states his belief
that the crookedness and the incivility of some of his humours
" had nothing to do with his heart and his hand when the one
told the other to give. Rogers's hospitality to poets," he adds,
" might be pleasant to himself, and no less so his handsome
reception of every handsome woman, but for the poor struggling,
suffering man of genius, and to the garret, . . . he was, I believe,
a deliberate almoner, a liberal distributor, and a frequent visitor.
Bilious, vicious, *cruel*, as he was with his tongue, Rogers was, I
know, a kindly and indefatigable friend to many humble men
and to a few less humble men."

We shall be pretty safe in accepting Chorley's estimate in
preference to Hall's, for after all, if Rogers had been everything
that Hall and Jerdan say he was, he would never have been for
more than half a century the centre of such a brilliant circle.
For all the members of that circle could not have been toadies;
there must have been *something* that attracted them to the man.
If he had been such a man as Hall and Jerdan say he was, can
we believe that Dickens would have accompanied his Dedication
of *The Old Curiosity Shop* with such a letter as this?—" Let me
have my ' Pleasures of Memory ' in connection with this book
by dedicating it to a poet whose writings (as all the world knows)
are replete with genius and earnest feeling; and to a man whose
daily life (as all the world does not know) is one of active sympathy with the poorest and humblest of his kind."—" As all the
world does *not* know." As Hall and Jerdan did *not* know; as
Dickens, we may be very sure, *did* know. There must have
been a side to the old man's character which was revealed only
to the few, and one of those few was Charles Dickens.

CHAPTER XXIII

THOMAS HOOD

AND now we come to a far more lovable man than either of the two from whom we have just parted. Naturally Tom Hood was one of Dickens's friends. We should expect to find a strong affinity between two such men. Each was a humorist who used his great gifts of humour for the highest purposes; each had a burning sympathy with the poor and suffering and an intense hatred of social injustice; the work of each was governed supremely by the heart.

Each had a high opinion of the other's work. Hood's article on the first volume of *Master Humphrey's Clock* is well known. It is the article in which he wrote of Dickens: "The poor are his especial clients. He delights to show Worth in low places— living up a court, for example, with Kit and the industrious washerwoman, his mother. To exhibit Honesty holding a gentleman's horse, or Poverty bestowing alms." It was to this article Dickens referred in his preface to the first cheap edition of *The Old Curiosity Shop* in 1845 :

> "I have a sorrowful pride in one recollection associated with ' Little Nell.' While she was yet upon her wanderings, not then concluded, there appeared in a literary journal, an essay of which she was the principal theme, so earnestly, so eloquently, and so tenderly appreciative of her and of all her shadowy kith and kin, that it would have been insensibility in me if I could have read it without an unusual glow of pleasure and encouragement. Long afterwards, and when I had come to know him well, and to see him stout of heart going slowly down into his grave, I knew the writer of that essay to be Thomas Hood."

The article appeared in 1840, and Dickens's words suggest that he was not personally acquainted with the poet then. But before that, Hood had many times expressed his appreciation of Boz's work. To Dilke, in 1839, for instance, he had written :

> "As regards Boz, his *morale* is better than his material, though that is often very good; it is *wholesome* reading;

the drift is natural, *along with the great human currents, and not against them.* His purpose, sound, with that honest independence of thinking, which is the constant adjunct of true-heartedness, recognising good in low places, and evil in high ones, in short a manly assertion of Truth *as* truth. Compared with such merits, his defect of overpainting, and the like, are but spots on the sun. For these merits alone, he deserves all the success he has obtained, and long may he enjoy them ! "

And Dickens had shown in the same year his sympathy with the poet, with whom, at the most, he was then very slightly acquainted. For it is in reference to this year that Forster says : " I find him noticing a book by Thomas Hood : ' rather poor, but I have not said so, because Hood is too, and ill besides.' " The book referred to was " Up the Rhine," and the review was written for the " Examiner."

When Dickens and Hood first met I cannot discover, but it is recorded that after that meeting the poet went home and told his wife to cut off his hand and bottle it, because it had shaken hands with Boz ! By 1841 they were close personal friends. " Didn't you enjoy *Pickwick* ? " writes the poet to a friend in April of that year. " It is so very English ! I felt sure you would. Boz is a very good fellow, and he and I are very good friends." In the following year Hood was one of the company at the Greenwich dinner to welcome Dickens back from America. I shall earn no one's ill-favour if I quote his account of that dinner, which he wrote to Mrs. Elliot.

" Jerdan was the *Vice*, and a certain person, not very well adapted to *fill* a Chair, was to have occupied the opposite *Virtue*, but on the score of ill-health I begged off, and Captain Marryat presided instead. On his right Dickens and Monckton Milnes, the poetical M.P. ; on his left Sir John Wilson, T. H., and for my left-hand neighbour Doctor Elliot*son*. . . . The Kelso man was supported by Forster and Stanfield the painter. Amongst the rest were Charles and Tom Landseer. . . . Father Prout and Ainsworth ; these two were at paper war—therefore some six, including a clergyman, were put between them. Procter, *alias* Barry Cornwall, and Barham, otherwise Ingoldsby, Cruikshank and Cattermole, a Dr. Quynne or Quin,[1] and a Rev. Mr. Wilde.[2] . . .

" Well, we drank ' the Boz ' with a delectable clatter, which drew from him a good warm-hearted speech, in which

---

[1] Quin, of course.   [2] ? The Rev. James White.

he hinted the great advantage of going to America for the pleasure of coming back again; and pleasantly described the embarrassing attentions of the Transatlantickers, who made his private house and private cabin particularly public. He looked very well, and had a younger brother along with him. . . . Then we had more songs. Barham chanted a Robin Hood ballad, and Cruikshank sang a burlesque ballad of Lord Bateman; and somebody, unknown to me, gave a capital imitation of a French showman. Then we toasted Mrs. Boz, and the Chairman, and Vice, and the Traditional Priest [1] sang the ' Deep deep sea ' in his deep, deep voice; and then we drank to Procter, who wrote the said song; also Sir J. Wilson's good health, and Cruikshank's and Ainsworth's. . . . Jerdan as Jerdanish as usual on such occasions—you know how paradoxically he is *quite at home in dining out.* As to myself, I had to make my *second maiden* speech, for Monckton Milnes proposed my health in terms my modesty allows me to repeat to *you ;* but my memory won't. However, I ascribed the toast to my notoriously bad health, and assured them that their wishes had already improved it—that I felt a brisker circulation—a more genial warmth about the heart, and explained that a certain trembling of my hands was not from palsy, or my old ague, but an inclination in my hand to shake itself with every one present. Whereupon I had to go through the friendly ceremony with as many of the company as were within reach, besides a few more who came express from the other end of the table. . . . Boz kindly sent me in his own carriage."

In 1844 Dickens promised a contribution to " Hood's Magazine and Comic Miscellany," and Hood wrote to him : " My dear Dickens,—I cannot say how delighted I was to learn from my friend Ward that you had promised me a little bit of writing to help me to launch afloat again. It has become a cruel business, and I really wanted help in it, or I should not have announced it, knowing how much you have to do." The " bit of writing " was *Threatening Letter to Thomas Hood, from an ancient Gentleman* [2]—a satire on the existing craze for the famous midget, Tom Thumb.

At the end of 1844 Hood took to his bed finally, yet there he wrote a review of *The Chimes.*

[1] Father Prout.　　　　　　　[2] See *Miscellaneous Papers.*

CHAPTER XXIV

LEIGH HUNT

THE friendship with Leigh Hunt was one of those formed through Forster in the first days of popularity. The poet, however, was never one of the inner Dickens circle. Indeed, it would be nearer accuracy to say that Dickens was a member of Hunt's circle, than that the author of " Abou Ben Adhem " was of the Dickens circle. For Hunt belonged to an older school, although he was only fifty-two years old when Dickens leaped into fame. He had suffered imprisonment for his political views, had known and loved Shelley, upon the immortal light of whose funeral pile he had gazed, had worshipped at the Byron shrine—had, indeed, been a planet in the firmament of letters, long before the Dickens planet had assumed the dimensions of a distant star. But there was a genuine friendship. Hunt recognised Dickens's genius, and appreciated his personal worth, whilst Dickens perceived the true sweetness of Hunt's character, and loved his oddities.

Dickens, as we have noted, was introduced to Hunt by Forster, and on the very next day that " mutual friend " received a letter from the poet, saying, " What a face is his to meet in a drawing-room ! It has the life and soul in it of fifty human beings." There are very few records of meetings between Hunt and Dickens, and not one of the novelist's letters to his friend seems to have been preserved; but from that first meeting there sprang a friendship which was not broken except by death. They must have met often, though obviously we should not expect to find Hunt sharing in those long country walks and rides indulged in almost daily by Dickens and Forster, Ainsworth, and Maclise. It would be difficult, for instance, to imagine Leigh Hunt tramping out to Jack Straw's Castle, and enjoying at that " good 'ouse " a " red-hot chop " ! But we find in 1839 Dickens writing to J. P. Harley : " This is my birthday. Many happy returns of the day to you and me. I took it into my head yesterday to get up an impromptu dinner on this auspicious occasion—only my own folks, Leigh Hunt, Ainsworth, and Forster. . . . Lord bless my soul ! Twenty-seven years old. Who'd have thought it ? I *never* did ! But I grow sentimental."

In 1847 Dickens gave evidence of the genuineness of the regard in which he held Hunt, and numbered himself among the many who had rendered practical aid to this least worldly and practical of men.   Hunt tells us in his " Autobiography " that throughout his life the multiplication table had been a mystery to him.   He had been indebted to Shelley and to Byron, whilst a relative of the former had made him an allowance, and still, with it all, he had always lived from hand to mouth.   Not because he was lacking in principle—as with Skimpole—but simply because though in the world, he was never of it.   And now, in his closing years, the literary men of a new generation were to help him, as those of his earlier years had done.   Dickens rallied round him that wonderful company of amateur actors to which reference has already been made so often.   It was decided to give perform- ances of " Every Man in his Humour " in London and the provinces, but while the arrangements were still incomplete Hunt was granted a Civil List pension of £200 a year, and in con- sequence the London performances were cancelled, and it was agreed to play only at Manchester and Liverpool.

And now to the unfortunate Skimpole incident.   Undoubtedly Dickens cannot be acquitted of a serious breach of good taste. The pity of it all was that men came to say, " Skimpole is Leigh Hunt."   It is not an exaggeration to say that this is the notion of the average man in the street to this very day.   And yet, on the testimony of every one who knew him, the notion is utterly wrong.   As a matter of fact, the whole of the trouble arose out of Skimpole's *un*likeness to his original—an apparent paradox but the actual truth.   Few English men of letters have been more charming or better men than Hunt.   Even S. C. Hall speaks well of him, which is saying much.   This is what he says of Leigh Hunt : " His famous sonnet, ' Abou Ben Adhem,' may have been inspired by an Eastern apothegm, but it was none the less an outpouring of his own large heart."   No higher praise was ever uttered of any man.   James Payn says that selfishness and baseness had nought to do with Hunt : " they were utterly opposed to his character."   Dickens himself says that Hunt's life was " of the most amiable and domestic kind, that his wants were few, that his way of life was frugal, that he was a man of small expenses, no ostentations, a diligent labourer, and a secluded man of letters."

How came Dickens, then, to pillory such a man as " a senti- mentalist, brilliant, vivacious, and engaging, but thoroughly selfish and unprincipled " ?   The most commonly accepted idea is that he merely wanted to transpose into his book the senti- mentalism, and the brilliant, vivacious, and engaging qualities of Hunt, and that he made the mistake of giving those qualities to a selfish and unprincipled man, never dreaming that with his readers the evil as well as the good would be attributed to Hunt—that, in short, he was charmed with Hunt's engaging ways, and desired to—shall we say immortalise them? Assuming that this is the whole truth, there would have been no harm in it if he had given those engaging ways to a pleasant character. In the very same book he treated another poet-friend in this way; but gave no offence, because he insisted on the innate tenderness and goodness underlying Boythorne's rough and brusque exterior—because, in fact, he gave a *complete* picture of the man. In the case of Leigh Hunt he placed all the charming oddities and whimsicalities upon a thoroughly odious character. It was bad taste; and that Dickens could have been guilty of it will never cease to astonish us.

But is this the whole truth? I have always had an idea that it is not. I cannot resist the thought that there was something more in it than this. However much Dickens might like Hunt, and however much he might be charmed with the poet's manner, is it not probable that he would dislike very strongly some of the extravagant—almost perverse—views on morality that Hunt was in the habit of expressing in print and in conversation? And is it not probable that the novelist tried to present an object lesson of their dangers? Dickens was as strong a believer as ever lived in the importance of self-reliance. Dilettantism was anathema to him: we recall how, even in his sincerely appreciative "In Memoriam" article on Thackeray he hints at his resentment of what he thought was that great writer's failure to take his art seriously. And though Hunt was undoubtedly a hard worker, there was a suggestion of the dilettante in him which would irritate Dickens. Forster quotes a passage from the "Tatler," which he says had "unluckily attracted Dickens's notice":

"Supposing us to be in want of patronage, and in possession of talent enough to make it an honour to notice us, we would much rather have some great and comparatively private friend, rich enough to assist us, and amiable enough to render obligation delightful, than become the public property of any man, or of any government. . . . If a divinity had given us our choice, we should have said—make us La Fontaine, who goes and lives twenty years with some rich friend, as innocent of any harm in it as a child, and who writes what he thinks charming verses, sitting all day under a tree."

To those who understand Hunt, Forster's hint that this must not be taken too seriously, as expressing its writer's own morality, is unnecessary. But there it is, printed and published for all to read. We may here quote a passage from the " Autobiography " :

> " I would not have missed the obligations I have had from my friends; no, hardly to have been exempt from all the cares of money; so little do I hold with that writer who spoke the other day of the ' degrading obligations of private friendship.' I see beyond that. But I do not the less hold with him that it is ' comely and sweet ' to be able to earn one's own sufficiency. I only think that it should not be made so hard a matter to do so as it very often is by the systems of society, and by the effects which we have in reserve for us even before we are born, and in our very temperaments as well as fortunes; and I think also that the world would have been the losers in a very large way— far beyond what the utilitarians suppose, and yet on their own ground—if certain men of a lively and improvident genius—humanists of the most persuasive order, had not sometimes felt themselves under the necessity of being assisted in a smaller way. But I desire, for my own part, not to be excused in anything, in which I do not take the whole of my fellow-creatures and their errors along with me. Let me not be left out of the pale of humanity for praise or for blame, and I am content. I desire only to teach and be taught, or if that be too presumptuous a saying, to learn and compare notes. . . ."

Now, there is truth in all this; and to those who knew the man it was unobjectionable, but it is a dangerous doctrine to be taught broadcast. Such sentiments might be moral enough coming from Hunt, but let a thriftless, unprincipled Harold Skimpole imbibe them, and the danger that lurks in them is very quickly recognised. Such, I think, may have been Dickens's object. He wanted to show how fine is the line that divides Leigh Hunt and Harold Skimpole—how easily such sentiments may be perverted from truth into mere sophistry.

This does not mean that we need doubt him when he says that " He had no more thought, God forgive him! that the admired original would ever be charged with the imaginary vices of the fictitious creature, than he has himself ever thought of charging the blood of Desdemona and Othello on the innocent Academy model who sat for Iago's leg in the picture." The trouble was that he did not stop to consider that it was a sheer

LEIGH HUNT

From a drawing by J. Hayter

CAPTAIN FREDERICK MARRYAT, R.N.

From a drawing by W. Behnes

134

impossibility to carry out his purpose without suggesting such an intention. To carry out such a purpose he was bound to give us a corrupt Leigh Hunt : there was no escape from it. The abyss was indicated while the book was in progress. He was genuinely surprised, and made many alterations, but it was too late : the damage was done. It was the old, old story :

> "Harm is wrought by want of thought,
> As well as want of heart."

Hunt did not recognise the likeness. It was left to " friends " to point it out. Dickens was more hurt than his victim. He recognised that there was only one course for him—full and frank apology. That was forthcoming, and that the relations of the two men, though temporarily strained, were not permanently affected is shown by the fact that Hunt wrote frequently for *Household Words*. In the very first number he had a poem, " Abraham, the Fire-Worshipper," and in 1853–4 there appeared the papers now known as " The Old Court Suburb."

CHAPTER XXV

CAPTAIN MARRYAT

WE have it on Forster's authority that among the first in Dickens's liking in these days was Captain Marryat. Unfortunately their friendship covered but a brief span of years. It did not start before 1837, for certain, probably not before 1839, and the gallant sailor and brilliant novelist died in 1848. The two men had a high regard for each other's genius, and in temperament they were not unlike. Both had "roughed it"—though in different ways—both had met all sorts and conditions of men, and their experience of the world had left them without any traces of cynicism; both were true humorists; both were at their best in the social circle. Forster, recording Dickens's delight in children's parties, says : "There was no one who approached him on these occasions, excepting only our attached friend Captain Marryat, who had a frantic delight in dancing, especially with children, of whom and whose enjoyments he was as fond as it became so thoroughly good-hearted a man to be."

Marryat's earliest reference to Dickens occurs in reply to an objection that had been taken to one of his stories appearing in serial form in the "Era."

"I would rather" (he said) "write for the instruction, or even the amusement of the poor than for the amusement of the rich; and I would sooner raise a smile or create an interest in the honest mechanic or agricultural labourer who requires relaxation than I would contribute to dispel the *ennui* of those who loll on their couches and wonder in their idleness what they shall do next. Is the rich man only to be amused? Are mirth and laughter to be made a luxury confined to the upper classes and denied to the honest and hard-working artisan? I have lately given my aid to cheaper literature, and I consider that the most decided step which I have taken is the insertion of this tale in a weekly newspaper—by which means it will be widely disseminated among the lower classes, who, until lately (and the chief credit of the alteration is due to Mr. Dickens), had hardly an idea of such recreation."

The man who spoke there would be likely to have much in common with Dickens. They met frequently, and Marryat was always a welcome member of the early Dickens circle. In 1842 he presided at the dinner at Greenwich at which Dickens was welcomed home from America by a few of his more intimate friends. Probably the fact that he, too, had toured America and had had very much the same experience as Dickens earned this honour for him.

In 1842 Dickens gave much offence in America on account of his stand on the copyright question. I think it is very probable that Marryat influenced him on this point. He had spent a couple of years (1837–9) in America, and had given offence in the same way. It was a very important principle that was at stake. Marryat had fought for it bravely; Dickens could not but know that his influence was even greater than his friend's, and he took up the fight. We have no evidence that Marryat did influence him, but I think there can be very little doubt on the point. Marryat greatly enjoyed Dickens's tilt at our cousins in *American Notes*. " It gives me great pleasure," we find Dickens writing to him in the summer of 1843, " to find that you like the tickling. I shall go in again before I have done, and give the eagle a final poke under his fifth rib."

Marryat settled at Langham in 1843, and thenceforward he took his place in the old circle but rarely. He became absorbed in farming—which proved an expensive hobby—and it was very difficult indeed to draw him to London. Stanfield tried in 1844 :

" Charles Dickens is about to leave England with his family for one whole year to visit foreign parts, previous to which we are about to bestow on the said Charles Dickens a complimentary dinner to be eaten at Greenwich. Now, Forster, Maclise, and myself, who have the arrangement of the above dinner, would be very glad indeed if you could, and *would,* make one amongst us on that occasion. I wish you would ! I really think a run up to town would do you good; at any rate, it would rejoice us much to have you with us on the present occasion."

But it was " no go "; even such an invitation as that could not tempt him. A little later, however, he ran up to town, and Dickens was among the friends he visited. At the end of the year Forster pressed him to come up for the forthcoming theatricals, but the reply was, " I dare not."

In 1843, however, he was happy in the anticipation of a visit from some of these old friends. Writing to Stanfield, he says :

" Although I shall be in town at the end of this month,
I write to you that we may not be disappointed in our
intended party down here in September, and I think you
had better at once make the arrangements as to the time
of coming so as to meet the wishes of all. I believe we have
only mentioned Landseer, Maclise, Dickens, Forster, and yourself. Are there any more that you would wish to add to the
list ? "

He evidently also wrote to Dickens, for on September 6 we
find the latter writing to him from Broadstairs : " I fear I cannot
say with any degree of certainty, sooner than the *third* week in
October for the pleasures of Langham, but, please God, I shall
be ready about the 19th or the 20th. I will make this known
to Maclise and Forster, and we will send you a threatening letter
when the time approaches." A month later—on October 9—
Marryat writes to Forster to know if the friends are coming.
There is no record as to whether the visit ever took place.

Marryat died in 1848. When the end was very near, the fact
was not recognised by his friends. He was at Brighton in March ;
so was Dickens, who wrote to him the following letter :

" I was coming round to see you this morning, but feel
myself obliged to go to London by the two o'clock train
with no time for preparation. As I shall not be back until
to-morrow night, and as I fear you will have left in the
interval, I write this to say that Kate and I were delighted
to find you had been here and were so happily recovered
from your illness. I assure you, my dear fellow, I was
heartily rejoiced and drank your health with all honours.
Do write me word in Devonshire Terrace some fortnight
hence, where you are and how you are ; and if you be within
reach let us foregather."

But he had not recovered from his illness, and there were to
be no more foregatherings. In August Marryat entered into the
higher life. His daughter tells us that as he lay dying, in his
semi-conscious condition produced by constant doses of morphia,
" he held imaginary conversations with Dickens, or Bulwer, or
some of his old shipmates."

CHAPTER XXVI

CHARLES KNIGHT

In the Shakespeare Society at this time Dickens was forming other friendships no less notable than those we have already considered. Talfourd and Maclise were members; so were Thackeray and Macready, Jerrold and Stanfield, Cattermole and the Landseers—two of them, at any rate, Charles and Tom. Others were Frank Stone, a well-beloved friend, B. W. Procter, Charles Knight, and Laman Blanchard, Jerrold's friend. Of the last named we will speak presently, but the other two may well find their places here.

Charles Knight—" Many-sided and true-hearted Charles Knight," as Forster called him—was a much older man than Dickens—he was editing a newspaper at Windsor when Dickens was born—and they had been acquainted from the earliest years of Dickens's authorship. I cannot find when they first met; Knight himself could not recall. But he does recall that in 1836 Dickens's uncle, Mr. Barrow, who was the conductor of " The Mirror of Parliament," sometimes meeting him at the printing office of Mr. Clowes, would tell him of his clever young relative who was the best reporter in the Gallery. He tells us also that he and Dickens were on tolerably familiar terms in the days of the Shakespeare Society. He says that the Society comprised too many members for readings and discussions as was originally intended, and its chance of promoting the friendly conviviality of men of congenial tastes was very soon destroyed. And then he describes the following incident which brought about the dissolution of the Society :

" There was a very full attendance at a dinner at which Mr. Dickens presided. His friend, Mr. John Forster, was at his side. I sat at a side table with a remarkable-looking young man opposite to me who I was told was the Michael Angelo Titmarsh of ' Fraser's Magazine.' Mr. Forster rose to propose a toast. He was proceeding with that force and fluency which he always possessed when there were some interruptions by the cracking of nuts and jingling of glasses

amongst the knot of young barristers, who were probably
fastidious as to every style of eloquence but the forensic.
The speaker expressed himself angrily; there were retorts
of a very unpleasant character. The Chairman in vain tried
to enforce order; but 'the fun,' if fun it could be called,
'grew fast and furious.' Previous to the dinner, Laman
Blanchard . . . had asked me to propose the health of the
Chairman. During a lull in the storm I was enabled to do
so, saying something about throwing oil upon the waves.
But it was all in vain. Mr. Dickens at length abandoned
the chair, and there was an end of the Shakespeare Club."

At this time there was but a bare acquaintance. We find,
however, a facetious reference to Knight in the amusing letter
that Dickens wrote to Forster announcing the death of his raven :
" I am not wholly free from suspicion of poison. A malicious
butcher has been heard to say that he would ' do ' for him : his
plea was that he would not be molested in taking orders down
the mews by any bird that wore a tail. Other persons have also
been heard to threaten : among others, Charles Knight, who has
just started a weekly publication price fourpence : *Barnaby* being,
as you know, threepence." Which reminds us that Knight was
the pioneer of cheap literature for the masses, and that in his
very valuable work in this direction he had, as might have been
expected, the earnest sympathy of Dickens. In 1844 he commenced the publication of " Knight's Weekly Volumes," and a
copy of the prospectus, entitled " Book Clubs for all Readers,"
he sent to Dickens. The scheme was to establish a cheap book
club—to publish high-class works at lowest possible prices, and,
by a system of small weekly contributions, to enable families to
acquire good libraries. Dickens's reply was : " I had already
seen your prospectus, and if I can be of the feeblest use in
advancing a project so intimately connected with an end on which
my heart is set—the liberal education of the people—I shall be
sincerely glad. All good wishes and success attend you."

In 1848 the two men were much more closely associated than
hitherto. In the announcement of the amateur theatricals
organised by Dickens and his friends it was set forth that the
Directors of General Arrangements would be Mr. John Payne
Collier, Mr. Charles Knight, and Mr. Peter Cunningham. When
the company went on tour Knight and Cunningham accompanied
them. During the tour Knight inevitably became more intimate
with Dickens, but still, he says, they rarely met in society. It
was *Household Words* that brought them into close relationship.
A week or so before the appearance of the first number, Dickens

wrote to Knight inviting him to become a contributor. The invitation was accepted, and from that time dated a close friendship between the men, a friendship so earnest that for years Dickens never failed to dine with Knight on the latter's birthday. In several of Dickens's letters we find references to this custom, whilst there can be no mistaking the heartiness of invitations. Indeed, there is no doubt but that they were true and fast friends, as the Editors of the *Letters* record. In July 1851 Dickens wrote from Broadstairs :

> " You say you are coming down to look for a place this week. Now, Jerrold says he is coming on Thursday by the cheap express at half-past twelve, to return with me for the play early on Monday morning. Can't you make that a holiday too ? I have promised him our only spare bed, but we'll find you a bed hard by, and shall be delighted to ' eat and drink you,' as an American once wrote to me. We will make expeditions to Herne Bay, Canterbury, where not ? and drink deep draughts of fresh air. Come ! They are beginning to cut the corn. You will never see the country so pretty. If you stay in town these days, you'll do nothing. Say you'll come ! "

I do not know whether that particular invitation was accepted, but we do know that in this year Knight spent a great deal of time with Dickens, especially at Broadstairs. The reference in this letter to the play reminds us that Knight was one of the " splendid strollers." In 1848, we have seen, he was one of the organisers of the theatricals. In 1851 he was one of the players. He was invited by Dickens to play Hodge in " Not so Bad as we Seem " in the Guild of Literature and Art performances. Referring to this, Knight says : " For myself, I should have been well contented with ' Hodge, the merry servant.' But my professional tastes and consequent histrionic capacity for playing the part of a scheming publisher of the days of Sir Robert Walpole were considered, and I had to rehearse the part of Jacob Tonson, the bookseller."

In 1864 Knight was in the Isle of Wight when his birthday came round, and Dickens wrote to him : " We knew of your being in the Isle of Wight, and had said that we should have this year to drink your health in your absence. Rely on my being always ready and happy to renew our old friendship in the flesh. In the spirit it needs no renewal, because it has no break."

Knight contributed regularly to *Household Words*, and we find Dickens, in his letters, frequently expressing his appreciation of his friend's work. His contributions included a series entitled "Shadows," and there are several references to these—always appreciative references, but often containing helpful criticisms and suggestions.

I doubt whether Knight was not of a rather too serious cast of mind to be entirely at home with Dickens at all times, but the two men had much in common. They were both strong believers in and advocates of the better education of the people. Knight's life was spent in bringing general knowledge and the best literature within reach of the masses. Many men who have rendered less service to their fellows and to human progress are better known to posterity, but he was in the truest sense a doer of good. Dickens's services to mankind are too widely acknowledged to need emphasis here. He served his fellows in many ways, and not least in his advocacy of education for the people. Here the two men had a common ground of sympathy, so that their friendship was, after all, the most natural thing in the world.

CHAPTER XXVII

" BARRY CORNWALL " AND HIS DAUGHTER

IN his book " John Forster and his Friendships," Mr. R. Renton quotes a letter from B. W. Procter to Forster, dated 1853, and says that it was written quite early in their friendship. That is obviously incorrect. Forster himself tells us that. Procter was one of the most prominent members of the Shakespeare Society which broke up in 1839, or thereabouts, and of which, as we have already seen, Forster was a leading spirit. Nay, they had both been friends of Lamb, who had died in 1834, so that Forster's friendship with Procter must have been one of the earliest he formed, dating from at least fourteen years, and probably twenty years, earlier than the year which Mr. Renton describes as " quite early in their friendship." We may take it as quite certain that Dickens came to know Procter through Forster. And from the first the novelist and the poet were on the best of terms. It was natural. Procter was a peculiarly lovable man, with a peculiar gentleness, " childlike, without being childish, with a keen, wholesome enjoyment of wholesome things, and an unfailing buoyancy of spirit." Such a man could not but have a strong attraction for Dickens.

From the beginning he loved the company of this friend, who, in the 'forties, was one of the innermost circle with Forster and Maclise and Ainsworth. Procter was one of the little company at the Greenwich dinner in 1842, and until he grew too old (he was twenty-five years older than Dickens) they had frequent social meetings.

For *Household Words* and *All the Year Round* he wrote a great deal, and Dickens valued his contributions very highly indeed. Chief among those contributions were his " Songs of the Trades," to which Dickens often refers in his letters. For instance, in December 1858 he writes :

" A thousand thanks for the little song. I am charmed with it, and shall be delighted to brighten *Household Words* with such a wise and genial light. I no more believe that your poetical faculty has gone by, than I believe that you

143

have yourself passed to the better land. You and it will travel thither in company, rely upon it. So I still hope to hear more of the trade-songs, and to learn that the blacksmith has hammered out no end of iron into good fashion of verse, like a cunning workman, as I know him of old to be."

And in March 1859 he writes : " I think the songs are simply ADMIRABLE ! and I have no doubt of this being a popular feature in *All the Year Round.*"

As Procter grew old Dickens saw less and less of him, but the friendship remained as deep as ever, and in 1854 it was peculiarly sweetened by the discovery that the " Miss Mary Berwick " who had contributed verses to *Household Words* which had won Dickens's unstinted praise was really his old friend's daughter, Adelaide, whom he had known from her childhood. That story does not need to be retold here. It was told by Dickens himself in the introduction he wrote to her " Legends and Lyrics," published shortly after her death. She had said at home : " If I send him, in my own name, verses that he does not honestly like, either it will be very painful to him to return them, or he will print them for papa's sake, and not for their own. So I have made up my mind to take my chance fairly with the unknown volunteers." That was in the spring of 1853. Dickens liked the verses for their own sake, and all contributions that " Miss Mary Berwick " cared to send were gladly welcomed. In that same year, 1853, she was invited to contribute to the Christmas number, and she responded with " The Angel's Story." In the following year, to *The Seven Poor Travellers* she contributed the third traveller's story.

" Happening," says Dickens, " to be going to dine that day with an old and dear friend, distinguished in literature as Barry Cornwall, I took with me an early proof of that number, and remarked, as I laid it on the drawing-room table, that it contained a very pretty poem written by a certain Miss Berwick. Next day brought me the disclosure that I had so spoken of the poem to the mother of its writer, in its writer's presence ; that I had no such correspondent in existence as Miss Berwick ; and that the name had been assumed by Barry Cornwall's eldest daughter, Miss Adelaide Anne Procter." The remainder of the introduction is a very beautiful tribute to the memory of a pure and beautiful life. Until her death in 1864, Adelaide Procter continued to contribute to *Household Words* and *All the Year Round.*

CHAPTER XXVIII

FRANK STONE AND HIS SON

" My father must have been a remarkable man," said Mr. Marcus Stone to me, as, seated in his studio one afternoon, he was recalling for my benefit the days when he was intimate with Dickens, and with nearly everybody who was anybody in the literary and artistic London of the mid-Victorian period. " Yes," he said, in a tone of affectionate remembrance, " a remarkable man. I often think of it. He was a Manchester man but moderately educated, a moderate artist who never made very much head-way in his profession; yet, within two years of his coming to London an utterly obscure man, he was the intimate of many of the most famous men of the time."

Frank Stone is remembered to-day chiefly as the father of Marcus Stone, but he must have been a man of marked indi-viduality and great personal charm. He had not the knack of making money, but he had something much better, the knack of making friends. And one of the most valued friends he ever made was Charles Dickens. There was a great intimacy and genuine affection between him and the novelist, which lasted from the beginning to the end without interruption. It is prob-able that it was the Shakespeare Society that brought them together : [1] anyhow they met when *Pickwick* was still running its course. And, say the Editors of Dickens's *Letters*, Stone was especially included in the category of Dickens's most affectionate and intimate friends. They spent many a holiday together at Broadstairs and elsewhere, and it was at Bonchurch in 1849 that the artist painted a portrait of Sydney Smith Haldimand Dickens, then two and a half years old, in which, says Forster, he very happily caught " a strange little weird, yet most attractive look in his large wondering eyes."

For some time Stone occupied a portion of Tavistock House, Tavistock Square, as a studio, his family living in the country. In 1851 he brought his family to London, and they went to live in a smaller house in the same square, Dickens taking Tavistock

---

[1] Stone was hon. sec., and the minute-book is still in the possession of one of his sons.

House. Henceforth, until Dickens moved to Gadshill, the two families were near and intimate neighbours.

Stone was one of the leading spirits in the amateur theatricals— " one of the leading heavy men," as his son puts it. He played Justice Clement in " Every Man in his Humour " at the Royalty Theatre in 1845. Two years later he took part in the perform- ances in aid of Leigh Hunt and John Poole. He was again prominent in the performances of 1848, but this time he played George Downright in Ben Jonson's comedy. He played the same part at Knebworth in November 1850, and in the Guild of Literature and Art performances in the following year he appeared as the Duke of Middlesex in " Not so Bad as we Seem," whilst in " Mr. Nightingale's Diary " he was Mr. Nightingale. During the rehearsals Dickens wrote to Lytton :

" . . . The Duke comes out the best man in the play. I am happy to report to you that Stone does the honourable manly side of that pride inexpressibly better than I could have supposed possible in him. The scene where he makes reparation to the slandered woman is *certain* to be an effect. He is *not* a jest upon the order of Dukes, but a great tribute to them. . . . I see, in the Duke, the most estimable charac- ter in the piece. . . . The first time that scene with Hardman was seriously done, it made an effect on the company that quite surprised and delighted me; and whenever and wher- ever it is done . . . the result will be the same."

Stone had the honour of doing three illustrations for *The Haunted Man*—" Milly and the Old Man "; " Milly and the Student "; and " Milly and the Children." When he submitted his rough sketch for the first of these illustrations, Dickens wrote to him :

" We are unanimous.
" The drawing of Milly on the chair is CHARMING. I cannot tell you how much the little composition and expres- sion please me. Do that, by all means. . . .
" I am delighted to hear that you have your eye on her in the students' room. You will really, pictorially, make the little woman whom I love."

These were the only illustrations that Stone did for his friend's books, but he designed the frontispiece for the first Cheap Edition of *Martin Chuzzlewit* in 1849, which shows Mark Tapley on his sick-bed. He also did one or two pictures of characters, in addition. He was commissioned by the novelist to paint a

CHARLES DICKENS IN HIS STUDY AT TAVISTOCK HOUSE

From a painting by E. M. Ward, R.A.

picture of 'Tilda Price, which picture in 1870 fetched £42.   He also did pictures of Kate Nickleby and Madeline Bray which were engraved by Finder, and published by Chapman and Hall in 1848.

Frank Stone died suddenly in 1859, to the very deep grief of Dickens.   He did not leave any very substantial worldly inheritance, but, said his son, Marcus, to the Boz Club a few years ago, " he gave me the splendid inheritance of the friendship of Charles Dickens—a more precious inheritance than the wealth of a millionaire."   Marcus Stone was, I am very certain, Dickens's favourite among all the young men that worshipped him in the last decade or so of his life.   The relations between them were, indeed, almost those of father and son.   Curiously enough, though his father had been intimate with Dickens before Marcus was born, the son was ten years old before he met the great man. In his address to the Boz Club in 1910 he recalled the first meeting :

> " I had only just come to live in London with my father, and had the blessed privilege of rummaging in his studio. . . . There was a window in the studio, and near that stood a screen.   One day I went behind the screen and looked into the garden, and there I saw a gentleman and two ladies. They were looking up at the house.   Then I was fetched, and I remember going downstairs and being presented to the ladies and gentleman, and being ashamed of a very black pair of hands which were grasped by that blessed, noble, generous hand of Charles Dickens.   That was the first time I saw him, when I was ten years old.   And from that time he was constantly in my field of vision."

Marcus Stone was a very precocious boy ; a bright, intelligent child ; and it was not long after this that he did his first Dickens illustration.   He drew a picture of Poor Jo, and while he was working on it Dickens saw it.   " That's very good," said the novelist.   " You must give that to me when it is done."   So he did ; and nearly eighteen months later he received from Dickens a copy of *A Child's History of England*, with this letter :

> " MY DEAR MARCUS,
>   " You made an excellent sketch from a book of mine which I have received (and have preserved) with great pleasure.   Will you accept from me in remembrance of it THIS little book ?   I believe it to be true, though it may be sometimes not as genteel as history has a habit of being."

That book is to-day the artist's most cherished possession.

From the beginning the boy was a warm favourite with the novelist, whose house was a second home to him. After his father's death Dickens's interest in him deepened, and Gadshill was Liberty Hall to him. He was, as he put it to me, a " sort of extra son." As he was growing up he stood, in a sense, between the novelist's eldest and younger sons. Charles was only three years older than he, but he married and left home very young; the other boys were younger than he. We know what a difference a couple of years will make between boys in their teens; but apart from that, Marcus Stone was older than his years. He was exhibiting in the Royal Academy when he was but seventeen; he was only nineteen when his father died, and he was called upon to battle with the world. Thus, though so young, he was a real companion to the novelist. He had the freedom of Gadshill : that is to say, he was told that he could come whenever he liked and stay just as long as he liked. He did not avail himself of the privilege so often as he would have wished, because he so early achieved success in his profession and was a very busy man, " but," he told me, " I spent, I should think, quite a month in his house every year, and I was always there at Christmas for about a fortnight. I saw him as nobody else saw him. I was, so to speak, nobody in the house. I came and went as I listed, and I saw the man himself. However intimate one may be with a guest, you know, there is inevitably some degree of self-consciousness. I was a nobody—that is, just a young man that did not count as a guest at all. I was one of the family. Thus I saw Charles Dickens as nobody else saw him. I saw him living his own, everyday, actual life, and as an observant boy, and as a mature man, I saw him. I used to take any work I could carry with me, and do it at Gadshill. I just ' walked in,' and was as much at home as one of his sons."

" What sort of man was Dickens ? " I asked the famous artist, and I am not likely to forget the fervent earnestness with which he answered me.

" He was quite the best man I ever knew. Yes "—and he gripped my arm and looked me earnestly in the eyes— " the best man I ever knew. He was such a good man that you put his greatness in the second place when you knew him. He occupied himself daily in some sort of work for somebody. The amount of work that he did, the amount of money that he took out of his pocket, was perfectly amazing. But the personal trouble that he took for people who had no sort of claim upon him ! He was the most compassionate creature that ever lived—in fact, almost to

a ludicrous extent at times. He forgave when he ought not
to have done so, and gave very often where he ought to
have withheld."

I realised then the truth of what he said to the Boz Club:
" The very mention of the name of Charles Dickens is always
followed in my case with a certain thrill of inward emotion."
If ever one man loved another, Marcus Stone loved Charles
Dickens. He asserts—and none need doubt that it is true—that
Dickens was the chief formative influence in his life.

In the " Gad's Hill Gazette," that entertaining little journal
printed and published by the novelist's boys, Marcus Stone's
name occurs frequently. There are several references to his skill
at billiards—which remained with him until recent years, when
his sight failed. " Only one game worthy of mention has been
played during the last week," we read in one place. " This was
a game between Messrs. M. Stone and C. Dickens, junr. (chiefly
remarkable for the large scores made by the former). Mr. Stone
began the game by giving his opponent a miss, which made a
difficult score for the latter: he however scored 2. The game
proceeded slowly till the marker called 24 (Mr. Stone) to 5. Then
the Champion made a break of 51, followed by another of 24,
winning the game by 91." In the number dated August 19,
1862, we read : " There has been little done at Gad's Hill during
the past week, as the weather has been so unpropitious. In
consequence of this, Billiards has been resorted to, in which
Mr. M. Stone has beaten all opponents." Not always, however,
did he triumph, as is shown by the following : " On Saturday
evening last two very scientific games were played between
M. Stone, Esqre. (the last week's champion), and C. Fechter, Esqre.
The former was the favourite, but to the astonishment of all, he
was beaten easily both games."

Another interesting fact recorded in the " Gazette " is that
" Mr. M. Stone has just completed a portrait in water-colours of
Mrs. Charles Collins.[1] In the painting of this little work of Art
there is a pose shown which is very creditable to the author, and
the portrait also is very like." And in a Supplement it is recorded : " In an article at the bottom of Page 2, we omitted
to mention that Mr. M. Stone has also painted a portrait (in
water-colours) of Gad's Hill House."

It is not necessary to do more here than recall the fact that
Marcus Stone illustrated *Our Mutual Friend*. With the question,
" Why did Dickens drop Phiz?" I have already dealt in my
chapter on Phiz, but I may observe that Mr. Stone confirmed me

---

[1] Kate Dickens ; now Mrs. Perugini.

in the conclusions at which I arrived there.   There was no quarrel of any kind whatsoever, but Dickens felt that Phiz's work was no longer suitable.   It had not advanced in character or quality since *Pickwick*, and Dickens decided to drop him after *Little Dorrit*.   He had no successor in view, but between *Little Dorrit* and *Our Mutual Friend* Frank Stone died, and Dickens saw the opportunity of helping his friend's brilliant son, who was also his friend.   " But," said Mr. Stone to me, " I want to be very clear on this point : regard for me or interest in me had absolutely nothing to do with the dropping of Browne.   I had not entered his head when he decided to do that.   The choice of me may have been actuated to some extent by personal feelings; on that I cannot speak; but I *know* that he had never even thought of me when he decided to drop Phiz."

It should also be recalled here that we are indebted to Marcus Stone for Mr. Venus.   Dickens had written nearly three numbers of *Our Mutual Friend*, when, says Forster, " upon a necessary rearrangement of his chapters, he had to hit upon a new subject for one of them.   ' While I was considering what it should be, Marcus, who has done an excellent cover, came to tell me of an extraordinary trade he had found out through one of his painting requirements.   I immediately went with him to St. Giles's, to look at the place, and found what you will see.'   It was the establishment of Mr. Venus, preserver of animals and birds, and articulator of human bones."

It is worthy of recording that the original drawings for *Our Mutual Friend* were subsequently sold for £66.   Marcus Stone also did the following illustrations for other of Dickens's works : the frontispiece to the first Cheap Edition of *Little Dorrit*, 1861; eight illustrations for the Library Edition of *Great Expectations*, 1862; four for the Library Edition of *Pictures from Italy*, 1862; four for the Library Edition of *American Notes*, 1862; eight for the Library Edition of *A Child's History of England*, 1862; and the frontispiece for the first Cheap Edition of *A Tale of Two Cities*, 1864.

Marcus Stone naturally had a part in the children's theatricals. He also assisted in the " grown-up performances " at Tavistock House.   In " The Lighthouse " he played the wind—off !; in " The Frozen Deep " he appeared on the stage, but had only one word to say.   His recollection of those happy days has not dimmed with the passage of years.   He often recalls with enjoyment how Thackeray rolled off his chair with laughing at the funniosities of one of the juvenile comedians.   He also recalls hearing Lord Campbell remark that he would rather have written *Pickwick* than be Lord Chief Justice of England.

In conclusion, it will not be out of place if I record one story that he told me. " I heard of Thackeray's death," he said, " from Charles Dickens. The news had not appeared in the morning papers. It was Christmas Eve, and I was going to Gadshill for the Christmas. I met another guest in the train—I forget who it was. Dickens was at the station to meet us. As soon as I saw him, I knew that something had cut him deeply. I went up to him, and said, ' What is it? ' and he said, in a breaking voice, ' Thackeray is dead.' I said, ' I know you must feel it very deeply, because you and he were not on friendly terms.' He put his hand on my arm, and said, so earnestly, ' Thank God, my boy, we were ! ' And then he told me about the reconciliation at the Athenæum Club. I know what a consolation it was to him to think of that meeting and reconciliation."

CHAPTER XXIX

SOME LIMBS OF THE LAW

SURPRISING indeed would it have been if Dickens had not numbered among his friends some distinguished limbs of the law. None of our novelists knew lawyers and lawyers' clerks and lawyers' chambers better than he did. He laughed at them all, and he laughed still more loudly and very much more scornfully at the law, but lawyers as a class have a keener sense of humour than most other classes, and from the beginning Dickens was a great favourite with them. Curiously enough, all his legal friendships were formed early in his career.

Sir Jonathan Pollock, who eventually became Chief Baron of the Exchequer, was one of these early friends. In his capacity as judge he on several occasions won the novelist's admiration. Pollock was much older than Dickens, but there was a strong mutual regard. When Dickens died, the Baron described him as " one of the most distinguished and honoured men England has ever produced; in whose loss every man among us feels that he has lost a friend and instructor." With the son, Sir Frederick Pollock, there was also a pleasant friendship. They met first at Broadstairs in 1850, and Pollock's first impression of Dickens's delightful manner was confirmed by subsequent friendly intercourse. It is rather curious that Dickens should not have met the son much earlier, but once they knew each other they became on splendid terms and saw much of each other.

A great judge to whom *Dombey and Son* made a special appeal was Lord Denman—Lord Chief Justice of England. " Isn't Bunsby good? " he exclaimed across the table at Talfourd's house to a fellow-guest. But he had been attracted to Boz in the very beginning, and we have Miss Edgeworth's word for it that he studied *Pickwick* on the bench while the jury was deliberating. There was much friendly intercourse with this excellent man for whom Dickens had a peculiar regard, as is shown by the following, written in 1844 :

" Denman delights me. I am glad to think I have always liked him so well. I am sure that whenever he makes a mistake it *is* a mistake; and that no man lives who has a grander and nobler scorn for every mean and dastard action. I would to Heaven it were decorous to pay him some public tribute of respect."

There was an equally hearty friendship with Lord Campbell, the man who declared that he would rather have written *Pickwick* than be Chief Justice of England and a peer of Parliament. The occasion was a supper party that followed a performance of " The Lighthouse " in 1855, and Forster in recording it adds a note which is further proof of the great judge's liking for Dickens's books. " Sitting at Nisi Prius not long before," he says, " the Chief Justice, with the same out-of-the-way liking for letters, had committed what was called at the time a breach of judicial decorum. ' The name,' he said, ' of the illustrious Charles Dickens has been called on the jury, but he has not answered. If his great Chancery suit had been still going on I certainly would have excused him, but as that is over he might have done us the honour of attending here that he might have seen how we went on at Common Law.' "

With Lord Brougham there was only a friendly acquaintance-ship. Dickens, of course, sympathised with Brougham's political opinions, and he found the lawyer a useful ally in the fight on the copyright question, but Brougham could never have made a very strong personal appeal to him. We read of Dickens receiving a letter from him in America in 1842 (probably on that copyright question), and we read of a meeting in Paris four years later, but there is not the least evidence of any genial intercourse. With Lord Cockburn, the friend of Jeffrey, there was a much greater friendship.

Sergeant Ballantine was almost a lifelong friend. They met on January 10, 1838, and Dickens died on the very day that he would have been elected a member of the Union Club on Ballan-tine's recommendation, so that their friendship extended over a period of thirty-two years. Ballantine was a great admirer of Dickens himself and of his books :

" I was very much attached to Charles Dickens ; there was a brightness and geniality about him that greatly fasci-nated his companions. His laugh was so cheery, and he seemed to enter into the feelings of those around him. He told a story well and never prosily ; he was a capital listener, and in conversation was not in the slightest degree dicta-torial. . . . No man possessed more sincere friends or deserved them better."

He records one amusing anecdote. Upon one occasion he

started from Boulogne with Dickens and Dr. Elliotson. " Neither of my comrades was a good sailor, and they knew it themselves. The illustrious author armed himself with a box of homœopathic globules; and the doctor, whose figure was rotund, having a theory that by tightening the stomach the internal movements which caused the sickness might be prevented, waddled down to the boat with his body almost divided by a strap. The weather was stormy, and neither remedy proved of any avail."

It is interesting to note, by the way, that Ballantine knew the originals of two of Dickens's characters very well. Of Mr. Laing, the original of Mr. Fang, the bullying magistrate in *Oliver Twist*, he says : " Notwithstanding an unfortunate temper, he was a thoroughly honourable gentleman, a good lawyer, and an accomplished scholar, very precise in his dress, but very sour looking." And of Sir Peter Laurie, the original of Alderman Cute in *The Chimes*, he says he was " a shrewd, far-seeing Scotchman, quaint and conceited, but with plenty of sound good sense, and an honourable character."

CHAPTER XXX

GORE HOUSE FRIENDS

" I HAD no means of knowing whether what the world said of this most beautiful woman was true or false, but I am sure *God* intended her to be good, and there was a deep-seated good intent in whatever she did that came under my observation. She never lost an opportunity of doing a gracious act, or saying a gracious word."

This is what Mrs. S. C. Hall wrote of Lady Blessington. It is the tribute of a good woman to the memory of a much-maligned woman, and its justice need not be doubted. Indeed, it may be said of her that she deserved to be good. She had many true friends among the greatest men of her time, and they all paid their tributes to her memory when, her glory faded, she died in poverty in Paris.

And as to D'Orsay, he certainly was " a rare sort of bird for our reticent land," but he was a remarkable man not at all deserving of unqualified condemnation. I suppose in our " moral " moods we condemn Micawber, but the " moral " mood is not the charitable mood, and both the Countess of Blessington and the Comte D'Orsay have very strong claims upon our charity when we are attempting to estimate their characters. Landor, Thackeray, Forster, Dickens, Carlyle, and many more men of the greatest ability and the highest character entertained for this pair feelings of the most earnest friendship. Miss Hogarth has told us that the Countess was " a lady for whom Chas. Dickens had a most affectionate friendship and respect for the sake of her own admirable qualities, and in remembrance of her delightful association with Gore House, where he was a frequent visitor. For Lady Blessington he had a high admiration and great regard, and she was one of his earliest appreciators; and Comte D'Orsay was also a much-loved friend."

One story that is told of D'Orsay is as follows : A major was telling his tale of woe. He was hampered with debt, and had come to London to sell his commission in order to pay his creditors. " Lend me £10," said D'Orsay. The money was lent, and the next day the Count handed to the major £750, with " It is yours. I gambled with your £10 last night, and won this. It is yours most justly, for if I had lost I should never have paid you the £10." How could Dickens be on terms of affection with such a man ? It is the obvious question, and the answer is equally obvious. There was—must have been—another side to D'Orsay's character. He lived grandly on nothing a year, but—let us quote H. F. Chorley :

> " There was every conceivable and inconceivable story current in London of the extravagance of the ' King of the French '; but it was never told that he had been cradled, as it were, in ignorance of the value of money, such as those will not believe possible who have been less indulged and less spoiled, and who have been less pleasing to indulge and to spoil than he was. . . . He was spoiled during most of his life by every one whom he came near. . . . It was a curious sight to see, as I often did in the early days of our acquaintance, how he seemed to take it for granted that everybody had any conceivable quantity of five-pound notes. . . . Never was Sybarite so little selfish as he. He loved extravagance—waste even. He would give half a sovereign to a box-keeper at a theatre as a matter of course and not ostentation; but he could also bestow time, pains, money, with a magnificence and a delicacy such as showed what a real princely stuff there was in the nature of the man whom Fortune had so cruelly spoiled. He had ' the memory of the heart ' in perfection."

All the men who knew him bear the same testimony. Such a man as Macready fell under the spell : " No one who knew him and had affections could help loving him. . . . He was the most brilliant, graceful, endearing man I ever saw—humorous, witty, and clear-headed." Indeed, the truth is that, nurtured in a more self-reliant school, D'Orsay might have been a great and good man. And Dickens, with that perception which never failed him, saw the solid qualities beneath the somewhat fantastic exterior, and loved the man for them.

In an article in *Household Words* in 1853 D'Orsay was written of as one " whose name is publicly synonymous with elegant and graceful accomplishment, and who, by those who knew him well, is affectionately remembered and regretted, as a man whose great abilities might have raised him to any distinction, and whose gentle heart even a world of fashion left unspoiled." This was not written by Dickens himself, but it passed his editorial scrutiny, and undoubtedly exactly expressed his feelings.

It has been stated, I know not on what authority, that Dickens met Lady Blessington—and presumably D'Orsay also—in 1841. I am inclined to doubt the accuracy of this. Forster had been a friend at Gore House since 1836, from which year his intimacy with Dickens also dated. It would seem extraordinary that he should so long have delayed introducing his brilliant young friend of whom he was so proud to the famous salon. Anyhow, whenever the introduction took place, certain it is that Dickens became a very close friend and one of the most frequent and welcome visitors at Gore House, which was then at the summit of its glory. The wonders of this salon have been described by many writers. Lady Blessington held her court in the library, " a magnificent apartment, lined with books, the edges of the shelves enamelled in ivory, and mirrors being dotted about. The fireplace was of beautifully carved marble, and in the centre were columns supporting an arch. Curtains of silk damask and a delicate apple-green shade; the same material, set in white and gold, being seen in the chairs and lounges."

Here they met frequently, all the brilliant men of a brilliant period—Landor and Disraeli, Dickens and Carlyle, Forster and Maclise, Bulwer and Ainsworth, Macready and Marryat, and Barry Cornwall—men differing in temperament as one star differeth from another in glory; all united in paying homage to this remarkable woman. Dickens fell under the spell at once, and Forster tells us what warmth of regard he had for her, and how uninterruptedly joyous and pleasurable were his associations with her.

In 1844 she was able to be of real service to him. On March 10 he wrote to her :

> " I have made up my mind to ' see the world,' and mean to decamp, bag and baggage, next midsummer for a twelve-month. I purpose establishing my family in some convenient place, from whence I can make personal ravages on the neighbouring country, and, somehow or other, have got it into my head that Nice would be a favourable spot for headquarters. You are so well acquainted with these matters that I am anxious to have the benefit of your kind advice. I do not doubt that you can tell me whether this same Nice be a healthy place the year through, whether it be reasonably cheap, pleasant to look at and to live in, and the like. If you will tell me when you have ten minutes to spare for such a client, I shall be delighted to come to you,

and guide myself by your opinion. I will not ask you to forgive me for troubling you, because I am sure beforehand that you will do so. . . ."

She gave him the advice asked for, and D'Orsay supplemented it : " Pray say to Count D'Orsay everything that is cordial and loving from me. The travelling purse he gave me has been of immense service. It has been constantly opened. All Italy seems to yearn to put its hand into it." Every one of the few letters of Dickens to Lady Blessington that have been preserved bears testimony to the regard in which he held her. For instance, writing from Milan, in November 1844, he says : " Appearances are against me. Don't believe them. I have written you in intention fifty letters, and I can claim no credit for one of them (though they were the best letters you ever received) for they all originated in my desire to live in your memory and regard." And in 1847 he wrote from Paris : " I feel very wicked in beginning this note, and deeply remorseful for not having begun and ended it long ago. But *you* know how difficult it is to write letters in the midst of a writing life; and as you know, too (I hope), how earnestly and affectionately I always think of you, wherever I am, I take heart, on a little consideration, and feel comparatively good again." In December 1844, when he made a hurried visit to England in order to read *The Chimes* at Forster's house, he found time to visit Lady Blessington, and on the day of his departure he wrote to her :

" Business for other people (and by no means of a pleasant kind) has held me prisoner during two whole days, and will so detain me to-day, in the very agony of my departure for Italy, that I shall not even be able to reach Gore House once more, on which I had set my heart. I cannot bear the thought of going away without some sort of reference to the happy day you gave me on Monday, and the pleasure and delight I had in your earnest greeting. I shall never forget it, believe me. . . . It will be an unspeakable satisfaction (though I am not maliciously disposed) to know under your own hand at Genoa that my little book made you cry. I hope to prove a better correspondent on my return to those shores. But, better or worse, or anyhow, I am ever, my dear Lady Blessington, in no common degree, and not with an everyday regard, yours."

When the " Daily News " was started in 1846, Lady Blessington was asked if she would supply the paper with " any sort of intelligence she might like to communicate of the sayings, doings, or movements in the fashionable world." She agreed, but asked £800 a year. This was considered too high a figure, and she was offered £400 a year, or £250 for six months, another agreement to be made at the expiration of that period if satisfactory to both parties. This latter offer was accepted, but at the end of the six months the Editor (John Forster) declined to renew the agreement.

It should be added here that Dickens was a contributor to "The Keepsake," which was edited by Lady Blessington. His contribution in 1843 was the verses entitled *A Word in Season*.

The novelist's regard for D'Orsay is shown by many references in his letters, but the best evidence is the fact that he named one of his sons after him. The late Mr. Alfred Tennyson Dickens was not named, as one might naturally conclude, exclusively after the poet laureate, "Alfred" being in compliment to the Count. It is interesting to note, also, that Dickens was influenced in some degree by D'Orsay's judgment to publish *Pictures from Italy*. These *Pictures* were practically a reprint of the letters he had addressed to Forster. Referring to them in a subsequent letter to that friend, he says : "Seriously, it is a great pleasure to me to find that you are really pleased with these shadows in the water, and think them worth looking at. . . . D'Orsay, from whom I had a charming letter three days since, seems to think as you do of what he has read in those shown to him, and says they remind him vividly of the real aspect of these scenes."

The glory of Gore House was but transient, and its sun set for ever in 1849. It had begun to sink behind the clouds two years before. Owing to the famine and distress in Ireland, Lady Blessington's income fell off, and her income from books diminished too. Eventually the house had to be shut against creditors and the sheriff's officer. At last, however, an entry was obtained. She was offered assistance by many friends, but she refused, and placed Gore House in the hands of an auctioneer, she and D'Orsay leaving England never to return. Gore House then became a scene of desolation.

Lady Blessington died but a few weeks after her arrival in Paris. D'Orsay lived on until 1852, and he dined with Dickens in the French capital in 1850.

The memories of these two friends, and of the happy days at Gore House, never left Dickens, and we find a reference to them in a letter he wrote to Landor in 1856, from Boulogne :

"There in Paris . . . I found Marguerite Power and little Nelly, living with their mother and a pretty sister in a very small and neat apartment, and working (as Marguerite told me) hard for a living.   All that I saw of them filled me with respect, and revived the tenderest remembrances of Gore House.   They are coming to pass two or three weeks here for a country rest, next month.   We had many long talks concerning Gore House and all its bright associations."

CHAPTER XXXI

THE HON. MRS. NORTON

In these days Dickens was acquainted with another brilliant woman, as unhappy as Lady Blessington—the Hon. Mrs. Norton. Indeed, they were very friendly. Speaking of a dinner at Devonshire Terrace in April 1849, Forster says that among the guests was " Lady Graham, wife of Sir James Graham, and sister of Tom Sheridan's wife, than whom not even the wit and beauty of her nieces, Mrs. Norton and Lady Dufferin, did greater justice to the brilliant family of the Sheridans; so many of whose members, and these three above all, Dickens prized among his friends." But there is positively no record of the friendship. This is Forster's only reference to it, and Mrs. Norton's biographer's only mention of Dickens is in connection with the performances at the St. James's Theatre in 1845. " We find," she says, " the Duff Gordons and Henry Reeve and Mrs. Norton all in a box together with Lord Melbourne at St. James's Theatre in November of that same year to see the first representation of ' Every Man in His Humour,' acted by some of the writers for ' Punch ' and other literary men of the time, notably Charles Dickens. We are told that Lord Melbourne found the play very poor . . , till suddenly between the acts he exclaimed in a stentorian voice, heard across the pit, ' I knew this play would be dull, but that it would be so damnably dull as this I didn't suppose.' " Miss Perkins makes one mistake. The first performance of the comedy had taken place two months previously at the Royalty Theatre.

Mention of Lord Melbourne recalls an interesting fact. All the world knows of the famous trial in which that peer was acquitted of misconduct with Mrs. Norton. Mr. Percy Fitzgerald makes the suggestion that Dickens obtained from it the idea for the *Pickwick* trial. He states, indeed, that the novelist parodied many of the incidents, and that Buzfuz's cross-examination was a reproduction. Referring to the great play made by Buzfuz with the two letters that had passed between Pickwick and Mrs. Bardell, he says :

" They were intended to satirise the trivial scraps brought forward in Mrs. Norton's matrimonial case—Norton *v.* Lord

Melbourne. My late friend, Charles Dickens the younger,
. . . in his notes on *Pickwick*, puts aside this theory as a
mere unfounded theory; but it will be seen there cannot
be a doubt in the matter. Sir W. Follett laid just as much
stress on these scraps as Sergeant Buzfuz did on his : he
even used the phrase ' it seems there may be latent love
like latent heat in these productions.' We have also ' Yours,
Melbourne,' like ' Yours, Pickwick.' . . . ' There is another
of these notes,' went on Sir William. ' " How are you ? "
Again there is no beginning, you see.' ' The next has no
date whatever, which is in itself suspicious,' Buzfuz would
have added. Another ran : ' I will call about half-past
four. Yours.' ' *These* are the only notes that have been
found,' added the counsel, with due gravity. ' *They seem*
to import much more than mere *words convey*.' After this
can there be any doubt ? "

Well, speaking for myself, I should think not. It seems to me
that Mr. Fitzgerald has made out an unanswerable case. Listen
to this for a moment :

" Two letters have passed between these parties. Letters
that must be viewed with a cautious and suspicious eye;
letters that were evidently intended at the time, by Lord
Melbourne, to mislead and delude any third parties into
whose hands they might fall. Let me read the first : ' How
are you ? ' There is no beginning, you see. ' How are
you ! ! ' Gentlemen, is the happiness of a sensitive and
confiding husband to be trifled away by such shallow artifices
as these ? The next has no date whatever, which is in itself
suspicious : ' I will call about half-past four. Yours.' It
seems that there may be latent love like latent heat;
these productions may be mere covers for hidden fire, mere
substitutes for some endearing word or promise, agreeably
to a preconcerted system of correspondence artfully contrived by Lord Melbourne, and which I confess I am not in
a position to explain."

Now the trial took place in June 1836. *Pickwick* had started
a couple of months before. All the world was talking about the
Norton *v.* Melbourne trial. Mrs. Norton's biographer says :
" There had been great talk beforehand of compromising letters
by Lord Melbourne, which were to be produced in evidence
against him, but on the day of the trial all that appeared were
several little notes of the utmost brevity and unimportance."

All the world had anticipated this correspondence which was going to be so incriminating; the trial was the sensation of the day; yet those trifling notes were the tiny mouse that the mountain of gossip and scandal brought forth of its labour!

Think of Boz, with his experience of the law, with his experience as a journalist; think of him full of enthusiasm over his first commission; think of him with a roving commission to take the Pickwickians where he liked and to do what he liked with them; think of him with all his keenness, with all his powers of observation, with his sense of the ridiculous, on the alert for material. Then think of this trial, *the* sensation of the hour just when his mind was fullest of *Pickwick*. And then read Sergeant Buzfuz's address in conjunction with Sir William Follett's address. Was ever anything clearer?

If for this reason only, Mrs. Norton is worthy of the place she has been given here. But she was unquestionably on friendly terms with Dickens, who had a great admiration for her gifts. And, it should be added, she contributed once or twice to *Household Words*.

CHAPTER XXXII

MISS COUTTS

THERE is another lady whose place is here, one of the most honoured friends that Dickens ever had, one at whose hands he received innumerable kindnesses, one of the noblest women that this country has ever produced. I mean Miss Coutts, known to a later generation as the Baroness Burdett-Coutts, the sweet and gracious woman whose lifelong devotion to the doing of good deeds won for her a final resting-place in the grand old Abbey, close to the friend to whom she was so kind, and who rendered her, through so many years, such devoted help in her efforts to make the world a happier place.

Forster's earliest mention of her relates to the year 1840, when, after naming a number of specially liked friends, he says : " Other friends became familiar in later years ; but, disinclined as he was to the dinner invitations that reached him from every quarter, all such meetings with those I have named, and in an especial manner the marked attentions shown him by Miss Coutts, which began with the very beginning of his career, were invariably welcome." So that the novelist had known Miss Coutts from his earliest days of fame. He had known her father, too. Sir Francis Burdett had been attracted by the onslaughts on the Poor-law in *Oliver Twist,* and in a speech at Birmingham referred to the young writer, and spoke approvingly of his advocacy of the cause of the poor.

Miss Coutts seems to have taken a particular liking to the novelist's eldest boy. For many years she sent him on his birth-day, which happened to be Twelfth Day, a Twelfth Cake, and there is an amusing reference to one of these confections in a letter written to Forster from Genoa in 1845 : " Miss Coutts has sent Charley, with the best of letters to me, a Twelfth Cake weighing ninety pounds, magnificently decorated ; and only think of the characters, Fairburn's Twelfth Night characters, being detained at the custom-house for Jesuitical surveillance ! But these fellows are—— Well, never mind ! " In 1846 she offered to take charge of Charley's education. The offer was accepted,

and the boy went to King's College. Forster says : " Munificent
as the kindness was, however, it was yet only the smallest
part of the obligation which Dickens felt that he owed this
lady."

In 1856 she did the novelist a kind service in respect of another
son, obtaining for Walter a cadetship in the 26th Native (India)
Infantry Regiment. It is not surprising that Dickens held this
kind friend in the highest regard, and entertained the deepest
respect for her. "She is a good creature, I protest to God," he
wrote on one occasion, " and I have a most profound affection
and respect for her." And he bore public testimony to the fact
in 1844, when he dedicated *Martin Chuzzlewit* to her " with the
true and earnest regard of the author." More than that, he
reciprocated her kindness all that lay in his power by rendering,
through many years, " unstinted service of time and labour, with
sacrifices unselfish as her own," to all her schemes for the benefit
of the neglected and uncared-for classes of the population.

His knowledge of the poor and their needs, his earnest desire
to see those needs supplied, and his sane, common-sense, business-
like character made him invaluable to her in her work, and until
the end of his life he was her most trusted confidant and adviser
in almost every one of her schemes. Indeed, it was he who
first showed her the way. It was he who introduced her to the
slums of London, taking her into the wretchedest parts of the
metropolis, and it was as a direct result of those visits to the East
End that she blotted out one of the worst plague spots of all—
Nova Scotia Gardens, Bethnal Green—and erected the Columbia
Square Buildings, the first model dwellings in London. It was
he, too, who secured her interest for the Ragged Schools. " I
sent Miss Coutts a sledge-hammer account of the ragged-schools,"
he wrote to Forster in September 1843, " and as I saw her name
for two hundred pounds in the Clergy Education subscription
list, took pains to show her that religious mysteries and difficult
creeds wouldn't do for such pupils. I told her, too, that it was
of immense importance they should be *washed*. She writes back
to know what the rent of some large airy premises would be, and
what the expense of erecting a regular bathing or purifying place ;
touching which points I am in correspondence with the authorities.
I have no doubt she will do whatever I ask her in the matter."

Again, in the establishment of the home for fallen women at
Shepherd's Bush, Dickens was Miss Coutts's right hand. He took
up the work with enthusiasm, and wrote an appeal to those
women which was printed as a pamphlet and given away in the
streets. (Has *no* collector ever yet lighted on a copy of that
appeal ?) Indeed, the whole of the work was carried through by

him, acting for Miss Coutts, and Forster declares that it largely and regularly occupied his time for several years.

Of social intercourse we do not read, but we do know that Dickens was a frequent guest at Miss Coutts's house, and we know that one of the things that delighted Hans Andersen most of all during his second visit to England was his introduction by Dickens to that house and its noble owner.

CHAPTER XXXIII

THE GOOD EARL

With that other great philanthropist of the time, the " good Earl of Shaftesbury," Dickens was also well acquainted, though perhaps he can scarcely be described as a member of the Dickens circle. That the greatest and most single-hearted social reformer of his or any other generation and the author of *Oliver Twist* and *Nicholas Nickleby* should come into personal contact was inevitable. But it was equally inevitable that there should be no comradeship, if I may so put it. The good Earl, we are told, had no sense of humour, never made a joke or saw the point of one. It is a difficult thing to believe of a man who so loved his fellows, but all the same it is not difficult to conceive of him as capable of reading *Pickwick* without a chuckle. Besides, his whole life was guided by a decidedly narrow set of Christian ethics, and Dickens's Christianity was of the broadest possible kind—so broad, indeed, that Lord Shaftesbury seems not to have been quite convinced of its reality. For in 1871 we find him noting in his Diary : " Forster has sent me his *Life of Dickens*. The man was a phenomenon, an exception, a special production. Nothing like him ever preceded. Nature isn't so tautological as to make another to follow him. He was set, I doubt not, to rouse attention to many evils, and many woes ; and though not putting it on Christian principles (which would have rendered it unacceptable), he may have been in God's singular and unfathomable goodness as much a servant of the Most High as the pagan Naaman ' by whom the Lord have given deliverance to Syria ' ! God gave him, as I wrote to Forster, a general retainer against all suffering and oppression."

Now that, it seems to me, reveals a mind with which Dickens could never have been absolutely at home. But he honoured the Earl as truly as any one did. The latter's biographer, Mr. Edwin Hodder, records : " Charles Dickens was always a warm admirer, and on several occasions aided materially some of his great labours for the poor." Mr. Hodder adds that in 1838 the novelist became an ally on the factory question, and he quotes a letter written to Mr. Edward Fitzgerald on December 29 in that year, in the course of which Dickens said :

" I went some weeks ago to Manchester, and saw the *worst* cotton mill. And then I saw the *best*. *Ex uno disce omnes*. There was no great difference between them. . . . On the eleventh of next month I am going down again only for three days, and then into the enemy's camp and the very headquarters of the Factory System advocates. I fear I shall have very little opportunity of looking about me, but I should be most happy to avail myself of any introduction from Lord Ashley which in the course of an hour or so would enable me to make any fresh observations.

" With that nobleman's most benevolent and excellent exertions, and with the evidence which he was the means of bringing forward, I am well acquainted. So far as seeing goes, I have seen enough for my purpose, and what I have seen has disgusted and astonished me beyond all measure. I mean to strike the heaviest blow in my power for these unfortunate creatures, but whether I shall do so in *Nickleby* or wait some other opportunity, I have not yet determined."

He did not strike the blow for some years—not, indeed, for sixteen years. For it was not until 1854 that he tackled the factory question in *Hard Times*. As all the world knows, that book was written largely under Carlylean influence, but it is worth remembering that it was Lord Shaftesbury's activities that first roused Dickens, and that when at last he dealt with the question he selected (as he had proposed to do years before) Manchester for the background of the story.

When the foregoing letter was written Dickens had not met Lord Ashley (as he then was), and another ten years passed before they became personally acquainted. But that his admiration for the man and his work became unlessened is shown by a letter written to Forster in 1841, in which he wrote that Samuel Rogers was much pleased with Lord Ashley for refusing a place in Peel's Government unless Peel would pledge himself to factory improvement, and added, " Much do I honour him for it." In 1851 he spoke at the dinner of the Metropolitan Sanitary Association, and proposed the toast of the Board of Health. He concluded his speech : " With the toast of the Board of Health I will couple the name of a noble lord, of whose earnestness in works of benevolence no man can doubt, and who has the courage on all occasions to face the cant which is the worst and commonest of all—the cant about the cant of philanthropy."

Forster records that " Lord Shaftesbury first dined with him in the following year at Tavistock House." They remained friends after that, but their association was never one of personal intimacy. Dickens admired Lord Shaftesbury, and the Earl found in him a man earnest in all good works, ready at all times to assist by pen and voice any cause for the moral or physical uplifting of his fellow-creatures. And how Dickens did assist it is unnecessary to point out. In *Household Words*, in *All the Year Round*, he again and again supported the reforms that Lord Shaftesbury advocated. As, for instance, his articles on the Ragged Schools.

CHAPTER XXXIV

LORD JOHN RUSSELL

AMONG authors, artists, actors, and lawyers Dickens formed many intimate friendships. There was one class, however, that scarcely found any place at all in his circle. I mean the politicians. He had a poor opinion of them as a class. Forster tells us that his observations while a reporter in the Press Gallery at the House of Commons had not led him to form any high opinion of the House or its heroes. In his letters he often speaks contemptuously of our legislators, and there are many similarly contemptuous references to them in his books, and in his articles for *Household Words* and *All the Year Round*. I fear that Dickens lent himself a little too readily to this sort of non-constructive criticism. That is an aside, however. There is the fact : Dickens had a contempt for our Parliament and its heroes, and politicians do not cut any considerable figure in the Dickens circle in consequence.

There were exceptions, of course. There was Lytton, for instance, but his political activities were an accident, so to speak. He came into the circle as a brother author, and in that respect only have we to consider him in his relations with Dickens. Sir Austen Layard was a member of Parliament, too, but not until after he had entered the Dickens circle, and his political activities were a sort of regrettable lapse from good taste in his friend's sight. Lord Shaftesbury was a politician, too, but he was one of the exceptional legislators who saw in their membership of Parliament but enhanced opportunities of doing good. Disraeli he knew quite well in the Gore House days, but never liked him and never had much to do with him. It is impossible to imagine Dickens on terms of friendship with so cynical an opportunist, and one is not the least bit surprised to find the novelist writing of " the Disraelis, Richmonds, and the other Impostors and Humbugs." With Gladstone there was but the merest acquaintance.

But there was one prominent politician for whom Dickens had profound respect and great personal liking. This was Lord John Russell. Apart, for the moment, from their personal friendship, Lord John in his public capacity was regarded by Dickens with an esteem that he entertained for no other statesman or politician of his time. In 1852 Dickens wrote to Foster : " Lord John's note confirms me in an old impression that he is worth a score of official men ; and has more generosity in his little finger than a Government usually has in its whole Corporation." Five years later, speaking at the annual dinner of the Warehousemen and Clerks' Schools, he proposed the health of Lord John, the President, and said :

> " He should do nothing so superfluous and so unnecessary as to descant upon his lordship's many faithful, long, and great public services, upon the honour and integrity with which he had pursued his straightforward public course through every difficulty, or upon the manly, gallant, and courageous character, which rendered him certain, in the eyes alike of friends and opponents, to rise with every rising occasion, and which, like the seal of Solomon, in the old Arabian story, enclosed in a not very large casket the soul of a giant."

And at the Liverpool banquet in 1869 he said : " . . . There is no man in England whom I more respect in his public capacity, whom I love more in his private capacity, or from whom I have received more remarkable proofs of his honour and love of literature."

Lord John had piloted the great Reform Bill through the House of Commons in Dickens's twentieth year, and the future novelist had sat in the press gallery recording the historic debates. He had not dreamed then that some day he would be on terms of intimacy with the little man who was fighting the People's battle so staunchly, but, Radical that he already was, he had recognised in Lord John the true champion of Progress, and had formed an admiration for him that lasted till the end of his life. Two years later he had reported the passage of the Poor Law Reform Bill in which again Lord John had taken an active part.

I imagine that there was scarcely a principle in regard to which Dickens was not in agreement with Lord John Russell. England never had a more consistent champion of civil and religious liberty than Lord John ; there never was a more tolerant man than Dickens. Lord John helped to reform our Poor Laws ; Dickens did even more than the statesman in that direction. Lord John was a life-long advocate of educational reform ; there was no subject which Dickens had closer to his heart. But there was another important characteristic that earned Dickens's esteem. In that same Liverpool speech from which I have already quoted Dickens said :

" When I first took literature as my profession in England, I calmly resolved within myself that, whether I succeeded or whether I failed, literature should be my sole profession. It appeared to me at that time that it was not so well understood in England as it was in other countries that literature was a dignified profession by which any man might stand or fall. I made a compact with myself that in my person literature should stand by itself, of itself, and for itself, and there is no consideration on earth that would induce me to break that bargain."

Now, no Prime Minister has ever done more to encourage letters and the arts than Lord John Russell. Dickens acknowledged his " honour and love of literature " in that same Liverpool speech. He was ever ready to encourage letters by all means in his power. He was an author of distinction himself and a friend of authors, and no appeal on behalf of letters was ever made to him in vain. It was the granting by him of a Civil List pension to Leigh Hunt in 1847 that altered the plan of the theatricals organised by Dickens for that author's benefit. The purpose had hardly been announced, says Forster, " when, with a statesman-like attention to literature and its followers for which Lord John Russell has been eccentric among English politicians, a Civil List pension of two hundred pounds a year was granted to Leigh Hunt."

The plan was modified in consequence, and the proceeds of the performances were devoted, after a certain sum had been set aside for the purpose of clearing Hunt of debt, to the benefit of the author of " Paul Pry "—John Poole. The latter was never a friend of Dickens's in any real sense, but he was a brilliant playwright who had fallen on hard times, and with that ever-glowing sympathy of his the novelist helped him all he could. Three years after these performances, when the money raised thereby was exhausted, he appealed to Lord John Russell to help. Lord John asked for full information, and this is what Dickens wrote in reply :

" Allow me to thank you for your ready and kind reply to my note, and to put you in possession of the exact state of Mr. Poole's case. . . . For some years past he has been living in a fifth storey in a house in the Rue Neuve Luxembourg in Paris (on the proceeds of an amateur theatrical performance for his benefit of which I undertook the management and stewardship, and which I dispensed to him half-yearly); and such is the nervous affection of his hands particularly that when I have seen him there trembling and staggering over a small wood fire it has been a marvel to me, knowing him to live quite alone, how he ever got into or out of his clothes. To the best of my belief, he has no relations whomsoever. He must either have starved or gone to the workhouse (and I have little doubt that he would have done the former) but for the funds I have doled out to him which were exhausted before you generously assisted him from the Queen's Bounty. He has no resources of any kind—of that I am perfectly sure. In the sunny time of the day he puts a melancholy little hat on one side of his head, and with a little stick under his arm, goes hitching himself about the boulevards; but for any power he has of earning a livelihood he might as well be dead. For three years I have been in constant expectation of receiving a letter from the portress of the house to say that his ashes and those of his wood fire, both of a very shrunken description, had been found lying together on the hearth. But he has lived on;[1] and for a few hours every day has so concealed his real condition out of doors that many French authors and actors . . . would stand amazed to know what I now tell you. . . . I don't think he would hold a pension very long. I need not add that he sorely needs it—and I do not doubt that the public are well acquainted with his name and works."

That letter was dated December 18 : the response was prompt, for on Christmas Eve Dickens wrote to Lord John :

"I have conveyed to Mr. Poole by to-night's post the joyful intelligence of her Majesty's gracious approval of your generous suggestion in his favour; and I do not doubt that he will endeavour to express to you (over that brighter fire) some of the happiness he owes to you."

Three years later we find him writing to Lord John from Boulogne :

"You will be interested, I think, to hear that Poole lives happily on his pension, and lives within it. He is quite incapable of any mental exertion, and what he would have done without it I cannot imagine. I send it to him at Paris every quarter. It is something, even amid the estimation in which you are held, which is but a foreshadowing of what shall be by-and-by, as the people advance, to be so grate-

[1] He lived on until 1872.

fully remembered as he, with the best reason, remembers you.
Forgive my saying this.   But the manner of that transaction,
no less than the matter, is always fresh in my memory in
association with your name, and I could not help it."

I have referred at length to this incident—reflecting, as it does,
so much credit upon both Dickens and Lord John—because it is
so admirable an example of not only the statesman's goodness of
heart, but his ever-glowing sympathy with letters which drew
Dickens to him so strongly.

Lord John Russell had an association—very indirect, but none
the less real—with Dickens's first success, *Pickwick*.   The Bath
scenes in that book are among the very best.   They reveal an
astonishingly intimate knowledge of the city and its people.
That knowledge was gained during a flying visit paid in 1835, a
visit of which Lord John was the direct cause.   He made a tour
of the West of England in that year, speaking at all the important
towns; and young Dickens followed him round reporting his
speeches for the " Morning Chronicle."   His reference to that
tour at the Press Fund dinner thirty years later all the world
knows.

Lord John proceeded from Exeter to Bristol, where he spoke
at a dinner, and the next day to Bath, Dickens following in his
train.   So that, but for Lord John Russell, we should never have
known Angelo Cyrus Bantam, Esq., M.C., or the Dowager Lady
Snuphanuph, or Mr. John Smauker; we should not have been
introduced to the " elite of Ba-ath "; but for him we should never
have visited the surgery of " Sawyer, late Nockemorf," at Bristol,
or tramped with Sam Weller across the breezy Downs and
witnessed the folding of the carpet.

How Dickens and Lord John became personally acquainted I
do not know, but they were on very friendly terms in Dickens's
very early days of authorship.   They did not meet very frequently in social life, because, of course, Lord John was absorbed
in public affairs always, but we have the authority of Dickens's
daughter and sister-in-law for it that the statesman was " a
friend whom he held in the highest estimation and to whom he
was always grateful for many personal kindnesses."   Several of
his letters confirm this, being expressions of gratitude for personal kindnesses, the nature of which is not indicated.   And if
further evidence of his regard for this friend were needed we
have it in the fact that *A Tale of Two Cities* was dedicated to him.

The friendship continued till Dickens's death.   So late as June
1869 we find Lord John writing : " I expect Dickens to visit us.
We went to see him last night in the murder of Nancy by Sikes,

and Mrs. Gamp." Some years after the novelist's death, he wrote to Forster: " I have read them (Dickens's letters quoted by Forster in his *Life* of his friend) with delight and pain. His heart, his imagination, his qualities of painting what is noble, and finding diamonds hidden far away, are greater here than even his works convey to me. How I lament he was not spared to us longer. I shall have a fresh grief when he dies in your volumes."

CHAPTER XXXV

THOMAS CARLYLE

"IT is almost thirty-two years since my acquaintance with him began; and on my side, I may say, every new meeting ripened it into more and more clear discernment of his rare and great worth as a brother man : a most cordial, sincere, clear-sighted, quietly decisive, just and loving man : till at length he had grown to such a recognition with me as I have rarely had for any man of my time."

So wrote Thomas Carlyle when Dickens died. To Forster he wrote : " I am profoundly sorry for *you*, and, indeed, for myself, and for us all. It is an event world-wide, a *unique* of talents suddenly extinct, and has ' eclipsed,' we, too, may say, ' the harmless gaiety of nations.' No death since 1866 has fallen on me with such a stroke. No literary man's hitherto ever did. The good, the gentle, high-gifted, ever friendly, noble Dickens—every inch of him an Honest Man."

Carlyle truly loved Dickens. They had much in common. They were both great humorists, and, therefore, both were men of profound sympathy; both were quickly moved to scorn and indignation at oppression and chicanery; both had a true and abiding faith in their fellow-men. Carlyle was undoubtedly, as the mother whom he loved so well said, " gey ill to live with," yet, though his biographer has done his worst for him, the " sage of Chelsea " is still revealed as an Honest Man, a chivalrous man, and, though the truth of it may not at first be obvious, a tolerant man withal. It is easy to gibe at Carlyle, and it is also rather fashionable. Somebody once said of him that he preached the gospel of Silence in forty volumes. That was rather clever, but it was rather silly, too. It was true, but it was not the truth, and the difference is enormous. And, however much " superior people " may gibe at Carlyle, the fact stands unchallengeable that he was a great and noble man, a man who suffered privations rather than be untrue to himself, who would have died before he would have lied or done a dishonest deed; a man who believed unshakably in the innate goodness of human nature, and never feared to denounce evil wheresoever he found it. On the surface, very " difficult," dyspeptic that he was, at heart a true Man.

Dickens, with that insight of his, which enabled him unfailingly to see the real man in a friend, saw him in Carlyle and loved him. Froude tells us so. He says, for instance, that in 1860 the sage was fixed to his garret room, rarely stirring out, except to ride, and dining nowhere save now and then with Forster to meet only Dickens, " who loved him with all his heart." And Forster says that Carlyle was " a most dear friend," and that " there was no one whom in later life he honoured so much, or had a more profound regard for."

In 1842, when Dickens was so gallantly fighting for international copyright in America, Carlyle stood by him, and wrote a letter which served him in good stead. Their acquaintance had only recently begun then, but that act served to cement the friendship, and very soon we find Carlyle exercising a remarkable influence over the novelist. The first sign of this appears in 1844, when, metaphorically speaking, Carlyle is at his elbow all the time he is writing *The Chimes*, and we find him writing to Forster : " Shall I confess to you, I particularly want Carlyle above all to see it before the rest of the world, when it is done ? " And then he proposes the reading which was to become historic : " Don't have any one, this particular night, to dinner, but let it be a summons for the special purpose at half-past six. Carlyle indispensable, and I should like his wife of all things : *her* judgment would be invaluable." Mrs. Carlyle did not attend, but her husband did, and in Maclise's drawing of the scene, he is shown occupying the post of honour at Dickens's right hand.

A few years later *Hard Times*—a book that reveals the influence of the sage in every chapter—was dedicated to Carlyle, and eight years after that, saturated with " The French Revolution," which we are told he carried with him wherever he went, he wrote *A Tale of Two Cities*.

Carlyle reciprocated the regard, as we have seen, and the fact is the more worthy of note, because it evidenced the triumph of the man Dickens over the novelist Boz; for Carlyle, Scotch Puritan and dyspeptic that he was, assuredly had a native prejudice against Boz the novelist—against fiction, I mean. As, for instance, in 1837, he wrote : " It is worth noting how loath we are to read great works, how much more willingly we cross our legs, back to candles, feet to fire, over some *Pickwick*, or lowest trash of that sort. The reason is we are very indolent, very wearied and forlorn, and read oftenest chiefly that we may forget outselves." Even so, he was presently constrained to admit that *Pickwick* was not such trash after all. Great humorist that he was, he was bound to recognise the genius of the book. Thus, by and by, we find him writing to Forster : " An Arch-

N

deacon, with his own venerable lips, repeated to me, the other night, a strange profane story of a clergyman who had been administering ghostly consolation to a sick person; having finished, satisfactorily, as he thought, and got out of the room, he heard the sick person ejaculate, ' Well, thank God, *Pickwick* will be out in ten days, anyway ! '—this is dreadful.''

The genuine humour of Dickens conquered Carlyle, and it is almost startling to observe how often he quotes from the novels in his letters and conversation. *David Copperfield* was an especial favourite, and for Mrs. Gummidge he seems to have had a high regard. In 1849 we find him writing to his wife after one of their unhappy estrangements—or, rather, misunderstandings : " Alas, my poor little Goody ! these are not good times at all. . . . Your poor hand and heart, too, were in a sad case on Friday. Let me hope you have slept well since that, given up ' thinking of the old 'un,' and much modified the ' Gummidge ' view of affairs. Sickness and distraction of nerves is a good excuse for almost any degree of despondency. . . . But we can by no means permit ourselves a philosophy a la Gummidge— ' poor lone critturs ' though we be." It is recorded also by Forster that on the occasion of the dinner held to celebrate the start of *Copperfield*, " it was a delight to see the enjoyment of Dickens at Carlyle's laughing reply to questions about his health, that he was, in the language of Mr. Peggotty's housekeeper, a lorn lone creature, and everything went contrary with him."

We have it, too, on Forster's authority, that Carlyle very highly appreciated *A Tale of Two Cities* and *Great Expectations*, and Forster records that " a dear friend now gone would laughingly relate what outcry there used to be on the night of the week when a number was due, for ' that Pip nonsense ! ' and what roars of laughter followed, though at first it was entirely put aside as not on any account to have time wasted over it." Yes, Dickens conquered Carlyle by sheer force of humour and sympathy, and Carlyle loved him for it.

It was in 1840, at a dinner at the Stanleys', that they first met, and Carlyle records his impressions of the young novelist as follows : " There at the dear cost of a shattered set of nerves, and head set whirling for the next eight-and-forty hours, I did see Lords and lions. . . . Know, Pickwick too was of the same dinner party, though they did not seem to heed him over much. He is a fine little fellow—Boz, I think : clear blue intelligent eyes that he arches amazingly, large, protrusive, rather loose mouth, a face of the most extreme *mobility*, which he shuttles about—eyebrows, eyes, mouth and all—in a very singular manner while speaking. Surmount them with a loose coil of common coloured hair, and set it on a small compact figure very small and dressed a la D'Orsay rather than well—this is Pickwick. For the rest, a quiet, shrewd-looking little fellow, who seems to guess pretty well what he is and what others are."

It cannot be counted an unfavourable first impression. Further meetings were brought about by Forster—who, of course, was one of Carlyle's most trusted friends, as he was everybody else's—and as the two men became more intimate and grew to know each other, there arose that mutual regard which presently ripened into sincere affection. They met very often—at Gore House, among other places, as we have seen—and Dickens always treated his friend with easy gaiety, yet with a deference that was unassumed. Carlyle seems to have been at home and at his ease in Dickens's company, and Mr. Percy Fitzgerald recalls a dinner at which the only company were Forster, Dickens, Carlyle and himself, when Dickens " played round " the sage as Garrick did round Johnson—affectionately in high good humour and wit, " and I could well see much pleasing the old lion."

It was a high tribute to his regard for the novelist when, in 1863, Carlyle attended one of Dickens's readings " to the complete upsetting of my evening habitudes and spiritual composure." But he enjoyed it, despite himself—" Dickens does do it capitally such as *it* is, acts better than any Macready in the world; a whole tragic comic heroic *theatre* visible, performing under one *hat*, and keeping us laughing—in a sorry way some of us thought—the whole night."

Yes, Dickens conquered Carlyle.

CHAPTER XXXVI

BULWER LYTTON AND LAMAN BLANCHARD

ONE of the most brilliant stars in the Gore House constellation was Edward Bulwer. With him in these days Dickens formed a friendship that was quite unalloyed, and lasted right until the end without any breach or lessening of regard. It must be confessed that at first blush this friendship is rather difficult to understand. Superficially, Lytton had few of those qualities that one imagines appealed to Dickens. There is very little evidence in his books or his plays of those broad human sympathies that we find in Dickens. The impression is one of considerably more head than heart. But it is quite unjust thus to dismiss Lytton. Had circumstances behaved a little more kindly towards him he would have been a very different man from what he was, and the world might have been far more indebted to him than it is. A spoiled child, he early found himself compelled to write against time for money, whilst for very many years his life was embittered by the tragic failure of his marriage, and the persecution he suffered from his wife. The only wonder is that his earlier books do not bear more traces than they do of having been " pot boilers," and that his later work is not overclouded with cynicism. Bred in a different school, blessed with a happy marriage, Lytton might have been a very great man. I think H. F. Chorley struck the right note when he wrote, Lytton " has a thoroughly *satin* character; but then it is the *richest* satin. . . . It is a fine energetic, inquisitive mind, if I mistake not, that has been blighted and bent too soon."

" All these things contributed to make me what I am," wrote Dickens once when recalling his boyhood, and so might Lytton have written. His life's story is indeed a very sad one; loneliness and lack of sympathy dogged him always, until in his later years he found much consolation in the affection of his son, Robert. His life, says his grandson, the present Earl Lytton, was on the whole a singularly lonely one. " Neither in literature nor in politics did he belong to any intimate set. He went little into Society, and he never stayed for many months in the same place." His domestic tragedy was no mere " skeleton in the cupboard ";

180

LORD LYTTON

it dogged him whithersoever he went; and the wonder is that he achieved half so much as he did.

But his nature at bottom was good. Prof. Jowett says, " He left upon me an impression of genuine kindness, and endless activity of mind, of great knowledge, and of a noble interest in literature and literary men." Many tales of his kindness are told. For Macready, for instance, he did much when the actor was struggling at Covent Garden. He was chiefly instrumental, too, in obtaining a pension for Tom Hood; whilst we shall see how he threw himself into the Guild of Literature and Art scheme. No man, in fact, ever showed more loyalty to his art, or was more ready to assist a brother artist, and to say this of any man is to give him high praise. The present Earl Lytton says, " There were many who loved him truly," and it is quite true. The greatest friend of his life was John Forster, for whom he had a very deep and lasting affection, and probably next to Forster in his regard came Dickens, with whom he really had more in common than is apparent. First and foremost, I think, so far as Dickens, at any rate, was concerned, there was the high regard in which they both held their art. It was always a very strong point with Dickens, this jealousy for the dignity and reputation of his art. Literature was to Dickens a noble calling, not at any time to be held lightly, and in this he and Lytton were in complete sympathy. Of him he was able to say : " In the path we both tread I have uniformly found him from the first the most generous of men; quick to encourage, slow to disparage, ever anxious to assert the order of which he is so great an ornament; never condescending to shuffle it off, and leave it outside state rooms, as a Mussulman might leave his slippers outside a mosque."

Then, of course, there was their joint interest in the Guild of Literature and Art, which was brought into being and given a degree of vitality for many years, as a result of their activity and earnestness. Another interest that they had in common was the study of the occult. This had a stronger hold over Lytton than over Dickens, but of the latter's interest in it there is ample evidence. And finally the mutual friendship of Forster must have been a strong tie.

Mr. R. Renton surmises that Lytton and Dickens first met at the house of Colborn, the publisher. He is probably correct, but, in any case, we are safe in assuming that the meeting was brought about by Forster. And it was in the early days of Dickens's fame, because in Macready's Diary for the late 'thirties we find him recording several visits paid to his green room by the two novelists, whilst Forster tells us that in 1840 Lytton was one of the many friends with whom there were many social foregatherings, adding, "Of the genius of the author of ' Pelham ' and ' Eugene Aram ' he had, early and late, the highest admiration, and he took occasion to express it during the present year in a new preface which he published to *Oliver Twist*." [1]

But although they were very friendly from the first, and met often, it was their association in the establishment of the Guild of Literature and Art that brought about their intimacy. " In the year of the establishment of *Household Words*, Dickens resumed what I have called his splendid strolling on behalf of a scheme for the advantage of men of letters, to which a great brother author had given the sanction of his name and genius." In these words Forster introduces the Guild. Recent experience of the success of the theatrical performances in aid of Hunt and Poole and Knowles " had shown what the public interest in this kind of amusement might place within reach of its providers; and there came to be discussed the possibility of making permanent such help as had been afforded to fellow-writers, by means of an endowment that should not be mere charity, but should combine something of both pension-list and college-lectureship, without the drawbacks of either. It was not enough considered that schemes for self-help, to be successful, require from those they are meant to benefit, not only a general assent to their desirability, but zealous co-operation. Too readily assuming what should have had more thorough investigation, the enterprise was set on foot, and the ' Guild of Literature and Art ' originated at Knebworth."

The scheme undoubtedly was the child of Dickens's brain, and he took it up with all the enthusiasm which characterised him in everything he ever undertook, but Lytton was scarcely less enthusiastic. They had seen enough to convince them of the need for some such scheme. Tom Hood, Leigh Hunt, John Poole, Sheridan Knowles—all had been helped nobly by brother artists, and Dickens and Lytton were determined to make an effort to place such assistance on a permanent and organised basis. It was the tragic case of poor Laman Blanchard that actuated them most of all. Blanchard was a friend of both men : he was one of that select gathering at Lincoln's Inn Fields which listened to Dickens's reading of *The Chimes*. Of him Lytton wrote :

" To most of those who have mixed generally with the men who in our day have chosen literature as a profession,

[1] " Sir Edward Bulwer's admirable and most powerful novel of ' Paul Clifford.' " See Preface to Third Edition. A similar complimentary reference to Dickens was made by Lytton in his Preface to " Night and Morning " in 1845, where he wrote of " that popular and pre-eminent observer of the age in which we live," intimating in a note that the reference was to Dickens.

the name of Laman Blanchard brings recollections of peculiar tenderness and regret. . . . They recall the memory of a competitor without envy, a partisan without gall; firm as the firmest in the maintenance of his own opinions; but gentle as the gentlest in the judgment he passed on others. Whom among our London brotherhood of letters does not miss that simple cheerfulness, that inborn exquisite urbanity, that child-like readiness to be pleased, with all that happy tendency to panygerise for merit and to be lenient to every fault . . . who, in convivial meetings does not miss and will not miss for ever that sweetness of those unpretending talents, the earnestness of that honesty which seemed unconscious, it was worn so lightly—the mild influence of that exuberant kindness which softened the acrimony of any disputants and reconciled the secret animosities of jealous rivals ? "

And here we may appropriately quote a letter of Dickens's to Blanchard, as showing the affection in which the Author of Pickwick held him :

"I cannot thank you enough for the beautiful manner and the true spirit of friendship in which you have noticed my *Carol*. But I *must* thank you because you have filled my heart up to the brim and it is running over.

"You meant to give me great pleasure, dear fellow, and you have done it. The tone of your elegant and fervent praise has touched me in the tenderest place. I cannot write about it, and as to talking of it, I could no more do that than a dumb man. I have derived inexpressible gratification from what I know was a labour of love on your part. And I can never forget it.

"When I think it likely that I may meet you (perhaps at Ainsworth's on Friday ?) I shall slip a *Carol* into my pocket and ask you to put it among your books for my sake. You will never like it the less for having made it the means of so much happiness to me.

"Always, my dear Blanchard, faithfully, your friend——"

Born in 1804, Blanchard early achieved notice as a writer of great promise, but, handicapped by a lack of this world's goods, he was compelled to lay aside his higher gifts, and devote himself to popular journalism. Yet, all the time, we are told, he looked forward to the period when he might realise the cherished dreams of his youth, " escape from his hurried compositions for the day and the hour, and return into his inner self and there meditate the production of some work which might justify the critics' belief in the promise of his early efforts." But it was not to be, and in 1845 he ended his life by his own hand.

It was the memory of poor Laman Blanchard that spurred Dickens and Lytton on to establish the Guild of Literature and Art. They determined that if they could prevent it no struggling author or artist should again be placed in the same predicament. " I do devoutly believe," wrote Dickens to Lytton, " that this plan, carried by the support which I trust will be given to it, will change the status of the literary man in England, and make a revolution in his position which no government, no power on earth but his own, could ever effect. I have implicit confidence in the scheme—so splendidly begun—if we carry it out with a steadfast energy. I have a strong conviction that we hold in our hands the peace and honour of men of letters for centuries to come, and that you are destined to be their best and most enduring benefactor. . . . Oh, what a procession of new years may walk out of all this for the class we belong to after we are dust." It was a noble scheme, which failed only because, as Forster puts it, " the support indispensable to success was not as Dickens too sanguinely hoped, given to it by literary men themselves." In 1897 the Guild had to be dissolved, and by Act of Parliament its endowment was divided between the Royal Literary Fund and the Artists' General Benevolent Institution. It had degenerated into a mere charity which was exactly what its promoters had been most anxious to avoid.

The Guild was inaugurated at Knebworth, where three private performances were given of " Every Man in His Humour," Lytton bearing the whole of the expenses. This was in November 1850. It was decided to give further public performances in aid of the scheme in London and the provinces. Lytton agreed to write a five-act comedy, and Dickens a farce. Lytton fulfilled his part of the bargain, and produced " Not so Bad as we Seem," but Dickens had to " cry off," and " Mr. Nightingale's Diary," by Mark Lemon, was substituted, Dickens, however, contributing so much fun to it that it was eventually billed as " by Mr. Charles Dickens and Mr. Mark Lemon."

The first performance, at Devonshire House, on Wednesday, June 18, 1851, in the presence of the Queen and Prince Consort, was a very brilliant affair, and the subsequent tour was a great success. At Manchester, which was the last place but one visited, a public dinner was held, and Lytton attended. " Bulwer," wrote Dickens to Forster, " spoke brilliantly at the Manchester dinner, and his earnestness and determination about the Guild was most impressive. It carried everything before it."

The writing of a comedy did not end Lytton's interest in the Guild by a very long way. In 1854 he carried through Parliament a Bill to incorporate it, and in 1863 he made a free gift of a piece of land upon his estate upon which three houses were built to form residences for more needy authors or artists. When these houses were opened the members of the Guild visited them, and were afterwards entertained at Knebworth by Lytton, whose health was proposed by Dickens :

> " In thanking him for the toast which he has done us the honour to propose, allow me to correct an error into which he has fallen. Allow me to state that these houses never could have been built but for his zealous and valuable cooperation, and also that the pleasant labour out of which they have arisen would have lost one of its greatest charms and strongest impulses, if it had lost his ever-ready sympathy with that class in which he has risen to the foremost rank, and of which he is the brightest ornament.

> " Now I am sure I shall be giving utterance to the feelings of my brothers and sisters in literature in proposing ' Health, long life, and prosperity to our distinguished host.' Ladies and gentlemen, you know very well that when the health, life, and beauty now overflowing these halls shall have fled, crowds of people will come to see the place where he lived and wrote. Setting aside the orator and statesman—for happily we know no party here but this agreeable party—setting aside all this, you know very well, that this is the home of a very great man whose connection with Hertfordshire every other county in England will envy for many a long year to come. You know that when this hall is dullest and emptiest you can make it when you please brightest and fullest by peopling it with the creations of his brilliant fancy. Let us all wish together that they may be many more—for the more they are the better it will be, and, as he always excels himself, the better they will be. I ask you to listen to their praises and not to mine, and to let them, and not me, propose their health."

Dickens and Lytton had been excellent friends from the beginning, but their association with the Guild of Literature and Art naturally brought them very close together indeed, and henceforth they were on the most affectionate terms. They exchanged visits frequently, and there were few whom Dickens welcomed more gladly at Gadshill.

In 1851, whilst the rehearsals for the Guild performances were in progress, Macready left the stage. Lytton presided at the banquet which was given in the actor's honour, and Dickens proposed his health in a glowing speech. On November 2, 1867, Lytton was in the chair at the great banquet which was given to Dickens on the eve of his departure for his American reading tour, and in proposing the Guest's health paid an affectionate tribute to his great literary rival and personal friend who had helped to refine humanity " by tears that never enfeeble and laughter that never degrades." Before we come to note briefly the purely literary associations of the friends, it is interesting to observe that in November 1858 they were rival candidates for the Lord Rectorship of Glasgow University, a third candidate being another of Dickens's most esteemed friends, the famous Lord Shaftesbury. And the result of the poll was Lytton 216; Shaftesbury 203; Dickens 68.

Dickens had a very high opinion of Lytton's judgment in regard to his art, and allowed it to influence him considerably. Over and over again we find him referring to Lytton's criticism of this book and that, always expressing gratification if the criticism is favourable and always speaking of anything in the shape of adverse criticism with the profoundest respect. But it is generally admitted that Lytton's judgment was at fault in the case of *Great Expectations* and that Dickens did unwisely in acting upon it. " You will be surprised," he wrote to Forster, " to hear that I have changed the end of *Great Expectations* from and after Pip's return to Joe's, and finding his little likeness there. Bulwer, who has been, as I think you know, extraordinarily taken by the book, so strongly urged it upon me, after reading the proofs, and supported his view with such good reasons, that I resolved to make the change. . . . I have put in as pretty a little bit of writing as I could, and I have no doubt the story will be more acceptable through the alteration." Forster comments : " This turned out to be the case, but the first ending nevertheless seems to be more consistent with the drift, as well as natural working out, of the tale." The first ending left Pip a lonely man, but, as George Gissing says, " by the irony of fate he was induced to spoil his work through a brother novelist's desire for a happy ending—a strange thing indeed to befall Dickens."

It would be easy to give many quotations from Lytton and from Dickens showing how highly each esteemed the other's art, but it must suffice to say that never did two competitors in the race for fame respect each other more truly—never were two literary men more free from jealousies.

In 1861 Lytton wrote, at Dickens's earnest request, a serial story for *All the Year Round.* This was " A Strange Story," which followed *Great Expectations.* Unfortunately, it did not please the readers of *All the Year Round,* and it fell flat.

It only needs to be added that Dickens entertained for his friend's son, Robert, a very high regard, and was delighted to welcome him as a contributor to *All the Year Round.*

CHAPTER XXXVII

TENNYSON

To these early days in particular belongs the friendship with Tennyson. It lasted till the end, but it was in the early 'forties that they saw most of each other. After his marriage in 1850 the poet practically dropped out of the Circle, and there is recorded only one instance of his subsequently rejoining it. That was in June 1851 when he attended the *Copperfield* dinner at the Star and Garter, Richmond. He was then living at Twickenham, but in 1853 he settled at Freshwater, and thenceforward he and Dickens met but rarely. Indeed, it is remarkable to note that there is no evidence that they met even when Dickens visited the Isle of Wight.

The friendship, however, was never an intimate one. Dickens had a great liking for the poet and a tremendous admiration for his poetry. " He never faltered in his allegiance to Tennyson," says Forster; and in another place, " To Alfred Tennyson, through all the friendly and familiar days I am describing, he gave full allegiance and honoured welcome." Mary Boyle tells us : " One day I went with his two daughters . . . and their aunt to meet him at the station. Lifting up the hand-bag which he always carried, he exclaimed : ' Here, girls, I have a treat for you—Tennyson's magnificent poem of " The Idylls of the King." Is it not glorious to think that having written for so many years, a man should now bring forth perhaps the noblest of his works ? ' " Of the " Idylls," he wrote to Forster :

> " How fine the ' Idylls ' are ! Lord ! what a blessed thing it is to read a man who can write ! I thought nothing could be grander than the first poem till I came to the third; but when I had read the last, it seemed to be absolutely unapproached and unapproachable."

I am able to state, on the authority of the poet's son, that the admiration was mutual. " Dickens *profoundly* admired my Father," writes Lord Tennyson. " My Father admired Dickens, and thought *Pickwick* his most original work. He did not like his pathos, except in one case, that of *Old Cheeseman,* of which story he thought highly."

Tennyson loved London as much as Dickens did, though his knowledge of it was not as " extensive and peculiar." " He always delighted in the ' central roar ' of London," says the present Lord Tennyson in his biography of his father. " Whenever he and I went to London, one of the first things we did was to walk to the Strand and Fleet Street." He adds that his father would often dine with his friends at the Cock and other taverns, and " a perfect dinner was a beefsteak, a potato, a pint of port, and afterwards a pipe (never a cigar). . . . Very genial evenings they were, with plenty of anecdote and wit, and ' thrust and parry of bright monostick.' " Dickens and Forster and Maclise were often among the company on such occasions.

There was a curious link between the novelist and the poet, for in his early days, the latter had lived at 58 Lincoln's Inn Fields, under the same roof as Forster. In March 1843 Dickens presented Tennyson with a set of his works, sending the following letter with the gift :

" MY DEAR TENNYSON,
　　　　" For the love I bear you as a man whose writings enlist my whole heart and nature in admiration of their Truth and Beauty, set these books upon your shelves; believing that you have no more earnest and sincere homage than mine,
　　　　　　　" Faithfully and Gratefully your Friend,
　　　　　　　　　　　" CHARLES DICKENS."

CHAPTER XXXVIII

THERE remains one small group who may be spoken of before we accompany the novelist on his American tours. Several publishers were prominent among his friends. There were misunderstandings with some of them, but only on business grounds, and the friendships were not seriously damaged.

First, naturally, we speak of Chapman and Hall. And we will reverse the order in which all the world ever speaks of them, for Hall was the first to meet Dickens. The incident is a very interesting one, constituting one of the red-letter events in the novelist's life. One evening in 1833 young Charles Dickens, newspaper reporter, stealthily, with fear and trembling, dropped into a dark letter-box in a dark office up a dark court in Fleet Street, the MS. of a short story. It was his first bid for fame. Some time afterwards, in December of that same year, he purchased at a shop in the Strand a copy of the " Old Monthly Magazine," and therein saw that same story in all the glory of type. " On which occasion I walked down to Westminster Hall, and turned into it for half an hour, because my eyes were so dimmed with joy and pride, that they could not bear the street, and were not fit to be seen there." Exactly two years later a gentleman called on him at his chambers in Furnival's Inn, and made the proposal which begot *The Pickwick Papers* and the young reporter's fame. Boz recognised his visitor as the man who had sold him the issue of the " Old Monthly Magazine " for December 1833. It was Mr. Hall, junior partner in the recently-established publishing firm of Chapman and Hall. A genuine friendship ensued between the two men. There were misunderstandings at times, though. Hall, for instance, dropped what Forster calls an inconsiderate hint with reference to putting a clause in the agreement respecting *Martin Chuzzlewit* into force. The clause was to the effect that if on the first five numbers the profits should fall below a certain point a certain sum should be deducted from the author's payments ; and the early sales of *Martin Chuzzlewit* were disappointing. Dickens was indignant—though he ought to have known his man a little better—and he proposed to break with the firm, and then to give Hall " a piece of his mind." On Forster's advice he did not carry out that proposal at the time, but presently disappointment with the *Carol* receipts stirred him, and he and Chapman and Hall parted company. The breach was not for long, however, and he returned to them again for good. In 1841 there had been another misunderstanding in connection with which Dickens had considered Hall to be " morally and physically feeble, though perfectly well intentioned." " Well intentioned " summed Hall up admirably, and Dickens could always make allowances for a well-intentioned man, and despite their differences he liked him and had much pleasant intercourse with him. Hall died in 1847, and Dickens sincerely regretted the loss of " poor Hall," whose funeral he attended with Forster.

Of Edward Chapman, the senior partner, Dickens seems to have had a higher opinion. When Hall was " morally and physically feeble," Chapman was " very manly and sensible." He came under the clouds as Hall's partner, of course, but there was a mutual respect and liking that was not really affected by the misunderstandings, and they remained good friends to the end. Frederic Chapman, who joined the firm in 1841, was a particularly hearty, good-natured man, and he and Dickens were always on the best of terms.

Macrone was Dickens's first publisher. In 1835 Ainsworth introduced him to this gentleman, who, in the following year, published *Sketches by Boz* in book form. We need not concern ourselves with him to any extent. Forster has told how, when Dickens found that unwittingly he had let himself in for an impossible amount of work through ill-considered agreements with publishers, Macrone was inaccessible to all arguments, and had to be bought out. He was an adventurer, as his solicitor admitted in a letter to Forster, though we must be just enough to remember that he had made a big speculation with the *Sketches*, and so ought not to be criticised too severely for desiring to benefit to the full from the unlooked-for success of *Pickwick*. Mr. Percy Fitzgerald says that Macrone was a fellow-resident of Dickens's at Furnival's Inn, and so must have been intimate with him. It does not follow, however, that because two men are next-door neighbours they are intimate with one another, and, as a matter of fact, Dickens and Macrone never met until 1835, and though they naturally came to know each other pretty well, I can find no justification for talking about intimacy.

At the close of 1836 Richard Bentley published *The Village Coquettes* (one's head reels at the contemplation of the quantity of work young Boz undertook at this time). The sixth number of *Pickwick* had not yet appeared, when, on August 22, 1836,

Dickens signed an agreement with Bentley to undertake the editing of a monthly magazine to be started the following January, to which he was to supply a serial story. Soon afterwards he had agreed with the same publisher to write two other tales. With *Pickwick* on hand, the task proved too much, and a compromise was arrived at amicably. Later a similar difficulty arose, and six months of wrangling followed. A further agreement was reached, but still difficulties continued, until at last a final settlement was reached, and Dickens linked himself with Chapman and Hall. Bentley seems to have been honest and fair in his intentions, and Forster has not dealt too charitably with him. As to Dickens's personal relations nothing can be said, for nothing seems to be known, but it is clearly evident that there was no friendship.

With Bradbury and with Evans relations were much more intimate. He went to them when he squabbled with Chapman and Hall in 1844, and remained with them until 1859. Then came a dispute which apparently arose out of their refusal to publish in " Punch " that unhappy manifesto respecting his domestic troubles. A law case ensued respecting *Household Words*, and the court ordered the property to be sold. Dickens bought it and killed it, and started *All the Year Round*. Bradbury and Evans promptly started " Once a Week," and the breach was complete. But in the years between 1844 and 1858 there was considerable friendliness with both Bradbury and Evans. They were familiar guests at Devonshire House, and with Evans, at any rate, there could not have been an absolute rupture of the friendship. For the novelist's eldest son had fallen in love with the publisher's daughter, and in November 1861 Charles Dickens the Younger was married to Miss Evans.

There is one other publisher who finds a place here by virtue wholly of his personal friendship with Dickens. Thomas Longman never published anything of Dickens's, but he was more intimate with the author than any one who did, save only James T. Fields. He was a friend from the earliest Broadstairs' days, and, says Forster, remained a special favourite always. It was to Longman, it will be remembered, to whom Dickens recommended young Marcus Stone shortly after Frank Stone's death.

CHAPTER XXXIX

AMERICAN FRIENDS—WASHINGTON IRVING

THE ovations which Dickens received in Scotland in 1841 were but a slight foretaste of what he was to receive in America in the following year. He went to a land where he was as loved as he was in his own land. In America his genius, his humanising influence, had been recognised as quickly as here, and *The Old Curiosity Shop* had completed the conquest. It was a letter from Washington Irving about that book that finally determined him to cross the Atlantic. The reception that was accorded him is historic. Never before had any visitor been so welcomed. Everywhere Boz was the idol, and his progress was one steady triumph. Owing to his plain speaking on the international copyright question he gave offence in some quarters, and when he returned home and wrote *American Notes* and *Martin Chuzzlewit* there was a general revulsion of feeling. The Americans became almost as noisy in their denunciations of Boz as they had previously been in their demonstrations of affection. But it was a passing anger. Our cousins went on reading his books, and gradually he reconquered them. After an interval of a quarter of a century he revisited the States and was given a reception which surpassed the former one in enthusiasm and affection. Never since has the sky been clouded. To-day the Americans are more enthusiastic Dickens lovers than we are ourselves.

With his travels and doings in America we are not concerned now. Our concern is with some of the friendships that he formed in that country. He went among a nation of friends, of course, but there were choice spirits with whom he became very intimate. The English friends whom he loved as he loved Washington Irving, for instance, were very few indeed. Longfellow he grappled to his heart with hoops of steel; so did he Prof. Felton. Later James T. Fields was established in his affection. Others with whom he became on very friendly terms were James Russell Lowell, Charles Eliot Norton, Oliver Wendell Holmes, Childs, Emerson, Dana, Bancroft, etc.

Best loved of them all was " Geoffrey Crayon." Mr. W. Glyde Wilkins in " Dickens and America " accepts the suggestion that the chief influence that decided Dickens to pay his first visit to

O
193

the States was his desire to see Cairo. I think a much stronger influence than that was his desire to meet in the flesh the author of " The Sketch Book." They had already corresponded. In 1841 Irving had written to Dickens " expressing my heartfelt delight with his writings, and my yearnings towards himself" and "that glorious fellow " had, as Forster says, answered him with more than his own warmth :

> " There is no man in the world who could have given me the heartfelt pleasure you have by your kind note. . . . There is no living writer, and there are very few among the dead, whose approbation I should feel so proud to earn. And with everything you have written upon my shelves, and in my thoughts, and in my heart of hearts, I may honestly and truly say so. If you could know how earnestly I write this, you would be glad to read it—as I hope you will be, faintly guessing at the warmth of the hand I autographically hold out to you over the broad Atlantic."

In October 1841 Irving wrote to his niece, Mrs. Storrow : " What do you think ? Dickens is actually *coming to America*. . . ." They first met in New York, and each was just what the other expected to find him—Boz breezy and generous-hearted, Crayon unaffected, homely, and lovable. And so the friendship, which had so far only existed " autographically," was cemented.

Before that first meeting, Irving's had been one of the signatures appended to an address of welcome from the citizens of New York. The dinner, an invitation to which had been included in that address, took place on the following day, and Irving was in the chair. About 800 guests were present, and in the course of his speech Dickens made a wholly delightful reference to his friend :

> " Washington Irving ! Why, gentlemen, I don't go upstairs to bed two nights out of the seven . . . without taking Washington Irving under my arm ; and when I don't take him, I take his own brother, Oliver Goldsmith. . . . Washington Irving—Diedrich Knickerbocker—Geoffrey Crayon—why, where can you go that they have not been there before ? Is there an English farm—is there an English stream, an English city, or an English country-seat, where they have not been ? Is there no Bracebridge Hall in existence ? Has it no ancient shades or quiet streets ? "

This was the occasion on which Irving broke down in his speech.

WASHINGTON IRVING

From an engraving by Joseph Brown

His and Dickens's common friend, Prof. Felton, has told the story. Irving, he says, always shrank with a comical terror from making an after-dinner speech, and on this occasion he was full of forebodings that he would break down.

> "He had brought the manuscript of his speech, and laid it under his plate. 'I shall certainly break down,' he repeated over and over again. At last the moment arrived. Mr. Irving rose, and was received with deafening and long-continued applause, which by no means lessened his apprehension. He began in his pleasant voice; got through two or three sentences pretty easily, but in the next hesitated; and, after one or two attempts to go on, gave it up, with a graceful allusion to the tournament and the troop of knights all armed and eager for the fray; and ended with the toast, 'Charles Dickens, the Guest of the nation.' 'There!' said he, as he resumed his seat under a repetition of the applause which had saluted his rising—'there! I told you I should break down, and I've done it.'"

Following the New York dinner, Dickens and Irving journeyed to Washington together, and there spent a few days. Then they said what both expected to be the last " good-bye " before Irving sailed for Spain, where he was to take up the duties of American minister. " Irving . . . *wept heartily* at parting," wrote Dickens to Forster, adding, " He is a fine fellow, when you know him; and you would relish him, my dear friend, of all things. We have laughed together at some absurdities we have encountered in company, quite in my vociferous Devonshire Terrace style." A day or two later he wrote to Irving himself:

> "We passed through—literally passed through—this place again to-day. I did not come to see you, for I really have not the heart to say 'good-bye' again, and felt more than I can tell you when we shook hands last Wednesday.
>
> "You will not be at Baltimore, I fear? I thought at the time that you only said you might be there, to make our parting the gayer. Wherever you go, God bless you! What pleasure I have had in seeing and talking with you, I will not attempt to say. I shall never forget it as long as I live. What would I give if we could have but a quiet week together! Spain is a lazy place, and its climate an indolent one. But if you ever have leisure under its sunny skies to think of a man who loves you, and holds communion with your spirit oftener, perhaps, than any other person alive—

leisure from listlessness, I mean—and will write to me in London, you will give me an inexpressible amount of pleasure."

They *did* meet again, in Baltimore, for Irving could not resist the opportunity of saying one more farewell. " Washington Irving has come in for another leave-taking, and dines with me to-day," Dickens wrote to Forster. It was indeed their last leave-taking. They never met in London, and when Dickens revisited the States, his friend had been dead nearly ten years. That farewell dinner at Baltimore on March 23, 1842, was always a happy memory with Dickens. During his second American tour he thus replied to a letter from Mr. Charles Lanman :

" Your reference to my dear friend Washington Irving renews the vivid impressions reawakened in my mind at Baltimore but the other day. I saw his fine face for the last time in that city. He came there from New York to pass a day or two with me before I went westward; and they were made among the most memorable of my life by his delightful fancy and genial humour. Some unknown admirer of his books and mine sent to the hotel a most enormous mint julep, wreathed with flowers. We sat, one on either side of it, with great solemnity (it filled a respectably-sized round table), but the solemnity was of very short duration. It was quite an enchanted julep, and carried us among innumerable people and places that we both knew. The julep held out far into the night, and my memory never saw him afterwards otherwise than as bending over it, with his straw, with an attempted air of gravity (after some anecdote involving some wonderfully droll and delicate observation of character), and then, as his eye caught mine, melting into that captivating laugh of his, which was the brightest and best I have ever heard."

There can be no irreverence in imagining these two friends, so close bound in life, recalling in the land of Shadows, that last happy night they spent together on earth, when the happiness was tinged with the sadness of farewell.

CHAPTER XL

AMERICAN FRIENDS (*continued*)—LONGFELLOW

NEXT to Irving, Dickens's best-loved American friend was Longfellow. The earliest reference to the poet in Forster's book is contained in a letter written by Dickens soon after his arrival in the States : " The professors at the Cambridge University, Longfellow, Felton, Jared, Sparks, are noble fellows." A little later he confirmed this first impression : " Longfellow . . . is a frank accomplished man, as well as a fine writer." The poet was a man of a type likely to appeal to Boz—frank, genial, capable of joviality, and ever ready to open his heart to those whom he counted his friends.

They met several times during Dickens's first American tour, and when in the autumn of the same year Longfellow came to England, Dickens was eager to welcome him and repay some of the kindness that he had received across the water. Needless to say, the door of Devonshire Terrace was flung wide open, and there were sounds of revelry by night during the poet's stay in London. " You and I," he wrote to Forster some years later, " were the jolliest of all the youths at Dickens's table in the autumn of 1842." Forster records how, twenty-six years later, the author of " Hiawatha " reminded him of two experiences of many that they enjoyed during the visit. " One of these was a day at Rochester, when, met by one of those prohibitions which are the wonder of visitors and the shame of Englishmen, we overleapt gates and barriers, and, setting at defiance repeated threats of all the terrors of law coarsely expressed to us by the custodian of the place, explored the castle ruins. The other was a night among those portions of the population who outrage the law and defy its terrors all the days of their lives, the tramps and thieves of London; when, under guidance and protection of the most trusted officers of the metropolitan prisons . . . we went over the worst haunts of the most dangerous classes."

Longfellow returned home by the " Great Western," Dickens travelling with him to Bristol, whence he sailed. They next met in America in 1867, and a warm welcome awaited the novelist at Sunnyside. " Dickens was here last night," wrote the poet to

197

Forster; " it is a great pleasure to see Dickens again after so many years, with the same sweetness and flavour as of old." Longfellow was one of the guests at the dinner which followed the great Walking Match between George Dolby (" the Man of Ross ") and James R. Osgood (" the Boston Bantam "). It will be remembered that in the humorous " Articles of Agreement " for this match, drawn up by Dickens (" the Gad's Hill Gasper ") the last two names of those who are to honour the dinner by their presence are " an obscure poet named Longfellow (if discoverable) and Miss Longfellow." The two friends met very often—daily, indeed, whenever Dickens was in Boston—and one of the happiest evenings of the tour was spent at Longfellow's house, when the following immortals dined together : Longfellow, Dickens, Agassiz, Lowell, Holmes, and Bayard Taylor. It is scarcely surprising to find Dolby recording that the dinner was a most enjoyable one, and that the fun flew fast and furious !

In June 1868 Longfellow paid his last visit to England accompanied by his daughters, and Dickens laid himself out to give his friend a right royal time : " At the arrival of friends whom he loved and honoured as he did these, from the great country to which he owed so much," says Forster, " infinite were the rejoicings at Gadshill." The weather was glorious, and though the poet's stay was short, the small house-party had, as Dickens wrote to Fields, " a really good time."

> " I showed them all the neighbouring country that could be shown in so short a time, and they finished off with a tour of inspection of the kitchens, pantry, wine-cellar, pickles, sauces, servants' sitting-room, general household stores, and even the Cellar Book of this illustrious establishment. . . . I turned out a couple of postilions in the old red jacket of the old red royal Dover road, for our ride; and it was like a holiday ride in England fifty years ago."

Just two years later, Longfellow was writing to Forster : " The terrible news from England fills us all with inexpressible sadness. Dickens was so full of life that it did not seem possible he could die, and yet he has gone from us, and we are sorrowing for him. . . . I never knew an author's death cause such general mourning. It is no exaggeration to say that this whole country is stricken with grief."

CHAPTER XLI

AMONG Americans, next to Irving and Longfellow in Dickens's regard came Cornelius Conway Felton, Professor of Greek at Harvard, to whom some of his best and most Dickensian letters were written. " A most delightful fellow " was Dickens's description of him, and we are told by the Editors of the novelist's *Letters* that he was one of the most heartily loved friends. They first met at Boston in 1842, they became firm friends at once, and when Dickens set out on his tour Felton accompanied him as far as New York. A little later we find Dickens writing to this " very dear friend " :

> " You carried away with you more than half the delight and pleasure of my New World; and I heartily wish you could bring it back again. . . . We shall be in Buffalo, please Heaven, on the 30th of April. If I don't find a letter from you in the care of the postmaster at that place, I'll never write to you from England. But if I *do* find one, my right hand shall forget its cunning, before I forget to be your truthful and constant correspondent; not, dear Felton, because I promised it, nor because I have a natural tendency to correspond (which is far from being the case), nor because I am truly grateful to you for, and have been made truly proud by, that affectionate and elegant tribute which —— sent me, but because you are a man after my own heart, and I love you *well*. And for the love I bear you, and the pleasure with which I shall always think of you, and the glow I shall feel when I see your handwriting in my own home, I hereby enter into a solemn league and covenant to write as many letters to you as you write to me, at least. Amen."

And the covenant was kept. In the whole of Dickens's published letters there are none so charming, so redolent of the spirit of the man himself as those written to Prof. Felton. Several of them contain diverting references to oysters. It seems to have been a joke which the pair kept to themselves, more's the pity.

It evidently arose out of some jovialities during their first stay together in New York.   For Felton was a jovial soul.

Their correspondence was regular after Dickens's return to England.   He was untiring in pressing Felton to cross the Atlantic, and all his letters are in the same hearty strain.   " Heavens ! if you were but here at this minute ! . . . With what a shout I would clap you down into the easiest chair, my genial Felton, if you could but appear, and order you a pair of slippers instantly ! " Or, " On the 4th of April I am going to preside at a public dinner for the benefit of the printers ; and if you were a guest at that table, wouldn't I smite you on the shoulder, harder than ever I rapped the well-beloved back of Washington Irving at the City Hotel in New York."   Or again : " Yesterday morning, New Year's Day . . . the postman came to the door with a knock, for which I denounced him from my heart.   Seeing your hand upon the cover of a letter which he brought, I immediately blessed him, presented him with a glass of whiskey, inquired after his family (they are all well) and opened the dispatch with a moist and oystery twinkle in my eye.   And on the very day from which the new year dates, I read your New Year congratulations as punctually as if you lived in the same house !   Why don't you ! . . . Countless happy years to you and yours, my dear Felton, and some instalment of them, however slight, in England, in the loving company of THE PROSCRIBED ONE.   Oh, breathe not his name ! "

" A few days of unalloyed enjoyment were given to the visit of his excellent American friend Felton."   It is disappointing that this should be Forster's only reference to Felton's long anticipated visit to England.   Nor can I find any reference elsewhere.   But it is not difficult to picture the meeting of the friends, the hearty smite upon the shoulder, the " gleaming spectacles " ;   or to hear in imagination their hearty laughter as they recalled that joke about the oysters (we may be sure they had an oyster feast together).   We can picture Dickens's " unalloyed enjoyment " as he welcomed his guest, and showed him the sights of London ; took him to the George and Vulture, or to the Belle Sauvage, or perhaps to the Spaniards and Jack Straw's.   It was the last time they met, though their correspondence continued uninterruptedly until Felton's death in 1862.

CHAPTER XLII

AMERICAN FRIENDS (*continued*)—HOLMES, LOWELL, AND OTHERS

OLIVER WENDELL HOLMES was only thirty-three years old when Dickens first met him in 1842, and he had to live another twenty years before achieving fame as the Autocrat. To the world at large he was quite unknown, but in Boston, where, in the previous year, he had started in general practice as a doctor, he moved in the best cultured circles, and was sufficiently prominent in the life of the city to be selected one of the vice-presidents of the dinner which was given in Boz's honour. One of the events of that evening was the singing of a song which Holmes had written specially for the occasion. He sang it himself, too, to the tune of " Gramachree."

During this first visit no friendship was formed, which is not surprising, for Holmes being an unknown man it was hardly likely he would be brought into personal touch with Dickens. But when Dickens returned to America twenty-five years later Holmes was famous, and well-beloved by the English-speaking peoples, and was one of America's chief citizens whom the novelist desired to know. He was one of the first to bid the traveller welcome, and whenever Dickens was in Boston, Dolby tells us, the Autocrat's society was a great pleasure to him. It is a pity they had not come to know each other long before, for they must have been kindred souls.

James Russell Lowell was still younger than Holmes, but in 1842 he already had to his credit a volume of poems which had found considerable favour. He was one of the committee which waited upon Dickens to invite him to the Boston dinner, but they did not become personally intimate until the novelist's second visit. Then they saw a great deal of each other, and formed a strong mutual regard. In 1869 Dickens welcomed Lowell's daughter to Gadshill with delight, and made her stay there with James T. Fields and his wife memorable.

There were other American friends whom Dickens liked well, with whom he was very friendly, who showed him many kindnesses, but with whom there was nothing of that intimacy that existed with Irving, Longfellow, and Felton. Emerson was one

201

of these, as might be supposed, and Dickens was glad to welcome him when he came to England. George William Childs was another. There were also George Bancroft (" a famous man, a straightforward, manly, earnest heart "); Washington Allston (" a fine specimen of a glorious old genius "); William Henry Channing (" just the man he ought to be "); John Lathrop Motley (who the late Frederick Locker-Lampson tells us was very fond of Dickens); Richard Henry Dana (" a very nice fellow "); Henry Clay (" a most *charming* fellow ") Fitz-Greene Hallack (" a merry little man "); David Colden (" I am deeply in love with his wife. Indeed, we have received the greatest and most earnest and zealous kindness from the whole family, and quite love them all "); William Cullen Bryant (" sad and very reserved "); W. H. Prescott (for whose work Dickens had a great admiration : " I wrote to Prescott about his book, with which I was perfectly charmed. I think his descriptions masterly, his style brilliant, his purpose manly and gallant always "); Bayard Taylor (whose visits to Gadshill in 1869 were a special enjoyment to the novelist); and Charles Eliot Norton.

There remain James T. Fields and his wife, and his partner, James R. Osgood, for whom a separate chapter is reserved.

CHAPTER XLIII

AMERICAN FRIENDS (*continued*)—MR. AND MRS. JAMES T. FIELDS

THERE never was a period in all his life when Dickens so needed friendship as during that tragic American tour of 1867–8, and he was indeed happy in the friendship of Mr. and Mrs. James T. Fields. They looked after him as though he were their only son, and again and again and again he speaks in his letters home of their unceasing kindness.

Dickens and Fields became acquainted in the way of business, for Fields was a partner in the famous publishing house of Ticknor and Fields. From his earliest days, however, Fields had been one of the novelist's most enthusiastic admirers, and he has recorded something of the enthusiasm he felt in his book, " Yesterdays with Authors."

They first met in London in 1859, though they had had business dealings some time prior to that date. Their acquaintance quickly ripened into a strong friendship as a result of personal inter-course. Fields spent a happy day at Gadshill, and within a month we find Dickens concluding a letter thus : " Believe me always (and here I for ever renounce ' Mr.' as having anything whatever to do with our communications, and as being a mere preposterous interloper), Faithfully yours, Charles Dickens." Fields was possessed by the desire that Dickens should read in America, and during this visit he urged it upon the novelist, but the Civil War came in 1860, and the idea had to be abandoned for years. But Fields never allowed the matter to drop, and his ambition was realised in 1867. And when at last Dickens crossed the Atlantic, Fields and his wife laid themselves out to make his stay in the land of the Stars and Stripes as happy and as comfortable as it could be made. Over and over again Dolby tells us how devoted the pair were to the novelist, and Dickens himself bears frequent testimony. In almost every one of his letters home, he told of their devotion to him : " Mrs. Fields is more delightful than ever, and Fields more hospitable. My room is always radiant with brilliant flowers of their sending." Again : " They are the most devoted of friends, and never in the way, and never out of it."

Of course, Fields entered into the fun of the great Walking Match. In the articles drawn up by the " Gad's Hill Gasper," he is described as " James T. Fields, known in sporting circles as Massachusetts Jemmy," and he is named as one of the " umpires, starters, and declarers of victory." Dolby was beaten because he allowed Osgood to get too far away from him, supposing that he had poor staying power. " My supposition," he says, " probably would have been confirmed had not Mrs. Fields arrived on the scene in her carriage, and turning round, accompanied Osgood the rest of the walk, plying him the whole time with *bread soaked in brandy!* We all, with the exception of Osgood, of course, felt that she showed great favouritism in this respect, but she frankly admitted that she would have done the same by me if she had met me first. . . ."

In a letter to his daughter, Dickens described the dinner which followed :

> " As she (Mrs. Fields) had done so much for me in the way of flowers, I thought I would show her a sight in that line at the dinner. You never saw anything like it. Two immense crowns; the base of the choicest exotics; and the loops oval masses of violets. In the centre of the table an immense basket, overflowing with bell-mouthed lilies; all round the table a bright green border of wreathed creeper, with clustering roses at intervals; a rose for every buttonhole, and a bouquet for every lady."

Says Fields, " David Copperfield, Hyperion, Hosea Biglow, the Autocrat, and the Bad Boy were present, and there was no need for set speeches. The ladies present, being all daughters of America, smiled upon the champion, and we had a great good time." Let us recall an incident of the dinner, and judge whether he is right in saying that the company had a great good time. Dickens had described the plan he adopted when preparing a speech, and he proceeded to give a practical illustration. They were to have a mimic election, and the candidates were to be Dolby and Biglow. Dickens was to voice the claims of the former, and Fields those of the latter. Dolby shall tell the rest :

> " In his endeavour to establish my claims as a fit and proper person to represent the borough, Mr. Dickens instanced the fact that I had no hair on the top of my head, whereas the rival candidate, being plentifully supplied with that article, could not be considered a desirable person to

represent any borough in the House of Commons. After he had finished his speech, which was of the most ludicrous description, Fields commenced his, but was never allowed to finish it, for he was continually interrupted by Mr. Dickens in a variety of voices and cries, such as ' Down with the hairy aristocracy ! ' ' Up with the chap with the shiny top ! ' etc.; the whole resulting in such an uproar that poor Fields had no chance. The outbursts of laughter were so loud and continuous, and the side-splitting pain so great in consequence, that it was with sheer exhaustion that we all gave up and retired for the night."

Such events as this, however, were but glimpses of the sun through the clouds, for throughout the tour Dickens was labouring against the utmost physical distress. All the time Fields and his wife were kindness personified. " The Fields were all and everything to him in his illness," says Dolby, " and the affectionate attention of Mrs. Fields, who, as usual, had decorated his rooms with flowers, and the genial society of Fields did much to make him forget his sufferings." To the end of his life he remembered all this with gratitude. The affection between the two men deepened, and when at last Boz set his face homewards, Fields was remembered among his best-loved friends.

In May 1869 Fields and his wife came to England, and needless to say, Dickens welcomed them with the utmost heartiness. Fields has told the story of that visit fully. Dickens showed him round London as well as round the beauty spots of Kent, and at his visitor's special request, mounted a staircase at Furnival's Inn, which he had not mounted for very many years, in order to show him the very room in which the first page of *Pickwick* was written. They visited some of the slums, and haunts of crime, and saw together the opium den which was afterwards literally described in *Edwin Drood*. They went over the General Post Office; they explored the Temple, Dickens taking his friend to Pip's room; they rambled through the quaint old city of Rochester, through the Cobham Woods to Cobham Park, and on to the Leather Bottle; and one glorious day the whole house-party drove over to Canterbury and trod the streets that little David Copperfield so often trod. On another day, Cooling was their destination; and yet another favourite walk was to Kit's Coty House. After a tour on the continent, the visitors again spent some pleasant days at Gadshill, and then they sailed for home, never again to see him whom they loved so truly.

With James R. Osgood and with Ticknor, Fields's partners, Dickens was on the best of terms, but neither has a claim to be classed with Fields among his intimate friends. To Osgood, however, he was particularly indebted for many kindnesses during the Reading Tour, and he acknowledges this in several of his letters.

CHAPTER XLIV

RICHARD MONCKTON MILNES

DICKENS'S return from America in June 1842 " was the occasion of unbounded enjoyment," says Forster. "A Greenwich dinner in which several friends (Talfourd, Milnes, Procter, Maclise, Stanfield, Marryat, Barham, Hood, and Cruikshank among them) took part, and other immediate gatherings followed." With all but one of these friends we have already dealt. Let us speak of him now.

The Marquis of Crewe suggests to me that his father was one of a group of " outer acquaintances " of Dickens's. He says : " Both he and my mother were on terms of pleasant and intimate acquaintanceship with Dickens, and I have a few letters and notes from him to both. But I do not think that they met regularly or often, and I am pretty sure that Dickens never stayed at Fryston, and that my father was never a guest at Gadshill." It is true that Milnes was not a member of the innermost Dickens circle; but there was more than one Dickens circle. We might say there were three circles—innermost, inner, and outer, and then we might place Milnes in the second of these. At one time, when both were in their heyday, they certainly did meet frequently. Forster couples him with Marryat as a welcome companion in the very early days, and later, dealing with the period 1848–51, he speaks of Milnes as " familiar with Dickens over all the period since, and still more prominent in Tavistock House days, when, with Lady Houghton, he brought fresh claims to my friend's admiration and regard." So early as 1840 they were sufficiently intimate for Dickens to address his letters with the familiar " My dear Milnes."

It was at about this time that Dickens received the inevitable invitation to breakfast (Carlyle, it will be remembered, said that if Christ were to come on earth Milnes would ask Him to breakfast), and his reply was : " I never went out to breakfast in my life, and am afraid to try how one feels under such circumstances ; but I will be with you next Friday at eleven o'clock for purposes of small talk—that being the day which did itself the honour of presenting me to the world twenty-eight years ago." But at some subsequent date unrecorded he summoned up his courage,

for in 1862 we find him writing : " Many thanks. But I have
been out to breakfast only twice in my life—both times ages ago
—once with Rogers, and once with you in Pall Mall. Moreover,
I read *Copperfield* on Thursday night. And when I do that, I am
in lavender on a shelf all day."

But let us refer again to the first of these two letters. Milnes
had evidently hinted at some humorous notion that he had, for
Dickens's letter continues :

" I really would immortalise myself, if I were you, by
presenting that national anthem of the Seven Dials. It is
a capital notion. Perhaps you have heard that song in the
streets about the Queen's marriage, whereof the burden is
(Her Majesty being supposed to sing it) :

> " ' So let 'em say whate'er they may,
>   Or do whate'er they can ;
>   Prince Halbert he vill allvays be
>   My own dear Fancy Man.'

" There is another prose composition in the form of a
catechism. This is performed by two gentlemen, and opens
thus :

" Question.—Vell, Mr. Bull, Sir, what is your private
opinions vith respectin' to German sassages—fresh and im-
ported, Sir, from Saxe Humbug and Go-to-her ?

" Answer (in a melancholy growl).—My opinion is, Sir, as
they comes very dear.

" Question.—Supposin', Mr. Bull, as these here foreign
sassages wos to cost the country a matter of thirty thousand
pound per annewum, who do you think ought to spend
that 'ere wast and enormous expenditer ?

" Answer.—Them as awails theirselves o' the sassages
aforesaid. (A laugh in the crowd.)

" Question.—Then, in your opinion, Mr. Bull, they're a
dear commodity ?

" Answer.—I consider, Sir, as they would be uncommon
dear at any price, and what I says is, let us revert to the
good wholesome home-made dairy-fed native sassages—the
Cambridge sassages of right down English manafacter—the
Protestant sassages as our forefathers and Marshal Blucher
fought and bled for. (Great applause.)

" (Both sing) :

> " Oh *didn't* the Prince look as sweet as new honey
>   Ven Melbourne said, Johnny should get the full money ;
>   And *isn't* his missis with Joe rayther vild,
>   Now they're almost too proud to vet-nurse the child."

Dickens had a very high regard for Milnes as a literary man, as a friend of literary men, as an enlightened and Liberal politician, as a champion of the oppressed, and as a man of very exceptional charm. Here is an estimate of this fine man taken from a mere book of reference : " A Mæcenas of poets, he got Lord Tennyson the laureateship, soothed the dying hours of poor David Gray, and was one of the first to recognise Mr. Swinburne's genius. . . . Besides this, he was a traveller, a philanthropist, an unrivalled after-dinner speaker, and Rogers's successor in the art of breakfast-giving. . . . He championed oppressed nationalities, liberty of conscience, fugitive slaves, the rights of women; and carried a bill for establishing reformatories." Add to this his culture and his great social charm, and it is very easy to understand that he possessed a very strong attraction for Dickens. His liberal views, we may be sure, appealed to Dickens, and his never-failing readiness to help literature and literary men could not but win him the regard of a man who was so jealous of the dignity and good name of his profession. The two men had much in common, and their friendship was very natural. Milnes had the same high opinion of Dickens's gifts that nearly all the world had, and he also came under the magic spell of the man's personality. Dickens, too, appreciated Milnes the poet. The latter sent him a copy of his " Palm Leaves " in 1844, and here is his acknowledgment :

> " I have not acknowledged the receipt of your highly esteemed present because I think it a poor compliment to thank an author for his book without having first read it. I am now in a condition to thank you, and honestly to assure you that the elegance, tenderness, and thoughtful fancy of the ' Palm Leaves ' have greatly charmed me, and have made an impression on me such as I believe you would yourself desire and would be satisfied with—fully."

In 1869 Milnes (then, of course, Lord Houghton) spoke at the Liverpool banquet to Dickens. He expressed regret that Dickens abstained from public life, and (in Forster's words) " half reproached him for alleged unkindly sentiments to the House of Lords." Dickens waxed rather vehement in denying the latter charge, and referring to the number of members of the upper House whom he counted personal friends, said : " Taking these circumstances into consideration, I was rather amazed by my noble friend's accusation." And he added : " When I asked him, on his sitting down, what amazing devil possessed him to make this charge, he replied that he had never forgotten the

P

days of Lord Verisopht. Then, ladies and gentlemen, I understood it all. Because it is a remarkable fact that in the days
when that depreciative and profoundly unnatural character was
invented there was no Lord Houghton in the House of Lords.
And there was in the House of Commons a rather indifferent
member called Richard Monckton Milnes."

Then he took up the other charge, prefacing his reply with
" here I am more serious." The reply was that well-known
passage in which he declared his life-long determination that
literature should be his sole profession by which he would stand
or fall. Commenting on this, Forster says : " Here, however, he
probably failed to see the entire meaning of Lord Houghton's
regret, which would seem to have been meant to say in more
polite form, that to have taken some part in public affairs might
have shown him the difficulty in a free state of providing remedies
very swiftly for evils of long growth." That difficulty Dickens
never seems fully to have realised.

But this little difference of opinion made no difference to their
friendship, and in another public speech—in his Literary Fund
address in 1866—Lord Houghton made a very appreciative reference to Dickens, who acknowledged it : " Many thanks for your
kindness in sending me the printed notes of your Literary Fund
address, and many more for your reference to myself. It is a
touching and acceptable reminder to me that a good many years
have gone by since we first knew each other."

With Lady Houghton, too, Dickens was on pleasant terms of
friendship, and I am able to quote one letter to her. It is dated
July 18, 1862 :

> " I think the photograph of your charming labour of love
> from the *Cricket* comes out exceedingly well : though it does
> not render full justice to the delicacy and beauty of your
> design. It is highly interesting to me to have it, and I
> thank you for it heartily.
>
> .   .   .   .
>
> " I am glad you like *Copperfield*. It is far more interest-
> ing to me than any of the other Readings, and I am half
> ashamed to confess—even to you—what a tenderness I have
> for it."

Lord Houghton's biographer [1] tells us that there was a very
old tie uniting the family at Fryston with the author of *Pickwick*.
" When Lady Houghton," he says, " was a girl at Crewe, the
person who filled the responsible office of housekeeper at Crewe

[1] T. Wemyss Reid.

Hall was a Mrs. Dickens, the grandmother of Charles." Lady Houghton, he adds, used to say that when she was a child the greatest treat that could be given to herself and her brother and sister was an afternoon in the housekeeper's room, " for Mrs. Dickens was an inimitable story-teller, and she loved to have the children round her, and to beguile them, not only with fairy tales, but with reminiscences of her own and stories from the pages of history. It was natural, therefore, that when, after her marriage, Lady Houghton became personally acquainted with Charles Dickens she should feel a peculiar interest in him. Not very long before Dickens's death a dinner was arranged at Lady Houghton's town house chiefly for the purpose of enabling the Prince of Wales and the King of the Belgians to make the acquaintance of the great writer."

When Dickens died, Lord Houghton wrote to his son, the present Marquis of Crewe : " I fear you never saw Charles Dickens. When he dined with us to meet the Prince of Wales he pressed us to visit Gadshill any day, and we might have been there at the time of his seizure. He has died happily in the zenith of his fame." But the son had met Dickens, for he writes to me : " I can well remember seeing the great man at Upper Brook Street, where my father then lived, my sister and I having come down after dinner. But no special point attaches to the recollection, though his appearance is vividly clear to my mind."

Proof that Lord Houghton was an intimate friend of Dickens's is provided by the fact that it was through him that Dean Stanley made the offer of a grave in Westminster Abbey.

CHAPTER XLV

THE private reading of *The Chimes* at Forster's chambers in December 1844, to which several references have been made, was of far-reaching influence in Dickens's life. It was the forerunner of the historic readings with which he took this country and America by storm in the last dozen years of his life, and which undoubtedly cut short that life. And out of it also arose those amateur theatricals which became so famous. There remain three who were present on that occasion to whom no reference has yet been made. Dyce was present as Forster's friend. By virtue of that friendship he was, of course, well acquainted with Dickens, but he was never a member of the Dickens circle, and calls for no more mention here. William Johnson Fox also was more Forster's friend than Dickens's, and never penetrated beyond the outer Dickens circle. I doubt if his personality was such as to appeal very much to Dickens, but, on the other hand, his ardent advocacy of every sort of reform that had Dickens's passionate sympathy could not but win him the esteem of the novelist. Intellectually—or rather, politically—they had almost everything in common. Fox, when Dickens first knew him, was a Unitarian minister, and we know that in those early days the novelist was much drawn to the Unitarian creed. He was, next to Cobden and Bright, perhaps the greatest of the anti-Corn Law orators, and Dickens felt very strongly on that question. But more important than that in Dickens's eyes, we may be sure, was Fox's advocacy of popular education. There was no reform which Dickens more earnestly and consistently urged all his life, and Fox was the first man to introduce a Bill into Parliament to bring it about.

But though on political questions the two men were absolutely at one, they had nothing else in common. Why, then, was Fox invited to the Lincoln's Inn reading? Mainly, in all probability, because he was one of the most powerful journalistic advocates of social reform, and in *The Chimes* Dickens was hoping to strike a great blow for the poor. Carlyle, Jerrold, Maclise, and Harness were invited for quite different reasons.

Fox's chief association with Dickens was in connection with

212

the " Daily News," on the staff of which he was engaged as a
leader-writer. We are told that the appointment was due to
Forster's influence with Dickens, but we may be sure that the
novelist was glad to secure the services of so able a journalist,
whose views were so completely in sympathy with the avowed
policy of the paper. Fox's daughter says : " The paper promised
to be as Radical as even Mr. Fox could desire, Dickens's enlightened
and enthusiastic views as to elevating the character of the press,
as to the crying need of popular education, and for generally
raising the status of the poor ; and for reform of various social
anomalies, were completely in sympathy with those long-advocated
by Mr. Fox."

That this was the case is proved by a note of Fox's to Miss
Eliza Flower : " Forster's position does not show him off well.
It brings out his worst points. Dickens and I are regularly
against him on almost everything involving a difference of opinion."
How autocratic Dickens was as editor even in those days is shown
by his note to Fox, dated January 21, 1846, in which he says :
" Your leader most excellent. I made bold to take out Bright's
name, for reasons I hinted at the other day, and which I think
have validity. He is unscrupulous and indiscreet, Cobden never
so." Which reveals a curious prejudice which history does not
justify.

When Dickens left the " Daily News," Fox remained, working
under Forster, but he had practically no association with the
novelist thenceforth.

The Rev. William Harness, who is depicted in tears in Maclise's
drawing, was almost an idolator where Dickens was concerned,
and he and his sister were sincerely esteemed by the novelist.
He was a simple sociable soul, and Forster speaks of occasional
days with him and his sister and of " social entertainments "
with him, but he was twenty-two years older than Dickens, and
a staid London clergyman, with views that were none too broad,
and there could not be any deep sympathy between the two.
I think the Rev. A. G. L'Estrange sums up their relations very
accurately in his " Literary Life of the Rev. William Harness."

" Dickens," he says, " was a very kind friend to Mr.
Harness ; he regarded him as one of the literary men of the
past, and occasionally asked his opinion and sent him little
presents, which were of course gratifying. Mr. Harness fully
appreciated the great novelist and his works, and was
supremely happy whenever he could persuade ' Charles ' to
be a guest at his table. When Dickens was giving readings
in his later years he told Mr. Harness that he would always

have a chair placed for him close to the platform; but Mr. Harness never accepted the kind offer, although he attended all his recitations, and on these appointed nights it was impossible to persuade him to accept any invitations."

On the one side, an enthusiastic admiration and worship; on the other, a genuine respect for a much older man who had achieved some distinction in the literary world before *Pickwick* was thought of : that is all. How could there be a very close sympathy between Dickens and a man who held the views that " people should be educated according to their stations " ! " It is certainly just and right," says the Rev. William Harness, " kind to the individual and advantageous to the public, that every man endowed with extraordinary talents such as Sir Robert Arkwright and Professor Lee should, however humble his circumstances, be afforded the educational means of raising himself above it. To effect this, if he be imbued with sound Christian principles as his guide, reading and writing—the ability of collecting the ideas of others and imparting his own—are quite sufficient."

We still meet with this point of view to-day : it was commoner sixty or seventy years ago, but Dickens never had any patience with it, and he could not have been in much sympathy with a man who could think thus.

The Rev. A. G. L'Estrange tells us that notes frequently passed between Dickens and Harness, but that they were unimportant, " though always neatly worded "; and he adds that Dickens was too fully engaged to write long letters, " even had he not been a man of too active a character to spend his time in that way." Which makes curious reading to those who know what a voluminous letter-writer the novelist was ! The truth is that Harness was not the man to whom Dickens could " let himself go " in any sense. He had the novelist's esteem, but there never existed anything like an intimacy.

CHAPTER XLVI

MR. AND MRS. WATSON

DICKENS spent the summer of 1846 in Switzerland, and at Lausanne formed some of the most appreciated friendships of his life. Chiefest among these was that with the Hon. R. and Mrs. Watson. It struck a note of earnestness and affection that was quite remarkable even for him. For both Mr. and Mrs. Watson he formed an extraordinary regard. " I loved him as my heart," he wrote to Charles Knight when Watson died, " I cannot think of him without tears." A few years later he wrote to Mrs. Watson : " I send you my sincere love, I am always truthful to the dear old days and the memory of one of the dearest friends I ever loved." And of Mrs. Watson he wrote to Mary Boyle in 1858 : " You know what an affection I have for Mrs. Watson, and how happy it made me to see her again."

During that summer of 1846 they had many happy days together, seeing all the sights, and the memory of those days lasted with Dickens to the end of his life.

His letters to Mrs. Watson (her husband died in 1852) were frequent and lengthy thenceforth, and in almost all of them we find some winsome reference to " the tender grace of a day that is dead." It was indeed, as Mrs. Watson's daughter has said, " a most remarkable friendship " that sprang up, and after Watson had gone, it was maintained in all its earnestness with the widow.

Dickens's first visit to Rockingham Castle, the Northamptonshire home of the Watsons, was paid at the end of 1849. During that visit he wrote an amusing letter to Forster :

" Picture to yourself, my dear F., a large old-fashioned castle, approached by an ancient keep, portcullis, etc., etc., filled with company, waited on by six-and-twenty servants ; the slops (and wine-glasses) continually being emptied ;[1] and my clothes (with myself in them) always being carried off to all sorts of places ; and you will have a faint idea of the

---

[1] The letter was written in the character of an American visitor to England, in parody of a book recently published. See *Miscellaneous Papers :* " An American in Europe."

mansion in which I am at present staying. I should have written to you yesterday, but for having had a very busy day. Among the guests is a Miss B.,[1] sister of the Honourable Miss B. (of Salem, Mass.) whom we once met at the house of our distinguished literary countryman, Colonel Landor. This lady is renowned as an amateur actress, so last night we got up in the great hall some scenes from the ' School for Scandal '; the scene with the lunatic on the wall, from the *Nicholas Nickleby* of Major-General the Hon. C. Dickens (Richmond, Va.); some conjuring; and then finished off with country dances; of which we had two admirably good ones, quite new to me, though really old. Getting the words, and making preparations occupied (as you may believe) the whole day, and it was three o'clock before I got to bed. It was an excellent entertainment, and we were all uncommonly merry. . . . Of all the country houses and estates I have yet seen in England, I think this is by far the best. Everything undertaken eventuates in a most magnificent hospitality. . . . At a future time it will be my duty to report on the turnips, mangel-wurzels, ploughs, and live-stock; and for the present I will only say that I regard it as fortunate for the neighbouring community that this patrimony should have fallen to my spirited and enlightened host. Every one has profited by it, and the labouring people in especial are thoroughly well cared for and looked after. To see all the household, headed by an enormously fat housekeeper, occupying the back benches last night, laughing and applauding without any restraint; and to see a blushing, sleek-headed footman produce, for the watch-trick, a silver watch of the most portentous dimensions, amidst the rapturous delight of his brethren and sisterhood; was a very pleasant spectacle, even to a conscientious republican like yourself or me. . . ."

Forster says : " Dickens, during the too brief time his excellent friend was spared to him, often repeated his visits to Rockingham, always a surpassing enjoyment; and in the winter of 1850 he accomplished there, with help of the country carpenter, ' a very elegant little theatre,' of which he constituted himself manager." And he adds that after the performance Dickens took part in a country dance, which lasted far into the morning, travelled 120 miles to London the next day, and dined with the Prime Minister in the evening. F. G. Kitton, in " The Dickens Country," also says that this performance took place in 1850, but as a matter

[1] Miss Mary Boyle.

ROCKINGHAM CASTLE, NORTHAMPTONSHIRE,
the home of the Hon. Mr. and Mrs. Richard Watson

THE HON. RICHARD WATSON   THE HON. MRS. RICHARD WATSON

of fact it was in January 1851. The pieces played were " Used
Up " and " Animal Magnetism," and for the latter Dickens wrote
a " tag " for the occasion, of which I quote the concluding lines :

> "Stay yet again. Among us all I feel
> One subtle, all-pervading influence steal,
> Stirring one wish within our heart and head ;
> Bright be the path our host and hostess tread !
> Blest be their children, happy be their race,
> Long may they live, this ancient hall to grace ;
> Long bear of English virtues noble fruit—
> Green-hearted Rockingham ! strike deep thy root."

At this time he was busy on *Copperfield*, which was to be dedicated to the Watsons. In July 1850 he had written : " Every one
is cheering *David* on, and I hope to make *your book* a good one.
I like it very much myself—thoroughly believe in it all, and go to
the work every month with an energy of the finest description."
The fact that he dedicated his " favourite child " to these friends
is strongest possible proof of the earnestness of the regard he had
for them.

The next book to *Copperfield* was *Bleak House*, and in this
he immortalised Rockingham Castle as Chesney Wold. There is
nothing speculative in this as there is with so many " Dickens-
land " identifications. We have his own authority for it, for in
a letter to Mrs. Watson he wrote : " In some of the descriptions
of Chesney Wold I have taken many bits, chiefly about trees and
shadows, from observations made at Rockingham."

In August 1852 Mr. Watson died, and Dickens was greatly
distressed. He had been at Rockingham in the spring, and had
been shocked by his friend's decline, but death was not anticipated,
and when it came the novelist was pained as he rarely was by such
an event.

> " I cannot bear," he wrote to the widow, " to be silent
> longer, though I know full well—no one better, I think, how
> your love for him, and your trust in God, and your love for
> your children will have come to the help of such a nature
> as yours, and whispered better things than any friendship
> can, however faithful and affectionate.
>
> " We held him so close in our hearts—all of us here—and
> have been so happy with him, and so used to say how good
> he was, and what a gentle, generous, noble spirit he had,
> and how he shone out among common men as something so
> real and genuine, and full of every kind of worthiness, that
> it has often brought the tears into my eyes to talk of him ;
> we have been so accustomed to do this when we looked

forward to years of unchanged intercourse, that now, when everything but truth goes down into the dust, those recollections which make the sword so sharp pour balm into the wound.   And if it be a consolation to us to know the virtues of his character, and the reasons that we had for loving him, O how much greater is your comfort who were so devoted to him, and were the happiness of his life !

"May God, who has received into His rest through this affliction as good a man as ever I can know and love and mourn for on this earth, be good to you, dear friends, through these coming years !   May all those compassionate and hopeful lessons of the great Teacher who shed divine tears for the dead bring their full comfort to you !   I have no fear of that, my confidence is certainty.

"If you should ever set up a record in the little church, I would try to word it myself, and God knows out of the fulness of my heart, if you should think it well.
"My dear Friend, yours with the truest affection and sympathy."

Mrs. Watson's daughter says that Dickens kept up his letter-writing to her mother "with the same bubbling over thoughts and rare good literature."   So he did, until he himself went to join his well-loved friend; and every letter breathed the sincerity and depth of his friendship.

CHAPTER XLVII

WILLIAM HALDIMAND, MONS. DE CERJAT, AND THE BROOKFIELDS

THE friendship with William Haldimand was, next to that with the Watsons, the most valued of those formed at Lausanne. Formerly a member of Parliament, he had left England and settled in Lausanne, where he had a fine seat just below Rosemont and where, as Forster says, " his character and situation had made him quite the little sovereign of the place." Inevitably Dickens met him directly he arrived in the town, and was so heartily received and so pleasantly entertained that a great friendship sprang up. He paid a tribute to those happy days and pleasant friendships by dedicating *The Battle of Life*, published in that same year, to his English friends in Switzerland—" a dedication," he wrote to Haldimand, " that is printed in illuminated capitals on my heart." Writing in November, he said :

> " I shall trouble you with a little parcel of three or four copies to distribute to those whose names will be found written in them, as soon as they can be made ready, and believe me, that there is no success or approval in the great world beyond the Jura that will be more precious and delightful to me than the hope that I shall be remembered of an evening in the coming winter time, at one or two friends' I could mention near the Lake of Geneva. It runs with a spring tide that will always flow and never ebb through my memory; and nothing less than the waters of Lethe shall confuse the music of its running, until it loses itself in that great sea, for which all the currents of our life are desperately bent."

In the following April the novelist's fifth son was born, and Dickens paid further tribute to that Lausanne holiday by inviting Haldimand to become godfather.

Meetings between the friends were of course rare—indeed, as far as I can find, they never did actually meet after 1847.

It should be added that M. de Cerjat and his wife—" clever and agreeable both far beyond the ordinary," says Forster—took part in most of the happy excursions at Lausanne, and after Dickens's return to England, de Cerjat began a custom of writing Dickens a long letter every Christmas. Practically without a break this custom was continued until de Cerjat's death in 1869, Dickens replying regularly. Most, if not all, of the novelist's letters are preserved, and they prove the depth of the friendship that he entertained for de Cerjat; they are among the longest and most charming of all his letters, and certainly are the most " newsy." I can find no record of it anywhere, but the following sentence in the last letter of the series, written in January 1869, certainly suggests that de Cerjat had visited England and been a guest at Gadshill : " You wouldn't recognise Gadshill now; I have so changed it and bought land about it." Certain it is that the friends met in 1853, for Dickens, in a letter from Milan, in October of that year, records that " Cerjat accompanied us on a miserably wet morning, in a heavy rain, down the lake."

There was a lesser friendship of which the seed was sown at Lausanne. Henry Hallam (with whom Dickens was acquainted) came on a visit to Haldimand. Writing to Forster about the visit, Dickens said : " Heavens ! how Hallam did talk yesterday ! I don't think I ever saw him so tremendous. Very good-natured and pleasant, in his way, but Good Heavens ! how he did talk. That famous day you and I remember was nothing to it. His son was with him, and his daughter (who has an impediment in her speech, as if nature were determined to balance that faculty in the family), and his niece, a pretty woman, the wife of a clergyman and a friend of Thackeray's. It strikes me that she must be ' the little woman ' he proposed to take us to drink tea with, once, in Golden Square. Don't you remember ? His great favourite ? She is quite a charming person, anyhow." This great favourite of Thackeray's was Mrs. Brookfield, wife of the Rev. W. H. Brook-field. The Editors of Dickens's *Letters* declare that the Rev. W. H. and Mrs. Brookfield were held in high estimation by the novelist. We may accept that readily enough, but I very strongly doubt if Brookfield was ever a friend. They were fairly well acquainted—sufficiently well for Dickens to seek Brookfield's advice in the choice of a tutor for one of his sons—but I cannot imagine what they could have had in common, save certain mutual friendships—with the Procters in particular. There was a con-sciousness of intellectual superiority about Brookfield that could never have had any charm for Dickens. There seems to have been, too, a decidedly un-Dickensian vein of uncharitableness in him. It is not pleasing to observe the tone in which he speaks in some of his letters of some of his brother clerics; one he dis-misses in charmingly Christian fashion as " the fool." There is an atmosphere of " superior person " about him all the time.

Five years before his wife met the novelist, he had written to her : " I detest *Humphrey's Clock* more than I can tell you—I really find no genius in it. Except Swiveller and Mrs. Jarley I have not found a natural character in the story. (All the rest are badly selected—badly conceived—badly overdrawn.) Not one of them is a type of a class. And for structure, surely never was a story worse. No—Dickens won't do." So away had gone Dickens with a sweep of the arm, in the true Podsnappian manner !

In 1845 he had written in his diary : " In the evening read Dickens's *Chimes*, as utter trash as was ever trodden underfoot." Two years later he wrote to his wife : " *Dombey*, if possible, viler than ever." In 1844 he attended the Artists' dinner, and wrote afterwards to his wife : " Dickens spoke shortly and well enough, but it had a very cut and dried air and rather pompous and shapely in its construction and delivered in a rather sonorous deep voice. Not a jot of humour in it. He looks like Milnes, same height and shape, still longer hair, but not his demoniacal good humour of expression." So we see that whilst he regarded Dickens's work as trash, he also refused to acknowledge that the novelist was a gifted public speaker, in which I declare positively he stands absolutely alone. Brookfield was on most intimate terms with one of Dickens's best loved friends—R. W. Procter; he was especially intimate with Thackeray, who was friendly with Dickens from the *Pickwick* days ; yet Dickens's letter from Lausanne makes it very clear that they had not met up to 1846. When they did meet I do not know, but the first recorded meeting was at the Procters' in January 1859. It seems inconceivable that he should have allowed another twelve years to elapse before becoming personally acquainted with the novelist, but it would appear that that was the case. The only possible conclusion to be drawn from all these facts is that Brookfield did not want to know Dickens. But, indeed, he was out of sympathy with Dickens and things Dickensian. The two men did become fairly well acquainted, but never in the least degree intimate. As the authors of " Mrs. Brookfield and her Circle " put it, Brookfield always kept up with him " a pleasant if not particularly close friendship." To sum up, Brookfield was too " superior " for the Dickens Circle ; Dickens could never have been at home in the Brookfield Set.

With Mrs. Brookfield there was a pleasant friendliness. She was a woman of exceptional charm, with a far greater capacity for friendship than her husband possessed, and Dickens certainly was one of her greatest admirers. She gave him an unpleasant task once. She sent him the manuscript of a novel she had written, hoping that he might find it suitable for *All the Year*

Round. He did not, and he " turned it down " in a letter that bears tribute alike to his friendship for her and to his consideration for the feelings of another. He told her why the book was unsuitable for publication in serial form, and then he offered some kindly and helpful criticism.

He thought the book might be successful in two-volume form, supposing " the polishing I have hinted at (not a meretricious adornment, but positively necessary to good work and good art) to have been first thoroughly administered," and he concluded : " Now, don't hate me, if you can help it. I can afford to be hated by some people, but I am not rich enough to put you in possession of that luxury."

It was not fair of Mrs. Brookfield to give Dickens so unpleasant a task. Adelaide Procter showed a much finer sense when she submitted her manuscripts to him under an assumed name so as not to embarrass him. But the task having to be performed it could not have been better done.

CHAPTER XLVIII

MARY BOYLE AND SIR WILLIAM BOXALL

OUT of the friendship with the Watsons sprang that with Mary Boyle. It was a peculiarly charming friendship. This vivacious young lady occupied almost a unique position in his regard; she seems to have stood in something of the relation of a daughter to the novelist, for Mr. Percy Fitzgerald tells us that " every night she enjoyed the special privilege of receiving a kiss from the amiable Boz, wishing him ' good-night,' and coming up to him shyly like a child, with her candle in her hand." Her brilliance, vivacity, wittiness, and imperturbable good-nature endeared her to Dickens and to all the members of his family. She was one of the most frequent and welcome visitors both at Tavistock House and at Gadshill, and she was an idolator of the novelist, whom she first met in 1849.

Her relative, Mrs. Watson, invited her to Rockingham Castle, and told her to look out at Euston for the Dickens family, who would be her fellow-travellers. She missed them at the station, but the guard brought Dickens to her carriage, and " a hand was held out to help me from the carriage, a hand that for twenty successive years was ever ready to grasp mine in tender friendship or cordial companionship, and whose pressure still thrills my memory." She adds : " It was difficult for two such lovers of the Drama as Charles Dickens and myself to meet under the same roof without some dramatic plotting; and so, during that visit we trod for the first time the same boards together in a hastily concocted scene from *Nicholas Nickleby*—that in which the mad neighbour from the top of the garden wall makes a passionate declaration to Mrs. Nickleby. My shabby-genteel costume with the widow's cap of the period attracted universal admiration from its appropriate fitness, while the amorous outbursts of my adorer were given in a manner worthy of the actor-author."

So impressed was Dickens with her ability as an actress that in September 1850 he recommended to Lytton that she should be given a part in connection with the Guild of Literature and Art performances, but owing to a family bereavement she was unable to accept the invitation.

By this time she was an intimate at Tavistock House. " The

very sound of the name," she says, " is replete with memories of innumerable evenings passed in the most congenial and delightful intercourse; dinners where the guests vied with each other in brilliant conversation, whether intellectual, witty, or sparkling—evenings devoted to music or theatricals.   First and foremost of that magic circle was the host himself, always ' one of us,' who invariably drew out what was best and most characteristic in others, who used the monosyllable ' we ' much more frequently than that of ' I,' and who made use of his superiority to charm and quicken the society around him, but never to crush or over-power it with a sense of inferiority."

Dickens's regard for this vivacious lady is very evident from the charming letters he wrote to her.   As for instance :

" It is all very well to pretend to love me, as you do. Ah ! If you loved as *I* love, Mary ! But when my breast is tortured by the perusal of such a letter as yours, Falkland, Falkland, madam, becomes my part in ' The Rivals,' and I play it with desperate earnestness.   As thus :

" FALKLAND (*to* ACRES).   Then you see her, sir, sometimes ?

" ACRES.   See her !   Odds beams and sparkles, yes.   See her acting !   Night after night.

" FALKLAND (*aside and furious*).   Death and the devil ! Acting, and I not there !   Pray, sir (*with constrained calmness*), what does she act ?

" ACRES.   Odds, monthly nurses and babbies !   Sairey Gamp and Betsy Prig, ' which, wotever it is, my dear (*mimicking*), I likes it brought reg'lar and draw'd mild ! ' *That's* very like her.

" FALKLAND.   Confusion !   Perhaps, sir, perhaps she sometimes acts—ha ! ha ! perhaps she sometimes acts, I say—eh ! sir ?—a—ha, ha, ha ! a fairy ? (*With great bitterness.*)

" ACRES.   Odds, gauzy pinions and spangles, yes !   You should hear her sing as a fairy.   You should see her dance as a fairy.   Tol de rol lol—la—lol—liddle diddle. (*Sings and dances.*)   *That's* very like her.

" FALKLAND.   Misery !   while I, devoted to her image, can scarcely write a line now and then, or pensively read aloud to the people of Birmingham.   (*To him.*)   And they applaud her, no doubt they applaud her, sir.   And she—I see her ! Curtsies and smiles !   And they—curses on them ! they laugh and—ha, ha, ha ! clap their hands—and say it's very good. Do they not say it's very good, sir ?   Tell me.   Do they not ?

"ACRES. Odds, thunderings and pealings, of course they
do ! and the third fiddler, little Tweaks, of the country town,
goes into fits. Ho, ho, ho, I can't bear it (*mimicking*);
take me out ! Ha, ha, ha ! O what a one she is ! She'll be
the death of me. Ha, ha, ha, ha ! *That's* very like her !

"FALKLAND. Damnation ! Heartless Mary ! (*Rushes
out.*)

"Scene opens, and discloses coals of fire, heaped up into
form of letters, representing the following inscription :

> "When the praise thou meetest
> To thine ear is sweetest,
> O then
>
> "REMEMBER JOE.

"*(Curtain falls.)*"

Or again : "Enclosing a kiss, if you will have the kindness to
return it when done with. I have just been reading my *Christmas
Carol* in Yorkshire. I should have lost my heart to the beautiful
young landlady of my hotel (age twenty-nine, dress, black frock
and jacket, exquisitely braided) if it had not been safe in your
possession. Many, many happy years to you ! " And in another
letter he writes : " You are among the few whom I most care for
and best love."

Mary Boyle was continually sending her idol some little token
of her admiration and regard for him. He writes on December 28,
1860, for instance : " I cannot tell you how much I thank you
for the beautiful cigar-case, and how seasonable, and friendly,
and good, and warm-hearted it looked when I opened it at Gadshill.
Besides which, it is a cigar-case, and will hold cigars ; two crowning
merits that I never yet knew to be possessed by any article claiming
the same name. For all these reasons, but more than all because
it comes from you, I love it, and send you eighteen hundred and
sixty kisses, with one in for the new year." On November 17
1861, he writes : " I am perfectly enraptured with the quilt. It
is one of the most tasteful, lively, elegant things I have ever seen ;
and I need not tell you that while it is valuable to me for its own
ornamental sake, it is precious to me as a rainbow-hint of your
friendship and affectionate remembrance." And on January 6,
1869, he writes : " I was more affected than you can easily believe
by the sight of your gift lying on my dressing-table on the morning
of the new year. . . . You may be sure I shall attach a special
interest and value to the beautiful present, and shall wear it as
a kind of charm. God bless you, and may we carry the friendship
through many coming years."

When he was on his reading tours this worshipper of his con-

Q

trived to send him a button-hole for almost every reading. Even when he was in America in 1867 she contrived to pay him this charming little attention, and we find him writing to Miss Hogarth from Boston : " I find by going off to the Cuba myself this morning I can send you the enclosed for Mary Boyle . . . whose usual flower for my button-hole was produced in the most extraordinary manner here last Monday night ! " The " enclosed " was the following letter : " My dear Meery; You can have no idea of the glow of pleasure and amazement with which I saw your remembrance of me lying on my dressing-table here last Monday night. . . . But you must go away four thousand miles, and have such a token conveyed to *you*, before you can quite appreciate the feeling of receiving it. Ten thousand loving thanks."

When Dickens removed to Gadshill, Mary Boyle was there almost as frequently as she had been at Tavistock House. Many were the summer days passed there, she says : " In the afternoon he sought relaxation and then the other inmates of the house came in for their share of his enviable society, and the basket carriage was brought to the door drawn by the ' sober Newman Noggs,' the harness adorned with musical bells which his friend Mr. Lehmann had brought him from Norway, and we would take long drives all round the picturesque neighbourhood. Sometimes we would alight at a distant point to return home on foot ; sometimes we would wend our way through green hop-gardens on one side and golden cornfields on the other for a distance of many miles; yet we never wearied."

.   .   .   .

A lesser friendship which Dickens owed to the Watsons was that with Sir William Boxall, R.A., the famous portrait painter, whom he met at Rockingham Castle in 1849.

In January 1850 Boxall took part in the private theatricals at Rockingham Castle, playing Fenel, the lawyer, in " Used Up," the part which was Egg's in the Guild performances. And it seems evident that he at least had a hand in the painting of the scenery for the special theatre which was erected. In the letter to Mrs. Watson announcing the dates, and so on, the novelist wrote :

" As your letter is *decided*, the scaffolding shall be re-erected round Charley's boots . . . and his dressing proceeded with. I have been very much pleased with him in the matter, as he never made the least demonstration of disappointment or mortification, and was perfectly contented to give in. (*Here I break off to go to Boxall.*) (*Here I return much exhausted.*)

.   .   .   .   .   .

" P.S.—As Boxall (with his head very much on one side and his spectacles on) danced backwards from the canvas incessantly with great nimbleness, and made little digs at it with his pencil, with a horrible grin on his countenance, I auger that he pleased himself this morning."

The only other reference we have to the friendship is Forster's statement that in 1856 Boxall was one of those whose presence in Paris contributed to Dickens's enjoyment of his stay there.

CHAPTER XLIX

AMATEUR THEATRICALS—LORD MULGRAVE

AND now we meet another remarkable group of friends. Dickens's passion for the theatre had been reawakened during his visit to Canada in 1842. We have seen in our first chapter how strong that passion had been in him in his youth; we know that only an accident—the accident of being prostrated by a bad cold on the very day that he was to display his histrionic gifts to Charles Kemble—had prevented him in those days from trying his fortune on the boards. Success in a higher realm of art came to him, and the passion slumbered. But only for a time. On the voyage to America in 1842 he had as fellow-traveller Lord Mulgrave, an officer in the Coldstream Guards, who was on his way to rejoin his regiment in Montreal. With him he struck up a marked friendship, and it was this officer who reawakened the old passion. First a word about this friend. He is mentioned first in a letter to Forster :

> " Lord Mulgrave (a handsome fellow, by-the-bye, to look at, and nothing but a good 'un to go) laid a wager with twenty-five other men last night, whose berths, like his, are in the fore-cabin, which can only be got at by crossing the deck, that he would reach his cabin first. Watches were set by the captain's, and they sallied forth, wrapped up in coats and storm caps. The sea broke over the ship so violently, that they were *five and twenty minutes* holding on by the hand-rail at the starboard paddle-box, drenched to the skin by every wave, and not daring to go on or come back, lest they should be washed overboard ! News ! A dozen murders in town wouldn't interest us half as much."

Arrived in America, Lord Mulgrave delayed rejoining his regiment as long as possible, in order to remain with the novelist, with whom he travelled as far as Boston. Later, of course, Dickens visited Canada, and at Montreal renewed his acquaintance with the officer. The officers of the Guards were organising some theatricals in aid of a charity, and Mulgrave, who was a member of the Committee, suggested that Dickens should take part. He agreed readily enough, and accepted the position of stage manager. Mulgrave played Mr. Selborne in " A Roland for an Oliver," and Crupper in " Deaf as a Post," whilst Dickens was Alfred Highflyer in the first-named piece and Gallop in the second, also appearing as Captain Granville in " Past Two O'clock in the Morning." Mrs. Dickens took part also, and did it " devilish well, too." How the novelist enjoyed these performances is revealed in the high-spirited accounts of them which he wrote to Forster.

Mulgrave remained one of Dickens's friends, and in after years, in England, their intercourse was intimate and frequent, but our chief interest in him lies in the fact that it was he who reawakened the old passion for " play-acting." Thenceforth it was strong in him, and the reading of *The Chimes* in 1844 served to revitalise it, so to speak. That very evening it was suggested—by Jerrold, no doubt—that some amateur theatricals might be organised, and in a more or less vague sort of way it was decided to do something of the kind when Dickens should return from Italy. Forster wrote to him in Genoa asking him whether he still thought they should have the play. " ARE we to have that play ? ? ? " Dickens replied : " Have I spoken of it, ever since I came home from London, as a settled thing ! " Forster should have known his friend better ! As though Dickens ever dropped an idea that had once taken possession of him ! Within three weeks of his return a play had been selected, and the parts had been cast. Miss Kelly's theatre was taken, and there, on September 21, 1845, " Every Man in his Humour " was played. This was a " strictly private " show, done for the sheer love of it, but the success was tremendous, and thenceforth, on any excuse, we find Dickens organising theatricals. In 1847 it was for Leigh Hunt's and John Poole's benefit ; in the following year it was for Sheridan Knowles's benefit ; in 1850 and 1851 it was for the benefit of the Guild of Literature and Art ; and then came a whole succession of performances " for love," at Tavistock House. With these many enterprises it is not our province to deal. Mr. T. Edgar Pemberton,[1] and Mr. S. J. Adair Fitzgerald [2] have told the whole story. We are concerned with the people who took part. With some of them we have already made acquaintance. There remain several others, some of them among the best loved friends that Dickens ever had.

[1] " Dickens and the Stage."   [2] " Dickens and the Drama."

CHAPTER L

FIRST comes John Leech. Not because he was the most active in the theatricals, for he was not; nor only because of his association with them. But because he had a foremost place in Dickens's regard—was one of the innermost circle, in which his was one of the most winning personalities. Like Stanfield, he was before all else a *lovable* man : modest, highly sensitive, for others as well as for himself; though of a somewhat melancholy temperament, yet capable of the heartiest mirth; a staunch friend, incapable of wounding, incapable of making an enemy, ever glad to do a kindness; he was, indeed, as true a gentleman as ever breathed. John Leech's art is John Leech himself—graceful and kindly—yet thoroughly masculine. For him Dickens had a very deep regard indeed.

Forster certainly implies that Leech was introduced to Dickens in 1845, in connection with the theatricals at Miss Kelly's theatre, only we know better, for he had illustrated the *Carol* nearly two years before. None the less, we may reasonably assume that it was Jerrold who made Dickens and Leech personally known to each other. They were members of the " Punch " staff; Leech was just building up his reputation, and it is probable that Jerrold recommended him as illustrator for the *Carol*. This supposition is confirmed by the statement of Mr. W. A. Fraser [1] that Leech first met Dickens in 1843.

But it is at least probable that they had met seven years earlier, when *Pickwick* was in its infancy, before Sam Weller had come into being. When Seymour shot himself before the second number had appeared, and the publishers were looking for his successor, Leech, like his old Charterhouse schoolfellow and life-long friend, Thackeray, applied for the honour. We know that Thackeray saw Dickens personally, and showed him some specimen drawings, which were not considered good enough. We do not know whether Leech also applied to Boz himself, but according to Joseph Grego in his " Pictorial Pickwickiana," Leech was asked by the publishers to do a specimen drawing and he accordingly submitted a pencil sketch, tinted in colours, of " Tom Smart and

[1] *The Dickensian*, December 1906.

230

JOHN LEECH

the Chair," which indicated promise. His art, at that date, was perhaps undeveloped, and in any case, Browne had been before him, and had been chosen. Leech was then but nineteen years old. At the time he was probably just sorry that he had failed to secure a fairly remunerative odd job; a few months later, when *Pickwick* was all the rage, the disappointment was probably a sore one. Within seven years, however, he was to be on terms of friendship with this great writer who had taken the town by storm, and to have secured a share in his friend's fame by illustrating that friend's noblest work—the *Carol*.

For this book he prepared eight designs, four of which were etched on steel, the impressions being afterwards coloured by hand, the remaining four being drawn on wood, and engraved by W. J. Linton.

In the following year Leech shared with Maclise, Doyle and Stanfield, in the work of illustrating *The Chimes*, for which he did five drawings, and gave us the picture of Trotty Veck, which must stand for all time like Seymour's Mr. Pickwick and Phiz's Sam Weller. Dickens was delighted with his friend's work. He had, indeed, a very high opinion of Leech's genius, and he expressed it in an article he wrote in the " Examiner " in 1848, in appreciation of the artist's " The Rising Generation." And in a letter written in 1847, he wrote of Cruikshank and Leech as " the best caricaturists of any time, perhaps."

In 1845, Leech contributed seven woodcuts to *The Cricket on the Hearth*. For *The Battle of Life*, in the following year, he did three drawings, and in connection with one of these he made a strange and unfortunate mistake. This is the illustration which closes the second part of the story, where Michael Warden is introduced into the elopement scene. Says Forster, " We did not discover this until too late for remedy . . . and it is highly characteristic of Dickens, and of the true regard he had for this fine artist, that, knowing the pain he must give in such circumstances by objection or complaint, he preferred to pass it silently. Nobody made any remark upon it, and there the illustration still stands . . ." And Forster quotes Dickens's letter to him on the subject :

" When I first saw it, it was with a horror and agony not to be expressed. Of course, I need not tell *you*, my dear fellow, Warden has no business in the elopement scene. *He* was never there ! In the first hot sweat of this surprise and novelty, I was going to implore the printing of that sheet to be stopped, and the figure taken out of the block. But when I thought of the pain this might give to our kind-hearted Leech, and that what is such a monstrous enormity to me, as never having entered my brain, may not so present itself to others, I became more composed; though the fact is wonderful to me. . . . Leech otherwise is very good, and the illustrations altogether are by far the best that have ever been done for any of the Christmas books."

For *The Haunted Man*, the last of the Christmas books, published in 1848, Leech did five illustrations. Thus, within twelve years of his *Pickwick* disappointment, he had been associated with Boz in every one of the writer's famous Christmas books.

In 1845 Leech took part, as we have seen, in the theatricals of Miss Kelly's theatre, playing Master Mathew in " Every Man in his Humour." Macready particularly refers to his, Dickens's, and Lemon's acting as " very fine for amateurs." In 1847 he took the same part in the performances in aid of Leigh Hunt and John Poole. In the humorous fragment that Dickens wrote, purporting to be an account of the tour in the north of England, written by Mrs. Gamp, Leech is referred to, though not by name. Mrs. Gamp has a conversation with the wig-man, Mr. Wilson :

> " ' Oh, Mrs. Gamp, I ask your pardon '—I never see such a polite man, Mrs. Harris ! ' P'raps,' he says, ' if you're not of the party you don't know who it was that assisted you into this carriage ! '
>
> " ' No, sir,' I says, ' I don't indeed.'
>
> " ' Why, ma'am,' he says, a wisperin', ' that was George, ma'am.'
>
> " ' What George, sir ? I don't know no George,' says I.
>
> " ' The great George, ma'am,' says he. ' The Crookshanks.'
>
> " ' If you'll believe me, Mrs. Harris, I turns my head, and see the wery man a making picturs of me on his thumb nail at the winder ! while another of 'em—a tall, slim, melancolly gent, with dark hair and a bage voice—looks over his shoulder, with his head o' one side, as if he understood the subject, and cooly says, " I've draw'd her several times—in Punch," he says, too ! the owdacious wretch ! '
>
> " ' Which I never touches, Mr. Wilson,' I remarks out loud— I couldn't have helped it, Mrs. Harris, if you had took my life for it !—' which I never touches, Mr. Wilson, on account of the lemon ! ' "

The reference here, of course, is to the fact that Leech very often gained inspiration for his famous cartoons from his friend's books. Mrs. Gamp also correctly records that Leech had a " bage voice." He could sing excellently, and his fine voice was always in demand on social occasions, though, we are told, he generally sang melancholy songs, his favourite being one about King Death.

In 1848, Leech again played Master Mathew in the performances for the benefit of Sheridan Knowles. He also played the same part, as well as that of the Marquis de Lancy in " Animal Magnetism " at the Guild of Literature and Art inaugural performances, at Knebworth, in 1850, but he had no share in the subsequent performances in London and the Provinces, nor did he participate, except as a spectator, in the theatricals at Tavistock House.

But he was ever a welcome guest at Dickens's house, and he shared with Mark Lemon the affection of the children. He was not boisterous, like Mark Lemon, but he was ever genial, and he could be merry, whilst there were a sweetness and tenderness about him that never failed to win the love of little children. In her book, " My Father, as I recall Him," Mamie Dickens tells how Leech and her father specially learned the polka so as to be able to dance it with her and her sister at a children's party. " None can imagine our excitement and nervousness," she says, " when the evening came in which we were to dance with our pupils. Katie, who was a very little girl, was to have Mr. Leech, who was over six feet tall, for her partner, while my father was to be mine. My heart beat so fast that I could scarcely breathe, I was so fearful for the success of our exhibition. But my fears were groundless, and we were greeted at the finish of our dance with hearty applause, which was more than compensation for the work which had been expended upon its learning."

The Dickens and Leech families spent several holidays together. During their stay at Brighton, in 1849, they had a very unpleasant experience, both the landlord and landlord's daughter suddenly going raving mad, and the lodgers having to be driven away to the Bedford Hotel.

Later in the same year, the two families spent a holiday at Bonchurch, I.W. Here they had rollicking times. During their stay they were visited by Forster, Lemon, Jerrold, Hablôt Browne, Talfourd, etc., and they one and all gave themselves up to the fun. But the merriment suffered an unfortunate interruption. While bathing one day, Leech was knocked over by a blow on the forehead from a big wave, causing congestion of the brain. A serious illness followed, and eventually it was only the exertion by Dickens of his hypnotic powers that saved his friend's life.

" My plans " (he wrote to Forster) " are all unsettled by Leech's illness; as of course, I don't like to leave this place

while I can be of service to him and his good little wife. . . .
Ever since I wrote to you Leech has been seriously worse. . . .
The night before last, he was in such an alarming state of
restlessness which nothing could relieve, that I proposed to
Mrs. Leech to try magnetism. Accordingly, in the middle
of the night, I fell to; and after a very fatiguing bout of it,
put him to sleep for an hour and thirty-five minutes. A
change came on in the sleep, and he is decidedly better. I
talked to the astounded little Mrs. Leech across him, when he
was asleep, as if he had been a truss of hay ! What do you
think of my setting up in the magnetic line, with a large
brass plate : ' Terms, twenty-five guineas per nap ' ? "

From that time, Leech steadily improved, and some days later,
he was so much better that Dickens was able to leave him and
return to London.

In March 1848 Leech, Dickens, Lemon and Forster had a trip
together to Salisbury Plain, and in the following November, the
first-named three had a trip to Norwich, visiting also Yarmouth,
Lowestoft, Blundeston, etc. In 1851, Dickens and Leech, with
the Hon. Spencer Lyttleton, made a short bachelor excursion to
Paris, and had a very enjoyable time. Again, in 1854, Leech and
his wife visited the Dickenses at Boulogne.

Finally, it should be mentioned that in *The Dickensian* for
December 1913, there was reproduced a pencil sketch portrait of
Dickens by Leech; an unfinished drawing, but revealing all the
artist's charm and skill. The date of this drawing is not known.

CHAPTER LI

MUCH more active in the theatricals was Mark Lemon. As in the case of Leech, Forster suggests that he was introduced to Dickens by Jerrold in connection with the performances at Miss Kelly's theatre. The suggestion is obviously wrong so far as it concerns Leech, but it is probably accurate in regard to Lemon. For many succeeding years he and the novelist were the best of friends. I do not think that there was ever that finer friendship that existed with some others, but they liked each other well, and Lemon's joviality and heartiness appealed to Dickens. At Twelfth Night parties, at the dinners and dances which followed the theatrical performances at Tavistock House, he was ever in great demand, rivalling Dickens himself as a provoker of merriment. What wonder that the children should love " Uncle Mark " ? This giant—who could play Falstaff without padding—this hearty, rollicking Lord of Misrule, was a prime favourite with them, and the fact must have strengthened the bond of friendship with their father. " My sister and I," writes Mrs. Perugini to me, " were greatly attached, when we were little girls, to the two little daughters of Mr. Mark Lemon—Lally and Betty—and he and his wife were extraordinarily kind to us, having us constantly at their house. Our affection for them in return was so strong that they were always ' Uncle Mark,' and ' Aunt Nelly,' to us, although there was no tie of blood between us."

From 1845 he was one of the leading spirits in all the amateur theatricals, and probably Dickens was his only superior as an actor in the company. Macready says that " the farce between Dickens and M. Lemon was very broad and laughable," whilst of his performance in the " Elder Brother," three months later, the great tragedian says, " the best-filled part in the play was Miramount by Lemon." Dickens, it may be added, described him as " so surprisingly sensible and trustworthy on the stage."

In April 1848 Lemon was present at the *Dombey* dinner, and in that same year he dedicated one of his books to Dickens's two little girls. Dickens acknowledged the compliment in the

following terms : " My dear Mark, I assure you, most unaffectedly
and cordially, that the dedication of that book to Mary and
Kate (not Catherine) will be a real delight to me, and to all of us.
I know well that you propose it in affectionate regard, and value
it and esteem it therefore, in a way not easy of expression."
Mrs. Perugini very kindly informs me that the book thus referred
to was " The Enchanted Doll."

In this same year came the performances in aid of Sheridan
Knowles and John Poole, Lemon playing Brainworm in " Every
Man in his Humour," and Falstaff in " The Merry Wives of
Windsor." In 1848 Lemon, with Dickens's hearty approval and
assistance, dramatised *The Haunted Man*. His version—a very
good one—was produced at the Adelphi. In 1863 it was revived,
J. L. Toole then achieving a success as Tetterby. Needless to
say, Lemon was present at *The Haunted Man* dinner.

In 1850 at the Guild of Literature and Art inaugural performances at Knebworth Mrs. Lemon played the part of Tib, owing
to Mrs. Dickens, who had previously sustained the part, having
sprained her ankle. To this accident, allusion was made in the
epilogue, which was written in the form of a dialogue between
old Knowell and Wellbred. Mrs. Dickens is alluded to, and
Knowell says :

> " A word on her sad accident; but, quite
> Impromptu, not intended for to-night.
> Oh, may she soon recover from her sprain,
> To tread with us, her friends, these boards again ! "

To which Wellbred replies :

> " That fall sank all our spirits; but in need,
> 'Tis said, a friend is found a friend indeed.
> Successful friendship has one's cares allayed."

Whereupon Knowell interrupts with :

> " Ay, and the case relieved by Lemon—aid."

Following these performances at Knebworth came the series in
London and the provinces. As we have seen, Dickens had to
ask to be absolved from his promise to write a farce, and instead
a farce by Lemon was chosen, " to which Dickens soon contributed so many jokes and so much Gampish and other fun of
his own, that it came to be in effect a joint piece of authorship."

It was " Mr. Nightingale's Diary " which is now published in the
Miscellaneous Papers as the joint work of Dickens and Lemon.
Dickens played half a dozen characters, and Lemon took the parts
of Slap, Mr. Tickle and a Virtuous Young Person. On the occasion

of the Devonshire House performance, Lemon was stage manager, Dickens being designated general manager.

In 1854 came the first of the children's theatricals at Tavistock House. It is delightful to read how Dickens and Lemon, and Wilkie Collins, gave themselves up to the entertainment of the youngsters on these occasions, and the memory of these theatricals, when the play was followed by high revels, must be very precious to " Mr. H. ——" [1] and " Miss Kate," who are the only survivors of those happy parties, of which Forster writes :

" These began with the first Twelfth Night at Tavistock House, and were renewed until the principal actors ceased to be children. The best of the performances were ' Tom Thumb ' and ' Fortunio,' in 1854 and 1855, Dickens now joining first in the revel, and Mr. Mark Lemon bringing into it his own clever children and a very mountain of child-pleasing fun in himself. Dickens had become very intimate with him, and his merry, genial ways had given him unbounded popularity with the young ' uns,' who had no such favourite as ' Uncle Mark ! ' In Fielding's burlesque he was the giantess Glumdalca, and Dickens was the ghost of Gaffer Thumb; the names by which they respectively appeared being the Infant Phenomenon and the Modern Garrick."

In the summer of 1855, Dickens " threw open to many friends his Tavistock House Theatre, having secured for its lessee and manager, Mr. Crummles, for its poet, Mr. Wilkie Collins, in an entirely new and original domestic melodrama, and for its scene painter, Mr. Stanfield, R.A." " The Lighthouse " was produced, its actors being Dickens, the author of the play, Mr. Lemon, and Mr. Egg, and the manager's sister-in-law and eldest daughter. Lemon played Jacob Dale, the third Light-keeper. Two years later " The Frozen Deep " was produced at Tavistock House, Lemon playing Lieutenant Crayford. It was followed by " Animal Magnetism," in which he appeared as Pedrillo.

As far as published records go, it might well be imagined that Dickens's associations with Lemon were almost exclusively of a dramatic character, but this was not the case. For several years they were on terms of intimacy, and they and their families frequently exchanged visits, their children, as may be gathered from Mrs. Perugini's letter which I have quoted, forming a strong bond between them. Dickens, in fact, took a strong liking to this big, hearty, jovial, " mountain of child-pleasing fun," this " most true-hearted and affectionate fellow," as he described him. The

[1] Now Mr. Henry F. Dickens, K.C. He was then less than five years old.

death of the novelist's infant daughter, Dora, in April 1851, gave Lemon an opportunity of showing that his friendship was of value. Dickens was in the chair at the General Theatrical Fund, and half an hour before he was to deliver his speech Forster was summoned out of the room to learn that his friend's child was dead. He decided to allow Dickens to make his speech before breaking the sad news to him.

> "As he went on to speak of actors having come from scenes of sickness, of suffering, aye, even of death itself, to play their parts before us, my part was very difficult. 'Yet how often is it with all of us!' he proceeded to say, and I remember to this hour with what anguish I listened to words that had for myself alone, in all the crowded room, their full significance, 'how often is it with all of us, that in our several spheres we have to do violence to our feelings and to hide our hearts in carrying on this fight of life, if we would bravely discharge in it our duties and responsibilities.' In the disclosure that followed when he left the chair, Mr. Lemon, who was present, assisted me, and I left this good friend with him next day, when I went myself to Malvern and brought back Mrs. Dickens and her sister."

As a matter of fact, Lemon sat with Dickens all that night. Four years later, when he was sorrowing in his turn, his friend recalled that night :

> "MY DEAR MARK,
>   "I will call for you at two, and go with you to Highgate, by all means.
>   "Leech and I called on Tuesday evening and left our loves. I have not written to you since, because I thought it best to leave you quiet for a day. I have no need to tell you, my dear fellow, that my thoughts have been constantly with you, and that I have not forgotten (and never shall forget) who sat up with me one night when a little place in my home was left empty.
>   "It is hard to lose any child, but there are many blessed sources of consolation in the loss of a baby."

In 1848 Dickens and Lemon, with Leech and Forster, had a pleasant excursion together. ". . . Obtaining horses from Salisbury," says Forster, "we passed the whole of a March day in riding over every part of the plain; visiting Stonehenge, and exploring Hazlitt's 'hut' at Winterslow . . .; altogether with

AUGUSTUS EGG, R.A.
From a painting by W. P. Frith, R.A.

MARK LEMON

so brilliant a success " that in the following November Dickens proposed to " repeat the Salisbury Plain idea, in a new direction in mid-winter, to wit, Blackgang Chine in the Isle of Wight, with dark winter cliffs and roaring oceans." But when winter came, it was decided that it would be better to " make an outburst to some old cathedral city we don't know." Accordingly Norwich was selected. During this excursion, Dickens saw Yarmouth and Blunderstone for the first time. In the summer of 1849, the Lemons spent happy days with the Whites and the Dickenses and the Leeches at Bonchurch. Great was the fun, one of the most amusing incidents being a race between " Uncle Porpoise " and Dr. Lankester, who also was abnormally stout, Macready acting as judge.

In 1858 came a most unfortunate estrangement, and though the friendship was eventually renewed, the old happy days had gone for ever. In the discussions which preceded the separation of Dickens and his wife, Lemon acted for Mrs. Dickens, and Forster for the novelist. A month or two later, Dickens published the famous letter in which he gave the lie direct to various statements that had become the subject of common gossip. Many of his friends tried to dissuade him from his purpose, and there are no two opinions to-day as to the unwisdom of the course he took. But he persisted, and the letter appeared in *Household Words*. Not satisfied with this he endeavoured to secure the publication in " Punch." Naturally Lemon could not listen to such a proposition, and Dickens took offence, with the result that for nearly ten years they were as strangers. It was Clarkson Stanfield who brought about a reconciliation, as we have seen, and over " Stanny's " open grave, the right hand of friendship was once more held out and grasped.

Both men had but three years left to them, Dickens following Lemon to the Great Beyond within a month.

CHAPTER LII

AUGUSTUS EGG

It is strange to find so little mention of Augustus Egg in Forster's *Life of Dickens*. His name never occurs except to record a bare fact—that he took part in some theatrical performance, or visited Dickens at Broadstairs, for instances—or when he is mentioned in a quoted letter of the novelist's. It is all the more curious because in the case of Egg, at any rate, Forster cannot be accused of prejudice or jealousy. Mr. Renton, in fact, declares that Egg has " no inconsiderable claim to be included amongst those friends of Forster's who so largely contributed to make his life the happy, pleasant thing it, in the main, really was." And with Dickens Egg was a very dear friend. That is quite certain; every member of the Dickens circle who has left any record at all tells us so. The fact seems to be that Egg was not a man of strong personality, capable artist though he was. Moreover, he suffered from very poor health. Dickens writes of him as a " dear gentle little fellow," and, again, as a " dear fellow . . . always sweet-tempered, humorous, conscientious, thoroughly good, and thoroughly beloved." Many others bear similar testimony. He was just a " dear gentle little fellow," simple-hearted, lovable, but with no striking individuality at all. This probably explains why no biography of him exists. It is a pity from the Dickensian's point of view, for the novelist most certainly had a very peculiar regard for him.

It was in 1847 that they first met, Egg being introduced—probably by Frank Stone—in order that he might help in the theatricals on behalf of Leigh Hunt and John Poole. At once a strong friendship was formed. That is shown by Mrs. Cowden Clarke's recollection that during the provincial tour Dickens " had a way of suddenly calling out to Egg during dinner or supper, ' Augustus ! ', and when he looked up, would exclaim with a half-serious, half-playful affectionateness, ' God bless you, Augustus ! ' " The Editors of the novelist's *Letters* say : " We much regret having been unable to procure any letters addressed to Mr. Egg. His intimacy with Charles Dickens began first in the plays of this year (1847); but Mr. Egg became almost immediately one of the friends for whom he had an especial affection, and was a regular visitor at his house, and at his seaside places of resort for many years after this date."

In the performances of 1847, and again in 1848, Egg played Master Stephen in " Every Man in His Humour," and John Brown in " Love, Law, and Physic." In this same year we find him visiting Dickens at Broadstairs, and in 1849 they were to- gether at Bonchurch. In 1851 in the private performances at Knebworth of " Every Man in His Humour," Egg took the part of Oliver Cobb, whilst in " Animal Magnetism " he was Jeffery.

In the following year there were the Guild performances of " Not so Bad as we Seem " and " Mr. Nightingale's Diary." I have never seen it remarked that for these productions Egg designed the dresses. The play-bill certainly states : " The Costumes (with the exception of the Ladies' Dresses and the dresses of the Farce, which are by Messrs. Nathan, of Titchborne Street) made by Mr. Barnett, of the Theatre Royal, Haymarket. Under the superintendence of Mr. Augustus Egg, A.R.A." But the following extract from one of Dickens's letters to Lytton makes it clear that Egg not merely superintended the making of the dresses, but actually designed them : " The dresses are a perfect blaze of colour, and there is not a pocket-flap or a scrap of lace that has not been made according to Egg's drawings to the quarter of an inch."

In Lytton's comedy Egg played Mr. David Fallen, and in the farce he was Tip and Christopher, whilst during the provincial tour he played Mr. Fennel in " Used Up." Of this tour he has left us a very interesting souvenir, in the shape of an admirable painting of Dickens as Sir Charles Coldstream in the last-named play. To complete the record of Egg's connection with the theatricals : he took part in the production of both " The Light- house " and " The Frozen Deep " at Tavistock House.

Continually during these years Egg was a favourite holiday companion of Dickens's. In 1853 they, with Wilkie Collins, had a memorable trip to Switzerland and Italy, and many a delightful adventure did they experience. Writing to Miss Hogarth from Milan, Dickens says : " We continue to get on very well together. We really do admirably. . . . Egg is an excellent fellow, too, and full of good qualities; I am sure a generous and staunch man at heart and a good and honourable nature." Forster makes no mention of him after this, but the friendship remained unchanged right up to Egg's death in 1863, when we find Dickens writing to Wilkie Collins :

" Ah, poor Egg ! I know what you would think and feel about it. . . . What a large piece of a good many years he

R

seems to have taken with him! How often have I thought, since the news of his death came, of his putting his part in the saucepan (with the cover on) when we rehearsed 'The Lighthouse'; of his falling out of the hammock when we rehearsed 'The Frozen Deep'; of his learning Italian numbers when he ate the garlic in the carriage; of the thousands (I was going to say) of dark mornings when I apostrophised him as ' Kernel'; of his losing my invaluable knife in that beastly stage-coach; of his posting up that mysterious book[1] every night! . . . In my memory of the dear gentle little fellow, he will be (as since those days he always has been) eternally posting up that book at the large table in the middle of our Venice sitting-room, incidentally asking the name of an hotel three weeks back! And his pretty house is to be laid waste and sold. If there be a sale on the spot I shall try to buy something in loving remembrance of him, good dear little fellow. Think what a great 'Frozen Deep' lay close under those boards we acted on! My brother Alfred, Luard, Arthur, Albert, Austin, Egg. Even among the audience Prince Albert and poor Stone! 'I heard the '—I forget what it was I used to say—' come up from the great deep '; and it rings in my ears now, like a sort of mad prophecy.

"However, this won't do. We must close up our ranks and march on."

Of more intimate records of this friendship we have none at all. But Egg was one of the inner Dickens circle for sixteen years; the two men were together at every opportunity, and in the novelist's home no one was more welcome than Egg, whilst W. P. Frith tells us that Dickens was often at Egg's house, Ivy Cottage, Black Lion Lane (now Queen's Road), Bayswater.

As far as I know, Egg never tried his hand at scenes or characters from his friend's books.

[1] His travelling journal.

CHAPTER LIII

MRS. COWDEN CLARKE, the famous compiler of the Shakespeare Concordance, was especially prominent in many of the theatricals. She was introduced to Dickens by Leigh Hunt at a party at the Tagarts' in 1848. "At once," she says, "with his own inexpressible charm of graceful ease and animation, Charles Dickens fell into delightful chat and riveted for ever the chain of fascination that his mere distant image and enchanting writings had cast about M. C. C., drawing her towards him with a perfect spell of prepossession. The prepossession was confirmed into affectionate admiration and affection that lasted faithfully strong throughout the happy friendship that ensued and was not even destroyed by death."

Twenty-two years later she read in an Italian paper "Carlo Dickens è morto," and, she says, "the sun seemed suddenly blotted out as I looked upon the fatal line." Through all those years, "genial, kind, most sympathetic and fascinating" had been his companionship, and "very precious to me was his friendship."

Mrs. Cowden Clarke was, indeed, one of the most sincere and loyal of Dickens's friends. But their association was confined mainly to the earlier theatrical performances in which she had a prominent share.

At that first meeting at the Tagarts' house, Dickens referred to her performance of Mrs. Malaprop in some recent theatricals, and she said that she understood he was organising an amateur company to play "The Merry Wives of Windsor," and that she would be delighted to play Dame Quickly. Dickens did not take the proposal seriously, but she was very keen on playing the part, and so wrote to him repeating the proposal. She received the following reply:

"I did not understand, when I had the pleasure of conversing with you the other evening, that you had really considered the subject, and desired to play. But I am very glad to understand it now; and I am sure there will be a universal sense among us of the grace and appropriateness of such a proceeding. . . . Will you . . . receive this as a solemn ' call-' to rehearsal of ' The Merry Wives ' at Miss Kelly's theatre, to-morrow (Saturday) *week*, at seven in the evening ?

"And will you let me suggest another point for your consideration ? On the night when ' The Merry Wives ' will *not* be played, and when ' Every Man in his Humour ' *will* be, Kenny's farce of ' Love, Law, and Physic ' will be acted. In that farce there is a very good character (one Mrs. Hilary, which I have seen Mrs. Orger, I think, act to admiration). . . . If you find yourself quite comfortable and at ease among us in Mrs. Quickly, would you like to take this other part ? "

She accepted the offer, and she also played Tib in Ben Jonson's comedy. Mrs. Clarke's enthusiastic eulogy of Dickens as a manager has often been quoted and there is no need to repeat it here. But she wrote of the tour even more enthusiastically, if that were possible :

"What enchanting journeys those were ! The coming on to the platform at the station where Charles Dickens's alert form and beaming look met one with pleasurable greeting; the interest and polite attention of the officials; the being always seated with my sister Emma in the same carriage occupied by Mr. and Mrs. Charles Dickens and Mark Lemon; the delightful gaiety and sprightliness of our manager's talk; the endless stories he told us; the games he mentioned and explained how they were played; the bright amenity of his manner at various stations; . . . his indefatigable vivacity, cheeriness, and good humour from morning till night—all were delightful."

" No man," she says, " could better make a ' party of pleasure ' truly pleasant and worthy of its name. . . . Charles Dickens— beaming in look, alert in manner, radiant with good humour, genial voiced, the very soul of enjoyment, fun, good taste, and good spirits, admirable in organising details and suggesting novelty of entertainment—of all beings the very man for a holiday season; and in a singularly exceptional holiday season was it my fortunate hap to pass every hour that I spent in his society."

As a souvenir of this tour Mrs. Clarke sent to Dickens a handsome blotting case which she had made. It was bound in green watered silk. In the corners were the names of the parts he had played; in the centre on the front was a leaf of heartsease and forget-menots, surrounding the initials " Y. G." [1] In the centre on the other side was a group of roses and rosebuds worked in gloss silks, and natural colours.

He received other little tokens of admiration from her :

" It is almost an impertinence to tell you how delightful your flowers were to me; for you who thought of that delicately-timed token of sympathy and remembrance, must know it very well already.

" I do assure you that I have hardly ever received anything with so much pleasure in all my life. They are not faded yet—are on my table here—but never can fade out of my remembrance. . . .

" Ever faithfully and gratefully your Friend."

In 1853 Dickens gave her a copy of *Bleak House*, requesting that she would give the book a place on her shelves and in her heart—" where you may always believe me." It should also be said that he invited her to take part in some of the later theatricals, but she was unable to do so.

In 1859 Mrs. Clarke wrote him in praise of *A Tale of Two Cities*, which was then appearing in serial form, and here is his warm acknowledgment :

" I cannot tell you how much pleasure I have derived from the receipt of your earnest letter. Do not suppose it possible that such praise can be ' less than nothing ' to your old manager. It is more than all else. Here in my little country house on the summit of the hill where Falstaff did the robbery, your words have come to me in the most appropriate and delightful manner. When the story can be read all at once, and my meaning can be better seen, I will send it to you . . . and it will be a hearty gratification to think that you and your good husband are reading it together. For you must both take notice, please, that I have a reminder of you always before me. On my desk, here, stand two green leaves which I every morning station in their ever-green place at my elbow. The leaves on the oak-trees outside the window are less constant than them, for they are with me through the four seasons.

.   .   .   .

The " two green leaves " referred to a porcelain paper-weight, another gift from this enthusiastic admirer. It had two green leaves enamelled on it, on either side of the initials " C. D."

[1] " Young Gas "—a name he had bestowed upon himself.

Later Mrs. Clarke and her husband left England and settled in Italy, and on their departure Dickens wrote, " I shall never hear of you or think of you without true interest and pleasure."　As we have seen, it was in Italy that Mrs. Clarke read " Carlo Dickens è morto."　" Often since then," she says, " the sudden blur of the sunshine comes over the fair face of Genoa, sea, sky, fortressed hills, which he described as ' one of the most fascinating prospects in the world '—when I look upon it and think that his loving eyes can never again behold a scene he loved so well; but then returns the bright clear light that illumined his own nature, making him so full of faith in loveliness and kindness as to shed a perpetually beaming genial effect upon those who knew him—and one's spirit revives in another and a better hope."

CHAPTER LIV

THE DUKE OF DEVONSHIRE

The (seventh) Duke of Devonshire is quite appropriately " placed " here. He never took part in any of the theatrical performances, of course, but his friendship with Dickens arose out of the Guild performances in 1851 in which he took a great interest, and for which he loaned his house in Piccadilly. He was never on intimate terms with the novelist, but he showed Dickens many kindnesses, and there was a great cordiality. The offer of Devonshire House was not spontaneous, but came in response to a direct appeal from Dickens. The response, however, was prompt and hearty, and the Duke in his princely way (says Forster) discharged all the expenses attending the performances. A movable theatre was built and set up in the great drawing-room, and the library was turned into a green-room.

Thenceforth great cordiality existed between Dickens and the Duke, and for some years they corresponded pretty frequently. Some of the novelist's letters are preserved and they are very hearty. From Boulogne in July 1856, for instance, Dickens wrote a long letter, acknowledging one from the Duke which had been received with " uncommon pleasure," and making interesting reference to the book then in hand.

" I am so glad you like Flora. It came into my head one day that we have all had our Floras, and that it was a half-serious, half-ridiculous truth which had never been told. It is a wonderful gratification to me to find that everybody knows her. Indeed, some people seem to think I have done them a personal injury, and that their individual Floras (God knows where they are, or who!) are each and all Little Dorrits! "

" We were all grievously disappointed that you were ill when we played Mr. Collins's ' Lighthouse ' at my house," the letter proceeds. " If you had been well, I should have waited upon you with my humble petition that you would come and see it; and if you had come I think you would have cried, which would have charmed me. I hope to produce another play at home next Christmas, and if I can only persuade you to see it from a special arm-chair and can only make you wretched, my satisfaction will be intense."

In the following December he wrote :

" The moment the first bill is printed for the first night of the new play I told you of, I send it to you, in the hope that you will grace it with your presence. There is not one of the old actors whom you will fail to inspire as no one else can ; and I hope you will see a little result of the friendly union of the arts, that you may think worth seeing, and that you can see nowhere else.

" We propose repeating it on Thursday, the Eighth ; Monday, the Twelfth ; and Wednesday, the Fourteenth of January. I do not encumber this note with so many bills, and merely mention those nights in case any one of them should be more convenient to you than the first.

" But I shall hope for the first, unless you dash me (N.B.— I put Flora into the current number on purpose that this might catch you softened towards me, and at a disadvantage). If there is hope of your coming, I will have the play clearly copied, and will send it to you to read beforehand."

The play, of course, was " The Frozen Deep." There is no record whether the Duke accepted the invitation, but it is more than probable that he saw the play at one of its many representations.

CHAPTER LV

MANY "SPLENDID STROLLERS"

AND now we come to some lesser luminaries who were prominent in the theatricals. That expression is used, not out of any disparagement of the men concerned, but merely in reference to their relations with Dickens. Those who are to be named in this chapter were not members of the inner Dickens circle.

It is true that Forster declares that Dickens had an old and great regard for George Henry Lewes, but that is all the evidence we have of it. I suppose we are bound to accept the assurance though I confess that I do not find it easy. Justin McCarthy records one remark of Dickens's about Lewes which hardly goes to corroborate Forster. When Lewes wrote a series of essays in the " Fortnightly Review," says McCarthy, on the principles of success in literature, Dickens asked : " Success in literature : what on earth does George Lewes know about success in literature ? " Not a particularly nasty remark, certainly, but it was not Dickens's way of talking about valued friends. And then, on the other side, there is Lewes's well-known article on Dickens which he wrote for the " Fortnightly " in 1871. Forster has dealt amply with that remarkable article—remarkable, not so much for the attitude it reveals, with which we are all quite familiar, as for its revelation of its writer's complete failure to understand a man whom he had known more or less intimately for years. One extract is sufficient : " Dickens once declared to me that every word said by his characters was distinctly *heard* by him ; I was at first not a little puzzled to account for the fact that he could hear language so utterly unlike the language of real feeling, and not be aware of its preposterousness ; but the surprise vanished when I thought of the phenomena of hallucination." The man who wrote that had palpably completely failed to understand Dickens, and where there is such a hopeless lack of understanding there cannot be an intimate friendship. So that though Dickens may have had a cordial regard for him, Lewes did not occupy a place in the inner Dickens circle. His chief association with the novelist was in connection with the theatricals of 1847 and 1848. He played Cattermole's old part, Wellbred, in " Every Man in his Humour," and Andrew in " Love, Law, and Physic."

Francis W. Topham was one of the artists who joined the company that produced " Not so Bad as we Seem " in 1851. He played Mr. Goodenough Easy. He was evidently a sociable individual, well liked by Dickens, for Forster records that he became a frequent guest at Devonshire Terrace. It should also be recorded that he painted three scenes from Dickens's books. One was from *Barnaby Rudge*, which he presented to the novelist, and which was sold in 1870 for £115 10*s*., and another was from *The Old Curiosity Shop*, representing Little Nell and her grand-father in the tent making bouquets for the racecourse, which he also presented to Dickens and which realised £288 15*s*. in 1870. The third was painted in 1856. It was entitled " Little Nell in the Churchyard," and it realised £325 10*s*. at the Gadshill sale.

Dudley Costello took part in the first theatricals at Miss Kelly's theatre in 1845, playing George Downright in " Every Man in his Humour."   Stanfield was to have played the part, but he backed out. It was offered to George Cruikshank, but he could not accept and Costello was invited. In 1847 he assisted at the performances in aid of Leigh Hunt and John Poole, and in 1848 he was Knowell in Jonson's comedy when it was performed in aid of the fund for the endowment of a perpetual curatorship of Shakespeare's house. Then, in 1851, he was the Earl of Loftus in Lytton's comedy, and Mr. Nightingale in " Mr. Nightingale's Diary."   There is absolutely no record of any intimacy between him and Dickens.

Peter Cunningham was associated with the tour of 1848 as business manager, or, as the Editors of Dickens's *Letters* put it, he " managed the *un*theatrical part of this Amateur Provincial tour."   In 1851, however, he came on to the stage, and played Lord Le Trimmer in " Not so Bad as we Seem."   He was one of the most popular members of the companies, and with Dickens he was a favourite.   Forster says :

> " His presence was always welcome to Dickens, and indeed
> to all who knew him, for his relish of social life was great,
> and something of his keen enjoyment could not but be shared
> by his company.   His geniality would have carried with it a
> pleasurable glow even if it had stood alone, and it was in-
> vigorated by very considerable acquirements.   He had some
> knowledge of the works of eminent authors and artists ; and
> he had an eager interest in their lives and haunts, which he
> had made the subject of minute and novel inquiry.   This
> store of knowledge gave substance to his talk, yet never
> interrupted his buoyancy and pleasantry, because only intro-

duced when called for, and not made matter of parade or display. But the happy combination of qualities that rendered him a favourite companion, and won him many friends, proved in the end injurious to himself. He had done much while young in certain lines of investigation which he had made almost his own, and there was every promise that he would have produced much weightier works with advancing years. This, however, was not to be. The fascination of good-fellowship encroached more and more upon literary pursuits, until he nearly abandoned his former favourite studies, and sacrificed all the deeper purposes of his life to the present temptation of a festive hour. Then his health gave way, and he became lost to friends as well as to literature. But the impression of the bright and amiable intercourse of his better times survived, and his old associates never ceased to think of Peter Cunningham with regret and kindness."

It is a sad story of talents wasted. And yet, can it be truly said that a man who leaves sweet memories with a host of friends has wholly wasted his life?

Among the " splendid strollers " of 1851 and 1852 was a young man named John Tenniel, destined presently to succeed John Leech as chief cartoonist for " Punch," to draw the weekly cartoon for half a century, and to leave behind him, when he died in 1914, an imperishable name. Undoubtedly recommended by his " Punch " colleagues, Douglas Jerrold and Mark Lemon, he was cast for the part of Hodge, in " Not so Bad as we Seem," and he took part in the first performance at Devonshire House on June 18, 1851. By the Editors of Dickens's *Letters*, Tenniel is described as " a new addition and a very valuable and pleasant one to the company." When the company went on tour in the provinces, and Forster was compelled to drop out, Tenniel, who had but a few weeks previously joined the staff of " Punch," and thus started his unique career, was promoted and given the part of Hardman. He proved a great success, and we find Dickens in a letter from Sunderland, paying special tribute to the excellence of his acting.

In the following year Tenniel played the Hon. Tom Saville in performances of " Used Up." This was the end of his association as an actor with Dickens, but he remained one of the novelist's most esteemed friends, and Forster tells us how the young artist was one of the most frequent guests at Devonshire Terrace. No one who knows his work in " Punch " will have any doubt as to his knowledge of and affection for Dickens's books. Over and over again he went to those books for inspiration, and one of the half-dozen best known of his cartoons is that in which Gladstone is depicted as " The Political Mrs. Gummidge." Tenniel was associated with other artists in illustrating *The Haunted Man*, and contributed six charming pictures to that Christmas story.

For Shirley Brooks, Lemon's successor in Mr. Punch's editorial chair, Dickens always had a cordial regard; that Brooks had at least an equal regard for Dickens is proved by the fact that he dedicated his first novel to him. They met pretty often and were always good friends. " To do Shirley a good turn was one of the best investments a man could make," says his biographer, Mr. George Somes Layard. Dickens made the investment in 1855. Brooks commenced to write " The Gordian Knot " for " Bentley's Miscellany," but failed to keep up the instalments, partly because he had more work on hand than he could do, and partly because of some domestic trouble. Bentley threatened legal proceedings, but Dickens, with memories, no doubt, of his own early days, stepped in, and as the result of his good offices the trouble was settled amicably. Not long before his own death, Dickens visited Brooks, who was ill and scarcely expected to live long, but yet was to live to write an In Memoriam leading article of the novelist for " Home News," and to purchase a souvenir of his friend at Christie's. He bought a bust of Landor for £25—which Mr. George Somes Layard purchased thirty years later for 4*s*. 6*d*.! Brooks played Bateson and Darker in the performances of " The Frozen Deep " in aid of Douglas Jerrold's family in 1847.

Forster does not even mention James Robinson Planché, but he was very prominent in connection with the Tavistock House performances. The late Canon Ainger, who, as a youngster, took part in these festivities, in his article entitled " Mr. Dickens's Amateur Theatricals " records :

> " Our first attempt was the performance of Albert Smith's little burletta of ' Guy Fawkes' . . . ;' at another time we played ' William Tell,' from the late Robert Brough's clever little volume, ' A Cracker Bon-bon for Evening Parties.' In those days there were still extravaganzas written with real humour and abundant taste and fancy. The Broughs, Gilbert à Beckett, and Mr. Planché could write rhymed couplets of great literary excellence, without ever overstepping the bounds of reverence and good taste."

Planché was, of course, the author of " Fortunio " which was played by the children in 1855.

Neither Lionel nor Robert Brough is mentioned by Forster,

CHARLES DICKENS AS SIR CHARLES GOLDSTREAM IN "USED UP"

From the painting by Augustus Egg, R.A.

but both, like Planché, were very prominent in connection with the children's theatricals, though they did not act. One year, as we have just seen, Robert Brough's " William Tell " was played, and with reference to this Canon Ainger says :

> " Extreme purists may regret that the story of the struggle for Swiss independence should ever be presented to children in association with anything ludicrous; but, those critics excepted, no other could object to the spirit of ' gracious fooling' in which Mr. Brough represented William Tell brought up before Gesler for ' contempt of hat '; Albert, his precocious son, resolving that, as to betraying his father, ' though torn in half, I'll not be made to split '; and when he confronts his father, about to shoot at the apple, by assuring him that he is ' game,' the father replying, ' Wert thou *game*, I would preserve, not shoot thee.' This is drollery, it seems to us, not unworthy of Sydney Smith or Hood, and in no way to be placed in the same catalogue with the vulgarities and inanities of a later brood."

Gilbert à Beckett stood closer to Dickens than most of those named in this chapter. With him and with his family there was a very cordial friendship; but there is practically no record of it. As Canon Ainger has told us, he was to the fore at Tavistock House, but years before that he had been associated with the theatrical performances, having played William in the very first presentation of " Every Man in his Humour " in 1845. When the performance was repeated a couple of months later, however, he dropped out, W. Eaton taking his place. But in 1844 he had been associated with Mark Lemon in dramatising *The Chimes*. The piece was produced at the Adelphi theatre with Dickens's entire approval in December of that year.

Robert Bell, who played Paddy O'Sullivan in " Not so Bad as we Seem " at the Hanover Square Rooms in 1851, had been friendly with Dickens for some years prior to that, and had been one of the company at *The Haunted Man* dinner. G. A. Sala says that he was an intimate friend of Dickens's. Certainly he was a frequent and welcome guest at the novelist's house. In July 1866 he appeared as Rogue Riderhood in a version of *Our Mutual Friend* entitled " Dustman's Treasure," which was produced at the Britannia Theatre. He was a frequent contributor to *Household Words* and *All the Year Round*. Percival Leigh was another of Mr. Punch's young men introduced for the performances of 1845. He was a frequent guest at Dickens's house, but never penetrated beyond the outer circle. He wrote occasionally for *Household Words*.

Mr. Francesco Berger, who is happily still with us, was a very young man when, as a music student in Leipzig, he met and formed a friendship with Dickens's eldest son, who was studying the German language in that city. That friendship naturally led to visits to Tavistock House, where he became popular. That was in 1854. In the following year, when preparations were commenced for the production of " The Lighthouse," Dickens asked this clever young musician to compose for it an original overture, and to arrange the incidental music. He did as he was asked, and in his " Reminiscences, Impressions, and Anecdotes " he has told of the happiness associated, not only with the performances themselves, but with the rehearsals too.

In 1857 Mr. Berger wrote the music for " The Frozen Deep " and conducted the orchestra. At the performance before Queen Victoria at the Gallery of Illustration copies of the overture, bound in satin, were handed to her Majesty and the Prince Consort.

At the conclusion of the Tavistock House performances Dickens sent the young composer a set of three shirt-front studs, each engraved " C. D. to F. B." They were " a little memorial," wrote the novelist, " in remembrance of our pleasant play and the obligations it owes to you. I can never forget the pains you have taken with it, or the spirit and genius with which you have rendered it high service." In 1857 Mr. Berger was associated with Dickens in the efforts to assist the family of Douglas Jerrold, and was one of the three conductors at the concert at St. Martin's Hall on June 27.

There were many others who took part in this performance or that, but who call for no mention here. They came simply to play certain parts, walked across the stage, and never entered into Dickens's life in any degree at all.

Perhaps, however, this is an appropriate place in which to mention James Sheridan Knowles, by reason of the fact that it was primarily for his benefit that the performances of 1848 were given. Dickens had been pretty well acquainted with him before that. They had quarrelled, too, and made it up again. This is clear from Dickens's letter to Knowles dated May 26, 1847 :

" MY DEAR KNOWLES,
        " I have learned, I hope, from the art we both profess (if you will forgive this classification of myself with you) to respect a man of genius in his mistakes, no less than in his triumphs. You have so often read the human heart well that I can readily forgive your reading mine ill, and greatly wronging me by the supposition that any sentiment

towards you but honour and respect has ever found a place in it.

"You write as few lines which, dying, you would wish to blot, as most men. But if you knew me better, as I hope you may (the fault shall not be mine if you don't), I know you will be glad to have received the assurance that some part of your letter has been written on the sand and that the wind has already blown over it."

They *did* get to know each other better, but there never developed a close friendship. Knowles was scarcely the man for that. He was a competent dramatist, and a fairly good actor; beyond that he and Dickens had nothing in common, and a letter of the novelist's written in January 1850 suggests that he made some demands upon the tolerance of his friends.

CHAPTER LVI

A GROUP OF ACTORS

NATURALLY Dickens numbered many professional actors among his friends. Of these, of course, Macready was far and away first in his regard. Later Fechter, of whom we shall speak more fully presently, exercised an extraordinary fascination over him. With these two he was especially intimate, but there were several others with whom he was on excellent terms. "Dear old Charles Kemble," for instance, with whom "occasional happy days" were spent, and there were Samuel Phelps, and John Parry, and Whitworth, Helen Faucit and Miss Dolby, "than whom none were more attractive to him."

Towards the Keeleys he was especially well disposed. Mrs. Keeley's acting as Smike in a "pirated" version of *Nickleby* in 1838, he described as excellent, and in 1844 he consented to the presentation by her and her husband of a version of *Chuzzlewit*. Keeley asked him for a prologue. He declined, but he wrote: "Believe me to be quite sincere in saying that if I felt I could reasonably do such a thing for any one I would do it for you." He was starting for Italy within the week, but he superintended one rehearsal. In 1845 Dickens requested Albert Smith to dramatise *The Cricket on the Hearth* for the Keeleys; and Mr. Keeley played Caleb Plummer, Mrs. Keeley, Dot, and their daughter Mary, Bertha. In 1846 Albert Smith prepared *The Battle of Life* for the stage, and the Keeleys produced it, Dickens travelling from Paris expressly to attend the rehearsals. That he thus countenanced such productions by the Keeleys is clear enough evidence of his high opinion of their acting and of their characters, too. And he counted them among his best friends.

With Benjamin Webster he was very friendly for a number of years—on hearty intimate terms, in fact. In 1868 Webster, while Dickens was in America, produced *No Thoroughfare* with Fechter in the leading part, and in connection with this production we have Dickens's own declaration of his high opinion of the man. For in a letter to Fechter concerning the play, he wrote: "Tell Webster, with my regard, that I think his proposal honest and fair; that I think it, in a word, like himself; and that I have perfect confidence in his good faith and liberality."

256

John P. Harley was one of the earliest friends that Dickens made in the theatrical world. *The Strange Gentleman*, the novelist's first serious dramatic venture, was produced at St. James's Theatre in September 1836, and Harley played the title rôle. It is declared by Theodore Taylor that Dickens himself took a part under an assumed name, but we have no other evidence to that effect. The piece ran for three months, and then was succeeded by *The Village Coquettes*, in which Harley played the part of Martin Stokes. In 1847 the book of words was published by Bentley, with a dedication to Harley. In March 1837 *Is She His Wife?* followed the *Coquettes*, with Harley as Felix Tapkins. On March 13—seven days after the first performance—Harley took his benefit, and the play bill announced : " Mr. Harley will, in the character of Mr. Pickwick, make his first visit to the St. James's Theatre and relate to a Scotch air his experiences of a ' whitebait dinner at Blackwall,' edited expressly for him by his biographer ' Boz.' "

These theatrical associations led to a personal friendship which was close and lasting. On June 27, 1837, we read that Harley dined with Dickens, Forster, and Macready at Doughty Street, and Macready records that he " laughed much at Mr. Harley's theatrical efforts to entertain." Harley was at the *Nickleby* dinner, and at the *Clock* dinner, too, and on February 7, 1839, we find Dickens inviting him to join his birthday party, which was to consist of Leigh Hunt, Ainsworth, and Forster.

In the following June we have a letter of the novelist's inviting Harley to Petersham : " Can you come if it's fine ? Say yes, like a good fellow as you are, and say it per post." Harley received a copy of *Nickleby*, inscribed : " J. P. Harley, Esquire, from his friend Charles Dickens," which seventy-six years later was sold for £125. Harley died in 1858, and to the end his friendship with the novelist remained unbroken.

John Hullah, who wrote the music for *The Village Coquettes*, was on very friendly terms with Dickens in those early days, and the novelist's letters to him at the time are quite familiar in tone. But very little is known of their later relations. Hullah outlived Dickens by fourteen years, and they certainly remained on good terms, but Forster ignores him utterly, and after 1836 he is mentioned in only one of the novelist's letters. That letter is dated October 24, 1860, and is addressed to Wilkie Collins. " Early in the morning, before breakfast," says Dickens, writing from Brighton, " I went to the nearest baths to get a shower-bath. They kept me waiting longer than I thought reasonable, and seeing a man in a cap in the passage, I went to him and said :

s

' I really must request that you'll be good enough to see about this shower-bath '; and it was Hullah ! waiting for another bath." In *Miscellaneous Papers* Dickens mentions Hullah once or twice, though only in regard to his musical fame. The references are all friendly in tone, however, showing that there had been no break in the good relations.

CHAPTER LVII

REV. JAMES WHITE

DICKENS was at the very zenith of his powers during the later Devonshire Terrace days and the Tavistock House days. The old friends he had and their adoption tried were firmly grappled to his heart, but he was ever making new friends, and in the period under notice there were attracted to him many fine men whom he valued for qualities of head and heart, who found themselves drawn to him by that breezy manliness, that earnest openness of heart, that hearty capacity for friendship that characterised him throughout his life. About many of these friendships there is not, to us now, that glamour that surrounds some of the earlier ones, but they were all sincere and deeply rooted. There was the Reverend James White, the Isle of Wight parson, for instance. Few friends were better loved, none was more worthy of the novelist's friendship. I do not know how they came to be "first acquaint." Possibly it was through Macready, who had produced with success White's play, "The King of the Commons "; but howsoever it was, and whensoever, we have plenty of evidence that their friendship was particularly close and hearty. " With Dickens, White was popular supremely for his eager good-fellowship," says Forster, " and few men brought him more of what he always liked to receive. But he brought nothing so good as his wife. ' He is excellent, but she is better,' is the pithy remark of his first Bonchurch letter. . . ."

In 1849 Dickens decided to spend his summer holiday at some other place than Broadstairs, and he selected the Isle of Wight, taking a house at Bonchurch. He was attracted there, says Forster, " by the friend who had made it a place of interest for him during the last few years, the Reverend James White, with whose name and its associations my mind connects inseparably many of Dickens's happiest hours !

"To pay him fitting tribute" (Forster adds) " would not be easy, if here it were called for. In the kindly, shrewd Scotch face, a keen sensitiveness to pleasure and pain was the first thing that struck any common observer. Cheerfulness and gloom coursed over it so rapidly that no one could question the tale they told. But the relish of his life had outlived its more than usual share of sorrow; and quaint, sly humour, love of jest and merriment, capital knowledge of books, and sagacious quips at men, made his companionship delightful."

It is interesting to note that it was during this holiday that Dickens's boys had as playmates a golden-haired lad named Algernon Charles Swinburne, whose parents lived in the island.

One might quote a great deal from Dickens's letters to White, but it is not necessary. The letters were frequent and lengthy and brimful of hearty friendship. The friends met fairly often, too, and White and his family were always enthusiastically welcomed at the novelist's home. It has to be added that White was a frequent contributor to *Household Words* from its commencement and to *All the Year Round*. In October 1852 he was invited to contribute to the Christmas number. "We are now getting our Christmas extra number together, and I think you are the boy to do, if you will, one of the stories. . . . The grandfather might very well be old enough to have lived in the days of the highwaymen. Do you feel disposed, from fact, fancy, or both, to do a good winter-hearth story of a highwayman? If you do, I embrace you (per post), and throw up a cap I have purchased for the purpose into mid air." White did feel disposed, and wrote "The Grandfather's Story"—"a very good story indeed," Dickens declared. Four years later he contributed "The Scotch Boy's Story" to *The Wreck of the Golden Mary*. These were all the Christmas numbers in which he appeared, but he often wrote for the weekly issues of both papers.

NO. 1 DEVONSHIRE TERRACE

From a photograph by H. Snowden Ward

CHAPTER LVIII

ANOTHER very special favourite was Sir James Emerson Tennent. When Dickens was in his prime—certainly from 1850 onwards—nobody was more welcome at his house; and the last book that he completed—*Our Mutual Friend*—was dedicated to Tennent. The friendship is not surprising. Tennent was a staunch supporter of reform. He was at Earl Grey's side in the final struggle over the Reform Bill in 1832, and later he supported Peel, though he was secretary to the Government of Ceylon when the Corn Laws were actually repealed. He was, in fact, an enlightened man, a widely travelled man, with genuine literary capacity, and he was gifted with the all too rare capacity for friendship.

In 1853 Dickens and the Tennents had many happy days together at Naples and elsewhere in Italy, and those days remained with Dickens a particularly pleasant memory. We find him writing in 1857, for instance : " I must thank you for your earnest and affectionate letter. It has given me the greatest pleasure, mixing the play in my mind confusedly and delightfully with Pisa, the Valetta, Naples, Herculanæum—God knows what not." The play referred to was " The Frozen Deep." The friendship continued and grew stronger. Tennent was frequently at Dickens's house, and he was one of the few friends for whom the novelist turned out a couple of postilions " in the old red jackets of the old red royal Dover road." In 1864 came the dedication of *Our Mutual Friend*, to which the following is an allusion : " I am heartily pleased that you set so much store by the dedication. You may be sure that it does not make me the less anxious to take pains, and to work out well what I have in my mind."

Tennent died in March 1869. Just at that time Dickens's health was failing, and he was soon to have that breakdown which was the beginning of the end. But he determined to attend his friend's funeral. On March 11 he read at York, and, says Forster, by shortening the pauses in the reading, he succeeded, after a violent rush, in catching the mail. He travelled through the night, and so reached London in time. " He appeared ' dazed ' and worn," says Forster. " No man could well look more so than he did that sorrowful morning." On the following day, in a letter to Austen Layard, Dickens referred sadly to those Italian days of sixteen years before : " I came to town hurriedly to attend poor dear Emerson Tennent's funeral. You will know how my mind went back, in the York uptrain at midnight, to Mount Vesuvius and our Neapolitan supper."

With the last named, Sir Austen Henry Layard, there was a very similar friendship. Layard had been of the company during those days in Italy; he, too, as all the world knows, was a great traveller; he, too, was a Member of Parliament, whose views on most questions coincided with Dickens's own; he, too, possessed literary tastes and gifts; he, too, had the capacity for friendship highly developed. With him, as with Tennent, there were many " social entertainments "; he was a frequent and heartily welcome guest at Dickens's house; for him, too, the postilions were turned out on the Dover road. They met about 1851, and the Editors of Dickens's *Letters* tell us that the novelist at once conceived for the great Nineveh traveller an affectionate friendship which went on increasing for the rest of his life.

Forster tells us that Layard held the same opinion of Dickens as Sir Arthur Helps—that he was " a man to confide in, and look up to as a leader, in the midst of any great peril." And he records that Layard was at Gadshill during the Christmas before Dickens went to America for the last time.

We have it on the authority of the Editors of Dickens's *Letters* that the Rev. Edward Tagart was a very highly esteemed and valued friend, and there is plenty of evidence in support of this statement both in the *Letters* and in Forster's book, though Tagart certainly had not the social qualities of Tennent and Layard. It was in the early 'forties that they came to know each other. Dickens found himself somewhat out of sympathy with the Established Church, and for two or three years took sittings at the Little Portland Street Unitarian Chapel, of which Mr. Tagart was minister, and although they had met before, it was during this period that their friendship was formed and cemented so firmly that it outlived Dickens's return to the Established Church. In 1844 we find Tagart and his family visiting the novelist at Albaro, and in 1849 they were at the *Copperfield* christening dinner, on which occasion, Forster tells us, the reverend gentleman was seated next to Carlyle, and " was soon heard launching at him various metaphysical questions in regard to heaven and suchlike." Forster adds : " The relief was great when Thackeray introduced, with quaint whimsicality, a story which he and I had heard Macready relate in talking to us about

his boyish days, of a country actor who had supported himself
for six months on his judicious treatment of the 'tag' to the
'Castle Spectre.'"

Which reminiscence suggests that the good Mr. Tagart (as
Forster calls him) was scarcely the friend for all occasions. He
was a solid, good man, for whose character and intellect Dickens
had high esteem, but his sense of humour was not highly developed,
and of intimacy such as existed with Tennent and Layard there
was really none.

Sir Joseph Oliffe was a valued friend of whose intimacy with
the novelist there is very little record. Forster never mentions
him at all, yet Dickens declares in one of his letters : " I loved
him truly. His wonderful gentleness and kindness years ago,[1]
when we had sickness in our household in Paris, has never been
out of my grateful remembrance. And, socially, his image is
inseparable from some of the most genial and delightful friendly
hours of my life." Oliffe was physician to the British Embassy
in Paris, and the reference in this letter is to 1855, when Dickens
and his family spent some time in the French capital during
the writing of *Little Dorrit*. With Lady Oliffe the friendship
was equally strong, as several letters show. Here is one as an
example. It is dated May 26, 1861.

> " Touching the kind invitations received from you this
> morning, I feel that the only course I can take—without being
> a Humbug—is to decline them. After the middle of June I
> shall be mostly at Gad's Hill—I know that I cannot do better
> than keep out of the way of hot rooms and late dinners, and
> what would you think of me, or call me, if I were to accept
> and not come !
>
> " No, no, no. Be still, my soul. Be virtuous, eminent
> author. Do *not* accept, my Dickens. She is to come to Gad's
> Hill with her spouse. Await her *there*, my child. (Thus the
> voice of wisdom.)"

Writing of the late Devonshire House days, Forster says : " It
will introduce the last and not least honoured name into my list
of his acquaintance and friends, if I mention his amusing little
interruption one day to Professor Owen's descriptions of a tele-
scope of huge dimensions built by an enterprising clergyman
who had taken to the study of the stars; and who was eager,
said Owen, to see farther into heaven—he was going to say, than

---

[1] The letter was written to Oliffe's daughter in March 1869, when her
father died.

Lord Rosse; if Dickens had not drily interposed, 'than his professional studies had enabled him to penetrate.' " This is Forster's only reference to so distinguished a friend as Sir Richard Owen, F.R.S., whom he declares to have been not the least honoured of the novelist's friends.

CHAPTER LIX

CHAUNCEY HARE TOWNSHEND

ONE of the most remarkable of all Dickens's friendships was that with Chauncey Hare Townshend, who worshipped the novelist with a devotion that was complete. Townshend was a most ardent hero-worshipper where Dickens was concerned, and was most demonstrative in his affection. Here, for instance, is an extract from a letter written by the novelist to his elder daughter in 1859 : " I wish you could have seen him alone with me on Saturday; he was so extraordinarily earnest and affectionate on my belongings and affairs in general, and not least of all on you and Katie, that he cried in a most pathetic manner, and was so affected that I was obliged to leave him among the flower-pots in the long passage at the end of the dining-room. It was a very good piece of truthfulness and sincerity, especially in one of his years, able to take life so easily."

No man was ever more capable of responding to such devotion than Charles Dickens, and he undoubtedly had a very tender regard for this eccentric clergyman. This is what he wrote to Miss Hogarth from America when Townshend died :

> " Just now . . . I received your sad news of the death of poor Chauncey. It naturally goes to my heart. It is not a light thing to lose such a friend, and I truly loved him. In the first unreasonable train of feeling, I dwelt more than I should have thought possible on my being unable to attend his funeral. I know how little this really matters; but I know he would have wished me to be there with real honest tears for his memory, and I feel it very much. I never, never, never was better loved by man than I was by him, I am sure. Poor dear fellow, good affectionate gentle creature. "

Townshend, eccentric that he was, had all the qualities that win love. He was gentle, affectionate, simply good. Bulwer Lytton says : " About this time (1821) I fortunately contracted an acquaintance with a young man some years older than myself.

Indeed, he had just taken his degree at Cambridge, where he gained the Chancellor's medal for a poem on Jerusalem. . . . He impressed me with the idea of being singularly calm and pure. In spite of a beauty of face which at that time attracted the admiration of all who even passed him in the streets, his manners and conversation were characterised by an almost feminine modesty." Speaking of him as he knew him many years later, Mr. Percy Fitzgerald says that Townshend had all the gentle amiability of Cousin Feenix, with a sort of old-fashioned simplicity and aristocratic bearing. Mr. Fitzgerald even suggests that Townshend was the original of Cousin Feenix, but as in another place he names him as the prototype of Mr. Twemlow, we should not, perhaps, take this too seriously. None the less, both these characters, though somewhat eccentric, are simple souls with aristocratic bearing, gentlemen by birth, breeding, and nature, and such characteristics might well have been taken from Townshend.

Dickens dedicated *Great Expectations* to this friend, and also gave him the manuscript of that book—very marked proof of the regard he had for him. Townshend, as is well known, selected Dickens as his literary executor—" I appoint my friend Charles Dickens, of Gad's Hill Place, in the County of Kent, Esquire, my literary executor; and beg of him to publish without alteration as much of my notes and reflections as may make known my opinions on religious matters, they being such as I verily believe would be conducive to the happiness of mankind."

It was a heavy and not very congenial task. The " Religious Opinions of Chauncey Hare Townshend " are poor stuff, in any case. Dickens was just returned from that tragic American reading tour, and was in poor health. Some of the papers were in Lausanne, some were in London; the religious opinions were the accumulation of years, some connected and prepared for the press, others " all over the place," so to speak, so that it was almost impossible to trace any sequence at all, and they were intermixed with journals of travel, fragments of poems, critical essays, old school exercises, etc. But Dickens went through with his task for the sake of the love that he had borne his friend, and the book was duly published.

CHAPTER LX

AN EDITOR AND AN HISTORIAN

The friendship with Lord Macaulay and John T. Delane do not come within the same category as those just recorded, but Dickens knew both men very well—Delane particularly. He was, in Forster's words, always a highly esteemed friend of Dickens's, but there is no record of the friendship. Forster himself mentions the famous " Times " Editor only twice, and each time it is a bare reference; there are only two references to the novelist in Mr. A. I. Dasent's " Life of Delane "—each a mere record that the two men had dined together, once at Dickens's house in 1857, and once at Lord Alfred Paget's in 1858; and there are only three references to Delane in Dickens's *Letters*. One of these is a record of the fact that it was Delane who recommended the school at Boulogne to which Dickens sent four of his boys; another is the novelist's letter to Delane thanking him for the recommendation; and the third is contained in a letter to Macready (1869), and is as follows : " I dined at Greenwich a few days ago with Delane. He asked about you with much interest. He looks as if he had never seen a printing office, and had never been out of bed after midnight."

To Dickensians, of course, Delane is remembered as the friend who did Dickens perhaps the greatest disservice of his life, though, of course, with good intent. For it was his advice which finally decided Dickens to publish his famous denial of the slanders which grew up around his separation from his wife. Forster, Lemon, and Yates, were all against publication, but Dickens remained unmoved by their arguments. At last Forster suggested that Delane should be asked for his advice, and Dickens agreed. He was for publication, and the statement appeared in *Household Words*, June 12, 1858. How the discreet adviser of Prime Ministers and Foreign Secretaries came to give such bad advice in this case is a lasting puzzle.

With Macaulay there was even less intimacy, though Dickens knew him before his American tour, and they remained on good terms until the historian died in 1859. We know practically nothing about their relations (though we do know that Macaulay had a high opinion of Dickens's works as a humanising influence); but it is quite certain that there was no intimacy between them. How could there be? Both were good men with strong humanitarian feelings; but what could Macaulay, the solemn, portentous Macaulay, scholar, politician, devourer of Latin and Greek classics, have in common with Dickens, the man of the world, the liver of life at full pressure, Dickens the uneducated, who knew no more Latin or Greek than Macaulay's valet? But they could value each other's fine qualities, none the less. We cannot doubt but that Macaulay's virtues and genius were appraised by Dickens at their true worth; and we know that Dickens's love of humanity and power of appealing direct to the heart were fully appreciated by Macaulay. The very last entry in the latter's Journal is:

" Have you seen the first number of *Dombey*? There is not much in it; but there is one passage which made me cry as if my heart would break. It is the description of a little girl who has lost an affectionate mother and is unkindly treated by everybody. Images of this sort always overpower me, even when the artist is less skilful than Dickens."

But, needless to say, Macaulay was not an undiscriminating admirer of the novelist. In 1842 he writes to the Editor of the "Edinburgh Review": "I wish Dickens's book to be kept for me. I have never written a word on that subject; and I have a great deal in my head. Of course I shall be courteous to Dickens, whom I know, and whom I think both a man of genius and a good-hearted man, in spite of some faults of taste." The book referred to was *American Notes*. A short time afterwards we find him writing:

" This morning I received Dickens's book. I have now read it. It is impossible for me to review it; nor do I think you would wish me to do so. I cannot praise it, and I will not cut it up. I cannot praise it, though it contains a few lively dialogues and descriptions; for it seems to me to be on the whole a failure. It is written like the worst parts of *Humphrey's Clock*. What is meant to be easy and sprightly is vulgar and flippant, as in the first two pages. What is meant to be fine is a great deal too fine for me, as the description of the Fall of Niagara. . . . In short, I pronounce the book, in spite of some gleams of genius, at once frivolous and dull. Therefore I will not praise it. Neither will I attack it; first, because I have eaten salt with Dickens; secondly, because he is a good man, and a man of real talent; thirdly, because he hates slavery as heartily as I do; and fourthly, because I wish to see him enrol in our blue and yellow corps, where he may do excellent service as a skirmisher and sharpshooter."

So Macaulay never wrote about Dickens, and the fact may be regretted. A pronouncement by him on the work of the great humorist would have been tremendously interesting. An article from Macaulay's pen on *Pickwick*, for instance !

He makes only one other reference to the novelist, which deals with the Leigh Hunt–Harold Skimpole controversy, and puts the case against Dickens very strongly.

CHAPTER LXI

SOME LESSER FRIENDSHIPS OF THIS PERIOD

THERE are several members of what I have called the outer Dickens circle who more or less belong to this period. Frederick Locker-Lampson first saw the novelist at a charity bazaar in the Painted Hall of Greenwich Hospital on July 1, 1841. Three years later he was introduced to him at an Odd Fellows' club dinner. Another four years passed before their next meeting at the Athenæum, but after that they met often.

It was Locker-Lampson who made Dickens and Dean Stanley acquainted, and it was through him, after the novelist's death, that Stanley made the offer of burial in the Abbey. His final estimate of Dickens is worth quoting : " Dickens was a very good fellow, a delightful companion, warm-hearted, gay-natured, with plenty of light-in-hand fun, and a great capacity for friendship. He was the devoted lifelong servant of the public, and in my opinion, to say the least of him, he was the most laughter-provoking writer that the world has ever known."

Tom Taylor, who succeeded Shirley Brooks as Editor of " Punch," was also very friendly—but, of course, Dickens was on friendly terms with all Mr. Punch's men. Certainly he was on excellent terms with Taylor from 1848. They were frequently together, but there is no record of their friendship, which was never really intimate.

With Lord Carlisle Dickens was on the best of terms for a great many years. The first evidence we have of their friendship is a letter written by Dickens to Lord Carlisle in July 1851 : " We shall be delighted to see you, if you will come down on Saturday. Mr. Lemon may perhaps be here with his wife, but no one else. And we can give you a bed that may be surpassed, with a welcome that cannot be. . . . You will have for a night-light in the room we shall give you the North Foreland Lighthouse. That and the sea air are our only lions. It is a very rough little place, but a very pleasant one, and you will make it pleasanter than ever to me." Dickens had much in sympathy with Carlisle, who had been a supporter of the great Reform Bill, and was always on the side of progress.

Lady Molesworth was one of the select few for whom the postilions were turned out at Gadshill. She was " an old and dear friend." But we have no record of this friendship, and none of Dickens's letters to her is preserved. We know, however, that she and her daughter, Mrs. Ford, were frequent guests at his house, and that he was as often their guest; whilst at Paris in 1863 they had many pleasant hours together.

No more can be written about Lord and Lady Lovelace. Forster mentions them only once, and their names do not occur in the *Letters*; but we do know that there was a very pleasant friendship, and that after Dickens's return from Italy in 1846 they were frequently guests at his house. Apparently this friendship arose out of the friendship with Sir George Crawford, with whom Dickens had had much pleasant intercourse in Genoa. He married Lovelace's sister, and thus Dickens came to know his lordship and his wife. We are told that Paul Dombey's death laid a strange fascination on Lady Lovelace.

Matthew Higgins was another with whom Dickens was very friendly, yet of whom Forster records nothing except that the postilions were turned out in his honour. That fact alone, however, is proof that he was held in special esteem. His gift of humour, and his enthusiasm for social reform, would be sufficient to account for it.

Giving a list of Dickens's most valued friends at this period Forster says : " Incomplete indeed would be the list if I did not add to it the frank and hearty Lord Nugent, who had so much of his grandfather, Goldsmith's friend, in his lettered tastes and jovial enjoyments." That is all we are told of a friendship that was very hearty and greatly valued. In regard to Lord Dudley Stuart we are in the same unfortunate position. " There was," says Forster, " a charm for him I should find it difficult to exaggerate in Lord Dudley Stuart's gentle yet noble character, his refined intelligence and generous public life, expressed so perfectly in his chivalrous face." No further reference to so valued a friend !

Sir Arthur Helps may find his place here. He was a well-liked friend. His son has told all there is to tell of his associations with the novelist, in his recent book.[1]

Dickens's first letter to Helps was dated January 3, 1854, at which time the two men were clearly not intimate. Helps made it a habit, his son tells us, to send to friends and to prominent men he had met copies of his books. From the letter which I quote it seems clear that he had met Dickens on some occasion and now had sent him a copy of " Friends in Council " with a reminder of the occasion. This is the letter :

[1] "Correspondence of Sir Arthur Helps, K.C.B., D.C.L." Edited by his son, E. A. Helps.

" Dear Sir,

" I too have a very pleasant remembrance of the evening to which you refer, and your name is so much a part of it that I required no other reminder.

" I shall take counsel with our ' Friends,' with the greatest interest in the subject that occupies their thoughts. Sanitary improvements are the one thing needful to begin with ; and until they are thoroughly, efficiently, and uncompromisingly made (and every bestial little prejudice and supposed interest contrariwise crushed under foot) even Education itself will fall short of its uses."

For some years after this there remained just an acquaintanceship, so far as I can gather, and it was not until 1861 that Dickens and Helps came really to know each other. In the summer of that year they met at Lytton's seat at Knebworth, and Forster tells us that then they visited, in company with Lord Orford, the so-called " Hermit " near Stevenage, whom Dickens described as Mr. Mopes in *Tom Tiddler's Ground.* Thenceforward they were on friendly terms, and they seem to have met fairly often. We know that Helps visited the novelist at Gadshill, for Forster tells us that the postilions were turned out for him.

But of course the most interesting feature of Dickens's friendship with Helps is that it brought about his famous interview with Queen Victoria. He told the Queen of some very interesting photographs of battlefields of the American Civil War which Dickens had shown him, and Her Majesty desired to see them. Dickens sent them to her, and she expressed a wish to meet him and thank him.

Mr. Helps quotes a letter from Dickens to his father, which is of peculiar interest, and which I had not seen before. It certainly is not published in *The Letters of Charles Dickens.*

It is dated from Hyde Park Place, Saturday, March 26, 1870, and is as follows :

" The binder reports to me to-day that he wants ' another fortnight ' for the completion of the set of my books which I have entrusted to him to bind for the Queen. Of course he must have it, or he will forever believe that I spoilt his work by driving him.

" *En attendant,* I send you for Her Majesty the first number of my new story which will not be published till next Thursday, the 31st. Will you kindly give it to the Queen with my loyal duty and devotion ? If Her Majesty should ever be sufficiently interested in the tale to desire to know a little

more of it in advance of her subjects, you know how proud
I shall be to anticipate the publication.

" You will receive soon after this a copy of your Godson's
most portable edition of his writings for yourself. I hope
you may like it, and, revising and abbreviating the Catechism,
' do one thing in his name ':—read it."

This letter makes one wonder whether Queen Victoria or Sir
Arthur Helps could have helped us to solve the *Drood* problem.

Thomas Milner Gibson was a staunch progressive in Parliament, for whose public work Dickens had a great admiration,
and with whom he was on most friendly terms. Dickens especially appreciated Gibson's efforts which were chiefly responsible
for the repeal of the advertisement duty, the newspaper stamp
duty, and the paper duty. But they had been friends long before
those important reforms were brought about—intimate friends :
indeed, this friendship was one of the pleasantest of the novelist's
life.

Forster never once mentions George Grove, Secretary of the
Society of Arts, Secretary and Director of the Crystal Palace Co.,
Editor of " Macmillan's Magazine," etc., and none of Dickens's
letters to him is preserved. But he was well acquainted with
the novelist, and when Sir Arthur Helps wrote for " Macmillan's " in 1870 an In Memoriam of Dickens he wrote to him
that " Dickens was the best and pleasantest person in the world
to tell a good story to. You saw that he was taking in every
word. As you went on, the sense of fun seemed to rise in his
face—his eyes shone and looked more and more knowing as you
neared the point; and the moment it was reached there was
just that explosion that was most gratifying."

Thomas Chapman, the Chairman of Lloyd's, was a " much-
valued friend " with whom there was frequent, kindly intercourse,
but we have no particulars of the friendship save that he obtained
a situation in the City for the novelist's younger brother, Augustus.
But the interest attaches to him that he was by many declared
to be the prototype of Mr. Dombey. Curiously enough, that
statement crops up occasionally in these days, despite the fact
that Forster declares that " few things could be more absurd or
unfounded."

Charles Reade, we are told by the Editors of Dickens's *Letters*,
was held as a writer and as a friend in the highest regard. Of
the friendship, however, we have no record. It was not until
fairly late in Dickens's life that they became acquainted—I
wonder if it was through Wilkie Collins ? We have at least one
record of Reade staying at Gadshill. " Charles Reade and

T

Wilkie Collins are here," Dickens wrote to James T. Fields in September 1867, " and the joke of the time is to feel my pulse when I appear at table, and also to inveigle innocent messengers to come over to the summer house . . . to ask, with their compliments, how I find myself *now*." In 1863, Reade's " Hard Cash " appeared in *All the Year Round*.

There is one little story of Reade which may well be retold here. It is related by Justin McCarthy, who says that an American friend of his asked Reade to go to America on a lecturing tour. Reade expressed himself as willing, but asked how much Dickens had. He was told, and he said that he would go for that amount. It was pointed out that Dickens's success had been something beyond all comparison or competition, but Reade insisted, and—the tour did not come off. Most likely this was just his eccentric way of refusing to undertake a tour. Of course, he was an eccentric, but his heart was sound enough, and so he was exactly the sort of man that would appeal to Dickens.

I have doubted whether Samuel Carter Hall should have a place in the Dickens circle. His wife was certainly counted a friend, but I am pretty sure he was not, though he was fairly well acquainted with the novelist. If one were to sit down to imagine the sort of man that Dickens would not like, the effort would cease when Hall came to mind. Listen to Samuel Carter Hall talking about Ainsworth's " Jack Sheppard " : " It became a sort of sacred book to the ruffians, demireps, and all who were dishonestly or immorally inclined amongst the lowest orders, and in fact made as well as encouraged thieves and other moral social pests of society. I hope before he died ' he repented of this evil.' God gave him time in which to do so." And he speaks of Walter Savage Landor as " the hoary old sinner." In the big gallery he gives us of the great men he has known, he has not an unqualified good word to say of half a dozen. I accept unhesitatingly the assertion that he was the prototype of Pecksniff. I do not mean that Hall was a rogue, or a humbug; but he was a moral man, oh, so moral ! In all mannerisms, methods of speech, in all the touches by which we know our Pecksniff, that character is a perfect reflection of the Hall that is self-revealed in his own writings. Friend of Dickens ! The thought is preposterous.

He had been in his early days a reporter in the Gallery for " The British Press," and he tells us that " Now and then came to the office a smart, intelligent active lad who brought what was then called, and is still, I believe, named ' Penny-a-line stuff '; that is to say, notices of accidents, fires, police reports, such as escaped the more regular reporters, for which a penny a

printed line was paid. The lad to whom I refer was that Charles
Dickens whose name not very long afterwards became known to
and honoured by the half of humankind." But as Hall definitely
fixes this at 1826, when Dickens was only fourteen years old, I
am like the Scotchman, " I ha'e ma doots." Nevertheless, the
two were certainly acquainted in early days.

Mrs. Hall was a good woman, with none of her husband's
failings; and she was a clever woman, too—a clever journalist
and novelist. For her Dickens certainly did entertain feelings
of friendship, and perhaps—who knows?—sometimes tolerated
her husband for her sake. She often visited his house, and she
has left some pleasing impressions of those visits.

Just two or three others may be mentioned with whom there
were hearty friendships, who were frequent guests at Dickens's
house. Isambard Brunel is classed by Forster with several with
whom Dickens's intercourse was intimate and frequent, and we
know that he was often a welcome guest at the novelist's table.
With him we may place Horace Twiss, Mowbray Morris, John
Harwick, Dr. Quin, and others.

There are one or two foreigners who may be mentioned in this
place, who cannot be claimed as in the real sense friends of Dickens,
but whom he knew well, for whose work and characters he had
high esteem. With Giuseppe Mazzini he became acquainted
through giving money to a begging impostor who made un-
authorised use of the great Italian's name. They became pretty
well known to each other. Dickens, it is not surprising to learn,
had a great regard for Mazzini's worth and character, and a
genuine sympathy with his ideals. When the Republic of Rome
fell in 1849, Dickens proved his sympathy with the cause very
emphatically, by penning " an appeal to the English People "
on behalf of the refugees who came to this country. In the
previous year, ere Mazzini had left England on this unsuccessful
enterprise, one Sunday evening was made memorable (as Forster
puts it) by the Italian taking the novelist and his friend to see
the school he had established in Clerkenwell for Italian organ
boys. On that evening Mazzini had dined at Dickens's house,
and in after years he was many times a guest there.

Alexander Dumas and Victor Hugo were but acquaintances.
Dickens dined with the former in Paris in 1847, as well as with
Eugène Sue, and other famous Frenchmen. In that same year
he was received by Victor Hugo " with infinite courtesy and
grace." Forster, who was present, says that the great French
writer " talked of his childhood in Spain, and of his father having
been Governor of the Tagus in Napoleon's wars; spoke warmly
of the English people and their literature. . . . To Dickens he

addressed very charming flattery, in the best taste; and my friend long remembered the enjoyment of that evening."

There were other famous Frenchmen whom Dickens met, but we need not name them—except, perhaps, Alphonse Lamartine, with whom, Forster tells us, there was much friendly intercourse during that stay in Paris in 1847.

CHAPTER LXII

A BIG GROUP OF ARTISTS

PROMINENT in the Dickens circle was a big group of artists. We have already met many of these; let us now shake hands with a few more.

First, there is Charles Robert Leslie. For a good many years he was on the best of terms with Dickens. He was a peculiarly likeable man, and the novelist held him in high regard. Though born in England, he spent his boyhood and youth in America, and when Dickens was still in his 'teens, he had illustrated Washington Irving, and it was " Geoffrey Crayon " who wrote to Dickens urging him to make the artist's acquaintance. He did so, and when he went to America in 1842 he not only carried with him a letter from Leslie to Irving, but also went out of his way to visit some of the artist's relatives. Leslie was a frequent and welcome visitor at Dickens's house, but he lacked social gifts, and his unassuming nature kept him in the background. He was often one of the company on the occasions of the theatrical performances, and if he took no active part in them, he has left us the best picture of Dickens as an actor that we possess—" Portrait of Charles Dickens, Esq., in the character of Captain Bobadil," painted in 1846.

E. M. Ward was another well-liked friend, and a frequent visitor to Dickens's house. The first mention of him in connection with the novelist that I can find relates to the year 1851, when he designed the card of membership for the Guild of Literature and Art. Three years later Dickens sat to him for a portrait—one of a series of oil sketches of the famous literary men of the day in their studies. In this latter year also Ward and his wife visited Boulogne and Paris with the novelist and his wife. The artist's widow only recently recalled her memories of that trip in a London newspaper.

On that occasion Mrs. Ward also related an incident which occurred at Dickens's house in which George Cruikshank figured unpleasantly. " Cruikshank," she wrote, " had suddenly developed a mania for total abstinence, and seeing me about to sip a glass of wine snatched the glass from me, to dash it on the

floor. I had never seen Dickens so angry. To Cruikshank he
said, ' How dare you touch Mrs. Ward's glass ? It is an un-
pardonable liberty. What do you mean ? Because some one
you know was a drunkard for forty years, surely it is not for you
to object to an innocent glass of sherry ! ' Cruikshank, one of
the largest-hearted creatures in the world—but given to acting
on impulse—was too taken aback to reply, and he disappeared
for the rest of that very pleasant evening."

W. P. Frith was a greatly liked friend. He was a young man
when his excellent paintings of Dolly Varden brought about an
acquaintance with Dickens, whom he worshipped, as did most
of the young men of the time. He has himself told the story of
the friendship that ensued, and to his account there is really
nothing to add. From his earliest days he was an enthusiastic
lover of Dickens's books, and sought for a subject in them that
would lend itself to his brush, but he was held back by the ugliness
of modern dress. But with the appearance of *Barnaby Rudge*
he discovered what he sought in the person of Dolly Varden.
He painted her in a variety of attitudes, and all the pictures found
ready purchasers, though for small sums. Then, in November
1842, he received the following letter from Dolly's creator :

> " MY DEAR SIR,
>   " I shall be very glad if you will do me the favour
> to paint me two little companion pictures ; one a Dolly
> Varden (whom you have so exquisitely done already), the
> other a Kate Nickleby."

The artist was transported with delight. " Mother and I,"
he says, " cried over that letter, and the wonder is that anything
is left of it, for I showed it to every friend I had, and was admired
and envied by all." He set to work with a will, and the pictures
delighted Dickens, who paid £40 for the pair, which, after his
death, fetched 1300 guineas at Christie's.

Henceforth Frith basked in the sunshine of Dickens's friendship,
and was a frequent and welcome visitor at the novelist's house.
To the end of his life he remained almost an idolater. " The
reading of Dickens's works," he says, " has no doubt engendered
a love for the writer in thousands of hearts. How that affection
would have been increased could his readers have had personal
knowledge of the man can only be known to those who, like myself,
had the happiness of his intimate acquaintance."

In 1859 Forster asked Frith to paint a portrait of Dickens for
him. He had made the suggestion in 1854, but Dickens had
grown a moustache, and his friend had decided to wait : " This

CHARLES DICKENS

(1859)

From a painting by W. P. Frith, R.A.

is a whim—the fancy will pass. We will wait till the hideous disfigurement is removed." The fancy did not pass, however, and the moustache was followed by a beard, and at last Forster gave it up as hopeless and commissioned the picture. It was while Dickens was sitting for this that he told Frith that a Library Edition of his works was to be published, and the artist begged to be allowed to be an illustrator. Dickens agreed, and Frith chose *Little Dorrit*, for which he did two small pictures. Dickens presented him with a complete set of the edition.

Of the portrait nothing needs to be said here. It is one of the best known of all the portraits of the novelist, and it is interesting because it is the first showing him with the beard. Dickens is said to have remarked of it that it made him look as if he had just heard that the house of his next-door neighbour, with whom he was on bad terms, was on fire ! But he liked it, all the same, and it pleased Forster, so that it cannot have been other than a good portrait.

A genuine, though not very intimate friendship was that with John Everett Millais, the lifelong friend of Charles Allston Collins, brother of Wilkie, and later Dickens's son-in-law. It was at Collins's house on April 18, 1852, that he met the novelist.

Dickens must have had some uncomfortable thoughts when he met the two Pre-Raphaelites, for in June 1850 he had written an article in *Household Words* entitled *New Lamps for Old Ones*, in which he had dealt with the Pre-Raphaelites with special reference to Millais's picture, " The Carpenter's Shop." It is worth while quoting from that article, I think :

" You will have the goodness to discharge from your mind all Post-Raphael ideas, all religious aspirations, all elevating thoughts; all tender, awful, sorrowful, ennobling, sacred, graceful, or beautiful associations, and prepare yourselves, as befits such a subject—Pre-Raphaelly considered—for the lowest depths of what is mean, odious, repulsive, and revolting.

" You behold the interior of a carpenter's shop. In the foreground of that carpenter's shop is a hideous, wry-necked, blubbering, red-headed boy, in a bed-gown; who appears to have received a poke in the hand from the stick of another boy with whom he has been playing in an adjacent gutter, and to be holding it up for the contemplation of a kneeling woman, so horrible in her ugliness, that (supposing it were possible for any human creature to exist for a moment with that dislocated throat) she would stand out from the rest of the company as a Monster, in the vilest cabaret in France, or the lowest gin-shop in England. Two almost naked carpenters, master and journeyman, worthy companions of this agreeable female, are working at their trade; a boy, with some small flavour of humanity in him, is entering with a vessel of water; and nobody is paying any attention to a snuffy old woman who seems to have mistaken that shop for the tobacconist's next door, and to be hopelessly waiting at the counter to be served with half an ounce of her favourite mixture. Wherever it is possible to express ugliness of feature, limb, or attitude, you have it expressed. Such men as the carpenters might be undressed in any hospital where dirty drunkards, in a high state of varicose veins, are received."

This is very interesting because of the facts that within a few months of the publication of that article Dickens was to meet the painter thus abused, and to form a friendship with him; that within ten years another of the Brotherhood was to marry his daughter; and that within twenty years he was to select a Pre-Raphaelite as the illustrator of his last book. For, as all the world knows, it was Dickens's wish that C. A. Collins should illustrate *Edwin Drood*. Which leads to another interesting fact; namely, that when Collins found himself unable, on account of ill-health, to proceed with the task, a young man named Luke Fildes was selected to take his place, entirely on the earnest recommendation of the painter of " The Carpenter's Shop " !

In 1860—the year that she became Mrs. Collins—Dickens's daughter served Millais for a model for one of his best pictures, " The Black Brunswicker." Ten years later the artist did a picture, not so well known, but much more interesting from the present point of view. His son, speaking of Dickens's death, says that Millais had " long entertained a tender regard for the novelist." He was one of the privileged few admitted to the dining-room at Gadshill while the great man lay dead, and his picture of Dickens on his death-bed is one of the best things he ever did.

He intended at first, we are told, to make it a little outline drawing only, but the features of the novelist struck him as being so calm and beautiful in death that he ended by making a finished portrait. He gave it to his old friend's wife—Kate Dickens.

It should be recorded that in 1886 Millais did an admirable picture of Little Nell and her Grandfather—so far as I have been able to trace, the only occasion on which he went to Dickens's books for inspiration.

Holman Hunt was well acquainted with Dickens, but he was

not so much a friend of Dickens's as a friend of Dickens's son-in-law.   For, of course, he was a lifelong intimate of Charles Collins, at whose wedding to Kate Dickens in 1860 he was a guest.

The novelist knew the great Turner, as we have seen, but the only meeting of the pair actually recorded was that already noted in our chapter on Carlyle, on the occasion of the dinner prior to Dickens's departure for Italy in 1844.   Another famous artist who was often a guest at Dickens's table was Sir Charles Eastlake. There were others, too, but with only one more have we any real interest.

Luke Fildes was but a young man when he first knew the novelist with whose name his own is indissolubly linked, and he knew him for only a few months, but in that time Dickens had learned to regard him as a friend, and he had learned to love the great writer. The young artist had, of course, already achieved some distinction in his profession before he was selected to illustrate *Edwin Drood*. He was twenty-five years old then, and had already exhibited at the Royal Academy, whilst he was known as a magazine illustrator.   I believe, indeed, that it was the excellence of one of his pictures in " The Graphic " that struck Millais, who went to Dickens with " I've found the very man you want."   The choice was the happiest Dickens ever made.   Better work than Fildes's illustrations to *Edwin Drood* was never done for any of his books, and that is saying much.

Of the personal relations of Dickens and his last illustrator there is very little to be said.   They had known one another for only a few months when the novelist was struck down.   That sorrowful event occurred on a Wednesday evening.   On the following morning Dickens was to have gone to London for the remainder of the week, and he was to have been accompanied on his return by the young artist, whose visit had been arranged so that he might become acquainted with the neighbourhood in which most of the scenes in the books were laid.   We know that he was to have accompanied the novelist to Maidstone gaol, there to see the condemned cell, with a view to a subsequent illustration.

Dickens had formed a great liking for the artist, and had a very high opinion indeed of his genius.   On the other side there was that admiration and reverence which Dickens never failed to inspire in young men.   A few years ago Sir Luke Fildes gave expression to his regard for the novelist in an indignant letter he wrote to " The Times."   A reviewer of Andrew Lang's book, " The Puzzle of Dickens's Last Plot " had suggested that the hints dropped by Dickens to Forster and to members of his family as to the plot, might have been intentionally misleading. " I know Charles Dickens was very anxious that his secret should not be guessed," wrote Sir Luke in reply, " but it surprises me to read that he could be thought capable of the deceit so lightly attributed to him." Then he related how Dickens had told him in confidence that Jasper was to strangle Drood, and he concluded :

> " I was impressed by his earnestness, as, indeed, I was at all my interviews with him . . . and it is a little startling, after more than thirty-five years of profound belief in the nobility of character and sincerity of Charles Dickens, to be told now that he probably was more or less of a humbug on such occasions."

That profound belief in the nobility of Dickens's character has always remained with Sir Luke Fildes.

Immediately after Dickens's death Sir Luke painted his famous picture " The Empty Chair," showing the study at Gadshill as it was left by the novelist when he laid down his pen for ever. That picture was engraved on wood, and published by " The Graphic " in December 1870. Copies of that engraving are now very rare, and are greatly valued by Dickensians. Sir Luke also did a drawing of the novelist's grave.

TOM SMART AND THE CHAIR

From a sketch for " The Pickwick Papers " by John Leech

CHAPTER LXIII

HENRY FOTHERGILL CHORLEY

On June 7, 1870, Charles Dickens wrote a letter to Henry Fothergill Chorley, the famous musical critic; on the 9th Chorley heard that Dickens was ill; on the 10th he heard of his friend's death. "Chorley's mental prostration when I called upon him shortly afterwards," says his biographer, Mr. Henry G. Hewlett, "was painful to witness." Writing to Benson Rathbone at the time, Chorley said : "God bless you for your kindness. For the hour I am best alone. . . . I had a letter from poor Mary.[1] If universal sympathy of the warmest kind in every form could soften the agony of such a trial they will have it in overflowing measure, but it will not give back one of the noblest and most gifted men I have ever known, whose regard for me was one of those honours which make amends for much failure and disappointment. I cannot express to any human being the void this will make for me to my dying day."

There was no exaggeration in this, for Mary Dickens tells us : "After my father's death, and before we left the dear old home, Mr. Chorley wrote and asked me if I would send him a branch off each of our large cedar trees in remembrance of the place. My friend, and *his* dear friend Mr. Lehmann, saw him lying calm and peaceful in his coffin with a large green branch on each side of him. He did not understand what this meant, but I did, and was much touched, as, of course, he had given orders that these branches should be laid with him in his coffin. So a piece of the place he loved so much for its dear master's sake went down to the grave with him."

Chorley is a figure calling for sympathy. He was a good man who went through life lonely, missing love; he suffered many sorrows and many trials, and he found in Charles Dickens a very true friend who understood and sympathised. The brightest part of his later years, Mr. Hewlett tells us, was that which was illumined by his friendship with Dickens. They became intimate in 1854, but they had met some years before that. During the last few years of the novelist's life they were in constant corre-

---

[1] Dickens's eldest daughter, Mamie.

spondence, and Mr. Hewlett says : " There was probably no other man of letters, with the exception of Forster, to whom his confidence was so entirely given.   Amid many differences of mental and moral constitution there was one salient feature in common. In Dickens the quality of *punctuality*, as Chorley used to describe it, was manifest in the minutest particulars.   He himself was less scrupulously methodical ; but in all essential points his thorough trustworthiness was equally prominent. . . . Though both the friends were probably self-conscious of possessing this characteristic, it seems to have been to each the object of special admiration in the other.   Both recognised in one another the presence of generous candour. . . ."

Mr. Hewlett adds :

> " Such other relics of Dickens's large correspondence with him as Chorley has preserved . . . attest the thorough sympathy that subsisted between the two.   On no occasion of his life when he needed help great or small, whether consolation under affliction, counsel in the settlement of a dispute, or as to the adaptation of his voice to a lecture-room, did Dickens fail to render it.   More than once during those years, when, bowed down by weight of loneliness, ill-health and sorrow, he was absorbed in moods of utter depression or driven to adopt the most fatal of expedients for removing it, the clear healthy sense of Dickens was felt by him as a tower of strength ; and it was doubtless a remembrance of the influence extended at such times that dictated the language of a grateful bequest to his friend as one by whom he had been ' greatly helped.' "

The bequest referred to was £50 for a ring.   Alas ! Dickens had gone before his friend.   There was also a bequest to Mamie Dickens of £200 a year for life.

We have seen that Dickens and Chorley became intimate in 1854.   Mamie Dickens tells us that the intimacy was brought about by their working together to obtain a pension for two literary friends.   Chorley was always a very welcome guest at Gadshill.   Says the novelist's eldest daughter :

> " People who were in the habit of seeing Mr. Chorley only in London would hardly have known him at Gadshill, I think.   He was a brighter and another being altogether there. . . . I believe he loved my father better than any man in the world ; was grateful to him for his friendship, and truly proud of possessing it, which he certainly did to

a very large amount. My father was very fond of him, and had the greatest respect for his honest, straightforward, upright and generous character. I think, and am very glad to think, that the happiest days of Mr. Chorley's life—his later years, that is to say—were passed at Gadshill."

Chorley at Gadshill. How many of his London friends could have pictured him as an amateur actor convulsing an audience with his comicalities! Yet so it was—at Gadshill. In No. 15 of " The Gad's Hill Gazette " we read of an entertainment " given by Messrs. H. and E. Dickens in the Theatre Royal Club Room." The farce, " The Rival Volunteers," was played; Mr. H. Dickens " managed " the orchestra, Mr. E. Dickens was stage manager, and " C. Dickens, Esq., as an aged gentleman, and H. F. Chorley, Esq., as a Turk, were intensely comic, and between all the scenes the laughter (caused by these gentlemen) was incessant."

If Dickens was whole-hearted in his encouragement of Chorley in his literary work, he, in his turn, valued very highly indeed his friend's opinion of his own books. Chorley reviewed in the " Athenæum " *Martin Chuzzlewit, David Copperfield, A Christmas Carol, Bleak House*, and *Our Mutual Friend.* In regard to his review of the last-named book, Dickens wrote to him : " I have seen the ' Athenæum,' and most heartily and earnestly thank you. Trust me, there is nothing I could have wished away, and all that I read there affects and delights me."

CHAPTER LXIV

WILKIE COLLINS

The great friend of Dickens's later years was William Wilkie Collins, for whom he entertained a regard that was quite exceptional and, to me, somewhat difficult of explanation. It was not merely a friendship in the ordinary sense : he came under Collins's spell to a remarkable degree, and one of the most astonishing of literary facts is the influence which the younger man exercised over the art of one who was famous and the acknowledged first of living novelists before he himself had left school. It is true, of course, that in so far as Dickens owed anything to anybody, he was chiefly indebted to Fielding and Smollett, but as he drew towards the close of his life the influence of those two masters gave way to that of a young writer who was his inferior in every respect save one, and never succeeded in crossing the line which divides the great writers from the first-class writers. Dickens recognised Collins's wonderful skill at plot construction and magnified its value and importance. It was the spell of Collins, undoubtedly, that prompted him to endeavour in *Edwin Drood* to prove himself an expert mystery unraveller, and it is equally beyond question that " if that book had been finished it would have shown that the pupil was at least the equal of his teacher." But even so, can we honestly say that we are glad of Collins's influence as revealed by this book? Frankly, I see no cause for gratitude to the author of " The Woman in White." I am not blind, I hope, to the art of this book, but I see little more than suggestions of those qualities that made Dickens famous and loved. *Edwin Drood* is a great fragment, but it is not the Dickens that will live—the Dickens of this book is not the great character drawer, the great enjoyer of life, the great friend of humanity that is revealed in every one of his other books, from *Pickwick* to *Our Mutual Friend*.

It may be that I misjudge Collins, but I confess that I find it at least as difficult to account for the affection in which he was held by Dickens. We are told by one writer that he was " highly gifted socially," and we are forced to believe that there was more in the man than any writer has revealed, yet all my reading has failed to make me believe that there was that *lovableness* about him that there was about the other members of the inner Dickens circle; it has only gone, indeed, to confirm the opinion expressed by Mr. Percy Fitzgerald : " I always think that Dickens's noble, unselfish, generous nature expanded itself somewhat vainly on such a character, certainly not endowed with anything likely to respond to such affection. Not that I knew him sufficiently to judge him, but he had not the warm and rather romantic tone of feeling that Boz looked for."

Still, there is the fact; Dickens had a genuine affection for Wilkie Collins. " You know," he wrote, " I am not in the habit of making professions, but I have so strong an interest in you, and so true a regard for you, that nothing can come amiss in the way of information as to your well-doing."

It was through Egg that the two novelists first became acquainted. It was in connection with the performance of " Not So Bad as we Seem " at Devonshire House. Forster tells us that Collins became " for all the rest of the life of Dickens, one of his dearest and most valued friends." He went with the company on tour, and in addition to Smart, in Lytton's comedy, played James, in " Used Up," and Lithers in " Mr. Nightingale's Diary." His love for the stage must have been almost as great as Dickens's and Mark Lemon's. They acted together many times, two of Collins's plays were specially written for and produced at Tavistock House, and they collaborated in the dramatisation of *No Thoroughfare,* the last of the famous Christmas numbers of *All the Year Round,* of which they were joint authors.

Let us deal with these stage associations first. In 1855 the first of the children's plays was produced at Tavistock House. This was " Fortunio." In the same year Collins wrote " The Lighthouse," which was produced on June 19, and repeated at Campden House in July for the benefit of the Bournemouth Sanatorium for Consumptive Patients. Collins himself played the second Light-keeper.

Two years later came " The Frozen Deep." Again Dickens wrote the Prologue, which was recited by Forster, but the original manuscript and the prompt-book reveal that he also contributed much to the play itself. The manuscript was sold by auction in 1890 and realised 300 guineas. To it was appended the following note in Collins's handwriting : " Mr. Dickens himself played the principal part and played it with a truth, vigour, and pathos never to be forgotten by those who were fortunate enough to witness it. . . . At Manchester this play was twice performed, on the second evening before 3000 people. This was, I think, the finest of all its representations. . . . Dickens surpassed himself. He literally electrified the audience."

The two novelists had close literary, as well as stage, associations. Few wrote more frequently for *Household Words* and *All the Year Round* than Wilkie Collins, whilst he collaborated with Dickens several times, more especially in connection with the Christmas numbers. His first story for *Household Words* was "Sister Rose," which appeared in April and May 1855, and which Dickens described as "an excellent story, charmingly written, and showing everywhere an amount of pains and study in respect of the art of doing such things that I see mighty seldom." It may be that here is one of the chief reasons for Dickens's admiration for Collins. The young writer possessed qualities of hard work and thoroughness, and few things appealed to Dickens more than "thorough-going earnestness." In 1856, "After Dark " and "The Diary of Anne Rodway" appeared in *Household Words*, and in the following year came "The Dead Secret."

In September 1857 Dickens and Collins made a tour to the North of England together for the purpose of writing *The Lazy Tour of Two Idle Apprentices*. "I have arranged with Collins," wrote Dickens to Forster, "that he and I will start next Monday on a ten or twelve days' expedition to out-of-the-way places, to do (in inns and coast-corners) a little tour in search of an article and in avoidance of railroads. . . . Our decision is for a foray upon the fells of Cumberland, I having discovered in the books some promising moors and bleak places thereabout." And so they went to the Lake District, but their trip was spoiled by a mishap which befell Collins, who sprained his ankle during the descent of Carrick Fell.

They completed their tour, however, and their account of it duly appeared in *Household Words*. The *Lazy Tour* is an unsatisfactory piece of work, and I never read it but I am glad that the desire that Dickens cherished for some time, that he and Collins should collaborate in the writing of a novel, was never realised. It is astonishing how Dickens, in this book, allowed his own personality to sink almost out of sight.

In 1858 *Household Words* came to an end, and in the following year *All the Year Round* was started. Its first serial was *A Tale of Two Cities*, and this was followed by "The Woman in White," which commenced on November 26. This, of course, was the book that finally established Collins as a novelist, and it also did much to establish the magazine in which it appeared. "No

Name " ran as a serial in 1861, and of this Dickens wrote : " It is as far before and beyond ' The Woman in White ' as *that* was beyond the common level of fiction writing." Later came " Armadale," and finally " The Moonstone." And by this time Dickens was tiring of Collins's style—tiring of the constant creaking of machinery. In a letter respecting " The Woman in White," he had put his finger right on his friend's weakness, the weakness which keeps Collins out of the first rank. He had written :

> " I seem to have noticed, here and there, that the great pains you take express themselves a trifle too much, and you know that I always contest your disposition to give an audience credit for nothing. . . . Perhaps I express my meaning best when I say that the three people who write the narratives in these proofs have a DISSECTIVE property in common, which is essentially not theirs but yours; and that my own effort would be to strike more of what is got *that way* out of them by collision with one another, and by the working of the story."

And now he wrote to a friend, " I quite agree with you about ' The Moonstone.' The construction is wearisome beyond endurance, and there is a vein of obstinate conceit in it that makes enemies of readers."

Collins had a hand in nearly all the Christmas numbers. He first appeared as the Fourth Traveller in *The Seven Poor Travellers*, 1854. In the following year he assisted with *The Holly-Tree Inn*, and in 1856 he wrote " John Steadman's Account " of the *Wreck of the Golden Mary*, and also " The Deliverance." In 1857 he wrote the second chapter of *The Perils of Certain English Prisoners*, Dickens writing the remainder of the number, and in the last *Household Words* Christmas number—*A House to Let*—he was the author of " Over the Way " and " Trottle's Report," whilst he and Dickens collaborated in the final chapter, " Let at Last."

His contributions to the *All the Year Round* Christmas numbers were as follow : To *The Haunted House* in 1859 " The Ghost in the Cupboard Room "; to *A Message from the Sea*, 1860, " The Seafaring Man," and, in collaboration with Dickens," The Money " and " The Restitution "; to *Tom Tiddler's Ground* in 1861 " Picking up Waifs and Strays "; and he collaborated with Dickens in the last of the series—*No Thoroughfare*—in 1867. When the friends were writing *A Message from the Sea*, they made a special trip to Cornwall and Devon in search of local colour. It should be noted that they evidently intended to

U

dramatise this story, because there is in the British Museum a small brochure whose title-page runs thus:

A MESSAGE FROM THE SEA

A Drama in Three Acts

by
CHARLES DICKENS
and
WILKIE COLLINS

An Outline of the Plot

LONDON.—Published by G. Holsworth
At the office of " All the Year Round,"
Wellington Street, Strand,
1861.

This manuscript traces the plot and action of Acts 1 and 2, and then " Act the Third passes in Tregarthen's cottage at Steepways and the story is unravelled as in the Christmas number of ' All the Year Round,' concluding the scene in Chapter V, ' The Retribution,' and ending with the villagers all coming in and cheering Captain Jorgan on his departure for America as heartily as they execrated him in Act 1." A list of the characters is also given.

And now let us glance briefly at the personal relations of these two novelists. Strangely enough, there is very little material, though from 1851 they were so intimate. They spent many holidays together. Their first trip was in 1853, when they went to Switzerland and Italy accompanied by Egg and had a good time. In February 1855 they made a short trip to Paris. Exactly a year later they were in Paris again, and in the summer of 1856, when the Dickens family were living at the Villa de Moulineaux, Boulogne, Collins joined them, and for many weeks took up his quarters in a little cottage in the grounds. In 1859 Dickens spent a short holiday with Collins and his brother at Broadstairs. But, though they spent all these holidays together, there is no evidence in Dickens's letters of that abandonment to pleasure-making that appears in letters respecting tours with other friends. There are very few of those merry, school-boyish letters to Collins such as Dickens wrote to many other friends, his letters to this friend reflecting a restraint which is very rare in his correspondence. There is plenty of friendship, of course, but he rarely " lets himself go " as in his letters to other friends. Very often he protests his friendship, however, and once he proves his sincerity. Here is that letter:

"Frank Beard has been here this evening . . . and has told me that you are not at all well, and how he has given you something which he hopes and believes will bring you round. It is not to convey this insignificant piece of intelligence, or to tell you how anxious I am that you should come up with a wet sheet and a flowing sail (as we say at sea when we are not sick), that I write. It is simply to say what follows, which I hope may save you some mental uneasiness. For I was stricken ill when I was doing 'Bleak House,' and I shall not easily forget what I suffered under the fear of not being able to come up to time.

"Dismiss that fear (if you have it) altogether from your mind. Write to me at Paris at any moment, and say you are unequal to your work, and want me, and I will come to London straight and do your work. I am quite confident that, with your notes and a few words of explanation, I could take it up at any time and do it. Absurdly unnecessary to say that it would be a makeshift! But I could do it at a pinch, so like you as that no one should find out the difference. Don't make much of this offer in your mind; it is nothing, except to ease it. If you should want help, I am as safe as the bank. The trouble would be nothing to me, and the triumph of overcoming a difficulty great. Think it a Christmas number, an 'Idle Apprentice,' a 'Lighthouse,' a 'Frozen Deep.' I am as ready as in any of these cases to strike in and hammer the hot iron out.

"You won't want me. You will be well (and thankless!) in no time. But there I am; and I hope that the knowledge may be a comfort to you. Call me, and I come."

The help was not needed, but the offer was made in good faith, and is as good evidence as one could need of the regard that Dickens had for Wilkie Collins.

CHAPTER LXV

DICKENS AS AN EDITOR—HIS FRIENDSHIP WITH W. H. WILLS

Now we come to a famous—I had almost said historic—group of friends—those who were associated with the novelist mainly, if not entirely, through *Household Words* and *All the Year Round*. A great deal has been written about Dickens as an Editor, and all the writers agree that in that capacity he had altogether exceptional qualities. His outstanding quality was his—shall we call it knack?—of discovering talent. Perhaps it cannot be claimed that he " discovered " Henry Morley, for Morley had already attracted Forster's attention, and it was Forster who recommended him to Dickens; nor did he " discover " Charles Knight, for Knight was famous long before *Household Words* came into being; he scarcely " discovered " Mrs. Lynn Linton, for she had established a fairly good reputation before he gave her a better and wider public than she had had hitherto; Harriet Martineau was famous before *Pickwick* was written. But George Augustus Sala owed his first chance to Dickens and *Household Words*; Percy Fitzgerald, J. C. Parkinson, W. Moy Thomas, Charles Kent, John Hollingshead—to name but a few of the best known —owed their first recognition and subsequent success to Dickens's ability to " spot " talent, and to his encouragement. As " Dickens's young men " they came to be known, and as " Dickens's young men " some of them will be remembered for long years to come.

And when we consider Dickens as an Editor we quickly realise one of the great differences between modern journalism and that of half a century ago. Contributions to *Household Words* and *All the Year Round* were, almost without exception, unsigned, and contributors had only the merit of their work to stand upon. The magazines themselves, likewise, had to stand or fall upon the intrinsic merit of their contents. To-day the prospectus of a new magazine invariably contains a list of names of well-known writers who have promised to contribute. It does not matter though some of them " slap off " anything anyhow; it does not matter though some of their contributions would have no chance of acceptance if submitted anonymously. The Editor relies upon their names. And if it be urged that these people " had to make their names," it can be answered soundly enough that in these days of commercialised journalism " names " may be easily made.

But all this by the way. Another noteworthy fact—and the fact with which we are primarily concerned—in regard to Dickens as an Editor is the personal relations that existed between him and his staff, some of whom became much loved personal friends. I do not propose to write of his relations with them all; some of them could not legitimately be described as of the Dickens circle. But a few of them undoubtedly were very welcome members of what may be termed the later Dickens circle. With most of these we may deal quite briefly; a few are entitled to chapters to themselves.

First of all there is W. H. Wills, sub-editor, assistant editor of both papers. There were few men for whom Dickens had a higher regard. Their association originally was entirely of a business nature, but Wills proved himself so trustworthy, and showed such a regard for his employer, that a friendship developed, and in the last years of his life there was no one, Forster excepted, in whom Dickens placed more trust and confidence. Their acquaint- ance began with the birth of the " Daily News " in 1846, but nearly ten years before that there had been an association. For in 1837 Wills sent two articles to " Bentley's Miscellany," and Dickens, as Editor, accepted one and invited further contributions.

Wills was a member of the original staff of the " Daily News." He was Dickens's right hand, and acted as the Editor's secretary. Dickens occupied the editorial chair only three weeks, but in that short time he had realised Wills's reliability, and shortly after his resignation we find him writing : " I miss you a great deal more than I miss the paper." And Wills continued to act as his almoner.

It is not surprising, therefore, that when Forster recommended Wills as sub-editor of *Household Words* Dickens should have acquiesced gladly, and never was a happier appointment made. Dickens was supreme, and exercised a very full supervision, but all details were left to Wills, in whom the utmost reliance was placed, and during the reading tours the control was necessarily almost entirely in his hands. They worked together, we are told by the Editors of *The Letters of Charles Dickens*, " on terms of the most perfect mutual understanding, confidence, and affectionate regard, until Mr. Wills's health made it necessary for him to retire from the work in 1868." As time passed, Dickens leaned on Wills more and more. He found in his assistant, not only a good journalist, but a competent man of business, a man of percep- tion to whom it was necessary but to indicate a wish in the vaguest way to see that wish carried into effect; and a tactful man capable of dealing with all sorts of contributors and would-be contributors, and offending none. Wills, indeed, was a positive godsend to Dickens.

Presently the novelist had an opportunity of showing his appreciation of his assistant's loyalty. In 1856 Forster relinquished his share in *Household Words* to Dickens, who gave a portion of it to Wills, to whom, in answer to a letter of thanks, he wrote :

> " I have just received your letter and am truly pleased to know that you are gratified by what I have done respecting the share. I hoped you would be ; and in this and in all other ways in which I can ever testify my affection for you, and my sense of the value of your friendship and support, I merely gratify myself by doing what you more than merit."

Years before this, however, he had recommended Wills to the Baroness Burdett-Coutts as confidential secretary, in which post his duty was to see that her charitable gifts were properly distributed. He had also obtained for him the post of secretary to the Guild of Literature and Art. He had invited Wills to take part in the performance on behalf of the Guild in 1851.

Wills declined. " I will not bore you," he wrote, " with all my reasons against it. One will suffice, for that is a strong one : there will be, I understand, not a few provincial performances ; and under present arrangements I think it would be extremely inexpedient for us both to be absent from *H. W.* together and as often as the performances will require." None the less, the objection does not seem to have been so very strong, for we read that he was " almost invariably one of the party in the provincial tour."

Mrs. Wills, however, was associated with Dickens in some of his Tavistock House theatricals. In April 1856 Dickens wrote to her husband as follows :

" MY DEAR WILLS,

CHRISTMAS.

" Collins and I have a mighty original notion (mine in the beginning) for another play at Tavistock House. I propose opening on Twelfth Night the theatrical season at that great establishment. But now a tremendous question. Is

MRS. WILLS !

game to do a Scotch housekeeper in a supposed country house

W. H. WILLS

From a drawing in possession of the proprietors of " Punch "

with Mary, Katey, Georgina, etc. ? If she can screw her
courage up to saying ' Yes,' that country house opens the
piece in a singular way, and that Scotch housekeeper's part
shall flow from the present pen. If she says ' No ' (but she
won't) no Scotch housekeeper can be.[1] The Tavistock House
season of four nights pauses for a reply. Scotch song (new
and original) of Scotch housekeeper would pervade the
piece.

YOU

had better pause for breath."

Mrs. Wills *did* consent, and played Nurse Esther in " The
Frozen Deep."

In 1859 when *Household Words* came to an end, and *All the
Year Round* was born, Dickens and Wills became partners, the
former as to three-quarters, and the latter as to one quarter,
in profits and losses. It was agreed that Dickens should have
£500 a year as editor, and that Wills should act as general manager,
with control, subject to Dickens, of the commercial department,
and also as sub-editor, at a salary of £420. The same old har-
monious relations continued. Here, for instance, is a letter
written by Dickens on January 2, 1862, from Birmingham station:

" Being stranded here for an hour . . . I write to you.
" Firstly to reciprocate all your cordial and affectionate
wishes for the New Year, and to express my earnest hope that
we may go on through many years to come as we have
through many years that are gone. And I think we can
say that we doubt whether any two men can have gone
on more happily and smoothly, or with greater trust and
confidence in one another.
" A little packet will come to you . . . almost at the same
time, I think, as this note.
" The packet will contain a claret jug. I hope it is a pretty
thing in itself for your table, and I know that you and Mrs.
Wills will like it none the worse because it comes from me.
" It is not made of perishable material, and is so far expressive of our friendship. I have had your name and mine
set upon it in token of our many years of mutual reliance
and trustfulness. It will never be so full of wine as it is
to-day of affectionate regard."

The business association of the two men ended with Wills's

---

[1] Mrs. Wills was a daughter of Robert Chambers, and Dickens was design-
ing to give her an appropriate part as a Scotchwoman.

retirement in 1868, but the personal friendship lasted until Dickens's death.

This is an appropriate place in which to deal with Dickens's friendship with Mr. and Mrs. Frederick Lehmann. Mrs. Lehmann was a niece of Mrs. Wills, and it was Wills who introduced her and her husband to Dickens at Sheffield during the "splendid strolling" on behalf of the Guild of Literature and Art. Their son, Mr. R. C. Lehmann, tells us that between his father and Dickens there was a special bond of intimacy, and this is undoubtedly true. We have, indeed, Dickens's word for it, for in a letter to Lytton in 1861 he wrote: "I am anxious to let you know that Mr. Frederick Lehmann who is coming down to Knebworth to see you . . . is a particular friend of mine, for whom I have a very high and warm regard." The Lehmanns were very frequent visitors at Tavistock House and at Gadshill, and they were with Dickens in Paris in 1862, doing "a course of restaurants" with him. In Lehmann's unfinished reminiscences we find many references to social meetings with the novelist, particularly to Sunday walks. With the family he was always at his best, for they were valued friends between whom and himself there undoubtedly existed a very special sympathy and understanding.

CHAPTER LXVI

EDMUND YATES

GREATEST favourite of all the band of " Dickens's young men " was Edmund Yates. We are told by the Editors of Dickens's *Letters* that for Yates he had always an affectionate regard, and we know how his esteem for this young man led him into one of the most unfortunate acts of his life—the quarrel with Thackeray. I cannot but think that this regard for a somewhat coxcombish young man arose more out of his sentiment for a day that was dead than out of any specially appealing qualities in Yates's character. Yates was a capable journalist, a successful novelist and lecturer, and a self-reliant man of the world. These were all qualities sure of recognition from Dickens in any young man, but they were possessed by other members of the band. Dickens was, as a matter of fact, specially inclined towards Yates because of memories of the days when Yates's father and mother were to him almost gods to be worshipped. For this young man's parents were bright lights of the English stage when Dickens was beginning his career, and Yates senior had appeared in adaptations of Dickens's books. Forster tells us that though once at the Surrey Theatre the novelist lay on the floor of his box almost throughout a performance of *Oliver Twist*, he was able to " sit through *Nickleby*, and to see merit in parts of the representation. Mr. Yates had a sufficiently humorous meaning in his wildest extravagance."

It is quite clear that this implied suggestion that Dickens was able more or less to tolerate Yates's performances is not at all fair to the actor from the following letter quoted by the latter's son, and written by Dickens at the time of the *Nickleby* performance :

" MY DEAR SIR,
        " I am very glad indeed that *Nickleby* is doing so well. You are right about the popularity of the work, for its sale has left even that of *Pickwick* far behind. My general objection to the adaptation of any unfinished work of mine simply is that being badly done, and worse acted, it tends

to vulgarise the characters, to destroy or weaken in the minds of those who see them the impressions I have endeavoured to create, and consequently to lessen the interest in their progress. No such objection can exist for a moment when the thing is so admirably done as you have done it in this instance. I feel it an act of common justice after seeing the piece to withdraw all objection to its publication, and to say this much to the parties interested in it without reserve. If you can spare us a private box for next Tuesday I shall be much obliged to you. If it be on the stage, so much the better, as I shall be really glad of an opportunity to tell Mrs. Keeley and O. Smith how much I appreciate their Smike and New-man Noggs. I put you out of the question altogether, for that glorious Mantalini is beyond all praise."

In regard to Mrs. Yates, Dickens had even more pleasing memories. When she died he wrote to her son : " *You* knew what a loving and faithful remembrance I always had of your mother as part of my youth—no more capable of restoration than my youth itself. All the womanly goodness, grace, and beauty of my drama went out with her. To the last I never could hear her voice without emotion. I think of her as a beautiful part of my own youth, and this dream that we are all dreaming seems to darken."

No wonder, then, that when, in 1854, Yates, with that self-assurance which ever characterised him, introduced himself to Dickens as his parents' son, he was given a hearty welcome. He was then only twenty years old. For the sake of his parents Dickens was kindly disposed towards him from the beginning, but, as we have already noted, he had qualities which in a young man always appealed to the novelist—punctuality and reliability.

In 1856 Yates made his first appearance in *Household Words* with a short story entitled " A Fearful Night," and thenceforward he was a frequent contributor. Then came that wretched trouble with the Garrick Club over his insult to Thackeray. In connection with this it is due to Yates to say that if Dickens was prepared to break with Thackeray for his sake, Yates, in return, wor-shipped Dickens. Exactly what Dickens thought of his young admirer is shown in a couple of letters. The first was written in response to an application for a reference when Yates was applying for an editorship :

" You cannot overstate my recommendation of you for the editorship described in the advertisement; nor can you easily exaggerate the thorough knowledge of your qualifications on which such recommendation is founded. A man even of your quickness and ready knowledge would be useless in such an office unless he added to his natural and acquired parts, habits of business, punctuality, steadiness and zeal. I so thoroughly rely on you in all these respects, and I have had so much experience of you in connection with them that perhaps the committee may deem my testimony in your behalf of some unusual worth. In any way you think best, make it known to them, and in every way rely on my help if you can show me further how to help."

The second was written to Messrs. Fields, Osgood, & Co., the famous American publishers, with whom Dickens's personal and business relations were so intimate :

" My particular friend, Mr. Edmund Yates, has asked me if I will give him a letter of introduction to you, advancing —if I can—his desire of disposing of early proofs for publication in America of a new serial novel he is writing called ' Nobody's Fortune.' Mr. Yates is the most punctual and reliable of men in the execution of his work. I have had the plan of his story before me, and have advised him upon it, and have no doubt of its being of great promise and turning upon a capital set of incidents. It has not been offered in America as yet, I am assured."

CHAPTER LXVII

PERCY FITZGERALD

A VERY special favourite among "Dickens's young men" was Percy Fitzgerald, whom we are all so glad to have still with us. Dickens had a strong personal liking for him. This is proved by the novelist's own letters. For instance, in 1867 he wrote to Mr. Fitzgerald's mother: "In regard to your son . . . let me honestly assure you that my editorial existence has had no pleasanter incident in it than its having made me acquainted with his very great abilities, and having made us private friends. It is impossible that he can have a more interested or appreciative reader than he has in me, and no man ever sets foot in my house whom I better like to see there."

It has been of late years rather the fashion among a certain class of critics to be very "superior" at Mr. Fitzgerald's expense, to sneer at his enthusiastic hero-worship. I am sure Mr. Fitzgerald will forgive me for recalling one little incident that goes to show that he is not at all the ridiculous undiscriminating Dickensian that these very superior critics would have us believe him to be. Some years ago he was showing me some of his treasures, and he picked up a note-book that had once belonged to Sir Walter Scott. "That is one of my most valued possessions," he said, "because Scott was a great man—a very great man—a much greater man than Dickens, don't you think?" I confess that I was surprised at the time, for only recently he had published his "Life of Charles Dickens, as revealed in his writings," in which his adulation of Boz had certainly been extravagant, and had brought down upon his head the ridicule of many critics. But, in very truth, anybody who knows Mr. Fitzgerald knows perfectly well that he is a man of wide tastes, a very competent judge indeed, with a sound idea of values. His published works of themselves prove the catholicity of his interests.

But Dickens was the literary hero of his youth and prime; he imbibed *Pickwick* in his boyhood; when he was a boy and when he was a young man, Dickens was the glorious planet round which contemporary stars revolved. When he came to manhood's estate, he found himself first a welcome contributor to the great man's magazine, and later a welcome guest at his house. How should we wonder that the glamour of Dickens has remained with him all his life?

Young Fitzgerald's introduction to *Household Words* was brought about by Forster—to whom he had rendered some service —in a characteristic way. He wrote a short story and submitted it to the " harbitrary cove," who marched off with it to Wellington Street, and put it down saying that they must see to it, " that there should be no official subterfuges, circulars, or the like; it MUST be considered and READ, mark you ! " It was accepted, and its author was forthwith engaged to help with the next Christmas number, *The Wreck of the Golden Mary*. That first short story was entitled " Down at the Red Grange," and appeared in the number dated September 20, 1856. For the next thirteen years Fitzgerald was one of the most regular contributors to *Household Words* and *All the Year Round*.

Dickens early formed a high opinion of his abilities, but he soon discovered a tendency which, I fear, has never been completely shaken off. The young man was apt to have too many irons in the fire at one time, and thus to prejudice the quality of his work. He had a tendency to carelessness, too, and that tendency has never been shaken off either. Dickens early recognised this, and wrote to the young man :

" You make me very uneasy on the subject of your new long story here, and by sowing your name broadcast in so many fields at one time. Just as you are coming on with us you have another serial in progress in the ' Gentleman's Mag.,' and another announced in ' Once a Week,' and so far as I know the art we both profess, it cannot be reasonably pursued in this way. I think the short story you are now finishing in these pages obviously marked by traces of great haste and small consideration, and a long story similarly blemished would really do the publication irreparable harm."

The young man wrote, he tells us, a penitent letter, and his hero replied : " Your explanation is (as it naturally would be, being yours) manly and honest, and I am both satisfied and hopeful." Mr. Fitzgerald has also recorded the receipt of the following letter : " For my sake—if not for Heaven's—do, I ENTREAT YOU, look over your manuscript before sending it to the printer. Its condition involves us all in hopeless confusion and really occasions great unnecessary cost."

But, these little weaknesses aside, Percy Fitzgerald was an able man, and a reliable man withal, devoid of the Bohemianism of

Sala or Horne, and there must have been something very winning about him in those days, too. It is not surprising, therefore, that he was a very welcome guest at Gadshill. He had been a contributor to *Household Words* some time before he met the novelist personally. The meeting took place in Dublin, where Dickens had been reading. Fitzgerald went to the railway station when the novelist was leaving, and when the great man arrived, " screwing up my courage, I went up to him, and said, rather nervously, ' I beg your pardon, Mr. Dickens, but my name is —— ' The keen eyes were looking with a sort of distorted anxiety—this was some intruder; but when he heard the name he changed in an instant. A warm and hearty shake of the hand —up and down—from him. ' And how do you *do ?* ' he said. ' Very glad to see you.' "

Thus began a friendship which lasted until the end. Soon came an invitation to Gadshill : " If you should be in England before this "—July 4, 1863—" I should be delighted to see you here. It is a very pretty country, not thirty miles from London ; and if you could spare a day or two for its fine walks, I and my two latest dogs, a St. Bernard and a bloodhound, would be charmed with your company as one of ourselves." The reference to the dogs reminds us that Mr. Fitzgerald once wrote an article on Dickens's dogs which greatly pleased the novelist, and he gave still more pleasure by the gift of an Irish bloodhound which received the name of Sultan, and is immortalised both in Forster's book and in several of the novelist's own letters.

In 1865 Fitzgerald formed one of the party that accompanied the novelist to Knebworth on the occasion of the formal opening of the almshouses that had been erected on Lytton's estate in connection with the Guild of Literature and Art, and " On the return to London," he says, " Dickens took the party to *Household Words* offices, where a dainty little repast was set out. Then on to Gravesend, and thence to Gadshill." In the following year Lytton wrote to Dickens in praise of a novel by Fitzgerald, and Dickens replied : " Fitzgerald will be so proud of your opinion of his ' Mrs. Tillotson,' [1] and will (I know) derive such great encouragement from it, that I have faithfully quoted it, word for word, and sent it on to him in Ireland. He is a very clever fellow (you may remember, perhaps, that I brought him to Knebworth on the Guild day), and has charming sisters and an excellent position." Those sisters were as welcome as he was at Gadshill. Their brother has again and again told of his visits to Dickens's home, and there is no need for any detailed reference here. Suffice

---

[1] " The Second Mrs. Tillotson," which Lytton thought was better than " Felix Holt."

it to say that through all the years they have been a glorious memory with him. It ought to be added that he more than once accompanied Dickens on his reading tours, and in Ireland they had many happy hours together.

Of Mr. Fitzgerald's writings for *Household Words* and *All the Year Round* very little need be said. He contributed to more than one Christmas number, he wrote many short stories and articles, he was sent on a special commission to Rome, and his serial stories included "Never Forgotten," "The Second Mrs. Tillotson," to which reference has already been made, and "Fatal Zero," of which Dickens wrote to Forster, "I think you will find 'Fatal Zero' a very curious bit of mental development, deepening as the story goes on into a picture not more startling than true." His last story for *All the Year Round* was "Doctor's Mixture."

Since Dickens's death Mr. Fitzgerald's affection for the memory of his master and friend has deepened with every year, and in a score of volumes he has raised a very sincere monument. More than that, he was the founder of the Boz Club, and the first President of the Dickens Fellowship; he never tires of bearing testimony to his love for Dickens, and in London and elsewhere are busts, modelled by his own hands, loving tributes to a cherished friendship. If hero-worship be a virtue—and who shall say that it is not?—Percy Fitzgerald possesses it in abundance. His loving care for Dickens's memory, and his pride in the recollection of his friendship with the great man, are sometimes laughed at, but only by those who do not know him. Those who know him know that in very truth there is something sacred in it all.

CHAPTER LXVIII

CHARLES KENT

As I have studied Dickens's relations with his friends I have wondered sometimes which of all the number loved him best. The "Dickens Circle" was a big one, indeed, but not in the case of one of its members is there a mere regard. Always affection reigned supreme. Forster, the friend of longest standing and of the greatest intimacy, loved him more deeply—more emotionally—than he—John Bull that he was—would have admitted; Maclise loved him; so did Stanfield, and Talfourd, and Landor, and Carlyle, and Hunt; Townshend and Chorley worshipped him; the younger men—Hollingshead, Fitzgerald, Payn, Yates—regarded him as a superman. But—putting Forster aside—I do verily believe that the most devoted of them all was Charles Kent, of whom it may be said, without exaggeration at all, that he would have given his life for the novelist. "This zealous friend," say the Editors of Dickens's *Letters*; "I doubt if I have a more genial reader in the world," wrote Dickens to him. To Kent Dickens was something more than human; something almost divine, and in his old age, if any one in his presence uttered a disparaging word of the novelist, or even of his works, the tears would course down his face.

Kent's regard for Dickens did not commence with their personal acquaintance. He had worshipped from afar off, when the idea of a personal friendship with the novelist did not enter his wildest dreams. It was, indeed, his veneration for Dickens that "made them first acquaint." He wrote a notice of *Dombey and Son* for the "Sun," on whose staff he was, and the notice so touched Dickens that he wrote to the Editor asking him to thank the writer of the review on his behalf. Kent, we are told, "replied in his proper person, and from that time dates a close friendship, and constant correspondence." Upon receipt of Kent's letter, Dickens wrote: "Pray let me repeat to you personally what I expressed in my former note, and allow me to assure you, as an illustration of my sincerity, that I have never addressed a similar communication to anybody, except on one occasion."

From that time dated a friendship which partook of hero-worship unadulterated on one side, and, on the other, of an unaffected appreciation of that hero-worship, coupled with a sincere recognition of a simply good character, and high literary gifts.

When Kent began to write for *Household Words* he must have felt curiously at home, for he and Blanchard Jerrold had some years previously rented the offices from which that paper was issued as the offices of the " Astrologer," a competitor with Zadkiel. While he was still writing for *All the Year Round* he became the proprietor of the " Sun," and Dickens wrote him a letter expressive of his friendship :

> " I meant to have written instantly on the appearance of your paper in its beautiful freshness, to congratulate you on its handsome appearance, and to send you my heartiest good wishes for its thriving and prosperous career. Through a mistake of the postman's that remarkable letter has been tesselated into the Infernal Pavement instead of being delivered in the Strand.
>
> " We have been looking and waiting for your being well enough to propose yourself for a mouthful of fresh air. Are you well enough to come on Sunday ? . . ."

The invitation conveyed in this letter is a reminder that during the last ten years of his life Dickens welcomed Charles Kent to Gadshill more heartily than he welcomed most people.

Kent was one of the guests at the wedding of Kate Dickens to Charles Collins, and it may be remarked that he is mentioned more than once in the " Gad's Hill Gazette," to which previous reference has been made.

In 1867, when Dickens was going to America for his reading tour, the suggestion of a send-off banquet was enthusiastically taken up by Kent, who undertook all the arrangements. Two years after Dickens's death Kent published " Charles Dickens as a Reader." This was a work undertaken with the novelist's express sanction, as the following proves :

> " Everything that I can let you have in aid of the proposed record (which, *of course*, would be far more agreeable to me if done by you than by any other hand) shall be at your service. Dolby has all the figures relating to America, and you shall have for reference the books which I read."

That letter was written on March 26, 1870. Less than three months afterwards Dickens wrote his last letter. It was to Kent :

x

Wednesday, eighth June 1870.

" MY DEAR KENT,

" To-morrow is a very bad day for me to make a call, as, in addition to my usual office business, I have a mass of accounts to settle with Wills.   But I hope I may be ready for you at 3 o'clock.   If I can't be—why, then I shan't be.

" You must really get rid of those Opal enjoyments.   They are too overpowering.

" ' These violent delights have violent ends.'   I think it was a father of your church who made the wise remark to a young gentleman who got up early (or stayed out late) at Verona ?

" Ever affectionately,
" C. D."

Little more than an hour after the ink had dried on that letter, Dickens was stricken unto death.   The letter was subsequently presented by Kent to the British Museum.

CHAPTER LXIX

HENRY MORLEY

NEXT to Wills, the most important member of the *Household Words* circle was Henry Morley, whom Mr. Percy Fitzgerald describes as " a sort of deputy sub-editor of immense use; in fact, a kind of handy man . . . a man of all work." He was a reliable, conscientious, level-headed man—" a thoroughly fine, earnest fellow," as Dickens declared, whose work for *Household Words* and for *All the Year Round* was of immense value. He was not a journalist in the sense that Sala was, or Hollingshead or Moy Thomas, but he was a sound man, well read and well educated, of a serious turn of mind, and he wrote ably and attractively on certain topics. To Wills he was an invaluable man, and Mr. Fitzgerald tells us that he could co-operate with any writer who wanted help.

Morley had a varied career. He started by practising medicine, and it was his articles on hygienic subjects, written in a novel and quaintly humorous way, that attracted Dickens. But, through no fault of his own, he made no headway in his profession and became a schoolmaster, making, by dint of hard and conscientious work, a success of private schools at Manchester and Liverpool. Whilst engaged in this work he wrote some articles on hygienic subjects for the " Journal of Public Health." In 1849, the " Examiner," at that time edited by Forster, reprinted one of these articles, and this led to his contributing to that famous newspaper. This, in its turn, led to an invitation to write for *Household Words*, and this again to an offer of a permanent position on the staff of that paper.

Morley's associations with Dickens were not very intimate. Dickens had a high opinion of him as a high-minded, conscientious man, describing him as one " whom one cannot see without knowing to be a straightforward, earnest man," but they were very different in temperament. It is difficult to imagine Morley convulsed with laughter at children's theatricals, or enjoying a rollicking evening at the Star and Garter. I doubt if he ever really understood Dickens, though he certainly liked him.

It was on April 5, 1850, that Morley received a letter from

Forster enclosing one from Dickens requesting that he would write on sanitary matters for *Household Words*, and we find the recipient writing to his future wife : " More compliment. If we begin so how shall we stop? Well, I must put my knuckles into my brains and root about. That's a fact. I do not care very much for *Household Words*, but this will lead to my making Dickens's acquaintance, and as I respect his labours heartily, I shall be glad of that." He was glad, too, to have a second pulpit from which to preach health to the people. Two days later he wrote his first article for *Household Words*. It was on City Abuses, and was entitled " Wild Sports in the City," and announcing its completion, he wrote of his admiration for Dickens, and of his belief that the novelist would take a place in literature next to Fielding. But as to Dickens's qualifications as an Editor he was less confident :

> " But he has no sound literary taste; his own genius, brilliant as it is, appears often in a dress that shows that he has more heart and wit than critical refinement. So I doubt whether he is the right man to edit a journal of literary mark, though it would be full of warm and human sympathies and contain first-rate writing from his own pen. Nous verrons. I shall be heartily rejoiced if my fears prove unfounded."

As all the world knows, they did.

Morley entered into his work for *Household Words* with all enthusiasm, and continued to write frequently for the paper until in June 1851 he was surprised to receive a letter from Dickens offering him a position on the *Household Words* staff at five guineas a week. It was a gratifying offer, but not one to be lightly accepted, for he had just succeeded in building up his school. He wrote to Forster, the sure friend of almost every literary man of his time, and the reply was : " Mr. Dickens is the kindest and most honourable of men; and in whatever you do for him you will be able to reckon steadfastly on his earnest acknowledgment and liberal desire to make it more and more worth your doing."

The offer was accepted, and Morley came to London, where he quickly justified the good opinion and high expectations that had been formed of him. We have it on Wills's authority that he " was the best fellow they ever had to do with." He was treated with great trust and honoured with several missions, and in everything he did he acquitted himself well. Of Dickens as an editor he soon formed a high opinion : " Dickens," he wrote, " reads every letter sent to him, and not a note to the office is pooh-poohed; every suggestion that may lead to good, however overlaid with the ridiculous, is earnestly accepted and attended to." That is the main art of editorship.

That Dickens appreciated Morley's work is shown in several letters. In reference to a paper entitled " The Quiet Poor," the novelist wrote : " You affected me deeply by the paper itself. I think it is absolutely impossible it should have been better done." And in 1855 he wrote : " I am very much touched by your article ' Frost-bitten Homes,' " proposing at the same time to visit with Morley a number of poor homes. Several such visits were made, and recalling them afterwards, Morley told of the tenderness and keen anxiety with which Dickens made his inquiries, and how, as he left each room after getting his facts, he also left half-crowns.

The *Household Words Almanac*, it should be recorded, owed its existence to Morley's suggestion. When *All the Year Round* was started, Morley continued to work for it as he had worked for its predecessor, but in 1865 he resigned his post. Three years later, when Wills was seriously ill, he filled his place for some months. Dickens, we are told, welcomed him back with rejoicing, and paid most liberally for his contributions, also greatly valuing the assistance of several new writers whom he was able to secure. And Wills wrote : " I am not in a hurry to get back; all the better for *All the Year Round*, I think. The numbers appear to me to be better than ever they were in my time."

It should be added that in 1853 Morley acted for a short time as tutor to Dickens's eldest son.

CHAPTER LXX

G. A. SALA

Most famous and most brilliant of all the famous and brilliant band of " Dickens's young men " was George Augustus Sala. When Dickens died, Sala wrote the obituary notice in the " Daily Telegraph," and he concluded thus :

" I have frequently asked myself in the course of this retrospect whether . . . I have over-estimated his powers, have exaggerated his qualities, have ranked him too high in the hierarchy of great men. . . . I can only plead that, if I have erred, the error must be attributed to ignorance—but to an ignorance which may be palliated by its sincerity. . . . And my fanaticism, if fanaticism it be, may lose some of its apparent insanity if I mention that when he first came before the world as an author I was an illiterate child, gifted with a strongly retentive memory, but Blind; that the chief solace in my blindness was to hear my sister read the *Sketches by Boz*; that when I recovered my sight, it was out of *Pickwick*, and by the same loving teacher that I was taught to read; and that finally I knew him from 1836 upwards, and, in literature, served him faithfully for nineteen years."

The " Telegraph " article, slightly extended, was reprinted in book form, and in the introduction to that little volume Sala wrote :

" My constant aim has been to suppress, as far as I possibly could, all mention of my personal dealings with him—dealings which have governed almost exclusively the tenor of my life. . . . He was my master; and but for his friendship and encouragement, I should never have been a journalist or a writer of books. My first coherent production was published by him in 1851; the first five-pound note I ever earned by literature came from his kind hand; I wrote for him, and for no other chief, for seven years; he sent me to Russia; we quarrelled (of course, I was in the wrong), and he laughingly forgave me my transgressions, my debts, and my evil temper; he urged me to enter into the lists of journalism, and watched with interest my progress in the newspaper with which I have been connected for thirteen years. . . . With the single exception of *No Thoroughfare,* no Christmas number of *Household Words* or *All the Year Round* was planned without his asking my co-operation; less than a year ago I wrote an article in the last-named publication; I was writing an article for him at the very moment when he was stricken down; and the last words he ever said to me . . . were ' God bless you ! ' And this is the whole history of my lettered life."

A good many years later Sala rather qualified this utterance, but its fundamental truth is unquestionable. In his autobiography he records his early interest in Dickens and his early association with the novelist. From infancy he breathed the atmosphere of the theatre, and he remembered having seen performances of *The Strange Gentleman* and *The Village Coquettes.* He was present at the first performance of the latter piece, and he remembered being taken behind the scenes, " where I found my mother talking to a very young gentleman, with long brown hair falling in silky masses over his temples; with eyes which, young as I was, at once struck me as full of power and strong will, and with a touching expression of sweetness and kindliness on his lips." A few years later he met the novelist again. He had left school and was intended for the profession of an artist. He was fifteen years old; his mother thought—with a mother's vanity—that his drawings were worthy of " Punch." " She did not know the original Editor of ' Punch,' " says Sala, " but she suddenly bethought herself that that genial gentleman was a friend of Charles Dickens; so she wrote the novelist . . . reminding him of the old St. James's Theatre days, and asking whether she might be allowed to wait upon him with myself and the inevitable portfolio crammed with pen-and-ink drawings." An appointment was made, and " Dickens received us with his usual cordiality; began to talk about the opera and play-houses, keeping all the while that wonderful eye of his very earnestly on me : and then we opened the portfolio, and he went quite as earnestly through the pile of drawings. His verdict was that he thought ' I should do,' and that ' something must be done,' and that Mr. Mark Lemon, the Editor of ' Punch,' was the man to do it; so the next day we called upon Mr. Lemon at his office in Whitefriars with a letter of introduction from the author of *Pickwick.*" Nothing came of the visit, but the incident shows that Sala had very good reasons for gratitude towards Dickens.

The years passed again, and then came Sala's start in journalism. The story of how he came to write " The Key of the Street " has been told many times, and need not be repeated here. He sent it to Dickens with a letter reminding him of their earlier acquaintance. Within four hours came a letter from the novelist accepting the article and enclosing a five-pound note.

> " ' The Key of the Street,' " says its author, " was literally the turning point in *my* career; yet I may add . . . that I at first entertained not the slightest hope, or, indeed, had a very lively desire, to contribute any more articles to *Household Words*; and when, a few days later, the assistant editor of that paper wrote to express Mr. Dickens's wish to have another article from my pen, I was for a considerable time in grave doubts as to what I should write about."

For Dickens had written to Wills : " There is nobody about us whom we can use in his way more advantageously than this young man. It will be exceedingly desirable to set him on some subjects." Thenceforth, week after week, year after year, scarcely a number of *Household Words*, or, later, of *All the Year Round*, appeared that did not contain an article from his pen. Oftentimes he had two articles in one number.

Most certainly Dickens treated Sala with generosity. The contributors' book of *Household Words* proves that; for it shows that this young man continually overdrew his account. He admits it : " I had always," he says, " *Household Words* as a stand-by. There was the five-guinea fee for every article I wrote; I often got through two in the course of one week, and if, as it more than once happened, I overdrew my account—I did so on one occasion to the extent of twenty pounds—and, on another, of seventy pounds—Dickens would, after a while, laughingly suggest the sponge should be passed over the slate and we should begin again."

On the other hand, I cannot but think that Mr. Percy Fitzgerald is not quite fair to Sala. He says : " At last he persuaded Dickens to send him to Russia to do for the *Journal* what he had so often done for his own paper, the ' Daily Telegraph,' that is, ' word paint ' all the manners, customs, and doings of the Muscovites. At last Dickens agreed. But G. A. S. had the fatal defect of ' growing tired ' of an enforced job." Mr. Fitzgerald says that Sala went to Russia towards the close of 1856, and in October his articles began to appear under the title of " A Journey due North." When he got to St. Petersburg, we are told, he was nearly tired; it was too much trouble to go and get information, so he wrote long rambling articles. He devoted column after column to

Russian cab-drivers, and that led him off to the cab-drivers of other countries. For weeks he wrote about the great street, the Newski Prospect, and at last Dickens stopped the series.

Now, to begin with, Sala is very definite that he first began to write for the " Daily Telegraph " in 1857; therefore Mr. Fitzgerald is wrong when he says that that paper had often sent him on similar tours previous to 1856. Again, Sala expressly says, " I was not expected to forward any copy to *Household Words* until I had left Russia," and he gives a very acceptable reason for that. If this be correct, then Mr. Fitzgerald's recollection is clearly at fault.

Nevertheless, this Russian trip led to a rupture with Dickens, and Sala's explanation is scarcely convincing. He tells how, long before he reached England, he had nearly exhausted his money. He wrote to Wills for a ten-pound note, and he says " this enabled me to pay my fare by Lille and Calais to London, to buy a few books and prints in Brussels, and to arrive at London Bridge with a couple of sovereigns in my pocket." He obtained an offer of £250 for the " Journey due North " in volume form; and then :

> " I quarrelled with Dickens. When, fourteen years afterwards, he died, I wrote a notice of him in the ' Daily Telegraph,' and shortly afterwards this notice was republished. . . . Now in this trifle I made a passing allusion to my misunderstanding with Dickens; [1] and, moved by I hope not ungenerous impulse, I added that in this feud I had been in the wrong. I revered the writer and I loved the man. . . . A spiteful critic . . . went out of his way, while professing to review a work of mine entitled ' Things I have Seen, and People I have Met,' to say that Dickens was very kind to me, and that it was at his expense that I went to Russia. Charles Dickens was kind to many youthful authors besides myself; and he was for five years exceptionally kind to me, for the reason that he had known me in early youth. But, confound it ! I gave him malt for his meal."

Just a word here. Admitting the quality of Sala's work for *Household Words*, we still have to remember that he was totally unknown when he wrote " The Key of the Street," and still a very obscure journalist when he undertook this trip to Russia. He says that it was this trip that first caused his name to be known. He received £5 for every article he chose to write for *Household Words*. This was generous payment to an unknown man, and his talk about his having given Dickens malt for his

[1] See p. 310.

meal was unworthy of him, more especially when we remember
his admission that he frequently overdrew his account—once even
to the extent of £70—and that Dickens often sponged the slate.
Let him proceed :

> " As to the statement of the spiteful critic, that I went to
> Russia at Dickens's expense, there is in it a suppression of
> truth which is more than a suggestion of falsehood.   In the
> last letter which he wrote me before I went away, he said,
> ' You shall have the means of travelling in comfort and
> respectability.'   I drew a certain sum to defray my expenses
> to St. Petersburg; and there I found, at Messrs. Stieglitz',
> a monthly credit of forty pounds.   In all, between April
> and November I received the sum of two hundred and forty
> pounds, eight-tenths of which I spent in subsistence and
> travelling outlay; and I landed in England, as I have said,
> with two pounds in my pocket.   It logically follows that if
> I went to Russia at Dickens's expense, I wrote the ' Journey
> due North ' at my own."

The logic is not self-evident.   He proceeds to relate how he
subsequently gave offence.   About half a dozen papers remained
to be written when he reached London.   He was dissatisfied
with what he unreasonably considered to be the ungenerous
treatment he had received; he found another excellent source of
income; and the delivery of the last half-dozen papers " hung
fire," as he puts it.   He yet had the impertinence to demand his
travelling expenses, however, and was referred to a solicitor for
his pains.   In face of these facts, in face of the frequent over-
drafts, and the " sponging of the slate "—of which, conceivably,
Dickens was growing rather tired—it is astonishing that Sala, at
almost the end of his career, should have talked about his " ungenerous treatment."   On his own admission, he had scarcely
" played the game," and Dickens had just cause for resentment.
The novelist, indeed, refused permission for the republication of
the papers, and so the rupture was complete.   However, in
1858 the embargo was removed; the book was published, and
the breach was healed.
There is another point in regard to which Mr. Fitzgerald is not
fair to Sala—if, that is, the latter's autobiography is to be accepted
as reliable.   He says that after a series of failures Dickens agreed
to take a novel from Sala, called " Quite Alone."   It commenced
in February 1864, and went on until September; then there appeared this notice : " The continuation of this story is postponed
until this day fortnight."   Next week there was this notice :

"The continuation of this story is postponed until next week."
Then, says Mr. Fitzgerald, it was resumed, and it concluded on
November 12. "I believe," he adds, "Sala supplied not another
line, and it is certain that Boz was compelled to call in the aid of
a deft emergency man—Andrew Halliday—who, in an incredibly
short time, contrived to finish off the tale, imitating the style and
peculiarities of his friend—for such he was—with due success."
Now, Sala does not mention anything about the copy of this
story having "hung fire," nor does he say anything about Halliday
having finished it, but he does state facts which would explain
the inconvenience caused. We must remember that at this time
his main source of income was the "Daily Telegraph," and that
whatever he wrote for Dickens was in the nature of an "aside."

> "I began," he says, "to write a novel myself in the
> summer of 1863; it was called 'Quite Alone.' . . . Dickens
> . . . secured it for *All the Year Round*; and my name was
> to be attached to it. . . . *It was about three-quarters finished
> when there came to me, quite unexpectedly, an offer from the
> proprietors of the 'Daily Telegraph' to proceed as a special
> correspondent to the United States, then in the midst of war.*"

The italics are mine. The sentence so printed is surely ample
explanation of any inconvenience that may have been caused,
and quite sufficient to dispose of the insinuation that Sala's
Bohemian habits were the origin of the trouble. It is, indeed,
conceivable, in the circumstances, that Halliday was called in at
his own suggestion and not at Dickens's.

But little need be said of Sala's more personal associations with
Dickens. He was never *persona grata* as Yates, Fitzgerald, and
Kent were, and he was not a frequent visitor at the novelist's
house, but he was well liked, and, if only for the sake of earlier
days, Dickens took a deep interest in him. He was a frequent
guest at dinners at Wellington Street, where the offices of *Household Words* were situated—"to my great glee and contentment,"
he says, "I used to get an invitation to dine at *Household Words*
office about once a month." He tells, also, how he met Dickens
in Paris, and was "in clover," and he says, "I learned once, quite
accidentally, from my friend Edmund Yates, that the Conductor
of *Household Words* had made strenuous, but fruitless, efforts to
obtain for me a position on the staff of 'Punch,' not as an artist,
but as a writer."

CHAPTER LXXI

MRS. LYNN LINTON

" Good enough for anything, and thoroughly reliable." So wrote Dickens against the name of Mrs. Lynn Linton in a list of contributors to *Household Words*, and in writing it I think he wrote all he felt in regard to her. That is to say, she was an acquaintance held in some regard, and a valued contributor, whilst he showed her many kindnesses, but to describe her as a friend would be a misuse of words. She herself tells us that she did not know Dickens intimately, and that her business relations with *Household Words* and *All the Year Round* were conducted with Wills. As a matter of fact, she was just that type of strong-minded woman that was more likely to repel than to attract Dickens, and the earnest efforts of her biographer notwithstanding, it is difficult to trace in her, strongly developed, those feminine traits that we know appealed to the novelist. Further, she did not like Forster, and she offended Dickens once by displaying that dislike in a review she wrote for him of his friend's " Life of Landor." Dickens returned the article, and wrote the review himself. On another occasion he rebuked her for an unnecessarily unkind reference to Lockhart in an article which she wrote for him.

On the other hand, she was a friend of one of his most cherished friends—Landor. This old man had had a great liking for her as a young girl, and it was he who introduced her to Dickens at Bath, when she was twenty-four years old. Of the occasion she says, " We had, I remember, a delightful evening. Dickens was sweet and kind and gay to me." She was an undoubtedly able writer, too, and Dickens was careful to entertain her goodwill, whilst the sorrow that came into her life earned for her his true sympathy. We find that she was occasionally a guest at his house. " I used to go to Mr. Dickens's parties, etc., with all the rest of the world," she wrote to the late F. G. Kitton. She had some hard struggles during her life, and more than once Dickens was her friend in need, his generosity as conductor of *Household Words* helping her across many a stony road. And, to her credit, she proved her gratitude when the opportunity came in 1859. *Household Words* died in that year, and *All the Year Round* took its place. Messrs. Bradbury and Evans at once commenced a rival

GAD'S HILL PLACE

Men standing : Wilkie Collins, C. A. Collins, C. Dickens, Junr., Hamilton Hume

Ladies : Mrs. C. Dickens, Junr.; the novelist's daughters, Mamie and Kate; and Miss Georgina Hogarth

Men on lawn : Fechter and Charles Dickens.

publication, " Once a Week," and made Mrs. Lynn Linton a valuable offer. But she remembered that Dickens's generous payments for articles had several times practically saved her from starvation, and so she wrote to him, telling him the facts, and asking whether he saw any objection to her accepting the offer made to her. It was a proper thing to do, of course, but not everybody would have done it.

Dickens replied that she could not write too much for *All the Year Round*, that whatever she wrote for him would, as a matter of course, be warmly welcomed, and that her contributions would always have precedence in his magazine. He added that he looked upon himself as her Editor of right, and made it very clear that any commerce with the opposition would be regarded as a personal injury. " Of course," says her biographer, Mr. Geo. Somes Layard, " such a reply was very gratifying, and forthwith she became his faithful lieutenant, and refused the tempting offer of his rivals."

But Mrs. Lynn Linton's more interesting association with Dickens has nothing to do with either *Household Words* or *All the Year Round*. It was from her that he purchased Gadshill. In February 1858 he wrote to Wills that he had seen a little house at Gadshill to be let, and that " the spot and the very house are literally ' a dream of my childhood.' " No need to recall the story of the " very queer small boy " who was told by his father that some day, if he grew up to be a good man, he might own that house. Mr. R. C. Lehmann says that the house referred to in the letter to Wills is not the famous house, but the one opposite, and that the negotiations for its purchase broke down. Mr. Lehmann is surely wrong, for when, in the same year, Dickens did purchase the house in which he was to die, he wrote to M. de Cerjat : " I have always in passing looked to see if it was to be sold or let, and it has never been to me like any other house."

This leaves no room for doubt but that the house which is now world famous, is the house referred to in the letter to Wills. It had belonged to Mrs. Lynn Linton's father, and she had lived there as a girl. Shortly after his death, Mrs. Lynn Linton met Wills at a dinner-party, and in the course of conversation told him that the estate would shortly be in the market. Wills informed his " chief," who eventually became the owner for £1700. An amusing fact is that the vendor asked £40 for the ornamental timber, and Dickens and Wills objecting, the matter went to arbitration, with the result that Dickens had to pay £70, which, as Mrs. Lynn Linton remarks, " was in the nature of a triumph."

She never saw Gadshill after she had sold it. " He used to always say I must *go down*," she wrote to the late F. G. Kitton, " but as no time was fixed I did not go."

CHAPTER LXXII

SOME MORE MEMBERS OF THE BAND

THERE are a few other members of the *Household Words* and *All the Year Round* circle who have unchallengeable claims to places here. Few contributed more frequently, few loved Dickens more truly than James Payn, for instance. Payn largely owed his success in life to Dickens's encouragement, and in his early days as a journalist his chief sources of income were *Household Words* and " Chambers's Journal," of which latter paper he was for a time Editor. His first article for *Household Words* was entitled " Gentleman Cadet," and described life at a Military Academy. It led to his acquaintance with Dickens. The Governor of Woolwich Academy read the article, took exception to it, and wrote to Dickens with some acerbity. He stated, " If your correspondent had been a cadet himself I should not have addressed you, but it is clear to me that he is an outsider."

As a matter of fact, Payn had been a cadet, and the Governor was so informed. He demanded the writer's name, and Dickens wrote to Payn for permission to disclose it. Thus began, we are told, " an acquaintance which presently ripened into friendship, none the less sincere though the obligations in connection with it were, from first to last, all on one side." Thenceforth no one contributed more frequently to *Household Words* : Payn had often two contributions in one number, and once no fewer than three.

Dickens and Payn met in the flesh for the first time in 1856, when the novelist went to Edinburgh in the course of his reading tour. The young man received a letter from the novelist inviting him to accompany him and his daughters to Hawthornden. The invitation was accepted, and Dickens related to Wills " we laughed all day." After that day, says Payn, " I discarded for ever the picture which I had made in my mind of him, and substituted for it a still pleasanter one taken from life."

The friendship lasted until Dickens's death, though intimacy was impossible owing to Payn being mostly resident in Edinburgh. But the novelist had a very strong liking indeed for him, and Payn had all his life regarded him as a literary idol.

John Hollingshead was a regular contributor of whose work

Dickens had a very high opinion. He commenced to write for *Household Words* in 1851. " Dickens," he tells us, " liked descriptive articles of life and odd corners of life, for in the early 'fifties the daily newspaper purveyed news only, with some social and political comment, and had not turned itself into a daily magazine. I supplied these articles freely, as they gave me outdoor employment which suited my active temperament; but I also occasionally wrote short stories." In September 1851 we find Dickens writing to Wills : " I have at Gadshill a pretty little paper of a good deal of merit by one Mr. Hollingshead." That paper was entitled " Poor Tom," and appeared in the number dated October 17, 1851. Thenceforth Hollingshead was one of the most regular contributors. He certainly contributed to more than one of the famous Christmas numbers, both of *Household Words* and of *All the Year Round*, and a print of the period shows him as a member of " The Committee of Concoction " planning *Tom Tiddler's Ground*. The other members of the Committee are Dickens, Wilkie Collins, and Sala.

But quite possibly Dickens had a rather closer interest in Hollingshead than in some others of his young men, because Hollingshead was so keen on the drama, his associations with which are historic. Mr. Percy Fitzgerald has recorded [1] how he once accompanied Dickens to the Gaiety to see Hollingshead's revival of " The Miller and His Men," a play that had charmed the novelist as a child.

But there was never any intimacy. Hollingshead was just one of that immortal band of " Dickens's young men "—a most capable and reliable contributor to the two periodicals edited by the novelist. Dickens was to him, however, a " superior creature," and to the end of his life he reverenced the great man.

I think J. C. Parkinson may be classed with Hollingshead. He was not quite the journalist that John was, but he was held in very similar regard by Dickens as a reliable, sound, competent man who could be trusted implicitly. He was only seventeen years old when *Household Words* started, and so he was not one of the earliest contributors to that magazine. But it was under Dickens's editorship that he commenced his journalistic career, and for Dickens he did much excellent work. He had a knack of making even a Blue Book interesting, and that was a quality which every reader of *Household Words* and *All the Year Round* knows appealed to the Editor of those magazines. And the young man worshipped Dickens as every one of that remarkable band of contributors did, and to the end of his days his associations with the novelist were a cherished memory.

[1] *The Dickensian*, December 1908.

Dickens's regard for Parkinson was shown in a letter written in 1868. Parkinson appealed to the novelist to recommend him to Mr. Gladstone for the vacant Commissionership of Inland Revenue. In reply Dickens wrote that he was diffident of approaching Mr. Gladstone, with whom his acquaintance was slight, but that Mr. Parkinson might make what use he liked of the following :

" In expressing my conviction that you deserve the place, and are in every way qualified for it, I found my testimony upon as accurate a knowledge of your character and abilities as any one can possibly have acquired. In my editorship of *Household Words* and *All the Year Round*, you know very well that I have invariably offered you those subjects of political and social interest to write upon, in which integrity, exactness, a remarkable power of generalising evidence and balancing facts, and a special clearness in stating a case, were indispensable on the part of the writer. My confidence in your powers has never been misplaced, and through all our literary intercourse you have never been hasty or wrong. Whatever trust you have undertaken has been so completely discharged that it has become my habit to read your proofs rather for my own edification than (as in other cases) for the detection of some slip here or there, or the more pithy presentation of the subject.

" That your literary work has never interfered with the discharge of your official duties, I may assume to be at least as well known to your colleagues as it is to me. It is idle to say that if the post were in my gift you should have it, because you have had for some years most of the posts of high trust that have been at my disposal. An excellent public servant in your literary sphere of action, I should be heartily glad if you could have this new opportunity of distinguishing yourself in the same character. And this is at least unselfish in me, for I suppose I should then lose you."

There are two or three others who may be dealt with very briefly. Walter Thornbury wrote frequently, and he was also associated with the novelist on the " Daily News." He was also an occasional guest at Dickens's house, but I can find no record of close friendship. But some of Dickens's letters to him respecting his contributions to *Household Words* and *All the Year Round* are of quite special interest as showing the novelist's care and conscientiousness as an Editor. Moy Thomas was one of the " young men " particularly valued, because of his reliability, but he was not, as far as I can ascertain, a friend as some others were. Richard Hengist Horne, the eccentric and erratic, was a very frequent contributor, but it would be absurd to describe him as a friend. Still, he is worthy of remembrance here because of his admirable chapter on Dickens in " The New Spirit of the Age."

Y

CHAPTER LXXIII

TWO LADIES—MRS. GASKELL AND MISS MARTINEAU

Two members of what Mr. Anthony Humm called " the soft sex " remain to be noted in this group of contributors to Dickens's two periodicals. Mrs. Gaskell, as the author of the first serial story for *Household Words*, certainly has claims to honourable mention here. She was on good, though not intimate, terms with Dickens; was an occasional visitor at his house, and was one of the company at the dinner which was held to celebrate the start of *David Copperfield*. He had a very high opinion of her abilities. That is shown by the following extract from his letter inviting her to write for his paper :

> " You may perhaps have seen an announcement in the papers of my intention to start a new cheap weekly journal of general literature.
>
> " I do not know what your vows of temperance or abstinence may be, but as I do honestly know that there is no living English writer whose aid I would desire to enlist in preference to the authoress of ' Mary Barton ' (a book that most profoundly affected and impressed me), I venture to ask you whether you can give me any hope that you will write a short tale, or any number of tales, for the projected pages.
>
> " . . . I should set a value on your help which your modesty can hardly imagine; and I am perfectly sure that the best result of your reflection or observation in respect of the life around you, would attract attention and do good. . . ."

The result was " Lizzie Leigh," which was followed by several other stories. Dickens's admiration for Mrs. Gaskell's work continued. In March 1852 he wrote to Forster : " Don't you think Mrs. Gaskell charming ? With one ill-considered thing that looks like want of natural perception, I think it masterly." This was a reference to a short story entitled " Memory at Cranford." And in 1855 he wrote to Mrs. Gaskell herself :

" Let me congratulate you on the conclusion of your story; [1] not because it is the end of a task to which you had conceived a dislike . . . but because it is the vigorous and powerful accomplishment of an anxious labour. It seems to me that you have felt the ground thoroughly firm under your feet, and have strided on with a force and purpose that MUST now give you pleasure."

And the letter proceeded :

" You will not, I hope, allow that non-lucid interval of dissatisfaction with yourself (and me ?), which beset you for a minute or two once upon a time, to linger in the shape of any disagreeable association with *Household Words*. I shall still look forward to the large side of paper, and shall soon feel disappointed if they don't begin to reappear.

" I thought it best that Wills should write the business letter on the conclusion of the story, as that part of our communications had always previously rested with him. I trust you found it satisfactory? I refer to it not as a matter of mere form, but because I sincerely wish everything between us to be beyond the possibility of misunderstanding or reservation."

This letter certainly tends to confirm the statement of Mr. Percy Fitzgerald that Dickens found Mrs. Gaskell a difficult person to deal with. Of her character, as of her abilities, he had nothing but admiration, but in his rôle of Editor he found her very " touchy." She had an absolute confidence in her own powers, and would not " stand any nonsense " in regard to her writings. Dickens was a brilliant Editor and a kindly Editor, ever ready to encourage and help, but he was undoubtedly an autocrat, and never hesitated to alter anybody's " copy " to bring it into compliance with his ideas or—the same thing—with the policy or spirit of his paper. Young men, on the threshold of their careers, like Parkinson, Fitzgerald, Sala, etc., were grateful for his suggestions and alterations, but, in justice to Mrs. Gaskell, we have to remember that she had an established position as a novelist before she began to write for *Household Words*, and we cannot in fairness condemn her for objecting to another novelist, even though it were Charles Dickens himself, altering the productions of her genius. So that I cannot follow Mr. Fitzgerald when he says : " In spite of soothing compliments and abounding homage, she was to be the cause of much worry and trouble to him, and, excellent as her performances were, it may be doubted

[1] " North and South."

whether her assistance was much gain to the paper." Even though she may have caused Dickens "much worry and trouble," it is decidedly difficult to understand why that fact should have prevented—say, " Lizzie Leigh " and "North and South " being of assistance to the paper ! Mr. Fitzgerald makes much of the fact that Mrs. Gaskell " once wrote to Wills declaring that she must particularly stipulate not to have her proofs touched even by Mr. Dickens." Surely a novelist whose fame was quite independent of *Household Words* or its Editor was entitled to make such a stipulation.

Harriet Martineau began to write for *Household Words* in 1850, and wrote frequently for three or four years. As to personal friendship, there really was none. She and Dickens met only once during her London life, and though after she had settled in the Lake District they seem to have met occasionally when she visited London, their relations were practically entirely of a business character. I rather think that it was as well. They never would have rubbed along together. They were both earnest reformers, but Dickens's views were the result of instinct and emotion ; Harriet Martineau's were the result of reasoning. She was kind-hearted, generous, sympathetic, but still, in her work for social reform and in her propagandist writings, there is revealed more brain than heart. The heart is not lacking, but the emotions are controlled by a strong, almost masculine mind. Dickens, on the other hand, was almost feminine in his liability to be swayed by his emotions. They would quickly have clashed in regard to their views on women, for instance. Indeed, they did, as we shall see in a moment.

Then, in matters of economy Dickens did not please her. But she had a great admiration for him, nevertheless. " Of Mr. Dickens," she says, " I have seen but little in face-to-face intercourse ; but I am glad to have enjoyed that little." She refers to his " erroneousness in matters of science" (quoting *Oliver Twist* and *Hard Times* in particular), and says " The more fervent and inexhaustible his kindliness (and it is fervent and inexhaustible), the more important it is that it should be well informed and well directed, that no errors of his may mislead his readers on the one hand or lessen his own genial influence on the other."

She was asked to write for *Household Words* when that periodical was first published. She hesitated. She disliked writing for magazines, but eventually she decided to make an exception in this case because its wide circulation went far to compensate for the ordinary objections to this mode of authorship. And for three or four years she wrote frequently—stories, picturesque accounts of manufactures and their productive processes, articles on personal infirmities (the treatment of blindness, deafness, idiotcy, etc.), and so on.

In 1854, however, she ceased to write for the paper. She disapproved of " the principles, or want of principles, on which the magazine was carried on," and she thought the proprietors " grievously inadequate to their function, philosophically and morally." She held that she could not write her views on the Woman's position in a magazine in which Dickens had already expressed his totally different views. There was logic in this. We must bear in mind that the articles in *Household Words* were not signed, and expressions of opinion contained in them were inevitably— and, I take it, designedly—accepted as Dickens's opinion. Therefore, such a complete inconsistency would have been absurd.

But later another difference arose. She was asked to write a tale for a Christmas number, and she wrote " The Missionary." [1] But it was rejected, " because the public would say that Mr. Dickens was turning Catholic," and because Wills and Dickens " would never publish anything, fact or fiction, which gave a favourable view of any one under the influence of the Catholic faith." She tells us that from that time her confidence and comfort in *Household Words* were gone, and she could never again write fiction for them, nor anything in which principle or feeling were concerned. So far, so good; but there presently appeared in *Household Words* a story in which a Catholic priest was held up to contumely. She wrote to Wills :

" The last thing I am likely to do is to write for an anti-Catholic publication, and least of all when it is anti-Catholic on the sly. I have had little hope of *Household Words* since the proprietors refused to print an historical fact (otherwise approved of) on the ground that the hero was a Jesuit : and now that they follow up this suppression of an honourable truth by the insertion of a dishonourable fiction (or fact— no matter which), they can expect no support from advocates of religious liberty or lovers of fair-play. . . . I might as well write for the ' Record ' newspaper; and, indeed, so far better, that the ' Record ' avows its anti-Catholic course. . . . No, I have no more to say to *Household Words*, and you will prefer my telling you plainly why, and giving you this much light on the views your course has occasioned in one who was a hearty well-wisher to *Household Words* as long as possible."

Here, it seems to me, her logic was at fault. She had urged

[1] Included in " Sketches from Life."

consistency in the case of the position of women, in this matter she objected to consistency. Dickens's attitude towards the Catholic Church was a very astonishing trait in one who in almost everything was so tolerant, and who numbered among his best-loved friends members of that Church; but, given the fact of his views, and remembering again the anonymity of the contents of his magazine, he was surely entitled to print something unfavourable or antagonistic to that Church, and to refuse to print something in its favour. Without being understood as approving of his point of view, one may surely say that if Miss Martineau wanted consistency it was surely inconsistent of her to object to it when it was offered to her.

Thus ended her connection with *Household Words*. There was no quarrel; she and Dickens and Wills parted friends, but I can find no record of any further intercourse at all.

CHAPTER LXXIV

ARTHUR AND ALBERT SMITH AND GEORGE DOLBY

IN the spring of 1858 Dickens commenced those readings which so took the world by storm, and made him personally better known to his readers than any other novelist, before or since. In connection therewith he had, at different times, three managers —Arthur Smith, Mr. Headlands, and George Dolby. The first was a well-beloved friend long before readings were ever thought of, the second was merely a servant and that only for a short time, the last-named, at first only a servant, became a trusted business confidant, a valued friend, and a much-liked companion.

Smith and his brother Albert were intimate with Dickens from the early years, though I cannot ascertain when they first became acquainted. His name first occurs in Forster's book in connection with the death of Douglas Jerrold, in the letter suggesting a series of theatrical performances, etc., for the benefit of the widow and family. " I have got hold of Arthur Smith," writes Dickens, " as the best man of business I know, and go to work to-morrow morning." In the following year the famous readings commenced with Smith as manager. One hundred and twenty-five readings were given between April 16, 1858 and October 1859, and Smith went with him everywhere as his " friend and secretary." Through all the tour his " zealous friendship and pleasant companionship " were a joy to Dickens, and almost every one of his letters written during the tour contains some hearty and genial reference to his manager. All these references, humorous, and breathing a deep friendship, also reveal how valuable Smith was to Dickens, taking every detail of business off his hands. Dickens simply had to read; Smith saw to everything else, and saw to it thoroughly. Needless to say, when the second series was fixed up, no other man was thought of as manager, but Smith's health, never, apparently, very good, broke down completely. The series commenced in 1861, and Smith superintended only the first six, which were all given in London. His illness was a grief to Dickens, not simply because he had come to regard the man as indispensable, but because he loved him.

The end came in October. " Poor dear Arthur is a sad loss to me," wrote Dickens to his daughter, " and indeed I was very fond of him." To Mr. H. G. Adams he wrote : " My readings are a sad subject to me just now, for I am going away on the twenty-eighth to read fifty times, and I have lost Mr. Arthur

Smith—a friend whom I can never replace—who always went with me, and transacted, as no other man ever can, all the business connected with them, and without whom, I fear, they will be dreary and weary to me." To Macready he wrote : " The death of Arthur Smith has caused me great distress and anxiety. I had a great regard for him, and he made the reading part of my life as light and pleasant as it *could* be made. I had hoped to bring him to see you, and had pictured to myself how amused and interested you would have been with his wonderful tact and consummate mastery of arrangement. But it's all over." And, finally, to Miss Hogarth he wrote during the tour : " I miss poor Arthur dreadfully. It is scarcely possible to imagine how much. It is not only that his loss to me socially is quite irreparable, but that the sense I used to have of compactness and comfort about me while I was reading is quite gone. And when I come out for the ten minutes, when I used to find him always ready for me with something cheerful to say, it is forlorn. I cannot but fancy, too, that the audience must miss the old speciality of a pervading gentleman."

Albert Smith had nothing to do with the readings, but the two brothers may well be linked together. He was a very popular member of the Dickens circle, particularly in the Tavistock House days. He had qualities that must have made his presence at those Twelfth Night parties a veritable delight. Mr. R. Renton says, " Albert Smith's great attraction was his buoyant, happy spirit, his careless, irresponsible nature, and his keen enjoyment of that Bohemian side of the life of his day, of which Dickens and his friends made the very most, and of which, in this twentieth century, there does not exist even the merest shred." This Bohemian of Bohemians, as Sir Frank Marzials calls him, enjoyed life at its fullest. Happiness, light-heartedness, generosity, always characterised Albert Smith, and it would have been surprising indeed if he had not been a prominent member of the Dickens circle. His marriage with a daughter of the Keeleys brought him into close touch with the circle, of which he was soon a very popular member. Canon Ainger has told us how Smith would drop in at Tavistock House " after a two or three thousandth ascent of Mont Blanc, but never refusing at our earnest entreaty to sit down to the piano and sing us ' My Lord Tomnoddy," or his own latest version of ' Gaglignani's Messenger.' " Be it noted that the first piece played by the children was Smith's burletta of " Guy Fawkes."

In 1845 Smith, with Dickens's approval and assistance, dramatised *The Cricket on the Hearth.* He worked from the proofs of the story so that the play was produced by the Keeleys at the Lyceum the same day that the book was published. In the previous year Smith had written a short prologue for Edward Stirling's adaptation of *Martin Chuzzlewit*—" Mrs. Harris "— which was played at the Strand Theatre. And in 1846 he drama- tised *The Battle of Life* for the Keeleys. Again he had Dickens's approval, and the novelist came home from Paris expressly to attend rehearsals.

Shortly before he died, Arthur Smith urged that his deputy, Headlands, should succeed him as manager of the readings. Dickens respected that wish, and Headlands was engaged, but he did not prove a success. He had been a good deputy, but he was not equal to the full responsibility, and throughout this second series Dickens had anxieties and worries that he had never known under Smith's management, and was not to know again.

When the third series was arranged in 1866, George Dolby was appointed to travel with Dickens as Messrs. Chappell's repre- sentative and manager. There was no thought of companion- ship. Dolby was there as a responsible servant, and W. H. Wills travelled with Dickens as companion, and, to a degree, as secre- tary. Dolby was scarcely thrown into the novelist's company at all. But presently the latter began to realise that he had found a first-class manager, and, of course, Wills could not be perpetually travelling up and down the country just to keep him company. So gradually the manager became more intimate, and at last developed into a congenial companion and well-liked friend. And when proposals for a tour in America became insistent, and Dickens was so unsettled as to whether to go or not, he had developed such confidence in Dolby, that he decided to send him across the Atlantic to see how the land lay, and to be guided by his report. We all know the result.

Dolby went to the United States as Dickens's manager, and through all that strenuous time proved a good and loyal friend. He has told the story of the tour, and I shall not touch upon it here, except to recall the watchful care with which he looked after " the Chief " whom he had come to love so well. Over and over again in his letters home Dickens makes reference to this watchful care. " He is as tender as a woman and as watchful as a doctor," is one of his tributes.

That tour cemented the friendship. Several times Dolby was a guest at Gadshill, and after the return from America he lunched with Dickens at *All the Year Round* office at least once a week. Dickens had visited him at his house at Ross before the tour, and after it—in January 1869—he spent a week-end there. He gave Dolby's little girl a Shetland pony, and stood sponsor to his manager's little son.

Dolby, of course, managed the final series of readings in this country.

CHAPTER LXXV

HANS CHRISTIAN ANDERSEN

HANS CHRISTIAN ANDERSEN'S friendship with Dickens was formed in 1847, but his chief associations with the novelist were during his visit to Gadshill, ten years later, and so I have left him until now. He was one of Dickens's most enthusiastic hero-worshippers. Indeed, it seems clear that his adoration of Dickens eventually became a real nuisance, so that the English novelist quietly dropped him. I cannot but think that the Dane must have been a disappointing sort of individual to a man like Dickens. The Englishman was emotional, of course, but he was always a man in the company of men. That can scarcely be said of Andersen. He was of a morbid turn of mind, and he was decidedly —yes, babyish. A kind word, and like a sensitive, delicate child, he would shed tears; a word of encouragement, and he was in the dust at the feet of him who had uttered that word; a harsh word, an adverse criticism, and he suffered agony. Very naturally Dickens felt drawn towards the author of " The Ugly Duckling," and he took some special notice of him in 1847. He saw but little of him then, however. Ten years later Andersen stayed at Gadshill, and then he was in paradise. His raptures over his host and his host's family, and the house and all the surrounding country, suggest the transports of an imaginative slum kiddie who finds himself in a green field for the first time in his life. To all his friends he wrote in the same strain, and when he returned to Denmark, Dickens received from him similar letters. This childish sort of conduct must have become very tiresome, but there was worse than that. Andersen lived in his friendship with the great English novelist whom he seems to have pestered with letters introducing this, that, or the other friend. Certain it is that at last Dickens cold-shouldered him, and this is the reason suggested by Andersen's biographer. Anyhow, with all the testimony that we have to Dickens's loyalty in friendship we may be quite sure that he did not turn Andersen down without some very good reason.

There is another point. If there is one thing more than another that would be assumed about Hans Christian Andersen from a reading of his books, it is that he must have had, in common

HANS CHRISTIAN ANDERSEN

From a drawing by E. M. Bærentzen

with Dickens, a great love for children. Not so, however. Andersen resembled a lot of people that we all know; he liked nice clean and bright little boys and girls, and to children that he liked he could be very charming; but childhood in itself had no special charms for him, and his fairy tales were never regarded by him as of very much account. Imagine Dickens reading those tales and saying enthusiastically : " Here is a man absolutely after my own heart ! " Imagine his coming to know that man intimately, and the shock that he would get when he learned the truth. In fact, Andersen was a shallow sort of man. In matters of friendship he had little to give and demanded a great deal.

I think there can be little purpose in pointing to the fact that Andersen, like Dickens, had hard struggles in boyhood. Indeed, I think the similarity—up to a point—of their early experiences must have rather accentuated their lack of sympathy in later years. Dickens never suffered quite such severe privations in boyhood as Andersen did. The latter's sufferings were physical; that is to say, he positively did starve at times and wandered the streets of a big city penniless and friendless. Dickens's sufferings were of a different kind. He was in poverty, certainly, but mother and father were with him, and we know that his father, at any rate, won his affection. His blacking factory experiences were painful, because he was a boy of imagination with a conviction—which was not begotten of snobbishness—that he was superior to his environment. It may be said that Andersen was the more fortunate of the two in that he found patrons—the State itself educated him—but I doubt it. Dickens, as his father put it, " may be said to have educated himself." He learned endurance and self-reliance, and he grew up to be a man of fibre. Andersen certainly did not.

Very likely Dickens first came to know of Andersen through William Jerdan, who was the first man to introduce the Danish writer to the English people. Andersen read Dickens's books very early, and in 1846 he wrote to Jerdan :

" How I should like to shake the hand of ' Boz.' When I read his books I often think I have seen such things, and feel I could write like that. Do not misunderstand me ; and if you are a friend of ' Boz ' and he sees these lines, he will not consider it presumption ; but I do not know how better to express myself than to say that what completely captivates me seems to become part of myself. As the wind whistles round his bell-rope, I have often heard it whistle on a cold wet autumn evening, and the chirp of the cricket I remember well in the cosy corner of my parents' humble room."

In the following year he paid his first visit to England, and he met Dickens at Lady Blessington's. To that lady Dickens had written : " I must see Andersen," and he came up to town from Broadstairs specially for that purpose. He did so a second time and brought with him a set of his books, in every volume of which he had written : " To Hans Christian Andersen, from his friend and admirer, Charles Dickens." At the end of his stay in England, Andersen visited Dickens at Broadstairs and dined with him, and the following morning Dickens walked over to Ramsgate pier to say " Good-bye ! " " We pressed each other's hands, and he looked at me so kindly with his shrewd sympathetic eyes, and as the ship went off, there he stood waving his hat and looking so gallant, so youthful, and so handsome. Dickens was the last who sent me a greeting from dear England's shore."

Not long afterwards, Bentley published " A Christmas Greeting to my English Friends," which contained seven of the fairy tales, and " A Poet's Day Dreams," containing fourteen new stories, and the dedication was to Dickens, the author declaring in his preface : " I feel a desire, a longing, to transplant in England the first produce of my poetic garden as a Christmas greeting, and I send it to you, my dear, noble Charles Dickens, who, by your works had been previously dear to me, and since our meeting have taken root in my heart."

Ten years were to pass before the two writers should meet again. They certainly corresponded during that period, but none of the letters has been preserved. In March 1857 Andersen wrote to Dickens that he proposed to visit England during the coming summer :

> " *Little Dorrit* enthrals me entirely. I would, and must admire you for the sake of this one book alone, even if you had not previously bestowed upon the world those splendid compositions *David Copperfield, Nelly,*[1] and the rest. When I last saw and spoke with you in England some twelve years ago, and felt a greater regard for you, if possible, than before, you presented me with your published works, which are a real treasure to me. I possess the later books, but you must give me a copy of *Little Dorrit* when we greet each other again, for it will certainly not find a more appreciative admiring reader than myself. . . . Keep a corner in your heart for me. . . . God's blessing and delight be yours as you delight us all."

In that same letter he wrote : " I beg you to send me a few

[1] Thus did he always write and speak of *The Old Curiosity Shop*.

lines, in April at the latest, to say whether you will be in London this summer . . . for it is not for London's sake I am coming to England. The visit is for you alone." He was sent into the seventh heaven by Dickens's reply, which was an invitation to stay at Gadshill. "Your letter has made me infinitely happy," he responded. "It has quite possessed me; I am overcome with joy at the thought of being with you for a short time, of living in your house and forming one of your circle! You do not know how much I value it, and how in my heart I thank God, yourself, and your wife!"

He came, and had whatever afterwards he declared was the happiest time of his life. The whole of his time was spent with Dickens, and he never went to London save in his host's company. He walked arm in arm through the London streets with Dickens, and he tasted of the joys of paradise. To all his friends he wrote rapturous accounts of his visit. To the Queen Dowager of Denmark, for instance, he wrote : " I have now been in England five weeks, and have spent the whole time with Charles Dickens in his charming villa at Gadshill. . . . Dickens is one of the most amiable men that I know, and possesses as much heart as intellect." And then he told how he had been one of the fifty honoured guests at the Gallery of Illustration when Dickens and his friends had played " The Frozen Deep " before the Queen, the Prince Consort, and the King of the Belgians. He attended the first Handel Festival at the Crystal Palace with the Dickens family, and he visited Miss Coutts with his host, whilst, needless to say, Dickens showed him all the beauties of Kent.

The visit came to an end on July 15, and Dickens accompanied his guest to Maidstone to see him off. " He was like a dear brother up to the last moment."

After his return to his native land, Andersen wrote often to Dickens in the same strain of enthusiastic hero-worship, and for a time Dickens replied cordially, but suddenly it all ceased, and in the last fifteen years of Andersen's life there is absolutely no mention of the English novelist. Andersen's biographer says : " The enthusiasm he felt for him in 1857 was too perfervid to last very long, and Dickens's very natural hesitation to foregather indiscriminately with all the Danes whom he was in the habit of sending from time to time with letters of introduction seems at last to have somewhat offended Andersen."

It was a pity, but still it is good to know that Charles Dickens and Hans Christian Andersen were, if only for a period, such close friends.

CHAPTER LXXVI

CHARLES ALBERT FECHTER

CHARLES ALBERT FECHTER came into the novelist's life and went out of it as a dream that passes in the night. For a brief span of years there was an extraordinary friendship, and the actor seems to have exercised a fascination over the novelist that was unique in the latter's life. Dickens was his backer in England and supported him with the greatest enthusiasm. Forster says : " He became his helper in disputes, adviser on literary points, referee in matters of management, and for some years no face was more familiar than the French comedian's at Gadshill or in the office of his journal." Dickens formed a tremendous estimate of Fechter's genius, and did all in his power to push him to the fore. And for the man himself he developed a positive hero-worship. There was no more frequent visitor at Gadshill, letters innumerable passed between the two, and again and again Dickens wrote in terms of praise and of cordial personal regard. " Count always on my fidelity and true attachment "; " I am, my dear Fechter, ever your cordial and affectionate friend "; " I shall be heartily pleased to see you again, my dear Fechter, and to share your triumphs with the real earnestness of a real friend "—and so on.

One can only wonder at Dickens's obsession. That such it was I am sure. I have heard friends of the novelist speak of it with wonderment, and speak slightingly of Fechter; and Forster seems to justify me when he says : " But theatres and their affairs are things of a season, and even Dickens's whim and humour will not revive for us any interest in them." Mr. R. Renton reads into this an unaccountable sneer at the theatre. If such it were, it would indeed be unaccountable in view of Forster's life-long liking for the theatre; but I do not so interpret it. Rather do I see in it a " letting down lightly " of the actor (who was still alive when Forster wrote), for whom few of Dickens's friends had any regard, whose fascination for Dickens was a puzzle to most of his friends.

How Dickens came to know Fechter is told by James T. Fields :

" His genuine enthusiasm for Mr. Fechter's acting was most interesting. He loved to describe seeing him first quite by accident in Paris, having strolled into a little theatre there one night. ' He was making love to a woman,' Dickens said, ' and he elevated her, as well as himself, by the sentiment in which he enveloped her, that they trod in a purer ether and in another sphere quite elevated out of the present. " By heavens ! " I said to myself; " a man who can do this can do anything." I never saw two people more purely and intensely elevated by the power of love. The manner also,' he continued, ' in which he presses the hem of the dress of Lucy in " The Bride of Lammermoor," is something wonderful. The man has genius in him which is unmistakeable.' "

It was entirely owing to Dickens's enthusiasm that Fechter came to London. He opened in " Ruy Blas " and took the town by storm. Then he appeared in Shakespeare, and his " Hamlet " created a sensation, and had a remarkable run. On December 26, 1867, he appeared as Obenreizer in *No Thoroughfare* at the Adelphi. The play ran there for 150 nights, and then was transferred to the Royal Standard Theatre, Shoreditch.

Fechter gave Dickens the Swiss châlet which he caused to be erected in the shrubbery at Gadshill. He furnished it, too, for we read in the issue of " The Gad's Hill Gazette," dated August 19, 1865, that " Mr. C. Fechter, who left on Sunday for Glasgow (where he intends to begin his provincial tour), has just completed his charming present of a châlet, by furnishing it in a very handsome manner." Writing of this châlet in that same year, Dickens says : " It will really be a very pretty thing, and in the summer (supposing it not to be blown away in the spring) the upper room will make a charming study." Forster tells us that it really did become a great resource in the summer months, and much of Dickens's work was done there. And it was in this châlet, in the room " up among the branches of the trees," that he wrote for the last time on that lovely June afternoon in 1870.

In 1869 Fechter went to America, and Dickens heralded him with an article in the " Atlantic Monthly," in which he spoke with the greatest enthusiasm of the actor's genius, and pointed out that his appreciation was not the result of personal regard, but that the personal regard had sprung out of his appreciation. " I cannot wish my friend a better audience than he will have in the American people," the article concluded, " and I cannot wish them a better actor than they will have in my friend." He died while Fechter was in America.

CHAPTER LXXVII

THE GREATEST OF THEM ALL

I HAVE always wondered at the neglect meted out to John Forster. It is said that he is known to the present generation only as the friend of Dickens, and I believe it is true. It is something to be sure of immortality as the friend of such a man as Dickens, but quite apart from that Forster was a very remarkable man who does not deserve the neglect that he suffers. I think I do not exaggerate when I say that no man exercised a greater influence upon Victorian literature than this self-made man, who established himself as one of the ablest editors of his time, one of the most authoritative and constructive dramatic, art, and literary critics, and, above all, as the trusted friend, confidant, and adviser of practically every writer of his time that mattered. Indeed, Forster was a greater man than this generation imagines. It cannot be said of him, as it was said by Johnson of Goldsmith : " Sir, he was a great man, a very great man " ; but we do him an injustice when we regard him just as the friend of Dickens, only that and nothing more. I am not, of course, intending to belittle his claim on that score; what I do want to insist upon is that if Forster had never met Dickens he would still have had strong claims upon our grateful remembrance. He was very nearly a great man, for certain. A little more play of fancy, a little less of the Podsnappian self-complacency, and he would have been one of our greatest biographers. As it is, he wrote some biographies that we could not afford to lose. He did not produce one truly great work, but he cannot be denied a place in the front rank of second-class biographers, even if his *Life of Dickens* does not (I am inclined to think it does) place him in the rear rank of first-class biographers. Add to the fact, the tremendous influence he wielded both as Editor of the " Examiner " and as the intimate friend of practically every contemporary writer of any pretensions at all, and we may reasonably echo Mr. Percy Fitzgerald's expression of surprise at the fact that Forster has never been included in any series of biographies of leading writers.

In this sense Forster's friendship with Dickens has counted rather to his disadvantage. Dickens was a man of overwhelming

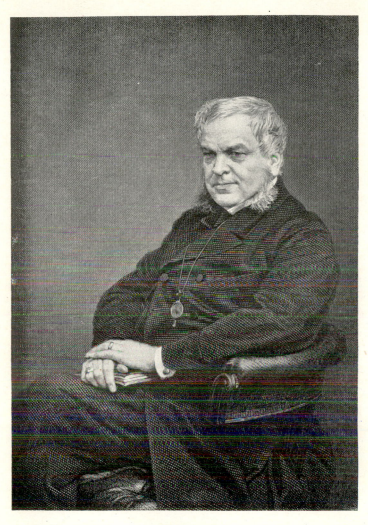

JOHN FORSTER

From an engraving by C. H. Jeens

and fascinating personality, and he has been allowed to over-shadow Forster, without whose staunch friendship, loyal service in business and family affairs, and reliable advice in literary matters, he might not have been the man he was. For it was advantageous to Dickens very often that the staid, level-headed, splendidly loyal John Forster was inevitably at hand to sit upon his coat tails, as it were, whenever necessary. By the present generation Forster is too lightly dismissed as "the friend of Dickens." He would be proud to be remembered in that capacity, of course, but we are unjust to him when we think only of that. His editorship of the "Examiner," and his indispensable books prove the injustice of a too scant dismissal of him as "Dickens's Boswell." Boswell was little more than tolerated by Burke and Reynolds and Hawkins and others because he was the friend of their common friend, Johnson. Forster was loved and trusted by Dickens's friends, or most of them, as he was by Dickens himself. If he had no other claim to a niche in the Temple of Fame he still has this one : that he was the champion Friend of his time. He was a friend of Lamb's, and Elia penned many delightful letters to him. He was *the* friend of Browning, *the* friend of Lytton; Carlyle loved him, and turned to him as he turned to nobody else save Froude; he was loved by Macready; he was the friend of Ainsworth, of Tennyson, of Landor, of Leigh Hunt, of Procter, of Gladstone—of almost everybody that mattered. On Forster's friendships, Mr. Richard Renton's book published a few years ago, is a positive revelation. That author points out this very noteworthy fact : that, with one exception, all Forster's friend-ships were lasting friendships. The exception was the greatest of all—save the Dickens friendship—namely, that with Browning, the quarrel with whom was the most lamentable incident in Forster's life. But that friendship lasted over many years, through much storm and stress, and how much the poet valued it is proved by his inscription in a presentation copy of "Pauline" : "To my true friend, John Forster," and by his inscription in a copy of "Paracelsus"—"To John Forster, Esq. (my early under-stander), with true thanks for his generous and seasonable public confession of faith in me." Carlyle—to whom Forster was "Fuz"—knew the value of this remarkable man. How com-pletely he trusted him is proved by this fact : when he wrote the story of his domestic life he entrusted the manuscript to Froude, with an injunction that it was not to be published within ten years of his death, and then in Froude's absolute discretion— absolute discretion, that is, save only that he might, if he so desired, consult John Forster.

But it is truly extraordinary how famous men of his time relied

z

upon Forster, and turned to him unhesitatingly, confident in his sound sense and level-headedness. And note how he helped and encouraged young men who were striving to make their way, and merited assistance. Henry Morley says :

> " The best actors, painters, poets, novelists, historians of his time were all his friends. They found constantly in the ' Examiner ' a definite appreciation of their work; prompt, hearty, and just appreciation, as distinguished from vague praise or commonplaces of reviewing. When afterwards they met their critic, came under the influence of his strong sympathy with all that was best in their aims, felt the sincerity of his nature, and learnt to rely on the soundness of his judgment, they were drawn inevitably into friendship. . . . There was not a young man of letters labouring for recognition and deserving it who could not find his way to the grasp of John Forster's strong hand, be encouraged by his ready smile, and helped by his sound counsel. He was intolerant of work with an unworthy aim, and quickened in all his friends ' the noble appetite for what is best,' that showed itself not only in his public writing, but also gave worth to his familiar conversation."

" Again and again," adds Morley, " the hearts of earnest men leapt out towards him who had been the first to know the meaning of their utterance, and with bold emphasis had been the first not only to call the world to listen, but clearly to set forth the reason of his faith in what they said or did."

And yet it is difficult to arrive at anything like a satisfying idea of what manner of man Forster was. " A harbitrary cove," the cabman called him, and so he was, but assuredly that is not all. The prototype of Podsnap, Mr. Fitzgerald says, but surely that is not sufficient. Mr. Fitzgerald also likens him to Dr. Johnson. I think the comparison is not unhappy. He was rough and uncompromising, says Mr. Fitzgerald again; lacking in breeding, says Macready, in one of his irritable moods, but probably with much truth. Sir Theodore Martin says : " Forster seemed to me a very dictatorial person." Douglas Jerrold, picking up a pencil stump, remarked that it was like Forster, " short, thick, and full of lead," which was just one of his facetious remarks, but contained a considerable degree of truth. Dr. John Brown said : " Forster is a ' heavy swell,' and has always been to me offensive, and he has no sense or faculty of humour."

Macready pays tribute again and again. We have to make allowance for that Irish quickness of temper in the famous tragedian which he himself was always lamenting. In his Diary we read some most outrageous things about many of his friends; most of them come under his lash at times : but these things were written during his " paddies," and must not be taken alone as indicating his real feelings. And so, though he writes in bitterest vein about Forster at times, the Diary as a whole conclusively proves his affection for the man. In it may be found many proofs of Forster's loyal friendship. Hablôt Knight Browne did not come within the same degree of friendship as Macready, but he was a friend of Forster's, and the following letter throws a light on the latter's capacity for rendering unassuming service :

" MY DEAR BROWNE,
            " They are getting a little anxious at White Friars. I enclose you a cheque—you charged too little for the design of the cover. I took the liberty of changing the five guineas into eight guineas, and you will find a cheque hereto corresponding. This liberty I am sure you will excuse, and believe me, my dear Browne, always and sincerely yours,
                                        "JOHN FORSTER."

And we have Bulwer Lytton's testimony as follows :

" A most sterling man with an intellect at once massive and delicate. Few indeed have his strong practical sense and sound judgment; fewer still unite with such qualities his exquisite appreciation of latent beauties in literary art. Hence, in ordinary life there is no safer adviser about literary work, especially poetry; no more refined critic. A large heart naturally accompanies so masculine an understanding. He has a rare capacity for affection which embraces many friendships without loss of depth or warmth in one. Most of my literary contemporaries are his intimate companions, and their jealousies of each other do not diminish their trust in him. More than any living critic he has served to establish reputations. Tennyson and Browning owe him much in their literary careers. Me, I think, he served in that way less than any of his other friends, but indeed I know of no critic to whom I have been much indebted for any position I hold in literature. In more private matters I am greatly indebted to his counsel. His reading is extensive. What faults he has lie on the surface. He is sometimes bluff to rudeness, but all such faults of manner (and they are his only ones) are but trifling inequalities in a nature solid and valuable as a block of gold."

That, I think, is the best picture of John Forster that has been drawn. "Harbitrary cove"? So he was, but how easy, and, alas! how common, it is to take hold of some catch phrase like that and repeat it until the world comes to think that it says all there is to be said. Forster's arbitrariness was really no more than a mannerism. He was, as Lytton says, a man of masculine understanding, a man with a rare capacity for affection which embraced many friendships without loss of depth or warmth in one, a rare literary critic utterly devoid of petty jealousies, who helped to make many a man and never lifted his hand to unmake or to injure any man, a man of staunch loyalty, and sound integrity, a man to be relied upon implicitly in any transaction.

Dr. John Brown says that Forster had no sense of humour. We may doubt that of a man who was a friend of Charles Lamb, Tom Hood, Douglas Jerrold, Mark Lemon, John Leech, R. H. Barham, and Charles Dickens. We may doubly doubt it of a man so full of human sympathy as he was. Macready says that Forster was lacking in breeding. Very likely he had not the manners of a D'Orsay. There was no veneer about him. He was the solid, unvarnished oak, rough cut, but finely grained, solid and steady. Mr. Renton sums up his character very aptly in the one word "reliable." Before all else and above all else, he was reliable. The famous authors of his time, the famous artists, the famous actors, yes, and the famous statesmen relied upon him implicitly, and he never failed them.

Yates says: "Forster, partly owing to natural temperament, partly to harassing official work, and ill-health, was almost as much over, as Dickens was under their respective years." Yates knew Forster only in the later years of the latter's life, but his remark applies to the man at any period. True, Forster writes of the joyous days in the late 'thirties and the 'forties with a sigh of regret for a day that is dead, but I never read of those boisterous frolics which he records without picturing him as the most sober and serious member of the party. When I read of the memorable trip to Cornwall—Dickens, Maclise, Stanfield, and Forster—and the merrymaking right into the wee small hours, I always picture Forster as the member of the party upon whom the others would rely for a reminder when bedtime came. Not that I mean to suggest that he was a drag upon the wheels of enjoyment, but he was what Dickens would call a "buttoned-up man." "All buttoned-up men are weighty," says the novelist, and that is exactly what Forster was. On these merry occasions he was the most ponderous—the most weighty man of the party, and though he entered into the enjoyment thoroughly, it is difficult to picture him giving way to that *abandon* that characterised

Dickens and Maclise, for instance. Dickens records that during the Cornwall trip, "the luggage was in Forster's department." It is symbolical. On this point Yates confirms me: "Though Forster's shrewd common-sense, sound judgment, and deep affection for his friend commanded, as was right, Dickens's loving and grateful acceptance of his views, and though the communion between them was never for a moment weakened, it was not as a companion ' in his lighter hour ' that Dickens, in his latter days looked on Forster. . . ." Though we must not forget that in his earlier days Forster was the companion, with Maclise and Ainsworth, and the Landseers, of all the " lighter hours."

The friendship with Dickens is really something of a puzzle, and I hope I run no risk of being misunderstood when I say that I think it was largely due to Dickens's perception of worth, and his ability, for worth's sake, to ignore qualities which, in the best of friends, may be trying. Never would Forster play second fiddle anywhere, if he could help it, Mr. Fitzgerald says. He was a despot, he was dictatorial—offensively so to those who could not or would not look beneath the surface. I am not prepared to assert that Dickens was a despot, but nothing is more certain than that he had to be " cock of the walk " in any company. Friendship between two such men, strong, lasting, heart-to-heart friendship is not common. And seeing that Forster had faults of manner which Dickens had not, seeing that undoubtedly the real nature and charm of the man were beneath the surface, there may be justification for the assertion that in the matter of tolerance Dickens had to give more than he demanded. The friendship puzzled many contemporaries. James Payn says :

" In friendship, which in all other points must needs be frank and open, this problem often remains unsolved— namely, the friendship of one's friend for some other man. D. and E. have the most intimate relations with one another, but for the life of him, E. cannot understand what D. sees in F. to so endear him to him. This was what many of Dickens's friends, and certainly the world at large, said of Forster. It is not my business, nor is it in my power to explain the riddle; I rarely met them together without witnessing some sparring between them—and sometimes without the gloves. On the other hand, I have known Forster to pay some compliments to ' The Inimitable ' in his patronising way which the other would acknowledge in his drollest manner. It is certain that Forster took the utmost interest in Dickens, even to the extent of seeing

everything he wrote through the press, and as to the genuineness of Dickens's regard for him I have the most positive
proof. I have already said that Dickens once wrote to me
spelling the word Foster (in Foster Brothers) with an *r*
' because I am always thinking of my friend Forster.' Long
afterwards, in acknowledging a service which I had been
fortunately able to do for him, in terms far more generous
than it deserved, he actually signed the letter, not Charles
Dickens, but John Forster ! When the biography of the
former appeared, and its editor (sic) was accused of mis-
representing himself as standing in a nearer relation to
Dickens than he really was, I thought it only fair to Forster
to send him those two letters, with which—though of course
he had no need of the corroboration on such a matter from
without—he expressed himself greatly pleased.''

Macready describes one of the contests in which the gloves
were removed. Under date August 16, 1840, he writes :

" Went to dine with Dickens, and was witness of a most
painful scene after dinner. Forster, Maclise, and myself
were the guests. Forster got to one of his headlong streams
of talk (which he thinks argument), and waxed warm, and
at last some sharp observation led to personal retorts between
him and Dickens. He displayed his usual want of tact, and
Dickens flew into so violent a passion as quite to forget
himself, and give Forster to understand that he was in his
house which he should be glad if he would leave. Forster
behaved very foolishly. I stopped him; spoke to both of
them, and observed that for an angry instant they were
about to destroy a friendship valuable to both. I drew
from Dickens the admission that he had spoken in passion
and would not have said what he said could he have reflected;
but he added that he could not answer for his temper under
Forster's provocation, and that he should do just the same
again. Forster behaved very *weakly ;* would not accept the
repeated acknowledgment communicated to him that Dickens
regretted the passion, etc., but stayed, skimbling-skambling,
and at last, finding he could obtain no more, made a sort of
speech accepting what he had before declined. He was
silent and not recovered—no wonder !—during the whole
evening. Mrs. Dickens had gone out in tears. It was a
very painful scene."

All of which proves very little more than that both Dickens
and Forster were essentially human. But in face of these facts,

I think it may be said that the friendship of these two men is very positive proof of the possession by both of the capacity for looking beneath the surface and seeing the true worth of a friend.

In November 1847 Macready writes in his Diary : " Forster dined to-day; was very sorry to hear him speak as if the long and intimate friendship between himself and Dickens was likely to terminate or very much relax.   They have both faults with their good qualities, but they have been too familiar.   I hope Dickens is not capricious—not spoiled; he has, however, great excuse." No, Dickens was not capricious : that charge was never brought against him.   Nor was he spoiled, though no man ever had greater excuse.   Two strong natures had clashed again, and there had been another " sparring bout," and Forster's pompous dignity had been hurt.   The friendship was to last another twenty-two years and more, and was to grow closer and closer, only to be broken by death. . . .

" And " (says Mr. Renton) " when at last the cords were loosed; the link snapped that had bound each to other for just upon forty years, what did it mean to Forster?

" Briefly this—

" There were not many to carry Charles Dickens to his burial.   His nearest and dearest only and a friend or two well-nigh as near and dear.

" Among the latter, the tall, still burly figure, bowed through grief and disease, of John Forster was sadly conspicuous.   Gone all that was autocratic and domineering about him; gone the dignity, the imperiousness, the harsh ' commandeering ' of all else human to his own will and pleasure.

" There remained only the true, inner, natural man, shaken with a sorrow such as is not given to every man to feel.   Himself hopelessly racked with physical pain, he appeared almost as if he were burying the better part of himself. . . . He had lost his chief object in existence; which, until he himself went to join his friend, was, I am convinced, mainly sustained in and by the occupation of writing that friend's life."

" He had lost his chief object in existence."   Verily, I believe Mr. Renton does not exaggerate.   From the days of their first acquaintance Forster loved Dickens with at least a brother's love.   There was an air of patronage in his affection, but it was the patronage of an elder brother.   For, as Yates says, though they were born in the same year, Forster was older than his years, and Dickens younger. He took Dickens under his wing, and positively would have stood up against the world in defence of his friend. He was constantly rendering service. He negotiated for his friend in the most intimate and delicate domestic affairs; he negotiated Dickens's business affairs for him; he served him early and late for the sake of the love that he bore him. Indeed, he was possessed of a very rare capacity for friendship. No man that ever breathed was possessed of a more sturdy independence, had less of toadyism in his nature, though he was the friend of almost every famous man of his time; yet in this particular case he was guilty of something like idolatry. He would have quarrelled with almost all his other friends for Dickens's sake. And maybe that air of patronage which sometimes appeared in his relations with the novelist was consciously assumed in the true English spirit (of which he was the very embodiment) to hide from the world the real depth of his feelings. He was jealous, as all men are when they love. He resented it when any other man gained the confidence of Dickens. He was even jealous of another's popularity. Did he not take umbrage at the success of Ainsworth's " Jack Sheppard," simply because it bade fair for a time to rival the popularity of Dickens's books !

And Dickens was as loyal a friend as was Forster. He knew the failings of the " Lincolnshire mammoth," as he called his friend, but he knew his worth thoroughly, and he accepted Forster's patronage with good-humour and with a complete appreciation of the devotion that was ever at his service. There are several instances on record in which he showed his loyalty. Take the case of Mrs. Lynn Linton. In his " Life of Landor " Forster dismissed that lady's friendship with the poet in a single sentence. It was grossly unfair, but a typical instance of that John Bullish prejudice which was his greatest failing. Mrs. Lynn Linton declared that Forster acted in this case out of jealousy, and she said that he used the " Life " as " a vehicle for his own laudation—diverging all other friendships to aggrandise and augment his own." Wilkie Collins said exactly the same thing about the *Life of Dickens*, and we will take note of the charge presently. Mrs. Lynn Linton was very much hurt, and when, at Dickens's request, she wrote a review of the book for *All the Year Round*, she commenced her article : " The Life of Walter Savage Landor has yet to be written." That could not have appeared in an anonymous magazine without the inference that it expressed the Editor's opinion. Dickens was too loyal to his friend. He wrote to the lady :

" Although your article on our old friend is interesting as a piece of personal remembrance, it does not satisfy my desires as a review of Forster's book. It could hardly be otherwise than painful to Forster that I, one of his oldest literary friends, and certainly, of all others, the most intimate and confidential, should insert in these pages an account of Landor without a word of commendation of a biography that has caused, to my knowledge, a world of care and trouble. I find from your letter to my son that you do not think well of the said book. Admitting that his life was to be written at all, I DO. And it is because I think well of it, and wish highly to commend it on what I deem to be its deserts, that I am staggered and stopped short by your paper and fear I must turn to and write another in its stead. I want you to understand the case on my own presentation of it, and hence I trouble you with this note."

And so, he wrote the review himself, nevertheless paying Mrs. Lynn Linton for the article which he did not use. And we have seen how, in the dispute with Bentley in 1839, Dickens stood loyally by Forster, and very nearly quarrelled with Ainsworth.

It would be absurd to attempt to follow Dickens and Forster through their friendship of thirty-four years. In that letter to Mrs. Lynn Linton just quoted Dickens described himself as one of Forster's oldest literary friends, and " certainly, of all others, the most confidential." How far he was in Forster's confidence there is no knowing, but it is certain that he confided in Forster as he confided in no one else. Forster, I think, had not the need for friendship in anything like the degree that Dickens had it. True-hearted, tender-hearted he was, but he had not that almost Celtic emotionalism that characterised his friend. Even if he had been a novelist he could never have written the death of Little Nell. In that sense he was even more English than Dickens. There was in him that typically English self-consciousness—fear of wearing his heart on his sleeve—that was not in Dickens. He lived in the material world far more than Dickens did, and though the latter was certainly no fool in business matters, it meant very much to him that he had a true and trustworthy friend always at hand to advise and assist and to conduct his business affairs for him. Living so strenuous an imaginative life as he did, Forster's friendship was of incalculable value to him. Indeed, without it, I doubt whether his gifts would have remained so fresh as they did, his imagination so vigorous and unfettered. From the very beginning, Forster, whom he described in his will as his " dear and trusty friend," was the man to whom he turned in everything. In disputes with publishers it was Forster who was his champion and negotiator, and in the saddest event of his life it was the same friend who acted on his behalf. So also was it to Forster that he turned first of all when he wanted to help Leigh Hunt, or the family of Douglas Jerrold. To Forster he sent all his proofs; it was Forster's advice in respect thereof that he valued most; it was Forster who saw his books through the press and negotiated with illustrators when he was abroad; and it was Forster whom he named as his executor in conjunction with Miss Hogarth.

It is perhaps curious that in his published letters to Forster we do not find those protestations of friendship that we find in letters to all other friends, but that may well be accounted for by the fact that nearly all such letters appear in Forster's book, and were sub-edited by him. There is one exception, however. In 1845 Forster's only brother died, and Dickens wrote to his friend from Genoa :

> " I feel the distance between us now, indeed. I would to Heaven, my dearest friend, that I could remind you in a manner more lively and affectionate than this dull sheet of paper can put on, that you have a Brother left. One bound to you by ties as strong as Nature ever forged. By ties never to be broken, weakened, changed in any way—but to be knotted tighter up, if that be possible, until the same end comes to them as has come to these. That end but the bright beginning of a happier union, I believe; and have never more strongly and religiously believed (and oh ! Forster, with what a sore heart I have thanked God for it) than when that shadow has fallen on my own hearth, and made it cold and dark as suddenly as in the home of that poor girl you tell me of. . . . I have many things to say, but cannot say them now. Your attached and loving friend for life, and for, I hope, beyond it."

But, indeed, such protestations were unnecessary; the understanding between them was too thorough. Much more curious is it that Dickens never dedicated a book to Forster. The latter, however, dedicated his " Life of Goldsmith " to Dickens, and he was godfather to his friend's eldest daughter.

But, of course, the consummation of this friendship is the book, the writing of which Mr. Renton says was the main solace of Forster's last few years. It was the fulfilment of Dickens's wish —of a sacred trust really. In 1847 the novelist first expressed the wish that if Forster should outlive him he should write his biography, and Forster says : " though, long before his death, I had ceased to believe it likely that I should survive to write about him, he had never withdrawn the wish at this early time strongly expressed, or the confidences, not only then, but to the very eve of his death reposed in me, that was to enable me to fulfil it." The writing of that book must have been torture to Forster, not merely because Dickens's death had meant the tearing away of a part of his very self, but because he was in wretched health and nearing his own end.   It seems to me to be reflected in the book. Always, in the record of the early days of their friendship there is a note of sadness, as though the writer were sighing for the days when the health and strength of early manhood made all the world so bright and gay, when all was promise—bright promise, and the sun shone sixteen hours out of the twenty-four.   And in the record of later years, there is the note of tiredness, not of dis-illusionment, but of sadness, and depression.   But it was a sacred task conscientiously carried out.   The book is criticised very freely, and when all has been said there is, and there can be, no answer to the question : " Who else could have written it ? " One recent critic compared it, to its disadvantage, with Boswell's immortal book.   Let us note Dickens's views on the point.   They are contained in a letter written to Forster himself in 1848.

" I question very much " (he says) " whether it would have been a good thing for every great man to have had his Boswell, inasmuch that I think that two Boswells, or three at the most, would have made great men extraordinarily false, and would have set them on always playing a part, and would have made distinguished people about them for ever restless and distrustful.   I can imagine a succession of Boswells bringing about a tremendous state of falsehood in society, and playing the very deuce with confidence and friendship."

With which, I think, we need not hesitate to agree.   In that same letter, Dickens, referring to his friend's " Life of Gold-smith," says : " I never will hear the biography compared with Boswell's except under vigorous protest.   For I do say that it is mere folly to put into opposite scales a book, however amusing and curious, written by an unconscious coxcomb like that, and one which surveys and grandly understands the characters of all the illustrious company that move in it." It is worth while bearing this in mind when we think of comparing Forster's *Life of Dickens* with Boswell's " Life of Johnson."   The letter concludes with these words : " I desire no better for my fame, when my personal dustiness shall be past the control of my love of order, than such a biographer and such a critic."

I do not share Dickens's opinion of Boswell, but it is difficult to controvert the suggestion that too many Boswells would bring about a state of insincerity in society that would destroy the value of biographies altogether. In any case, such a comparison as that under notice is futile for this reason : that Dickens was not a Johnson. He was a great man, but of a totally different type. Forster tells us that Dickens had no conversation. A recent critic has suggested that that was a " get out," if I may be permitted the colloquialism. It was nothing of the kind. It is perfectly true that Dickens had no conversation in the real sense. Many who knew him have written about him, and they all tell us that he was the life and soul of any company he was in ; but I have never yet come across a suggestion that he shone in conversation. He was too restless to do that, and—he was lacking in education. Splendid letter-writer he certainly was ; but the qualities that make a good letter-writer do not necessarily make a good conversationalist. By contrast, Johnson's letters are rarely of any special value.

Forster has been criticised for not having given us more facts than he did. There is very little in the criticism. If we bear in mind how near to Dickens's life he was writing we must surely admit that he omitted very little that he might have included. True, he did not mention all the houses in which his friend lived or stayed, but is that the normal duty of a biographer? Surely his duty is, in the main, to deal only with facts that affect the trend of his subject's life, or help to shape his character? To record that Dickens once stayed at Hyde Park Place, for instance, or to indicate every particular house in which he lived, is the legitimate business of a Robert Allbut or an F. G. Kitton, but not of a Forster. Such, at any rate, is my submission. I do not think that an instance can be pointed to of Forster having omitted a *vital* or *essential* fact. Some say that he should have told us more about Dickens's domestic trouble. Admitting that it is our business, it again has to be borne in mind that Forster wrote within a very few years of Dickens's death, when Mrs. Dickens and most of her children were still alive. Of course, here arises the old difficulty. It has been said that the friend, writing too soon after a man's death, cannot deal frankly and fully with the facts that he knows, whilst, later on, there is no one who has first-hand knowledge of the facts or knew the man. On which argument, no biography should ever be written. But the difficulty is a real one, and it must have handicapped Forster considerably. He

CHARLES DICKENS
(1868)
From a photograph by Ben Gurney of New York

erred on the right side—on the side of caution. Nevertheless, there were incidents in Dickens's life, illuminative incidents, that might well have been recorded more fully. The story of the quarrel with Thackeray, for instance, might have been told without offence to any one. The story of Dickens's interest in the Italian Refugees of 1849 might have been, ought to have been told. It is simply referred to.   Herein lies one of Forster's greatest faults. He assumes more knowledge in his reader than he has any justification for assuming; he writes more for his own circle than for the man in the street. If he mentions a dinner to Macready, he speaks of it as though he were simply recalling for the pleasure of a few friends a happy event in which they and he took part. So does he speak of great men with whom Dickens was acquainted as though all his readers knew them as well as he did.

But the most common criticism of Forster is that which Mrs. Lynn Linton expressed, namely, that he glorified himself at the expense of Dickens's other friends. It is certain that some of Dickens's friends were offended by Forster's treatment of them —Shirley Brooks records that Wilkie Collins and G. H. Lewes described the book to him as " The Life of John Forster, with notices of Dickens "—and in one or two cases it cannot be denied that they had cause for feeling hurt, but I cannot see any justice in the criticism of the principle upon which he worked. It seems to me that he was bound to reason somewhat like this : " Dickens was a very exceptional man, particularly in regard to the number of his friendships. I might appeal to them for material. I should be swamped—overwhelmed. My task would become herculean. My health is bad ; I am nearing the end of my life ; it is even doubtful if I shall live to complete this new task. But I knew Dickens more intimately and over a longer period than anybody else ; I loved him probably better than anybody else, and certainly better than I ever loved any other man. He wrote to me more frequently, more fully, and more intimately than to anybody else. From the days when he first became an author, right down to the very end, there was nothing in his life in respect of which I was not his confidant ; he had no interest in which I was not associated with him. I saw him in the company of all his other friends ; I saw him in every circumstance and in every mood. After all, who is there that could amplify my knowledge of him, or usefully extend the material that I have in my possession now ? "

What objection can there be to such a point of view ? We are told that Forster refused to make use of letters addressed by Dickens to other friends, and that in doing so he was actuated by jealousy. As a general charge it is sheer nonsense. Wilkie

Collins uttered the indictment, and possibly he had some personal grounds for it, but it was not true in a general sense, and no one who knows Forster would utter it now. The man had too big a mind and too big a heart. And when it comes to the point, would these letters have helped him to any material extent? Dickens's letters to Wilkie Collins have been published. Do they supply any vital deficiencies in Forster's book? A representative selection of letters addressed to other friends has been published. How far do they supply deficiencies? There may be one or two that help to illumine Dickens's character for us, but read the letters that Forster quotes, and say to what extent Forster's book, *as a biography*, would have been improved if he had had this mass of additional material in his hands. His task, already a heavy one, really a burden borne for the sake of the love he had had for his friend, would have been enormously increased to very little effect.

I see no point in the suggestion that Forster should have made plentiful use of other people's impressions of Dickens. That is not how biography is written—except, of course, when the biographer is writing of a man he never saw. Apart from the fact that such material would have been sufficient for a big volume in itself, it must be remembered that Forster was seeking solely to give the material facts in Dickens's life, and to reveal his friend's personality as he knew it. Was it not his proper aim, and did he fail in his purpose?

The argument that Forster did not go sufficiently into detail is not a weighty one. The Dickensian keen on topography grumbles when he cannot find in Forster information as to the exact identity and location of the home of this character or that; another complains that the author does not record the identity of the prototype of this character or that; another is cross because Forster does not record that Mrs. Dickens was " a large woman, with a great deal of colour, and rather coarse." Forster did not know that he was writing for the modern Dickensian; he did not know that all these details would be sought after some day; but even if he could have foreseen all this, he could not have included these minute—and comparatively trivial—details in his book. Indeed we must be careful what we ask of a biographer. Is he to be expected to record the full postal address of every house in which his subject ever dined? To ask that—and some Dickensians do seem to ask for it—is to reveal a misconception of the scope and purpose of biography. That purpose—the main purpose, at any rate—is to reveal character, and after we have read all that Dickens's friends have to say about him, can it be fairly suggested that Forster's book does not fulfil that purpose?

Boswell, of course, uses a different method of revealing his subject's character, but it is absurd to quote him against Forster in particular. He might be quoted with exactly the same amount of force against every other biographer in any language whatsoever. Remember, too, that Boswell's method would be impossible with nine hundred and ninety-nine biographers out of any thousand. Compare him with Forster for a moment. He knew Johnson for twenty years; Forster knew Dickens for thirty-four years. Boswell saw his friend twice a year at the most; Forster saw his almost every day. Only rarely did letters pass between Boswell and Johnson; between Forster and Dickens not a week passed but there was an exchange of letters. With these facts in mind, how ridiculous it is to criticise Forster for not being a Boswell!

In very truth Forster had a difficult task. He had the choice of two stools, as it were, and he surely is to be congratulated upon the fact that he avoided the fate that is proverbially said to befall the person placed in such a predicament. He chose one of the stools, planted himself firmly upon it, and he sits there immovable for all time.

And now let us consider the charge that Forster was unjust or unfair to others of Dickens's friends. He did, I think, in just one or two cases, allow his personal feelings to govern him. It is difficult to doubt that he was jealous of one or two of the friends of later years. He was always jealous of any one who came very close to his friend. Now, the friend of later years for whom Dickens had most regard was Wilkie Collins. There is no doubt about the closeness of his friendship with the younger novelist. It puzzles me, it has puzzled many others, but it was a fact. Just note how Collins was associated with Dickens in everything during the latter half of the latter's literary career. Need we be surprised if Forster feared sometimes that he was in danger of being supplanted? I think there can be no doubt but that he did. In addition to—probably partly because of, that fact, Forster had no great liking for Collins. I have already quoted James Payn on the difficulty one sometimes experiences in feeling a friendship towards one's friend's friend. In respect of Wilkie Collins, Mr. Renton makes exactly that point. He says that Collins was not to Forster what Forster was to Dickens (which hardly needed saying), and he adds : " My friend whom I introduce to you, is, by virtue of that introduction, your friend also, but not as I am your friend, or you mine." Of course it is true; and though Forster was friendly enough with Collins, it was only because Collins was his friend's friend. He had no particular regard for the man, and because of Dickens's strange regard for him, was also rather jealous of him. And the result was that when he came to write Dickens's life he did not treat Collins fairly. There are nineteen references to Collins in the book (according to the best index that we possess). Three of those references are to the appearance of serial stories in *All the Year Round*, most of the others are to Collins accompanying Dickens on journeys, and the remainder are to theatrical matters. There is not a reference of an intimate character, except the first, which, speaking of Collins's appearance in " Used Up " in 1852, says that he " became, for all the rest of the life of Dickens, one of his dearest and most valued friends "—surely a curt dismissal of a friend who influenced Dickens's literary work as no one else ever did ! Collins had reason for feeling aggrieved. He was entitled to better treatment.

Collins's is the most glaring case, but it does not stand alone. It is quite easy, in reading Forster's books, to tell which of Dickens's friends he liked and which he did not like. We know he liked Maclise and Stanfield and Lemon, for instance. We know he " was not so keen on " certain others. But, after all, the offence is not rank. Forster was *the* friend of Dickens. He loved the novelist with a love rarely found to exist between men. With that love there went, hand in hand, a real jealousy. Further, he had no particular regard for some of his friend's friends ; and he was human. Recognise these facts, and recognise—as I think we must—the soundness of the plan upon which he worked, and there is very little substantial ground for complaint. Consider fairly all the criticisms of his book that have been offered, and admit that in some of them there is a grain of truth, but when all is said and done we are forced to agree that Forster's *Life of Dickens* is a noble tribute to, and memorial of, a great and rare friendship which will last for all time.

INDEX

PRINTED IN GREAT BRITAIN BY
RICHARD CLAY & SONS, LIMITED,
BRUNSWICK ST., STAMFORD ST., S.E. 1,
AND BUNGAY, SUFFOLK.

THE MEMORIAL EDITION

OF THE

LIFE OF CHARLES DICKENS

By JOHN FORSTER

Illustrated with 500 Portraits, Facsimiles and other Illustrations, including

3 PHOTOGRAVURES AND 5 STEEL PLATES

Collected, Annotated, and arranged with Introduction

By B. W. MATZ

Editor of "The Dickensian."

Two Volumes = = Demy 8vo. - - 30/= net

LONDON: CHAPMAN AND HALL, LTD.

CHARLES DICKENS'S COMPLETE WORKS

BOOKS ON DICKENS

THE PAGEANT OF DICKENS.
By W. WALTER CROTCH. Third Edition. Demy 8vo, 5s. net.

THE SOUL OF DICKENS.
By W. WALTER CROTCH. Demy 8vo, 6s. net.

SHORT PLAYS FROM DICKENS.
By H. B. BROWNE. Crown 8vo. Second Edition. 3s. net.

SYNOPSES OF DICKENS'S WORKS.
By J. WALKER McSPADDEN. 18mo, 2s. 6d. net.

SCENES AND CHARACTERS FROM THE WORKS OF CHARLES DICKENS:
Being 866 Pictures Printed from the original Wood Blocks engraved for "The Household Edition" by FRED BARNARD, "PHIZ," J. MAHONY, CHARLES GREEN, A. B. FROST, GORDON THOMSON, Sir LUKE FILDES, R.A., and others. Imperial 8vo, 10s. 6d. net.

"THE DICKENSIAN":
A Magazine for Dickens Lovers. Edited by B. W. MATZ. Illustrated. Monthly, 4d. Yearly volumes, 4s. 6d. net.

THE FIRST EDITIONS OF THE WRITINGS OF CHARLES DICKENS AND THEIR VALUES:
A Bibliography. By JOHN C. ECKEL. Fully Illustrated. Demy 8vo, 12s. 6d. net (*out of print*). Large Paper Edition, £1 5s. net.

THE COMPLETE "MYSTERY OF EDWIN DROOD."
By J. CUMING WALTERS. Illustrated. Demy 8vo, 6s. net.

CHARACTERS FROM DICKENS:
A Portfolio of 20 Vandyck Gravures from the Drawings of F. G. LEWIN with an Introduction by B. W. MATZ. Large 4to, 3s. 6d. net.

THE CHARLES DICKENS AUTOGRAPH BOOK.
Compiled by J. W. T. LEY. With an Index to Subjects, and Portrait. Crown 8vo, 1s. 6d. net.

RAMBLES IN DICKENS LAND.
By ROBERT ALLBUT, with Illustrations by HELEN M. JAMES. Crown 8vo, 3s. 6d. net.

READINGS FROM THE WORKS OF CHARLES DICKENS.
As arranged and read by himself. With Portrait of Dickens giving a public reading, by ALFRED BRYAN, and an Introduction, entitled "Dickens as a Reader," by the late JOHN HOLLINGSHEAD. Crown 8vo, 3s. net.

LONDON: CHAPMAN AND HALL, LTD.

Redwood Library

SELECTIONS FROM THE RULES

1. Three volumes may be taken at a time and only three on one share. Two unbound numbers of a monthly and three numbers of a weekly publication are counted as a volume.

2. Books other than 7-day and 14-day ones may be kept out 28 days. **Books cannot be renewed or transferred.**

3. Books overdue are subject to a fine of one cent a day for fourteen days, **and five cents a day for each day thereafter.**

4. Neglect to pay the fine will debar from the use of the Library.

5. No book is to be lent out of the house of the person to whom it is charged.

6. Any person who shall soil (deface) or damage or lose a book belonging to the Library shall be liable to such fine as the Directors may impose; or shall pay the value of the book or of the set, if it be a part of a set, as the Directors may elect. All scribbling or any marking or writing whatever, folding or turning down the leaves, as well as cutting or tearing any matter from a book belonging to the Library, will be considered defacement and damage.